CATHOLIC
SOCIAL
TEACHING

"A true treasure and necessary companion for those who want to understand how Catholic social teachings relate to our daily and communal lives. McKenna writes clearly and organizes his materials to facilitate easy reference through excellent summaries and guided theological reflections."

Carolyn Y. Woo
President and CEO

~~Catholic Charities U.S.A.~~

"McKenna's text is an important study guide to Catholic social teaching and its impact on both of the Church and the global community. His presentation shows how this teaching continually challenges forces of injustice, violence, and oppression."

Sr. Marianne Farina, C.S.C.
Department Chair of Theology
Dominican School of Philosophy and Theology
Graduate Theological Union, Berkeley

"This book lays out the reasons Catholics advance social justice in their spheres of influence. McKenna provides a concise and pastorally useful presentation of the Catholic social tradition. Any Catholic wanting to understand social doctrine—especially those working in parish, university, diocesan, or agency settings—will find this to be a great tool."

Bill Purcell
Associate Director for Catholic Social Tradition
Center for Social Concerns
University of Notre Dame

"Here the most inspiring kernels of the major social encyclicals and pastoral letters are made accessible to everyone. Though he is also a scholar, McKenna is first a fine parish pastor, who builds upon the six major themes of Catholic social teaching, linking them with prayer, sacraments, and action. This little volume packs a real treasure trove for anyone seeking to learn, act, teach, or preach on Catholic social teaching."

Sr. Dawn M. Nothwehr, O.S.F.
The Erica and Harry John Family Endowed Chair in Catholic Ethics
Catholic Theological Union

"The Vatican's official summary of Catholic social doctrine runs nearly 450 pages. Father McKenna accomplishes the same task in clear style in 160 pages. McKenna's book includes a valuable glossary, a timeline, a homily guide for social themes, and more. His tone reflects just who he is: a workaday parish priest with a great passion for justice."

William Droel
Editor
National Center for the Laity

KEVIN E. MCKENNA

CATHOLIC
SOCIAL
TEACHING

REVISED EDITION

ave maria press AmP notre dame, indiana

Founded in 1865, Ave Maria Press® is a ministry of the United States Province of Holy Cross.

www.avemariapress.com

Paperback: ISBN-10 1-59471-438-X, ISBN-13 978-1-59471-438-2

E-book: ISBN-10 1-59471-439-8, ISBN-13 978-1-59471-439-9

Cover image © CORBIS

Cover and text design by David Scholtes.

Printed and bound in the United States of America.

Library of Congress Cataloging-in-Publication Data

McKenna, Kevin E., 1950-

 A concise guide to Catholic social teaching / Kevin E. McKenna. -- Revised Edition.

    pages cm

 ISBN 978-1-59471-438-2 (pbk.) -- ISBN 1-59471-438-X (pbk.)

 1. Christian sociology--Catholic Church. 2. Catholic Church--Doctrines. I. Title.

 BX1753.M38 2013

 261.8088'282--dc23

                            2013022202

DENNIS W. HICKEY

Auxiliary Bishop of Rochester

A true gentleman and a scholar

Requiescat in pace

Contents

INTRODUCTION

Perhaps the most important contribution the Roman Catholic Church has made to the world community during the last two ~~· ·~~ ~~development of the cohesive body of thought~~

social teachings stem from the seismic cultural ~~shifts brought on by~~ the Industrial Revolution in the Western World. These teachings have taken a variety of forms, primarily encyclicals, which are formal papal documents that present the Church's position regarding some issue of concern. Leo XIII was the first pope to present such teaching with his 1891 encyclical *Rerum Novarum*. This great work addressed some of the problems that were emerging in shifting and often volatile relationships between management and labor in the industrializing nations of the world. Every pope thereafter would utilize his office to address pressing social concerns.

A Concise Guide to Catholic Social Teaching distills major papal teachings as well as teachings from the episcopal conference of the United States (United States Conference of Catholic Bishops) into summary form. This is not an exhaustive summary of Catholic social teaching but rather presents several major Church documents that have provided clear guidance in regard to perplexing social issues. Included are several pastoral letters and responses from the US hierarchy often built upon the encyclical teachings, making them relevant to the local scene by providing concrete domestic applications. These documents have been summarized and paraphrased while seeking to maintain the strength and vigor of the original, which should always be consulted as the official teaching. It is hoped, however, that the reader nonetheless will obtain a useful sense of these milestone developments in Catholic social thought. The numbers of the sections summarized from the original document are provided throughout where possible. Exact section references are omitted in instances where they are not supplied in the original document.

In 1998, the United States Conference of Catholic Bishops provided a key framework for discussing Catholic social teaching in their document *Sharing Catholic Social Teaching: Challenges and Directions*. Here they offered seven key themes that we find throughout the Church's social teaching and that serve as the framework for this book:

Life and Dignity of the Human Person
Call to Family, Community, and Participation
Rights and Responsibilities
Option for the Poor and Vulnerable
The Dignity of Work and the Rights of Workers
Solidarity
Care for God's Creation

At times, similar themes are repeated in several of the social documents summarized here, but for the most part, each document is explored under the broad theme with which it seems most naturally identified.

Since the Second Vatican Council the Church has become particularly concerned with the need to promote Catholic social teaching. Toward that end, many parishes have developed social action committees or their equivalents. In many places, these groups have been very effective in mobilizing parish resources to provide economic assistance to those who are in financial need in their parishes, neighborhoods, or dioceses as well as those who are in urgent need in other areas of the United States or even abroad. However commendable or laudatory these initiatives, it can sometimes happen that efforts are focused on the *results* while losing sight of the rationale for the works of Gospel justice. A careful, consistent, and frequent reflection on the themes of justice and charity that are predominant in the scriptures and, consequently, of the social teachings of the Church, can be a helpful resource that combines prayer and action. In addition, such reflection and study can encourage new initiatives, as parish committees (or even parish pastoral councils) review the concrete proposals and suggestions that are often recommended in various Church documents.

The uses of this book are not limited to parishes. It can also be used with effectiveness by diocesan social ministry offices, such as Catholic Charities, who do on a larger scale what is often done by individual parishes. Religious orders, which often have committees or similar structures organized for coordinating the social concerns of their particular community, find the book helpful for their work, especially in

useful to begin its regularly scheduled meeting with some type of continuing education. This might be accomplished by assigning one of the chapters of this book for reading before the next meeting, and then using the dialogue questions (or a single question) to be discussed for a few minutes as time allows. In this way, the council is exposed gradually to some of the major themes of Catholic social teaching and is pressed to consider how these teachings can be put into practice within the parish setting. Such a practice can easily be expanded and adapted to be used by any parish committee or organization, for example, evangelization, Christian formation, etc. Just as it is important that we *act* on behalf of the Gospel, so too is it important that we know *why* we are doing what we do.

This work is also intended for use by the busy parish priest, deacon, or lay leader, providing a preaching or teaching resource that can be helpful in addressing the social concerns that are raised in the scriptures. In appendix A, various homiletic or catechetical themes related to Catholic social teachings are identified by reference to the Sunday lectionary of Mass readings. Thus, during the course of scriptural exposition and teaching that occupies the homilist or other parish leader during the course of the liturgical year, suggested connections with the heritage of our social teachings are provided.

Appendix B offers a sample Penance service that can be adapted for use in a variety of settings. Many parish communities gather during the Advent and Lenten seasons to celebrate God's plentiful mercy. A parish may wish to use a continuing education program or a retreat experience during these sacred times to study Catholic social teaching. The service provided here can conclude such programs by providing an opportunity for personal and communal reflection, leading to a service of reconciliation in the area of social justice.

Appendix C provides biographical information on the popes who have most recently contributed with their encyclicals to our Catholic social tradition. The creation of the teaching of the Church did not come from a vacuum. In a certain sense, the popes have translated a *sensus fidelium* (sense of the faithful) about important areas of justice and love of neighbor into a strong critique that provides a clear and consistent teaching framed within the imperatives of the Gospel. It can be helpful, in studying the development of Catholic social teaching, to know something of the background of those who have influenced the production of important teachings, as well as the times in which they lived. Closely related to these biographical sketches is appendix D, which presents a timeline or chart of milestones in the history of Catholic social teaching. All of the material in the appendices is also available as free downloadable documents via avemariapress.com. Once you get to the book's page, just click on the "More" tab.

Following the appendices, a glossary of terms is provided that highlights terms used in the text that may not be immediately understandable due to their nearly exclusive use within the context of the Church's social teaching. A short description of the documents referenced in this work can also be found in the glossary. Finally this book offers lists of sources cited and suggestions for further reading along with an index for easy reference.

I am grateful to those who have assisted me in this project, especially as they have attempted to live the message of these profound Church teachings in their daily lives. I am particularly indebted to Dr. Marvin Krier Mich and Dr. Patricia Schoelles, who were kind enough to review the manuscript and offer invaluable guidance, direction, and suggestions.

May the Lord bless the efforts of all those who work to be a light to the nations of God's saving love, mercy, and justice. May the insights and teachings of the Church in regard to its social mission given by

Christ continue to move us all to be witnesses of the Master to a world that seeks so consistently to find him.

ABBREVIATIONS

APT   *A Place at the Table: A Catholic Recommitment to Overcome Poverty and to Respect the Dignity of All God's Children*

BSTU   *Brothers and Sisters to Us, a Pastoral Letter on Racism*

CA   *On the Hundredth Anniversary of* Rerum Novarum (Centesimus Annus)

CP   *The Challenge of Peace: God's Promise and Our Response*

CPUN   *Statement on Capital Punishment*

CRFFF   *For I Was Hungry and You Gave Me Food: Catholic Reflections on Food, Farmers, and Farmworkers*

CV   *On Integral Human Development in Charity and Truth* (Caritas in Veritate)

DCE   *God Is Love* (Deus Caritas Est)

EJFA   *Economic Justice for All: Pastoral Letter on Catholic Social Teaching and the U.S. Economy*

EV   *The Gospel of Life* (Evangelium Vitae)

LE   *On Human Work* (Laborem Exercens)

MM   *On Christianity and Social Progress* (Mater et Magistra)

PP   *On the Development of Peoples* (Populorum Progressio)

PT   *Peace on Earth* (Pacem in Terris)

QA   *On Reconstructing the Social Order* (Quadragesimo Anno)

RN   *On the Condition of Labor* (Rerum Novarum)

SRS   *On Social Concern* (Sollicitudo Rei Socialis)

SS   *Saved in Hope* (Spe Salvi)

1.

LIFE AND DIGNITY OF THE

ries that follow in this chapter are taken from:

- ➲ *Pastoral Letter on Racism: Brothers and Sisters to Us*, United States Conference of Catholic Bishops, 1979

- ➲ *Statement on Capital Punishment*, National Conference of Catholic Bishops, 1980

- ➲ *The Gospel of Life* (Evangelium Vitae), Pope John Paul II, 1995

Pastoral Letter on Racism: Brothers and Sisters to Us
United States Conference of Catholic Bishops, 1979

- **Racial and Economic Justice**
- **The Church and Prejudice**
- **Presence of Racism in the United States Today**
- **Christian Response to Racism**

Racism is an evil that endures in our society, despite advances and significant changes in the last two decades. The majority of Americans realize that discrimination is both unjust and unworthy of this nation.

It cannot be denied that the ugly external features of racism that marred our society in the past have in part been eliminated. At the same time, however, it cannot be denied that too often what has happened has been only a covering over and not a fundamental change. The climate of crisis engendered by demonstrations and protests has given way to a mood of indifference.

Racial and Economic Justice

Attention should be called to the persistent presence of racism and in particular to the relationship between racial and economic justice. Although racism and economic oppression are distinct, they are interrelated forces that can dehumanize our society.

Major segments of the population are being pushed to the margins. As economic pressures tighten, racial minorities slip further into the unending cycle of poverty, deprivation, ignorance, disease, and crime.

The Church and Prejudice

The Church cannot remain silent about racial injustices in society and in its own structures. Discrimination belies our civil tradition and constitutional heritage that recognizes the equality, dignity, and inalienable rights of all its citizens. We are, as well, heirs of a religious teaching that proclaims that all men and women, as children of God, are brothers and sisters.

Racism is a sin that divides the human family by proclaiming that some human beings are inherently superior because of race. It is a denial of the truth of the dignity of each human being revealed by the mystery of the Incarnation.

We look to Christ for the strength to overcome racism. In Christ Jesus "there is neither Jew nor Greek, male nor female; for all are one . . . " (Gal 3:28). In Christ Jesus the Church finds the central cause for its commitment to justice and the struggle for the human rights and dignity of all persons.

Presence of Racism in the United States Today

The continuing existence of racism in our country is apparent when we look beneath the surface of our national life as, for example, in the case of unemployment figures. For many minority groups, being denied adequate access to employment opportunities has been a crushing burden for decades. A disproportionate number of families in these groups continue to face the generational poverty that this reality helps create. Racism can also be seen in housing patterns in our major cities and suburbs. The gap between rich and poor is widening, not decreasing.

Racism can be noted in the disproportionate minority population in prison and the violent crime that is the daily companion of a life of poverty and deprivation. The victims of such crimes are li

_____ ___ government-funded programs for the disadvantaged. At times, protestations claiming that all persons should be treated equally reflect the desire to maintain a status quo favoring one race and social group at the expense of the poor and the non-white.

The contribution of each racial minority is distinctive and rich. Each racial group has sunk its roots deep in the soil of our culture and has contributed in some way to giving this country its unique character and diverse coloration.

Racism is manifest in the tendency to stereotype and marginalize whole segments of the population whose presence is seen as a threat. It can be seen in the indifference given to the minority poor often perceived by some as expendable. The new face of racism is the computer printout, the graph of profits and losses, the pink slip, the nameless statistic. Racism today flourishes in the triumph of private concern over public responsibility, individual success over social commitment, and personal fulfillment over authentic compassion.

Christian Response to Racism

New forms of racism must be brought face to face with the figure of Christ. The Christian response to the challenges of our times is to be found in the good news of Jesus. God's word proclaims the oneness of the human family. All are created in the image of God. The Church is truly universal, embracing all races. The Church has a duty to proclaim the truth about the human being as disclosed in the truth about Jesus Christ.

Catholics must acknowledge a share in the mistakes and sins of the past, as prisoners of fear and prejudice. At times conformity to social pressures has replaced compliance with social justice.

The prophetic voice of the Church must not be muted—especially not by the counter-witness of some of its own people. The Church must strive to make every element of human life correspond to the true dignity of the human person. The Church must continue to proclaim that the sin of racism defiles the image of God and degrades the sacred dignity of humankind, revealed in the mystery of the Incarnation.

Conversion is the continuing task of each Christian. Christians must try to influence the attitudes of others by expressly rejecting racial stereotypes, racist jokes, slurs, and remarks. It is important to become more sensitive as to how social structures inhibit the economic, educational, and social advancement of the poor, and to commit to work with others in political efforts to bring about changes on behalf of justice.

Particular care should be taken to foster vocations to priestly and religious life among minority groups. There should also be a fostering of spiritual gifts of the various races and peoples within the liturgy as noted in the *Constitution on the Sacred Liturgy* (10, 37, 39, 40).

Special attention should be given to the plight of undocumented workers. Catholic institutions that are employers should examine carefully their policies to see that they faithfully conform to the Church's teaching on justice for workers and respect their rights. Investment portfolios should be examined to determine whether racist institutions and policies are inadvertently being supported.

It is recommended that Catholic institutions avoid the services of agencies and industries which refuse to take affirmative action to achieve equal opportunity and that the Church itself always be a model as an equal opportunity employer.

Leadership training programs should be established on the local level in order to encourage effective leadership among racial minorities on all levels of the Church, local as well as national.

Active spiritual and financial support should be given to associations and institutions organized by African-American, Hispanic, Native

American, and Asian Catholics within the Church for the promotion of ministry to and by their respective communities.

There should be a continuation and expansion of Catholic schools in the inner cities and other disadvantaged areas. The Church in the United States has been distinguished by its efforts to educate the poor and disadvantaged.

The difficulties of today demand a new visi̇

Statement on Capital Punishment
National Conference of Catholic Bishops, 1980

- **Purposes of Punishment**
- **Christian Values in the Abolition of Capital Punishment**
- **Difficulties Inherent in Capital Punishment**
- **Conclusions**

Criticisms of the criminal justice system in the United States call for careful and prayerful reflection on the question of capital punishment by the Christian community, showing a respect and concern for the rights of all. The public debate about capital punishment deals with values of the utmost importance: respect for the sanctity of human life, the protection of human life, the preservation of order in society, and the achievement of justice through law. Many factors must be considered, including the need to provide safety for members of society and concern for law enforcement officers who may be endangered in the midst of violent crime. There are no simple answers to this complex topic, but it is necessary to look to the claims of justice and to the example and teaching of Jesus.

Purposes of Punishment

Catholic teaching has accepted the principle that the state has the right to take the life of a person guilty of an extremely serious crime and that the state may take appropriate measures to protect itself and its citizens from grave harm. The question for judgment is whether capital punishment is justifiable under present circumstances.

Since punishment involves the deliberate infliction of evil on another, it is always in need of justification. The three traditional justifications advanced for punishment are retribution, deterrence, and reform.

The deterrence of actual or potential criminals from future deeds of violence by the threat of capital punishment is far from certain. There are strong reasons to doubt that many crimes of violence are undertaken in a spirit of rational calculation. Reform cannot be used as justification for capital punishment since it necessarily deprives the criminal of the opportunity to develop a new way of life. Although the need for retribution or the restoration of order justifies punishment, it does not need or require taking the life of a criminal.

The forms and limits of punishment must be determined by moral objectives which go beyond the mere infliction of injury on the guilty.

The forms of punishment must be determined with a view to the protection of society, the reformation of the criminal, and his or her reintegration into society (which may not be possible in certain situations).

In the conditions of contemporary American society, the legitimate purposes of punishment do not justify the imposition of the death penalty. There are serious considerations which should prompt Christians and all Americans to support the abolition of capital punishment.

Christian Values in the Abolition of Capital Punishment

The abolition of the death penalty would promote values that are important to Christian citizens. Abolition sends a message that the cycle of violence can be broken, that it is not necessary to take life for life, and that more humane and effective responses can be envisioned in response to violent crime.

It is also a manifestation of the belief in the unique worth and dignity of each person from the moment of conception, a creature made in the image and likeness of God. It gives further testimony that God is the Lord of life and is consonant with the example of Jesus who both taught and practiced the forgiveness of injustice and who came to "give his life as a ransom for many" (Mk 10:45).

Difficulties Inherent in Capital Punishment

Infliction of the death penalty extinguishes the possibilities of ref-

can bring with it great and avoidable anguish for the criminal, his or her family and loved ones, and those who are called on to perform or to witness the execution. Executions also attract enormous publicity, much of it unhealthy, stirring up considerable acrimony in public discussion.

There is widespread evidence that many convicted criminals are sentenced to death in an unfair and discriminatory manner. The legal system and the criminal justice system both work in a society that bears in its psychological, social, and economic patterns the mark of racism. Those condemned to die are nearly always poor and are disproportionately of African American descent.

Conclusions

The abolition of the death penalty is not proposed as a simple solution to the problems of crime and punishment. There is a special need to offer sympathy to and support for the victims of violent crime and their families. A firm determination is needed to help victims of violent crimes and their families. It is the special responsibility of the Church to provide a community of faith and trust in which God's grace can heal the personal and spiritual wounds of those victimized.

Important changes are needed in the correctional system in order to make it truly conducive to the reform and rehabilitation of convicted criminals and their reintegration into society. Also to be emphasized is the importance of restricting the easy availability of guns and other weapons of violence. Opposition must be made to the glamorizing of violence in entertainment with its detrimental effects on human moral development, especially among children and youth. Educational efforts must be undertaken to promote respect for the human dignity of all people.

We are called to contemplate the crucified Christ who set us the supreme example of forgiveness and of the triumph of compassionate love.

The Gospel of Life (Evangelium Vitae)
Pope John Paul II, 1995

- **Present-Day Threats to Human Life**
- **Attacks by the State**
- **Culture of Death**
- **The Pro-abortion Culture**
- **The Right to Life**
- **The Christian Message concerning Life**
- **Jesus and the Proclamation of Human Dignity**
- **God's Holy Law**
- **The Death Penalty**
- **The Crime of Abortion**
- **Embryo Experimentation**
- **Prenatal Diagnostic Techniques**
- **Euthanasia**
- **Suicide**
- **Proclaiming the Right to Life in a Democratic Society**
- **Toward a New Culture of Human Life**
- **Education in Values**
- **The Role of Women**

The gospel of life is at the heart of Jesus' message. In presenting the heart of his redemptive mission, Jesus says: "I came that they may have life, and have it abundantly" (Jn 10:10). Believers in Christ must defend and promote the right to life. Through his incarnation, the Son of God has united himself in some fashion with every human being and established the incomparable value of every human person. The gospel of God's love for each person, the gospel of the dignity of the person, and the gospel of life are a single and indivisible gospel (1–3).

The proclamation of life is ever more urgent due to the increase and gravity of threats to the life of individuals and peoples. For example, broad sectors of public opinion justify certain crimes against life in the name of the rights of individual freedom. Such initiatives are even being given cognizance by legislators in many countries. The individual conscience is finding it more and more difficult to distinguish between good and evil in what concerns the basic value of h...... ......

.... the first

fratricide, every murder is a violation of the spiritual kinship uniting humankind in one family. All kinds of ideologies can attempt to justify and disguise atrocious crimes against human beings.

God is merciful, even when he punishes. He places a mark on Cain lest anyone who comes upon him should kill him (Gn 4:15). In this, the paradoxical mystery of the merciful justice of God is shown.

Attacks against human life still continue through human history, from a variety of sources, including murder, war, slaughter, and genocide. Violence continues against children who are forced into poverty, malnutrition, and hunger due to an unjust distribution of resources.

Attacks by the State

There is another category of attacks which affects life in its earliest and in its final stages. In many cases the state gives these attacks legal recognition and makes them available through the free services of healthcare personnel. Such attacks strike human life at its greatest frailty, when it lacks any means of self-defense.

There are many factors involved, including a profound crisis of culture, the complexity of society, acute poverty, and anxiety or frustration in which the struggle to make ends meet can make the choice to defend life so demanding as sometimes to reach the point of heroism.

Culture of Death

There has been an emergence of a veritable structure of sin in the form of a "culture of death," a war of the powerful against the weak. A life which would require greater acceptance, love, and care is considered useless, or held to be an intolerable burden, and is therefore rejected in one way or another.

To facilitate abortion, enormous sums of money have been invested in pharmaceutical products which can kill the fetus without recourse to any medical assistance. Such developments become capable of removing abortion from any kind of control or social responsibility.

The Pro-abortion Culture

The pro-abortion culture is especially strong where the Church's teaching on contraception is rejected. In some instances, contraception and abortion are rooted in a hedonistic mentality unwilling to accept responsibility in matters of sexuality. The life which could result from a sexual encounter becomes an enemy to be avoided at all costs, and abortion becomes the only possible decisive response to failed contraception. Prenatal diagnosis all too often becomes an opportunity for proposing and procuring an abortion.

Serious threats hang over the incurably ill and the dying as well. Culture today considers any suffering as the epitome of evil, to be eliminated at all costs. Euthanasia is sometimes justified by a utilitarian motive of avoiding costs which bring no return and which weigh heavily on society.

There is also a demographic argument made today in support of attacks against life. The more powerful countries fear that the most prolific and poorest people represent a threat to the well-being and peace of their own countries. Sometimes, the economic help that the richer countries could provide is made conditional on the acceptance of an anti-birth policy.

The Right to Life

The process that once led to discovering the idea of "human rights"—rights inherent in every person—is today marked by a surprising contradiction. In an age when the inviolable rights of the person are solemnly proclaimed and the value of life is publicly affirmed, the very right to life is being denied or trampled upon, especially at the moment of birth and the moment of death. The roots of this remarkable contradiction lie in today's cultural and moral nature. There exists a mentality of extreme subjectivism that recognizes as a subject of rights only the person who enjoys full or at least incipient autonomy and who emerges from a state of total dependence on others. Th

, and universal truth, then the person ends up no longer taking the truth about good and evil as the point of reference for choices. Rather, the criterion becomes only a subjective and changeable opinion—selfish interest and whim.

Such a view of freedom leads to a distortion of life in society, a mass of individuals placed side by side but without any mutual bonds. Social life ventures on to the shifting sands of relativism. Everything is negotiable, everything is open to bargaining—even the first of the fundamental rights, the right to life.

Simultaneously, there is within culture an eclipse of the sense of God and of the human. When a sense of God is lost in a secularized culture, the sense of the human being is also threatened—the human no longer sees the transcendent character of the human being. In such a context, suffering, a factor of possible personal growth, is always seen as an evil, to be opposed and avoided. The body is seen then as pure materiality, a complex of organs, functions, and energies to be used, according to the sole criteria of pleasure and efficiency. Sexuality is depersonalized and exploited. Interpersonal relations are seriously impoverished.

Christ's blood reveals to humanity the greatness of the human being and the true vocation: the sincere gift of self. The blood of Christ is the instrument of communion, the richness of life for all. It is from the blood of Christ that all people draw the strength to commit themselves to promoting life. The unconditional choice for life reaches its full religious and moral meaning when it flows from, is formed by, and is nourished by faith in Christ. The Church is becoming more aware of the grace and responsibility that come to it from the Lord of proclaiming, celebrating, and serving the gospel of life (7–9, 11, 13, 15, 16, 18–23, 25, 28).

The Christian Message concerning Life

The gospel of life is concrete and personal, consisting of the proclamation of the person of Jesus, who said, "I am the way and the truth and the life" (Jn 14:6). Through the words, actions, and person of Jesus, humanity is given the possibility of knowing the complete truth concerning the value of human life. It can also be known in its essential traits by human reason.

The fullness of the gospel message about life was prepared for in the Old Testament. The Lord revealed himself to Israel as its Savior, with the power to ensure a future to those without hope. In coming to know the value of its own existence as a people, Israel grows in its perception of the meaning and value of life itself.

Revelation progressively allows the first notion of immortal life planted by the Creator in the human heart to be grasped with ever-greater clarity.

Jesus and the Proclamation of Human Dignity

Just as God reassured Israel in the midst of danger, so the Son of God proclaims to all who feel threatened and hindered that their lives are a good to which the Father's love gives meaning and value. The crowds of the sick and the outcasts who follow him and seek him out find in Jesus' words and actions a revelation of the great value of their lives and of how their hope of salvation is well founded. It is by his death that Jesus reveals the entire splendor and value of life.

The human being has been given a sublime dignity based on the intimate bond that unites each individual to God: in the human being shines forth a reflection of God. All who commit themselves to following Christ are given the fullness of life: the divine image is restored, renewed, and brought to perfection in them. Whoever believes in Jesus and enters into communion with him has eternal life because that person hears from Jesus the only words that reveal and communicate to his existence the fullness of life. The dignity of this life is linked not only to its beginning, to the fact that it comes from God, but also to its final end, to its destiny of fellowship with God in knowledge and love of him.

God is the sole Lord of this life. God does not exercise this power in an arbitrary and threatening manner, but rather as part of his care and loving concern for his creatures. The sacredness of life gives way to its inviolability. The commandment "Y...

... jesus, with the many healings he performed, shows God's great concern even for the individual's bodily life. No one can arbitrarily choose whether to live or die. The absolute master of such a decision is the Creator alone.

By his death, Jesus sheds light on the meaning of the life and death of every human being. Life finds its center, its meaning, and its fulfillment when it is given up (29, 31, 32, 36–39, 41, 47, 50).

God's Holy Law

The gospel of life is both a great gift of God and an exacting task for humanity. Scripture presents the precept "You shall not kill" as a divine commandment. God proclaims that he is the absolute Lord of the life of each individual, and thus human life is given a sacred and inviolable character. The commandment not to kill implicitly encourages a positive attitude of absolute respect for life.

The Death Penalty

Legitimate defense is not only a right but also a duty for someone responsible for another's life. Unfortunately it sometimes happens that the need to render the aggressor incapable of causing harm sometimes involves taking a life.

The problem of the death penalty should be examined in the context of a system of penal justice ever more in line with human dignity and with God's plan for humanity and society. Public authority must redress the violation of personal and social rights by imposing on the offender an adequate punishment for the crime as a condition for the offender to regain the exercise of his or her freedom. The public authority therefore defends the public order and ensures people's safety while offering the offender an incentive to change his or her behavior. For these purposes to be achieved, the nature and extent of the punishment must be carefully evaluated and decided upon. The punishment ought not to go to the extreme of executing the offender except in cases of absolute necessity: when it would not be possible otherwise to defend society. Today such cases are very rare, if not practically nonexistent.

Faced with the progressive weakening of individual consciences and in society of the sense of the absolute and grave moral illicitness of the direct taking of all innocent human life, the Church's magisterium has spoken out with increasing frequency in defense of the sacredness and inviolability of human life. *The direct and voluntary killing of an innocent human being is always gravely immoral.* No one can in any way permit the killing of an innocent human being whether a fetus or an embryo, an infant or an adult, an old person or one suffering from an incurable disease, or a person who is dying. Furthermore, no one is permitted to ask for this act of killing, either for himself or herself or for another person entrusted to his or her care, nor can he or she consent to it, either explicitly or implicitly. Nor can any authority legitimately recommend or permit such an action.

The Crime of Abortion

Among all the crimes that can be committed against human life, procured abortion is particularly serious and deplorable. Today, in many people's minds, the perception of its gravity has become progressively obscured. The moral gravity is apparent if we realize that we are dealing with murder since the one being eliminated is a human being at the very beginning of life. No one more absolutely innocent could be imagined. Sometimes the decision made by the mother for an abortion is not made for purely selfish motives; however, that can never justify the deliberate killing of an innocent human being.

Others can influence a decision to have an abortion, including the father, the wider family circle, and friends. Also responsible can be legislators who promote and approve abortion laws, and healthcare facilities and their personnel where abortions are performed. Even culture and society have an effect when it encourages sexual permissiveness.

Some attempt to justify abortion by claiming that the result of conception, at least up to a certain number of days ~~~ ~~

... ~~~~~~~~~ of the morality of abortion is to be applied also to intervention on human embryos. The use of human embryos or fetuses as an object of experimentation constitutes a crime against their dignity as human beings who have a right to the same respect owed to a child once born, just as to every person. Also to be condemned are procedures that exploit living human embryos and fetuses "produced" for this purpose by in vitro fertilization—either to be used as "biological material" or as providers of organs or tissue for transplants in the treatment of certain diseases. The killing of innocent human creatures, even if carried out to help others, constitutes an absolutely unacceptable act.

Prenatal Diagnostic Techniques

Attention must be given to evaluating the morality of prenatal diagnostic techniques. Sometimes it happens that these techniques are used with the intention to accept selective abortion in order to prevent the birth of children affected by various types of anomalies. This attitude is seen as reprehensible, since it presumes to measure the value of human life only within the parameters of "normality" and physical well-being.

Euthanasia

To many today, life seems valued only to the extent that it brings pleasure and well-being. Suffering seems like an unbearable setback. Death is considered "senseless" if it suddenly interrupts a life still open to a future of new and interesting experiences. But it becomes a "rightful liberation" when life is seen as no longer meaningful because it is filled with pain and doomed to even greater suffering.

There can be a temptation to have recourse to euthanasia, to take control of death and bring it about before its time. Euthanasia must be distinguished from the decision to forego so-called aggressive medical treatment, when it is seen as disproportionate to any expected results or because it imposes an excessive burden on the patient and his or her family. In such situations, when death is clearly imminent and inevitable, one can in conscience refuse forms of treatment that would only secure a precarious and burdensome prolongation of life so long as the normal care due to the sick person is not interrupted. It is licit to relieve pain by various types of painkillers and sedatives, even when this risks the shortening of life. In such a case, death is not sought, but rather simply a desire to ease pain effectively is desired.

Suicide

Suicide is always a morally objectionable choice, since it represents a rejection of God's absolute sovereignty over life and death. To concur with the intention of another to commit suicide and to help in carrying it out through so-called assisted suicide means to cooperate and at times be the actual perpetrator of an injustice. True compassion leads to sharing another's pain. It does not kill the person whose suffering we cannot bear. The height of arbitrariness and injustice is reached when certain people, such as physicians or legislators, arrogate to themselves the power to decide who ought to live and who ought to die.

Proclaiming the Right to Life in a Democratic Society

In the democratic culture of our time it is commonly held that the legal system of any society should limit itself to taking account of and accepting the convictions of the majority. At the basis of these tendencies is an ethical relativism that characterizes much of present-day culture. Democracy cannot be idolized to the point of making it a substitute for morality or a panacea for immorality. The moral values of a democracy are not automatic; rather, democracy depends on conformity to the moral law, the "natural law" written in the human heart, to which it must be subject. There is therefore a need to recover the basic elements of a vision of the relationship between civil law and moral law. Civil law must ensure that all members of society enjoy respect for certain fundamental rights which innately belong to the person, rights that every positive law must guarantee. First and fundamental among these is the inviolable right to life of every innocent h⸺

⸺ ... to refuse to take part in committing an injustice is not only a moral duty but also a basic human right.

The commandment "You shall not kill" even in its more positive aspects of respecting, loving, and promoting human life is binding on every individual human being (52, 54, 56–60, 63–66, 69–71, 73, 74, 77).

Toward a New Culture of Human Life

The Gospel of Christ has been received by the Church as a gift. The Church exists in order to evangelize, to proclaim the Gospel message. The gospel of life is an integral part of the Gospel that is Jesus Christ himself. Everyone has a responsibility of being at the service of this gospel of life, which proclaims that human life, as a gift from God, is sacred and inviolable. In preaching such a gospel, we must not fear hostility or unpopularity, and we must refuse any compromise or ambiguity which might conform us to the world's way of thinking.

Education in Values

Education aimed at encouraging vocations to service and practical projects inspired by the Gospel are needed. Agencies and centers of service to life need to be directed by people who are fully aware of the importance of the gospel of life. To implement the gospel of life requires certain forms of social activity and commitment in the political field. Civil leaders particularly have a duty to make courageous choices in support of life. Likewise, on the issue of population growth, public authorities have a responsibility always to take into account and respect the primary and inalienable responsibility of married couples and families. They cannot employ methods that fail to respect the person and fundamental human rights, beginning with the right to life of every innocent human being.

This cultural change demands courage from everyone to adopt a new lifestyle—making practical choices at the personal, family, social, and international level—on the basis of a correct scale of values: *the primacy of "being" over "having."* Other people are not rivals from whom we must defend ourselves, but brothers and sisters to be supported. The mass media has an important role to ensure the messages that they transmit will support the culture of life.

The Role of Women
Women who have had an abortion should know that the Church is aware of how painful and even shattering such a decision is in many cases. Although it is terribly wrong, such women should not give in to discouragement and should not lose hope. They should try to understand what happened and trust in repentance. With expert help, and as a result of one's own painful experience, it is possible to become eloquent defenders of everyone's right to life.

The gospel of life is for the whole of human society. To be actively pro-life is to contribute to the renewal of society through the promotion of the common good. There can be no true peace unless life is defended and promoted (78, 79, 81, 82, 88–99).

For Reflection and Dialogue

1. Why is racism considered to be sinful?
2. What are some indications that racism is still present in your own community today?
3. What steps could be undertaken by your faith community to address the issues of racism in a concrete and constructive way?

4. Why is capital punishment such a controversial issue today?

5. After reading summaries of *The Gospel of Life* (Evangelium Vitae) and the bishops' statement on capital punishment, have your own thoughts in regard to the death penalty changed at all? Why or why not?

6. Why do the bishops believe that capital punishment does not serve

... you believe are the most serious contemporary threats to life and its respect?

10. What examples can you give of what John Paul II referred to as the "culture of death"?

11. What steps could a parish take to increase awareness of life issues in the parish? The wider community?

12. Do you believe that the Church's position concerning the death penalty is consistent with its position on other issues concerning human life? Why or why not?

13. What educational efforts could be made by your parish/social action committee/local community to raise consciousness in regard to the issues raised in *The Gospel of Life* (Evangelium Vitae)?

14. Which practical recommendations found in *The Gospel of Life* (Evangelium Vitae) could be implemented in your area?

2.

CALL TO FAMILY,

~~COMM~~

...~~ry government~~ has the responsibility of protecting, supporting, and encouraging the family for the basic well-being of the entire society. The Church has also recognized the importance of a global vision of family, an interdependence that invites nations to work cooperatively for the common good. This chapter includes summaries from the following:

➲ *On the Condition of Labor* (Rerum Novarum), Pope Leo XIII, 1891

➲ *On Reconstructing the Social Order* (Quadragesimo Anno), Pope Pius XI, 1931

➲ *On the Hundredth Anniversary of* Rerum Novarum (Centesimus Annus), Pope John Paul II, 1991

➲ *The Gospel of Life* (Evangelium Vitae), Pope John Paul II, 1995

➲ *On Integral Human Development in Charity and Truth* (Caritas in Veritate) Pope Benedict XVI, 2009

On the Condition of Labor (Rerum Novarum)
Pope Leo XIII, 1891

- **Each Family Possesses Certain Rights**

Each Family Possesses Certain Rights

The parents of a family have the obligation, imposed by nature itself, to see that their offspring are provided with all the necessities of life. Families possess the rights, at least equal to civil society, in choosing those things that are necessary for protection and just liberty. Civil power should respect the family and not interfere with its operation unless there is a grave violation of mutual rights within the family itself (20–21).

On Reconstructing the Social Order (Quadragesimo Anno) Pope Pius XI, 1931

* **Support for the Worker and Family**

Support for the Worker and Family

The wage paid to the worker must be sufficient for the worker and the worker's family. Reforms are in order when such a wage is not paid. However, it is not just to demand wages that are so high that an employer cannot pay them without financial ruin. Employers and employees should join their efforts to overcome these difficulties and obstacles, aided by the wise measures of the public authority.

On the Hundredth Anniversary of Rerum Novarum (Centesimus Annus) Pope John Paul II, 1991

* **"Human Ecology": The Family**

"Human Ecology": The Family

The first and fundamental structure of "human ecology" is the family where each individual learns what it means to be a person. It often happens that people are discouraged from creating the proper conditions for human reproduction. Individuals are led to consider themselves and their lives as a series of sensations to be experienced rather than as work to be accomplished. The result is a lack of freedom, which causes a person to reject a commitment to enter into a stable relationship with another person and to bring children into the world. It leads people to think of children as one of the many "things" which an individual can have or not have, according to taste, and which compete with other possibilities.

It is necessary to see the family as the sanctuary of life. The family is indeed sacred, the place in which life . . .

. . . . . in order to live, then economic freedom loses its necessary relationship to the human person and ends up alienating and oppressing the individual.

The Church has no models to present for an effective economic system, since these can only arise within the framework of different historical situations and from the efforts of those responsible with confronting concrete problems. But the Church can offer its social teaching as an indispensable and ideal orientation which recognizes the positive value of the market and of enterprise, but points out that at the same time these must be oriented toward the common good (30–39, 43).

The Gospel of Life (Evangelium Vitae)
Pope John Paul II, 1995

- **Role of the Family**
- **Mobilization of Consciences**

Role of the Family

The family has a decisive responsibility as the domestic Church to proclaim, celebrate, and serve the gospel of life. It celebrates the gospel of life through daily prayer, both individually and as a family. The actual daily life together as a family, as a life of love and self-giving, becomes a service to the gospel of life.

Special attention must also be given to the elderly, who must be considered the object of our concern who also have a valuable contribution to make to the gospel of life. The rich treasury of experiences they have acquired through the years are a source of wisdom and witness of hope and love.

Mobilization of Consciences

Urgently needed is a general mobilization of consciences and a united ethical effort to activate a great campaign to support all life. This must begin with the renewal of a culture of life within Christian communities themselves. We need to promote a serious and in-depth exchange about basic issues of human life with everyone, including non-believers. The first and fundamental step toward cultural transformation consists in forming consciences with regard to the incomparable and inviolable worth of every human life. There is a need for education about the value of life from its very origin, helping the young to understand and appreciate the experience of sexuality and love and the whole of life according to their true meaning and in their close interconnection. Education is needed for couples concerning true parenthood. Education is also needed concerning the realities of suffering and death, grief, and loss (92–98).

On Integral Human Development in Charity and Truth (Caritas in Veritate) Pope Benedict XVI, 2009

- **On Integral Human Development**
- **Fraternity, Economic Development, and Civil Society**
- **The Development of Peoples and Technology**

On Integral Human Development

Besides the good of the individual, there is a good linked to living in society which is the common good. It is the good of all those in the society, a good not sought for its own sake, but for all the people who belong to the community. To desire the common good is a requirement of justice and charity. It becomes a dimension of the entire human family as we become ever more globalized (7).

Fraternity, Economic Development, and Civil Society

Man has conviction that he is self-sufficient and can eliminate evil in the world by his own conviction. This leads to the false ~~...~~

economy is ~ ·

~~...~~ market is subject to the principle of commutative justice, which regulates relations between the giving and receiving parties. But the Church's social doctrine highlights also the importance of distributive justice and social justice for the market economy. Without the internal forms of solidarity and mutual trust, the market cannot fulfill its proper economic function. The poor are not to be considered as a "burden," but rather a resource. It is erroneous to hold that a market economy must have an inbuilt quota of poverty and underdevelopment to function at its best (35).

Economic activity cannot solve all social problems by the application of commercial logic. This activity must be pursued with the common good in mind. Grave imbalances occur when economic action is conceived only as an engine for wealth creation and detached from political action when conceived as a means for pursuing justice through redistribution.

The market does not exist in a pure state, but is shaped by cultural configurations which define it and give it direction. The instruments of economy and finance are not good or bad in themselves; it is individuals with their moral conscience and their personal and social responsibility who must be called to account. Because the economic sphere is an integral part of humanity, it must be structured and governed in an ethical manner. The challenge is to demonstrate that in our economic ethics the traditional principles of transparency, honesty, and responsibility are maintained along with commercial relationships that accentuate the principle of gratuitousness and the logic of gift as an expression of fraternity.

The Church's social doctrine maintains that justice must be applied to every phase of economic activity. Every economic decision has a moral consequence. The canons of justice must be observed from the outset, not afterward or incidentally (CV 37).

The unity of the human family does not submerge individual identities but rather makes individuals, peoples, and cultures more transparent to each other and links them together in their diversity (53).

The Persons of the Trinity within one divine Substance show us the communion to which we are called to be united (54).

Some cultural and religious attitudes do not embrace the principles of love and truth and can obstruct authentic human development. Discernment is needed in regard to the contribution of cultures and religions, especially on the part of those who wield power. This discernment is based on the criterion of justice and peace. Christianity, with its "God who has a human face," contains this criterion within itself (55).

The contribution of Christian religion and other religions can only be made if God has a place in the public realm. If religion is excluded from the public square it will hinder an encounter between people and their collaboration for the progress of humanity. Reason is always in need of purification by faith. Religion must be also purified by reason to show its authentically human face (56).

A guiding criterion for cooperation between believers and non-believers is the principle of subsidiarity. This is a form of assistance wherein individuals and groups that are unable to accomplish something on their own are aided by a higher or broader authority. The governance of globalization must be marked by subsidiarity with different levels that can work together. The needed authority must be marked by subsidiarity if it is not to infringe upon freedom (57).

This principle of subsidiarity must be closely linked to the principle of solidarity and vice versa, taken broadly into consideration when addressing issues concerning international development. Aid must be distributed with the involvement of not only governments but also economic agents and the bearers of culture within society, including local churches. The most valuable resources in countries receiving development aid are human resources. In the economic sphere, the principal form of assistance is allowing and encouraging developing countries to penetrate the international market. The establishment of international trade regulations and stronger financing for development is needed to increase productivity of these economies (58).

Cooperation for development provides the opportunity for encounters between cultures and peoples. The ⋯⋯⋯ ⋯

⋯⋯ ⋯⋯p stimulate forms of welfare solidarity from below (60).

The Development of Peoples and Technology

The development of peoples is closely linked to the development of individuals. We are capable of making choices. A person compromises their development if they believe they are solely responsible for what they become. But the development of peoples goes awry if we also believe that humanity can re-create itself through technology. Man needs to look within himself to recognize the fundamental norms of the moral law, which God writes on our hearts (68).

Technology today enables us to exercise dominion over matter, reduce risks, save labor, and improve our conditions of life. It reveals man and his aspirations toward development and in a sense is a response to God's command to till and keep the land (cf. Gn 2:15) that he has entrusted to humanity (69).

There exists the possibility that the process of globalization could replace ideologies with technologies that could hold us back from encountering being and truth. We could then be evaluating and making decisions about life situations from a technocratic cultural perspective without being able to discover a meaning that is not of our own making. The key to development is a mind that is capable of thinking in technological terms but grasping the fully human meaning of human activities within a holistic meaning of the individual's being. Our actions always remain human, which is an expression of our responsible freedom. Human freedom is authentic only when responding to technology with decisions that are the fruit of moral responsibility (70).

Development is never guaranteed through automatic or impersonal forces. It is impossible without financiers and politicians finely attuned to the requirements of the common good. When technology takes over, the sole criterion for action in business is thought to be maximization of profit, in politics the consolidation of power, and in science the findings of research (71).

Even peace can be considered a technical product, merely the outcome of agreements between governments or of initiatives aimed at ensuring effective economic aid. If efforts that require diplomatic contacts; economic, technological, and cultural exchanges; joint strategies to curb the threat of war; and rooting out the causes of terrorism are all to have lasting effects, they must be based on values rooted in the truth of human life. The voices of the people affected must be heard. One must be aligned with the many individuals deeply committed to bringing people together, including members of the Christian faithful (72).

The means of social communication are integral to humankind today, but we are called to reflect on their influence, especially in regard to the ethical-cultural dimension of globalization and the development of peoples. They can have a civilizing effect when they are understood not only as possibilities of communication, but also as working toward a vision of the human person and the common good that reflects universal values. They need to focus on the promotion of the dignity of the human person and to be clearly inspired by charity and placed at the service of truth (73).

A crucial battleground today is in the field of bioethics. The question is asked today: is man the product of his own labors or does he depend on God? With an exclusive reliance on technology, reason without faith is doomed to flounder in an illusion of its own omnipotence (74).

In vitro fertilization, embryo research, and the possibility of manufacturing clones and human hybrids are being promoted in a disillusioned culture that believes it has mastered every mystery. We must not underestimate the disturbing scenarios that threaten our future or the powerful new instruments that are at the disposal of the culture of death. Underlying these scenarios exist cultural viewpoints that deny human dignity.

Unprecedented injustices seem to be widely tolerated. The poor of the world continue knocking on the doors of the rich, and the world of affluence runs the risk of no longer hearing those knocks due to a conscience that can no longer distinguish what is human (75).

The question of development is closely linked

...count (76).

The true development of peoples and individuals must consider the spiritual dimension, requiring a new heart capable of rising above the materialistic vision of human events, allowing the integral development that takes its direction from the driving force of charity in truth (77).

Without God, man does not know which way to go or who he is. In the vast work that lies ahead we are sustained by our faith in God who is present in those who come together to work for justice. God's love calls us to move beyond the limited and gives us courage to continue seeking and working for the benefit of all (78).

Development needs Christians, through prayer and moved by the knowledge that truth-filled love, *caritas in veritate*, is not produced by us, but given to us. Development requires attention to the spiritual life—the experiences of trust in God, spiritual fellowship in Christ, reliance upon God's providence and mercy, love and forgiveness, self-denial, acceptance of others, justice, and peace (79).

For Reflection and Dialogue

1. How does the state hinder and help parents in their parental responsibilities?

2. What are the most serious economic challenges parents (and especially single parents) face today?

3. What most challenges the ability of a family to develop a God-centered family orientation?

4. How did Pope Benedict XVI expand our understanding of family and global linkage?

5. Why is the common good inextricably linked to society and family?

6. Why did Pope Benedict teach that thinking of unity in the human family does not submerge individual identity?

7. How does cooperation in economic development flow naturally from the concept of the global family?

8. Why did Pope Benedict teach that development in nations must contain not only a material but also a spiritual dimension?

3.

RIGHTS AND

topic include:

➲ *Economic Justice for All: Pastoral Letter on Catholic Social Teaching and the U.S. Economy*, National Conference of Catholic Bishops, 1986

➲ *Socially Responsible Investment Guidelines*, United States Conference of Catholic Bishops, 2003

➲ *On Integral Human Development in Charity and Truth* (Caritas in Veritate), Pope Benedict XVI, 2009

Economic Justice for All:
Pastoral Letter on Catholic Social Teaching
and the US Economy
National Conference of Catholic Bishops, 1986

- **The Church and the US Economy**
- **The Christian Vision of Economic Life**
- **The Various Dimensions of Justice**
- **Social Sin**
- **Economic Policy Issues**

The Church and the US Economy

The United States plays a preeminent role in an interdependent global economy. Nations separated by geography, culture, and ideology are linked in a complexity of financial, technological, and environmental networks. An increasing global interdependence can sometimes be perceived by less developed countries as a pattern of domination.

There exists a number of challenges to the domestic economy, in that the promise of the "American dream"—freedom for all persons to develop their God-given talents in full—remains unfulfilled for many millions in the United States today. Harsh poverty continues to plague the country and the gap between rich and poor widens. The lack of a supportive relationship between family life and economic life is one of the most serious problems facing the United States today.

A strong moral vision is needed to face these problems. The fundamental moral criterion for all economic decisions, policies, and institutions must be that they are at the service of all people, especially the poor (10, 13, 16, 18, 24).

The Christian Vision of Economic Life

The basis for all that is believed about the moral dimension of economic life is its vision of the transcendent worth—the sacredness—of human beings, created in the image of God (Gn 1:27). Wherever our economic arrangements fail to conform to the demands of human dignity, they must be questioned and transformed. God has entered into a sacred covenant with humanity through the people of Israel, our forerunners in faith. God is described as a God of justice. The justice of a community is measured by the treatment that is extended to its most powerless members.

Jesus enters into history and proclaims the reign of God, challenging us to seek ways in which God's revelation of the dignity and destiny of all creation might become incarnate in history.

Jesus challenges his followers to a change of heart: to proclaim God's reign and to follow his example in taking the side of those most in need, physically and spiritually. The vision of Jesus challenges the Church to see things from the side of the poor and powerless, and to assess lifestyle, policies, and social institutions in terms of their impact upon the poor.

The Christian is a member of a new community of hope, in the new creation of Christ that can reconcile a broken world. The Word made flesh into human history gives strength and hope to overcome injustice (28, 35, 38, 45, 52, 55).

g-- ------ ------ individuals or private social groups. Such a perspective demands respect for the equal dignity of all persons in economic transactions.

Distributive justice requires that the allocation of income, wealth, and power in a society be evaluated in light of its effects on persons whose basic material needs are unmet.

Social justice implies that persons have an obligation to be active and productive participants in the life of society and that society has a duty to enable them to participate in this way.

Christian faith imposes certain limits on how we can view material goods. Americans are challenged today as never before to develop an inner freedom to resist the temptation to seek more.

Positive action is needed so that social and political institutions will be created that will enable all persons to become active members of society.

As individuals and as a nation, we are called to make a fundamental option for the poor and to evaluate social and economic activity from the viewpoint of the poor and the powerless (66, 69–71, 75).

Social Sin

Basic justice demands the establishment of minimum levels of participation in the life of the human community for all persons. Such marginalization, when actively determined by a person, people, or government, can be described as a form of social sin. Respect for human rights and personal and community responsibility are closely linked. A new order must be created that guarantees the minimum conditions of human dignity in the economic sphere for every person.

To address these issues, the active participation of government will be necessary, under the auspices of "subsidiarity." Governments should undertake only those initiatives that exceed the capacity of individuals or private groups acting independently.

All members of the Christian community are called to a discernment of the hurts and opportunities of the world around them, in order to respond to the pressing needs and thus build up a more just society (77, 79, 81, 87, 124).

Economic Policy Issues

Employment

Full employment is the foundation of a just economy. Employment is a basic right that protects the freedom of all to participate in the economic life of the society. It is a deep conviction of American culture that work is central to the freedom and well-being of people. The nation cannot afford the economic costs, social dislocation, and enormous human tragedies caused by unemployment. Discrimination in employment is one of the causes for high rates of joblessness.

A consensus must be developed that everyone has a right to employment. The burden of securing full employment falls on everyone—policymakers, business, labor, and the general public.

The general economic policies of the government are essential tools for encouraging steady economic growth (69, 141, 147, 153).

Poverty

Poverty is a condition experienced at some time by many people in different walks of life. Many remain poor for extended periods of time.

Most distressing is the number of children who are affected. Many poor families with children receive no government assistance, have no health insurance, and cannot pay medical bills. Due to their mother's lack of access to high-quality prenatal care, poor children are disadvantaged even from birth.

There has also been a significant rise in the number of women in poverty. This has been the result of many factors, including wage discrimination.

Racial minorities are especially susceptible to poverty, oftentimes due to discrimination. Despite gains that have been made toward racial equality, the effects of past discrimination, as well as discrimination in our own time continues to make it d

The most appropriate and fundamental solutions to poverty will be those that enable people to take control of their lives. We must continue to develop sound social welfare programs with a new creativity and commitment.

The search for more humane and effective ways to deal with poverty is not limited to short-term reform measures, but rather includes a variety of creative efforts to fashion a system of income support that protects the basic dignity of the poor (174–178, 181, 182, 185, 188, 192, 215).

Food and Agriculture

Many farmers face serious challenges to their economic well-being, including persistent high interest rates. US international trade policies have also affected the farmer, since past emphasis on producing for overseas markets has contributed to a strain on our natural resource base.

The diversity and richness in American society are being lost as farm people leave the land and as rural communities decay.

The US food system is an integral part of the larger economy of the nation and of the world. There must be a determination that the United States will play an appropriate role in meeting global food needs and a commitment to bequeath to future generations an enhanced natural environment and ready access to the necessities of life (223, 226, 250).

The US Economy and Developing Nations

The demands of Christian love and human solidarity challenge all economic actors to choose community over chaos. Basic justice implies that all peoples are entitled to participate in the increasingly interdependent global economy. Respect for human rights, both political and economic, implies that international decisions must be shaped by values that are more than economic. The special place of the poor means that meeting the basic needs of the millions of deprived and hungry people in the world must be the number one objective of international policy (EJFA 258).

Socially Responsible Investment Guidelines
United States Conference of Catholic Bishops, 2003

- **Principles for USCCB Investments**
- **USCCB Investment Policies**

Principles for USCCB Investments

The National Conference of Catholic Bishops (NCCB) and the United States Catholic Conference (USCC) were merged in 2001 to form the United States Conference of Catholic Bishops (USCCB). The USCCB is called to exercise faithful stewardship in managing its financial resources. It draws its values, directions, and criteria from the Gospel, universal Church teaching, and conference statements. To carry out its mission properly, the conference depends on a reasonable return on investment. Religious mandate and fiscal responsibility suggest a need for clear and comprehensive policies to guide the conference's investments.

The pastoral letter *Economic Justice for All: Pastoral Letter for Catholic Social Teaching and the US Economy* emphasized the following three themes related to this topic.

Church as Shareholder and Investor

Individual Christians and those responsible within Church institutions who are shareholders must see to it that the invested funds are used responsibly. As part owners, they must cooperate in shaping policies through dialogue with management, voting at corporate meetings, introduction of resolutions, and participation in investment decisions. The bishops support efforts to develop alternate investment policies, especially those that help foster economic development in depressed communities and help the Church to respond to local and regional needs.

Shareholder Responsibility

endeavor apply to the Church and its agencies. The Church must be exemplary in this regard.

The principles of wise stewardship of financial resources and socially conscious investment criteria are carried out by consistent strategies. These strategies seek to avoid participation in harmful activities, pursue the good, and use the conference's role as stockholder for social stewardship.

- To do no harm refers to a refusal to invest in companies whose products and/or policies are counter to the values of Catholic moral teaching. It may also refer to divesting or refusing to invest based on the principle of cooperation and the avoidance of scandal. In these cases prudence is the guiding principle.

- Pursuing the good refers to a positive strategy of seeking to invest in companies that promote values consonant with Catholic social teaching while earning a reasonable rate of return. It also refers to "alternate investments" which may result in a lower rate of return but advance the Church's preferential option for the poor or produce some truly significant social good.

- Social stewardship refers to a strategy of active corporate participation, actively seeking to influence the corporate culture and to influence corporate policies and decisions.

USCCB Investment Policies

At the present time the USCCB investment policies cover the following areas: protecting human life; promoting human dignity; reducing arms production; pursuing economic justice; protecting the environment; and encouraging corporate responsibility.

Protecting Human Life

- *Abortion:* Absolute exclusion of investment in companies whose activities include direct participation in abortion.

- *Contraceptives*: The USCCB will not invest in companies that manufacture contraceptives.

- *Embryonic stem cell/ human cloning:* The USCCB will not invest in companies engaging in scientific research on human fetuses or embryos that results in the end of prenatal human life; makes use of tissue derived from abortions or other life-ending activities; or violates the dignity of a developing person.

Promoting Human Dignity

- *Human rights:* The USCCB will use selected shareholder resolutions and other means to encourage companies to provide sufficient wages, working conditions, and other social benefits that enable employees and families to promote a respect for fundamental human rights.

- *Racial discrimination:* The USCCB will divest from those companies whose policies are found to be discriminatory of varied ethnic and racial backgrounds historically disadvantaged and will actively promote and support shareholder resolutions directed toward equal opportunities for minorities.

- *Gender discrimination:* The USCCB will divest from those companies whose policies discriminate against women and seek to invest in companies that actively seek to promote corporate policies of equal pay and promotion opportunities for women.

- *Access to pharmaceuticals:* The USCCB will encourage companies to undertake programs that make life-sustaining drugs available to those in low-income communities and countries at affordable prices.

- *Curbing pornography:* The USCCB will not invest in a company that derives a significant portion of its revenues from products or services intended exclusively to appeal to prurient interest in sex.

sonnel landmines.

Pursuing Economic Justice

- *Labor standards/sweatshops:* The USCCB will actively promote shareholder resolutions directed toward avoiding the use of sweatshops in the manufacture of goods.

- *Affordable housing/banking:* The conference will not invest funds in a financial institution that receives less than a "satisfactory" rating from federal regulatory agencies.

- *Protecting the environment:* The USCCB will promote and support shareholder resolutions which encourage corporations to preserve the planet's ecological heritage and create environmentally sensitive technologies.

- *Encouraging corporate responsibility:* The USCCB will encourage companies to report on social and environmental performance, as well as financial.

On Integral Human Development in Charity and Truth
(Caritas in Veritate)
Pope Benedict XVI, 2009

- **The Development of People: Rights and Duties;
  The Environment**

The Development of People: Rights and Duties;
The Environment

Appeals are made to alleged rights and arbitrary duties accompanied by the demand that they be recognized, while elementary and basic rights are unacknowledged and violated in many parts of the world. Claims to excess wealth within affluent societies are ignored, while areas of the underdeveloped world lack adequate food, drinkable water, basic instruction, and elementary healthcare. An overemphasis upon rights can lead to a disregard for duties. Duties reinforce rights and call for their defense and their promotion as a task to be undertaken in service to the common good. If the basis of human rights is only to be found in the deliberations of an assembly of citizens, these rights can be changed at any time and are no longer seen as inviolable. The sharing of reciprocal duties is a more powerful incentive than the assertion of rights (43).

It is a mistake to consider population growth as the primary cause of underdevelopment, even from an economic point of view. There is a need to defend the primary role of the family in the area of sexuality, as opposed to the state. Morally responsible openness to human life is a social and economic resource. The decline in birth rates in some formerly prosperous nations puts a strain on social welfare systems, increases their costs, eats into savings and the financial resources needed for investment, reduces the availability of quality laborers, and narrows the "brain pool" upon which nations can draw for their needs. States are called to enact policies which promote the centrality and integrity of the family founded on marriage between a man and a woman, the primary cell of society (44).

The economy is in need of moral values to function correctly, an ethics which is people-centered. It is advisable to use discernment when using the term "ethical" since the adjective can be easily misused. It can lead to interpretations which include decisions that are contrary to justice and authentic human welfare. The Church's social doctrine can make a specific contribution since it is based on man's creation in the image of God (Gn 1:27), which gives rise to the inviolable dignity of the human person and the transcendent value of natural moral norms. Efforts are needed to ensure that the whole economy and the whole

social welfare, and the diversified world of the so-called civil economy and the economy of communion. This reality includes the private and public spheres which does not exclude profit but considers it a means for achieving human and social ends and a more humane market and society (46).

For Reflection and Dialogue

1. What areas concerning economic justice could be reflected on in your local community?

2. How does the vision of Jesus Christ challenge the Church in the area of economic justice?

3. How can a society be said to be committing "social sin"?

4. How can a parish/local community assist in the programs recommended by the bishops in the area of employment? Poverty? Food and agriculture? U.S. economy and developing nations?

5. What should be considered as a rationale for shareholder decisions concerning investment policies?

6. How can Christian investors practice socially conscious stewardship as recommended in the investment policy of the USCCB?

4.

OPTION FOR THE POOR
~~AND V~~

beyond one's own boundaries to concern for appropriate development in especially disadvantaged areas throughout the world. Included in the documents that address this topic are the following:

- *On Christianity and Social Progress* (Mater et Magistra), Pope John XXIII, 1961

- *On the Development of Peoples* (Populorum Progressio), Pope Paul V, 1967

- *On Social Concern* (Sollicitudo Rei Socialis), Pope John Paul II, 1987

- *A Place at the Table: A Catholic Recommitment to Overcome Poverty and to Respect the Dignity of All God's Children,* United States Conference of Catholic Bishops, 2002

- *For I Was Hungry and You Gave Me Food: Catholic Reflections on Food, Farmers, and Farmworkers,* United States Conference of Catholic Bishops, 2003

- *On Integral Human Development in Charity and Truth* (Caritas in Veritate), Pope Benedict XVI, 2009

> ## On Christianity and Social Progress (Mater et Magistra)
> ## Pope John XXIII, 1961
>
> - **The Encyclical Rerum Novarum**
> - **Development of the Teachings of Rerum Novarum**
> - **New Aspects of the Social Question**
> - **Reconstruction of Social Relationships in Truth, Justice, and Love**

Jesus Christ established the Catholic Church as mother and teacher of nations. The teaching of Christ embraces the whole person, soul and body, intellect and will. For 2,000 years the Church has held aloft the torch of charity through teaching and example. The most notable evidence of the social teaching and action is the encyclical by Pope Leo XIII, *Rerum Novarum*, which resolved questions regarding workers' conditions in conformity with Christian principles (1, 6, 7).

The Encyclical *Rerum Novarum*

When the encyclical *Rerum Novarum* was written, it was held by many that no connection existed between economic and moral law, whereby those engaged in economic activity need look no further than their own gain. During this era, trade unions in many different countries were sometimes forbidden, sometimes tolerated, and sometimes recognized in private law. Workers labored under conditions where there were dangers to health, moral integrity, and religious faith. The specter of unemployment was ever present. As a consequence, many workers were indignant at the state of affairs and publicly protested.

Pope Leo XIII in his encyclical proclaimed a social message based on the requirements of human nature itself, conforming to the Gospel and reason. He taught that the human person cannot be treated as a commodity. Remuneration is not to be thought of in terms of merchandise, but rather according to the laws of justice and equity.

Private property is a natural right possessed by all, which the state must not suppress. The state must as well take interest in the economic activity of its citizens and promote a sufficient supply of material goods. In addition, the state should see to it that labor agreements are entered into according to the norms of justice. Workers and employers should regulate their mutual relations in a spirit of human solidarity.

The encyclical *Quadragesimo Anno* (On the Fortieth Anniversary of *Rerum Novarum*) by Pope Pius XI continued many of the themes of *Rerum Novarum*. It confirmed the natural-law character of private prop-

so that those involved in economic activities can carry out their tasks in conformity with the common good.

In a radio broadcast of June 1, 1941, Pope Pius XII declared that the Church had competence to decide whether the bases of a given social system are in accord with the unchangeable order which God has fixed both in the natural order and revelation (1, 2, 6, 7, 11, 13–15, 18–21, 27, 31–33, 37–39, 42).

Development of the Teachings of *Rerum Novarum*

Intervention of Public Authority in Economic Life
It is necessary that public authorities take interest to increase the output of goods and to further social progress for the benefit of all citizens. The intervention of public authorities is based on the principle of subsidiarity—that one should not withdraw from individuals and commit to the community what they can accomplish by their own enterprise and industry. Inasmuch as every social activity should prove a help to members of the body social, it should never destroy or absorb them. Precautionary activities by public authorities in the economic field should avoid restricting the freedom of private citizens and increase the basic rights of each individual person. There cannot be a prosperous and well-ordered society unless both private citizens and public authorities work together in economic affairs.

Our times are known for the multiplication of social relationships, a daily more complex interdependence of citizens. This reality is both a symptom and a cause of the growing intervention of public authorities in private life.

People are joining associations to accomplish goals which they cannot achieve alone, including economic, social, cultural, recreational, and political. An advance in social relationships brings numerous services and advantages. At the same time, opportunities for free actions by individuals are restricted within narrower limits.

Advances in social organizations and their objectives must be accompanied by a correct understanding of the common good by public authorities. As relationships multiply, binding people together more closely, the commonwealth must keep in mind the freedom of individual citizens and groups of citizens as the state regulates their undertakings.

Concern for the Working Class

It is distressing to see great masses of workers throughout the world who do not receive a just remuneration in wages for their work. Many times these workers live in conditions that are completely out of accord with human dignity.

It also happens in some of these nations that, in contrast with the extreme need of the majority, there exists great and conspicuous wealth.

Moreover, in economically developed countries, it frequently happens that great, or sometimes very great, remuneration is given for the performance of some task of lesser importance or doubtful utility. Meanwhile, the diligent and profitable work that whole classes of hardworking citizens perform receives low payment that is insufficient for the necessities of life.

It must be reaffirmed, once again, that just as remuneration for work cannot be left entirely to unregulated competition, neither may it be decided arbitrarily at the will of the more powerful. The norms of justice and equity should be strictly observed. This requires that workers receive a wage that is sufficient to lead a life worthy of humanity and to fulfill family responsibilities.

In determining this wage, many factors must be considered, including the economic state of the enterprise within which the worker is employed. Although the standards of judgment in this matter are binding everywhere and always, the measure in which they are to be applied cannot be established unless account is taken of the resources on hand.

The economies of various countries continue to evolve rapidly. The strict demand of social justice calls for a corresponding social development. The economic prosperity of any people is to be

goods and services for a better life. At the same time, efforts must be made either to eliminate or keep within bounds the inequalities that exist between different sectors of the economy. Finally, a humane way of existence must be passed on to the next generation.

Justice is to be observed not merely in the distribution of wealth but also in regard to the conditions under which people engaged in productive activity have an opportunity to assume responsibility and to perfect themselves by their efforts. An economic order is considered to be unjust if the organization and structure be such that human dignity of workers is compromised, or their sense of responsibility is weakened, or their freedom of action is removed.

The right of private property is permanently valid. The right of private individuals to act freely in economic affairs is recognized in vain unless these persons are given the opportunity of selecting and using things necessary for the exercise of this right. It is a right which continually draws its force and vigor from the fruitfulness of labor and which is an effective aid in safeguarding the dignity of the human person.

It is not enough to assert that the person has the right of privately possessing goods unless at the same time an effort is made to spread the use of this right through all ranks of the citizenry.

What has been said does not preclude ownership of goods pertaining to production of wealth by states and in other public bodies. The principle of subsidiarity is to be strictly observed.

It has always been taught that in the right of private property, there is rooted a social responsibility. Whoever has received a larger share of blessings must use them, in addition to one's own perfection, for the benefit of others (52, 53, 55, 56, 60, 62, 65, 67–74, 79, 82, 83, 109, 112, 113, 116, 117, 119).

New Aspects of the Social Question

Readjustment of the Relationship between Workers
and Management
The progress of events and of time makes it increasingly evident that the relationship between workers and management must be readjusted according to the norms of justice and charity. Within the human community, many nations have not made identical progress in economic and social affairs.

Concern for the Agricultural Enterprise
In agriculture, many farmers have abandoned their productive enterprises, which they see as not offering them a more comfortable life. They should be provided with insurance and social security benefits comparable to those in other professions. Agricultural products should be price protected, worked out by economic experts. In rural areas it is fitting that industries be established and common services be developed that are useful in preserving, processing, and transporting farm products. The family farm will be firm and stable only when it yields income sufficient for decent and humane family living.

In rural areas farmers should join together in fellowships especially when the family itself works the farm. It is proper for rural workers to have a sense of solidarity. Toward this end they should set up mutual aid societies and professional associations. But when wishing to make their influence felt, rural workers should refer, as should other categories of workers, to the common good.

Concern for Less Economically Advanced Countries
Perhaps the most pressing problem today is the relationship between economically advanced nations and those in the process of development. Nations that have abundance cannot ignore those nations that are overcome by poverty and hunger, unable to enjoy basic human

rights. For wealthier nations to destroy or to waste goods necessary for the lives of people in need runs counter to our obligations in justice and humanity.

Scientific, technical, and financial cooperation must be enlisted in the effort to assist those in need. Efforts should be made to ensure that improved social conditions and economic advancement occur simultaneously in the agricultural, industrial and various

growth, particularly in the more economically deprived nations, these problems should not be posed and resolved in a way that promotes means contrary to the dignity of the human person. These questions can only be resolved if economic and social advances preserve and augment the genuine welfare of individual citizens and of human society as a whole. All must regard the life of the human being as sacred, from its moment of conception. It is the important duty of parents to educate their children, who should be raised with a secure faith in the providence of God.

Cooperation and Mutual Assistance among Nations

Since the relationship between countries is closer today in every region of the world, it is proper that peoples become more and more interdependent. Because states must on occasion complement one another, they must take into account the interests of other nations. It is necessary for commonwealths to cooperate among themselves and provide mutual assistance. Unfortunately, peoples and states have fear of one another. Energies and resources are widely directed toward destruction rather than the advantage of the human family. That mutual faith may develop among leaders and nations, the law of truth and justice must be acknowledged and preserved on all sides. The guiding principles of morality and virtue must be based only on God (122, 124, 135, 137, 141, 143, 146, 147, 157, 161, 168, 173, 179, 192–194, 200, 202, 204, 207).

Reconstruction of Social Relationships in Truth, Justice, and Love

Role of Religion in Technological and Economic Development
A false opinion is today popularized holding that a sense of religion implanted in individuals by nature is imaginary and inconsistent with this day and age. Whatever the progress in technology and economic life, there can be no justice as long as individuals fail to realize their great individual dignity. Mutual relations among people absolutely require a right ordering of the human conscience in relation to God, the source of all truth, justice, and love. No folly seems more characteristic of our age than the desire to establish a firm and meaningful temporal order without God, its necessary foundation.

The individual person is the foundation, cause, and end of all social institutions. This principle, the dignity of the human person, must be applied to the systems and methods that the various situations of time or place either suggest or require. It is important that this social teaching of the Catholic Church be widely studied and disseminated. This teaching, which has truth as its guide, justice as its end, and love as its driving force, must also be applied.

The teachings in regard to social matters are put into effect in three stages: first, the actual situation is examined; then the situation is evaluated carefully in relation to these teachings; and finally it is decided what can and should be done in order that the traditional norms may be adapted to circumstances of time and place. These three steps can be expressed as *observe, judge,* and *act*. Members of the Church are reminded that in fulfilling their duties and pursuing their goals, they do not allow their consciousness of responsibilities to grow cool or neglect the order of the more important goods (213, 215, 217, 219, 221, 226, 236, 245).

> ## On the Development of Peoples (Populorum Progressio)
> ## Pope Paul VI, 1967
>
> - **Universality of the Problem**
> - **Nature of the Problem**
> - The Church's Role in Development

Universality of the Problem

The extent of poverty is worldwide, and the people who hunger are making urgent appeals for help. Concrete action must be taken to encourage social justice among all nations and to offer less developed nations the means whereby they can further their own progress (5).

Nature of the Problem

Many are seeking freedom from oppression of any kind, especially from that imposed by lack of subsistence, healthcare, and fixed employment. They seek freedom from violence to their dignity as human beings and better education—to seek to do more, know more, and have more in order to be more. Most especially this applies to newly developing nations, once subject to a colonial power. While the wealthy continue to enjoy rapid economic growth and development, the poor develop slowly, setting the stage for an increasing imbalance and social conflict. The new technologies of modern civilization can sometimes threaten traditional cultures and values (6–8, 10).

The Church's Role in Development

The Church has attempted continuously to foster human progress. Especially through missionaries, it not only has sought to bring the

Gospel to nations but has constructed hospitals, schools, and universities as well. Concerted efforts by all are now needed to assist developing nations with a clear vision of all economic, social, cultural, and spiritual aspects. The Church offers to the world what is one of its characteristic attributes: a global vision of the person and of the human race.

Development cannot be limited to economic growth. It must be complete and promote every person and the whole person. The vocation of each individual is to develop and fulfill his or her potential. Through Christ, a more complete fulfillment takes place, the highest goal of personal development.

Each person is a part of society and a part of humankind, and this human solidarity imposes a duty of mutual concern for the development of others. All people are called to work for a "new humanism," a more human condition that may be found by embracing the higher values of love and friendship, prayer and contemplation. Such humanism will help overcome oppressive social structures and foster an increased esteem for the dignity of others (14, 15, 17, 20, 21).

Action That Must Be Undertaken

God intended the earth and all that it contains for the use of every human being and people. All other rights, including property and free commerce, are subordinate to this principle. Private property does not constitute for anyone an absolute and unconditional right. No one is justified in keeping for his or her exclusive use what is not needed, when others lack basic necessities.

While industrialization in the modern world is a necessity for economic growth, it must always be remembered that the economy is at the service of the human being. Work must be seen as the mission of sharing in the creation of the supernatural world.

Urgent reforms are needed and programs must be undertaken that will reduce inequalities, fight discrimination, and free individuals from various types of servitude. Social progress demands growth in literacy, respect for the family, and the promotion of respect for different cultures. Developing nations must be taught to carefully discriminate concerning what is truly necessary and what is being imposed by other nations, which may not always be for their best interests (22, 23, 25, 33, 34, 36, 40, 41).

A Spirit of Solidarity

It is in the mutual spirit of understanding and friendship among peoples and nations that a common future can be built for the future of

financial aid is used to its full advantage, and that developing nations no longer risk being overwhelmed by debts whose repayment swallows up the greater part of their gain.

A worldwide collaboration of which a common fund would be created could be both a means and a symbol in assisting the most destitute of the world.

Nations whose industrialization is limited are faced with serious difficulties when they must rely on their exports to balance their economy and to carry out their plans for development. International trade must be humane and just. International agreements should establish general norms for regulating certain prices, guaranteeing certain types of production, and supporting new industries.

There is a duty to welcome others, especially for developed nations to welcome those from less developed areas. Between civilizations as between persons, sincere dialogue creates brotherhood.

To wage war on misery and to struggle against injustice is to promote, along with improved conditions, the human and spiritual progress of all people, and therefore the common good of humanity (43, 44, 51, 57, 61, 67, 73, 76).

On Social Concern (Sollicitudo Rei Socialis)
Pope John Paul II, 1987

- **Survey of the Contemporary World**
- **Some Particular Guidelines**

The social concern of the Church directed toward the authentic development of the individual and society, respecting all dimensions of the human person, has expressed itself in varied ways. One such means is through papal encyclicals such as *Populorum Progressio* (March 26, 1967) in which Pope Paul VI attempted to apply the teachings of the Second Vatican Council. This encyclical may be seen as a response to the Council's appeal, especially to those who are "poor or in any way afflicted," which are the "joys and hopes, the griefs and anxieties of the followers of Christ" (*Pastoral Constitution on the Church in the Modern World* [Gaudium et Spes], 1).

The encyclical, in taking up the theme of development, stresses the legitimacy of the Church's involvement in this concern, in continuity with previous encyclicals. The ethical and cultural character of the problems connected with development demand comment and concern from the Church. Paul VI in this encyclical presented a moral obligation to political leaders and citizens of rich countries to take into account the interdependence of their conduct and the poverty and underdevelopment of many millions of people.

True development cannot consist in the accumulation of wealth if this is to be gained at the expense of the development of the masses and without due consideration of the social, cultural, and spiritual dimensions of the human being.

The question is raised: how can one justify the fact that huge sums of money which could and should be used for increasing the development of peoples are instead used for the enrichment of individuals or groups, or assigned to the increase of stockpiles of weapons, both in developed and undeveloped countries? If "development is the new name for peace," war is the major enemy of the integral development of peoples (1, 5, 8–10).

Survey of the Contemporary World

We must confront and address the reality of an innumerable multitude of people—children, adults, and the elderly—who are suffering under the intolerable burden of poverty. There is a persistent and widening gap between the areas of the so-called developed North and the developing South. This picture is complex, especially with the differences of culture and values systems b̶e̶t̶w̶e̶e̶n̶ ̶t̶h̶e̶

...y ̶o̶f̶ ̶t̶h̶e̶ poor remains. Among the specific signs of underdevelopment which increasingly affect the developed countries are two in particular: the *housing crisis* and *unemployment*. Millions of people lack adequate housing, experienced universally and due in large measure to the growing phenomenon of urbanization. Also, with the high rate of population growth, the sources of work seem to be shrinking and the opportunities for employment are decreasing rather than increasing.

Another important phenomenon which must be mentioned as indicative of the interdependence between developed and less developed countries is the international debt. The availability of capital to developing nations, although originally welcomed as a possible investment for development projects, must now be reconsidered, since the debtor nations must now export the capital needed for improving their standard of living.

The developing countries, instead of becoming autonomous nations concerned with their own progress, become parts of a machine, cogs on a gigantic wheel, due to the influence of the northern hemisphere.

The possibility and willingness to contribute widely and generously to the common good only justifies a leadership role among nations. If a nation closes in upon itself and fails to meet the responsibilities following from its superior position in the community of nations, it falls short of its clear ethical duty.

The arms trade is equally to blame as a disorder in regard to the fulfillment of true human need. There exists a strange phenomenon: while economic aid and development plans meet with innumerable obstacles, arms circulate with almost total freedom all over the world.

There exists the festering wound that reveals the imbalances of this world in the form of the millions of refugees who have been deprived of home, employment, family, and homeland. Another painful wound in today's world is the phenomenon of terrorism. Christianity forbids seeking solutions by ways of hatred and the murdering of defenseless people.

It is alarming to see governments in many countries launching systematic campaigns against birth, often the result of pressure and financing from abroad, sometimes made as a condition for granting economic aid. This exhibits an absolute lack of respect for the freedom of choice of the parties involved. It is a sign of an erroneous and perverse idea of true development.

Included, however, in a positive assessment of the issues in development is the full awareness among large numbers of men and women of their own dignity and that of every human being. The influence of the *Declaration of Human Rights*, promulgated in December 1948 by the General Assembly of the United Nations, has been considerable in this regard.

Also, the growing conviction of a radical interdependence and need for solidarity among nations has been helpful. People are recognizing that they are linked together by a common destiny, which is to be constructed together (13–19, 22–25).

Authentic Human Development
Development is not a straightforward process, automatic and unlimited. Nor must "superdevelopment" be held as the ideal, which consists of an excessive availability of every kind of material good for the benefit of certain social groups, easily making people slaves of possessions and of immediate gratification. This is the so-called civilization of consumption or consumerism, which involves so much throwing away and waste. As taught by the Second Vatican Council, "to have" does not in itself improve the human person unless it contributes to the maturing and enrichment of that person's human vocation.

One of the greatest injustices in the contemporary world consists precisely in this: that the ones who possess much are relatively few and those who possess almost nothing are many. The evil consists not so much in having but rather in possessing without regard for the quality and the ordered hierarchy of the goods one has.

Development must be measured according to the reality and vocation of the human being in its totality.

The obligation to commit oneself to the development of peoples is not just an individual duty and still less an individualistic one. It is an imperative that obliges each and every man and woman as well as societies and nations. The Catholic Church is ready to collaborate with other churches and ecclesial communities in this effort. Such collaboration is a duty of all toward all. Peoples and nations have a right to their own full development that includes economic and social aspects as well as individual cultural identity and openness to the transcendent. Such development must also respect and promote human rights. Development must be achieved in the framework of solidarity and freedom. True development must be based on the love of God and neighbor (22, 28–33).

A Theological Reading of Modern Problems
Because of the essentially moral character of development, it is clear that the obstacles to development likewise have a moral character. The main obstacles to development will be overcome only by means of essentially moral decisions.

It is not out of place to speak of "structures of sin," rooted in personal sin, always linked to the concrete acts of the individuals. God has a plan for humanity, which requires from people clear-cut attitudes, which are expressed in actions or omissions toward one's neighbor. This also involves interference in the process of the development of peoples, the delay or slowness of which must be also judged in this light.

Two particular structures, created as a result of the actions and attitudes opposed to the will of God and the good of neighbor, deserve attention: the all-consuming desire for profit and the thirst for power *at all costs*. Not only individuals but also nations and blocs fall victim to these attitudes of sin.

One would hope that men and women, even those without explicit faith, would be convinced that the obstacles to integral development not only are economic but also rest on profound attitudes which human beings can make into absolute values. For Christians, there is a change of behavior called "conversion," a relationship to God, to the sin committed, to its consequences, and hence to one's neighbor.

There is an emerging sense of interdependence in the world with important moral consequences. When it becomes recognized as a system determining relationships in the world, in all its economic, cultural, political, and religious elements, its response becomes the virtue of "solidarity." This is not a feeling of vague compassion but a firm and persevering determination to commit oneself to the common good because we are really responsible for all. This determination is based on the solid conviction that what is hindering full development is the desire for profit and thirst for power.

There also exists a growing awareness of solidarity among the poor themselves in their efforts to support one another. The Church feels called to take a stand beside the poor and to discern the justice of their requests and to help satisfy them.

The same criterion must be applied by analogy to international relationships, with interdependence transformed into solidarity, based on the principle that the goods of creation are meant for all. The stronger and richer nations must have a sense of moral responsibility for the other nations in order that a strong international system may be established, resting on the foundation of the equality of all peoples and on the necessary respect for their legitimate differences.

Solidarity helps us to see the other—whether a person, people, or nation—not just as some kind of instrument but also as a neighbor. One's neighbor is not only a human being with his or her rights and a fundamental equality but also the living image of God, redeemed by the blood of Jesus Christ and placed under the permanent action of the Holy Spirit.

The structures of sin can be overcome only through the exercise of the human and Christian solidarity to which the Church calls us, which it tirelessly promotes (35–40).

Some Particular Guidelines

The Church does not have technical solutions to the problem of und...

...ply g ... truth to concrete situations. The instrument used for reaching this goal is the Church's social doctrine, a formulation that is the result of a careful reflection on the complex realities of human existence in the light of the Church's tradition. It attempts to guide human behavior and a commitment to justice.

Highlighted must be the preferential option for the poor, a primacy in the exercise of Christian charity. This preference for the poor and the decisions it inspires must embrace the immense multitudes of the hungry, the needy, the homeless, those without medical care, and above all, those without hope for a better future. Our daily lives, as well as our decisions in the political and economic fields, must be marked by these realities. Likewise, leaders of nations and the heads of international bodies must keep in mind the true human dimension as a priority in development plans.

The characteristic principle of Christian social doctrine is that the goods of the world are originally meant for all. The right to private property is valid and necessary, but it does not nullify the value of this principle.

The motivating concern for the poor must be translated into concrete actions. For example, the international trade system frequently discriminates against the products of the young industries of the developing countries and discourages the producers of raw materials. The world monetary system is marked by excessive fluctuation of exchange rates and interest rates to the detriment of the balance of payments and the debt situation of the poorer countries.

Development also demands a spirit of initiative from the underdeveloped countries. Each must discover and use to the best advantage its own area of freedom. Each developing country should favor the self-affirmation of each citizen and whatever promotes literacy and the basic education, which completes and deepens it as a direct contribution to true development. These nations must identify their own priorities and clearly recognize their own needs.

Some nations will need to increase food production in order to have always available what is needed for subsistence. Other nations need to reform their political institutions in order to replace corrupt, dictatorial, and authoritarian forms of government with democratic and participatory ones.

This can only be accomplished with the collaboration of all—especially the international community in the framework of solidarity, which includes everyone, beginning with the most neglected (41–45).

A Place at the Table: A Catholic Recommitment to Overcome Poverty and to Respect the Dignity of All God's Children
USCCB, 2002

The realities of poverty are shaped by economic, moral, and cultural forces, including the rapid pace of globalization. Many people are left behind, lacking the education, skills, and access to compete. These include the hungry and homeless, subsistence farmers, victims of discrimination, those suffering from AIDS, those caught in violent conflict, immigrants, and refugees.

Concern for the poor is a constant theme of the scriptures—a passion of the prophets, the witness of Jesus, and the example of the early Church. We are called to treat all people with dignity and respect.

The social doctrine of the Church provides principles for reflection, criteria for judgment, and guidelines for decisions that we must make each day. The presence of Christ in the poor requires the Church to make a preferential option for the poor and vulnerable. The principle of solidarity reminds us that we are members of one family and neighbor to each other. Our faith gives us the strength to continue, as a Church, to put into action the call to be Christ to others.

Efforts to serve and stand with the poor are the work of four institutions, or "legs of the table":

ishes and Catholic schools can be a beacon of hope and centers of hope for the poor.

- *What the private sector can do:* The private sector must be a reflection of our values and priorities and a contributor to the common good. Workers and farmers need living wages, access to healthcare, vacation time and family and medical leave, a voice and real participation in the workplace, and the prospect of a decent retirement.

- *What the government can do:* Government must provide a safety net for the vulnerable, help overcome discrimination, and ensure equal opportunity for all. It must work to help overcome structures of injustice and misuse of power to address problems beyond the reach of individual and community efforts.

Work on overcoming poverty should not be distorted by ideological agendas. We need more debt relief and development assistance but also more transparency and accountability to make sure that these investments are improving the lives, education, and housing of the poorest. Every Catholic and our communities of faith are called to join in the search for moral values and virtues and for just policies that will help people escape the trap of poverty.

Preaching, education, and formation are essential in reflecting the option of the Church for the poor. Every day we are presented with choices that can help us promote justice: raising our children with a

passion for justice; contributing to a workplace that is safe and respectful; supporting businesses that contribute to the common good; treat-
ing workers fairly; and not exploiting the poor and vulnerable. As consumers we can live more simply so there might be enough at the table
for all.

For I Was Hungry and You Gave Me Food:
Catholic Reflections on Food, Farmers, and Farmworkers
USCCB, 2003

- **Our Faith Tradition: Scripture**

Our Faith Tradition: Scripture
The Old Testament calls us to care for the land and to provide food for
the poor and outcast.

Jesus warned against selfishness and called us to feed the hungry and
show concern for those who are poor.

One of the fundamental measures of our lives will be how we cared
for people who were in need.

On Integral Human Development in Charity and Truth
(Caritas in Veritate)
Pope Benedict XVI, 2009

- **The Message of *Populorum Progressio***
- **Human Development in Our Time**

The Message of *Populorum Progressio*
As taught in the encyclical of Pope Paul VI, *Populorum Progressio*, the
whole Church—when she proclaims, celebrates, and performs works
of charity—is engaged in promoting integral human development.
Authentic human development concerns the whole of the person in
every dimension. Institutions by themselves are not enough, because
human development is a vocation, involving assumption of responsibility in solidarity on the part of everyone. It requires a transcendent

vision of the person, needing God. Only through an encounter with God are we able to see another person as something more than just another creature (11).

The Christian vocation to development helps to promote the advancement of all people and the whole person. In promoting development the Christian faith relies on Christ to whom every authentic vocation to

understand it and mobilize ourselves at the level of the heart to ensure that current economic and social processes evolve toward fully human outcomes (20).

Human Development in Our Time

The economic growth that we see today continues to be weighed down by malfunctions and dramatic problems and presents us with choices that cannot be delayed. Global interrelationships, the damaging effects on the economy of badly managed and largely speculative financial dealings, large-scale migration of peoples, and the unregulated exploitation of the world's resources lead us to reflect on the measures that are necessary to provide solutions to problems that impact the present and future good of humanity. The crisis is an opportunity for discernment to shape a new vision for the future (21).

Today, although the world's wealth continues to grow, new sectors of society are succumbing to poverty and new forms of poverty are emerging. In some areas of the world we see glaring corruption and illegality, while some large multinational companies sometimes fail to respect the human rights of workers. International aid is sometimes diverted from its proper ends (22).

Progress in economic and technological development is never sufficient in itself. Emerging from economic backwardness does not resolve the complex issues of human advancement (23).

In today's world, various states find themselves limited by a new context of international trade and finance. It is necessary that the state's public authorities reevaluate their role and their powers to resolve the economic challenges of today (24).

Today's global market stimulates a search in rich countries for areas to outsource production at a low cost to reduce the prices of goods and make for greater availability of consumer goods for the domestic market. Consequently, the market has prompted new forms of competition between states as they seek to set up foreign production centers. This leads to a downsizing of social security systems with grave danger for the rights of workers. Trade union organizations experience greater difficulty in carrying out their task of representing the interests of workers, sometimes limited by the economic utility of governments. The promotion of workers' associations must be honored today even more. The mobility of labor and an uncertainty over working conditions can create new forms of psychological instability. Being out of work and dependent on public or private assistance can undermine freedom and creativity of the person and the family. The primary capital that must be safeguarded is the human person in his or her integrity (25).

Today there are more possibilities for interaction between cultures, providing new opportunities for intercultural dialogue. However, we see today a cultural eclecticism often assumed uncritically, where cultures are simply placed side by side and viewed as substantially equivalent. This cultural relativism emerges where cultures remain side by side but separate. The opposite dynamic is also possible, of cultural leveling, with an indiscriminate acceptance of conduct and lifestyles. Cultures then can no longer define themselves within a nature that transcends them, and the human person is reduced to a mere cultural statistic (26).

Hunger still continues to ravage the earth and its elimination has become a requirement for safeguarding the peace and stability of the planet. Needed are economic institutions that are capable of guaranteeing access to sufficient food and water supplies. The crisis needs to be addressed within a long-term perspective, eliminating the structural causes that give rise to it while promoting agricultural development in poorer countries. The right to food, similar to the right to water, has a place within the pursuit of other rights, beginning with the fundamental right to life. Through support of poor countries by means of financial plans inspired by solidarity, true economic growth can be generated (27).

Development cannot be detached from respect for life. The presence of poverty provokes high infant mortality rates. Some governments promote demographic control, limiting population growth. Some development which is linked to specific head

spiritual strength necessary for attaining integral human development (29).

Integral human development requires a commitment to foster the interaction of the different levels of human knowledge in order to foster the authentic development of peoples. The joint action of implementation of the socioeconomic measures needed have to be given direction, because all social action involves a doctrine. Since the demands of love do not contradict those of reason, intelligence and love are never in separate compartments (30).

Moral evaluation and scientific research must go hand in hand. The Church's social doctrine allows faith, theology, metaphysics, and science to collaborate together in service to humanity (31).

New elements in the picture of the development of peoples demand new solutions. The dignity of the human person and the demands of justice require that economic choices do not cause disparities in wealth to increase in an excessive and morally unacceptable manner. We must continue to prioritize the goal of access to steady employment for everyone.

The reduction of cultures to the technological dimension in the long term impedes reciprocal enrichment. There is a need to enter into a deep reflection on the meaning of the economy and its goals—given the dysfunctions and deviations caused in part by ecological problems and the cultural and moral crisis of today (32).

The ferocious pace of globalization presents new opportunities for cooperation among nations, but without the guidance of charity in truth unprecedented damage could be created. Charity in truth invites a perspective of a "civilization of love" whose seed God has planted in every culture (33).

For Reflection and Dialogue

1. What insights of Pope John XXIII could be kept in mind as more and more aspects of citizens' lives are regulated by the state?

2. What are the particular concerns today that come from those engaged in the agricultural sector? What solutions as proposed by Pope John XXIII could be considered today?

3. Does the Church have a role today in assisting in the economic development for poorer nations? Why or why not? Is foreign aid a good thing?

4. How does the Church understand God's intention and humanity's use of the earth's natural resources? What are the consequences of improper stewardship of our natural resources? What steps could a local community take in this regard?

5. How would you assess the progress that has been made in economic development to combat inequality among nations since the document *Populorum Progressio* was issued in 1967?

6. What can be a danger to poorer nations in accepting aid from wealthier countries?

7. Why should the Church enter into questions regarding the development of peoples?

8. What areas of development do you believe have become worse since the publication of Paul VI's encyclical on development? What hopeful signs do you see?

9. What do you see, in the area of development, as one of the "greatest injustices" in regard to the differences between the rich and poor nations?

10. What are the "structures of sin" which can prevent or delay true development? How can they be overcome?

13. What basic principles of Catholic social teaching require that economic choices do not cause disparities in wealth to increase "in an excessive and morally unacceptable manner"?

5.

THE DIGNITY OF WORK

⊥ safe working conditions, association, disability protection, security in retirement, and economic initiatives. In these teachings, labor is given priority over capital. The documents that address the topic of labor include:

- ➲ *On the Condition of Labor* (Rerum Novarum), Pope Leo XIII, 1891

- ➲ *On Reconstructing the Social Order* (Quadragesimo Anno), Pope Pius XI, 1931

- ➲ *On Human Work* (Laborem Exercens), Pope John Paul II, 1981

- ➲ *On the Hundredth Anniversary of* Rerum Novarum (Centesimus Annus), Pope John Paul II, 1991

- ➲ *For I Was Hungry and You Gave Me Food: Catholic Reflections on Food, Farmers, and Farmworkers*, USCCB, 2003

- ➲ *On Integral Human Development in Charity and Truth* (Caritas in Veritate) Pope Benedict XVI, 2009

On the Condition of Labor (Rerum Novarum)
Pope Leo XIII, 1891

- **Purpose for Employment**
- **Distinctiveness of the Human Being**
- **Proper Order within Society**
- **Rich and Poor Must Not Be Understood as Adversaries**
- **Duties of the Worker**
- **Duties of Employers**
- **The Church Reminds the Rich of the Gospel Mandate**
- **How People Are to Use Their Possessions**
- **Poverty Is Not a Disgrace**
- **The Church Must Tend to Worldly Matters as Well as the Divine**
- **The State Must Provide Aid When Needed**
- **Peace and Good Order Needed for the State**
- **Protection of Rights by the State**
- **Payment of Wages**
- **Workers' Associations**

Purpose for Employment

The primary purpose for engaging in work is to procure property for oneself. By using his energy to work for the sake of an employer, the laborer does so in order to obtain a livelihood. It is wrong for employers to set up a system whereby the goods of private individuals are transferred to the community at large, since it takes away from people the right to own property for which they may dispose of their wages (9).

Distinctiveness of the Human Being

What makes the human being unique is the use of reason. The human may use goods for the achieving of desired ends, using these goods for the best use in the present and in the future. God gave the whole human race the earth to use, and not just certain individuals. It is for institutions of peoples to determine the limits of private possessions, but the earth never ceases from serving the common interests of all. Those lacking resources supply labor and receive compensation (11, 14).

Proper Order within Society

Rich and Poor Must Not Be Understood as Adversaries
It cannot be taken for granted that one class of society is naturally opposed to another. Each is dependent upon the other, and it is the Church which can bring together and unite the rich and the poor by recalling for them their mutual duties, especially those duties that derive from justice (28, 29).

Duties of the Worker
Included among the duties of the worker is to perform entirely and con-scientiously whatever work has been voluntarily and equitably agreed on. It is also expected that the employee will not injure the property or do harm to employers, to refrain from violence (30).

Duties of Employers
Workers are not to be treated as slaves. Justice demands that workers always be treated with human dignity, since labor, as gainful employ-ment, is an honorable means of supporting life. It is shameful and inhuman to use people as things for gain. It is also important that the spiritual dimension of the person be honored: employers should see to it that employees are free for adequate periods to attend to religious obligations.

Likewise, the employer should make sure that the employee is not alienated from proper care of family. Work should not be such that it threatens the worker's health, or engages the worker in labor that is not suitable for the person's age or sex.

Among the most important duties for employers is to give every worker what is justly due them. Pay schedules should be established in accord with justice, and to defraud anyone of wages justly due is a great crime (31, 32).

The Church Reminds the Rich of the Gospel Mandate

Jesus Christ is the teacher of the Church and reminds both the rich and poor of the values of life, including the immortality of life and the promise of a life yet to come. Only when we have left this life do we truly begin to live. Whether we abound in the riches of this life or lack them is of no importance in relation to eternal happiness. Jesus by his sufferings has wondrously lightened our burdens and shows us the way to eternal glory. Those who are rich in this life have been admonished by the Lord that wealth is of no avail in entering the kingdom of God, and may make it even more difficult to obtain. One day God will call the wealthy to an accountability for their use of the material resources which they have received (33, 34).

How People Are to Use Their Possessions

Although to own goods privately is a natural right, each person should share of their goods when seeing that someone else is in need. When the demands of necessity have been sufficiently provided for, it is a duty to give to the poor out of that which remains. Whoever has received from the bounty of God a greater share of goods has received them that they might be employed for the benefit of others (36).

Poverty Is Not a Disgrace

The Church teaches that poverty is not a disgrace and no one should be ashamed because of the labor performed. True dignity is established not by wealth accumulated, but rather by virtue obtained, equitably available to all classes of people, whether poor or rich. God seems to incline more toward the unfortunate since Jesus called the poor to be blessed, embracing with special love the lowly and those harassed by injustice. We should reflect on those things which unite us. All people share in a commonality, since all people have been equally redeemed by the blood of Christ (37, 38).

traditionally instituted works of charity to assist especially the working class in some of their material need. Many religious organizations and societies have been founded and sponsored by the Church that the variety of human ills could be properly cared for (42–44).

The State Must Provide Aid When Needed

Those governing the state have the responsibility to ensure the well-being of the entire commonwealth, including the workers. Public authority should show proper concern for the worker so that what the worker contributes to the common good may be returned, that each laborer may be housed, clothed, and secure, living without hardship.

Since the power of governing comes from God and is a participation in God's sovereignty, it should be administered according to the example of Divine power, which looks to the well-being of individuals and to that of all creation (51, 52).

Peace and Good Order Needed for the State

It is vitally important for the public welfare and the private good as well that there be peace and good order in the state. Within limits, the state ought to be free to intervene if disorder is threatened due to strikes or concentrated stoppages of work, or if any threat exists to the integrity of the workers such as practice of their religion and protection of family values. The worker should be free from unjust burdens or anything which would degrade them. Intervention by the state, especially by use of law, should be appropriate and not go further than the remedy requires (53).

Protection of Rights by the State

Rights must be religiously protected, but most especially the rights of private individuals with special consideration of the poor and the vulnerable within society. Justice does not forbid us from striving for better things, but it does preclude us from taking from another what properly belongs to that individual.

The state should ensure that situations that lead to labor strikes—including work that is too long and hard with inadequate pay—are remedied. Such disruptions can inflict damage upon both the employer and the employee, making it well within the interests of the state to anticipate and prevent by removing the causes.

The power of the state should also protect the goods of the worker's soul, which bears the image and likeness of God. For this reason, it is important that workers be given the opportunity to practice their religion and worship, keeping holy the Sabbath day.

The state should protect the worker from labor that is excessive, extracted merely for the benefit of the employer's greed. Working conditions should be such that rest is provided and that proper safeguards are used regarding the employment of women and children. Proper time for days off and vacation should be provided, that energy may be restored after labor has been expended (56–60).

Payment of Wages

It has been taught that free consent fixes the amount of a wage between employer and employee. But underlying such an agreement must be natural justice. It is in the interest of the employer and society that the worker be given a sufficiently large wage to provide comfortably for the worker and the worker's family. Thus a just wage, plus the right to private property, can reasonably insure against violence or public disorder. It is also important that crushing taxes imposed by the state do not drain private wealth away (65–67).

Workers' Associations

Employers and employees, uniting in institutions and agencies to assist the poor, can accomplish much. It can also be opportune for workers to organize into associations. Such private associations can provide a forum where the worker may be better enabled to ensure benefits from the toil expended, and to ensure adequate retirement benefits for the

---

On Reconstructing the Social Order
(Quadragesimo Anno)
Pope Pius XI, 1931

- **Partnership between Employer and Employee**
- **Individual and Social Character of Labor**
- **Subsidiarity**

Partnership between Employer and Employee

The wage contract between employer and worker should be modified when possible by a contract of partnership, in which wage earners are made sharers in some way of the ownership, management, or profits.

Individual and Social Character of Labor

Human society must form a social and organic body, where labor is protected in the social and juridical order, and where various forms of human endeavor are united in mutual harmony and mutual support. Brains, capital, and labor must combine for common effort or labor cannot produce due fruit.

The wage scale should be regulated with a view toward the economic welfare of the whole people and the common good. Opportunities need to be provided for those who are willing and able to work. To lower or raise wages unduly, with a view toward private profit and disregard for the common good, is contrary to social justice. By union of effort and goodwill, a scale of wages should be established which offers the greatest number of opportunities for employment and for securing a suitable means of livelihood.

Subsidiarity

Due to the change in social conditions, much that was formerly done by small bodies can now be done only by large corporations. Just as it is wrong to withdraw from the individual and commit to the community at large what private enterprise and industry can accomplish, so too is it an injustice for a larger and higher organization to claim for itself functions that can be performed efficiently by smaller and lower bodies.

The primary responsibility of the state and of all good citizens is to abolish conflict between classes with divergent interests and thus foster and promote harmony between the various ranks of society.

On Human Work (Laborem Exercens)
Pope John Paul II, 1981

- **The Dignity of Labor and the Laborer**
- **The Individual and Work**
- **A Right Order of Values**
- **Worker Solidarity**
- **Labor and Personal Dignity**
- **The Priority of Labor over Capital**
- **Work and Ownership**
- **Rights of Workers**
- **A Spirituality of Work**

The Dignity of Labor and the Laborer

New questions and concerns are always arising concerning labor and the worker, providing fresh hopes, but also fears, connected with this basic dimension of human existence. With new developments in technology, the economy, and politics, it is always important for the Church to call attention to the dignity and rights of all who work and to call attention to those situations in which the dignity and rights of those who work are violated (1).

The Individual and Work

that the person is destined for work and called to it, work is for the person and not the person for the work (6).

A Right Order of Values

The worker should never be seen solely as an instrument of production. Errors can occur when the individual is treated on the same level as a means of production and not in accordance with the true dignity of the laborer's work (7).

Worker Solidarity

The reaction against the degradation of the person as the subject of work and exploitation in the area of wages, working conditions, and social security led in the past to worker solidarity and various methods of associating. Great strides and advances have been made by such cooperative efforts. Regretfully, various ideological or power systems have sometimes thwarted these efforts and have allowed flagrant injustices to continue. There must continue, therefore, the study of work and living conditions of workers. New means of creating solidarity among workers must be promoted whenever there is a degradation or exploitation of the worker. The Church commits itself to this cause as its mission and service, in order that the dignity of human work will not be violated (8).

Labor and Personal Dignity

Work is a universal calling and is good for the human person. Through work, the person not only transforms nature, but also achieves fulfillment as a human being, and to a certain extent becomes even more a human being. Work is the foundation of family life, indeed work makes it possible to form family since a family requires some means of subsistence. Work likewise influences the process of education in the family.

Each individual also belongs to a greater family, that of the great society, to which the person is joined by particular cultural and historical links. This link allows each person to combine a deep human identity with membership in a nation thereby identifying the individual's labor with the common good of the entire society (10).

The Priority of Labor over Capital

The Church has always taught the principle of the priority of labor over capital. The concept of capital includes the whole collection of means by which the individual appropriates natural resources and transforms them in accordance with the person's needs. All these means are the result of the historical heritage of human labor. Everything that is at the service of work, including modern technology, is itself the result of work. Therefore, the Church stresses always the primacy of persons over things. Capital can never be separated from labor. Always to be avoided is the error of materialism, the conviction of the primacy and importance of the material, which directly or indirectly places the spiritual in a position of inferiority and subordination (12, 13).

Work and Ownership

Christian tradition has never upheld an absolute or untouchable claim to private ownership. It has always understood this right within the broader context of the right for all to use the goods of the whole of creation, that goods are meant for everyone. The position of "rigid" capitalism, which defends the exclusive right to private ownership of the means of production as an untouchable dogma of economic life, is not acceptable. From this conviction has come forth many proposals from the Church, including joint ownership of the means of work, sharing by workers in the management and/or profits of businesses, so-called shareholding by labor, etc. The principle of the priority of labor over capital is an important principle of social morality. The laborer needs not only recompense for work performed but also to know that the labor performed does not make the worker just "a cog in the wheel." Work involves not only the economy but also, and especially, personal values (14, 15).

in order to be maintained and developed.

Involved in employment are "indirect employers," that is, all the agents at the national and international level responsible for the whole orientation of labor policy. Respect for the objective rights of the worker—every kind of worker: manual or intellectual, industrial or agricultural, etc.—must constitute the fundamental criterion for shaping the whole economy. The fundamental issue of providing suitable employment for all who are capable of it needs always to be addressed. It is particularly painful when the young who, after technical and professional preparation, fail to find work. To meet the dangers of unemployment these agents need to make provision for overall planning, organizing work in a correct and rational way, matched by a suitable system of instructing and education. Thus not only will mature human beings be developed, but at the same time, people will be prepared for the world of work.

The justice of a socioeconomic system can be evaluated by examining whether or not the worker's labor is properly remunerated. Wages are the practical means by which the vast majority of people have access to those goods intended for the common good. Just remuneration for the work of an adult responsible for a family means a wage that properly maintains the family and provides security for its future. Women who desire to join the workforce must not be discriminated against and must not be excluded from jobs for which they are capable. Their family aspirations must likewise be respected, especially their role as mothers.

Various social benefits should be accorded to workers, including medical assistance, healthcare, vacation time and days off, pension, and insurance for old age and accidents at work. Also of importance is the right to a working environment that is safe both physically and morally.

Workers also enjoy the right of association, by which they may participate in labor unions where the interests of workers are protected. Just efforts, however, to secure the rights of workers who are united by the same profession should take into account the limitations imposed by the general economic situation of the country. Care should be taken that such unions not "play politics" in the sense that they be subject to the decisions of political parties. Rather, their efforts can profitably be directed toward education and training efforts for workers.

The use of strikes or work stoppages must never be abused, especially for political purposes. When essential community services are in question, means may be needed on behalf of the common good, including appropriate legislation.

Also to be remembered is the importance of agricultural work, which provides society with the goods needed for daily sustenance. In many situations, radical changes are needed to restore to agriculture and to rural people their just value as the basis for a healthy economy.

It must likewise not be forgotten that disabled people deserve consideration in their quest to participate in all aspects of society, including in the workforce. Disabled people should be offered the opportunity to work according to their capabilities.

Immigrants, whether in a permanent situation or as a seasonal worker, should not be placed at a disadvantage in comparison with other workers in that society in the matter of working rights. Immigrants in search of work must never become an opportunity for financial or social exploitation (16–23).

A Spirituality of Work

The word of God contains the truth that the individual created in the image of God shares by his or her work in the activity of the Creator. The Book of Genesis is in a certain sense the first "gospel of work," proclaiming that the human should imitate God the Creator in working, because the human being alone has the unique characteristic of likeness to God. Each person should also imitate God's creative activity under the form of work and rest. Christians are convinced that the triumphs of the human race are a sign of God's greatness and a mysterious unfolding of God's divine plan. By means of work, men and women share in this great work of creation.

On the Hundredth Anniversary of Rerum Novarum (Centesimus Annus) Pope John Paul II, 1991

- **Toward the "New Things" of Today**
- **The Error of Socialism**
- **The Use of "Subsidiarity" by the State to Promote Reform**
- **Private Property and the Purpose of Material Goods**
- **The Gift of Work and Land**
- **The Poor and the Modern Business Economy**
- **The Role of Profit in Business**
- **Relations between Poor and Wealthy Nations**
- **The Danger of Consumerism**
- **Respect for the Earth and Environment**
- **State and Culture**
- **The Development of Authentic Democracy**
- **The Economic Activity of the State**
- **The Person as the Way of the Church**

Toward the "New Things" of Today

Pope Leo XIII, in his encyclical *Rerum Novarum*, which addressed "New Things" of his day, especially in terms of the Industrial Age, predicted that the social order proposed by socialism would be a danger to the masses and a radical solution to the "question of the working class" of the time.

The Error of Socialism

The fundamental error of socialism is the consideration of the individual person as an element within the social organism, so that the good of the individual is completely subordinated to the functioning of the socioeconomic mechanism. It likewise maintains that the good of the individual can be realized without reference to the person's free choice. This makes it difficult for the person to recognize his or her dignity as a person and hinders progress toward the building of an authentic human community.

The first cause of the mistaken concept of the nature of the person is atheism. The denial of God deprives the individual of his or her foundation and leads to a reorganization of the social order without reference to the person's dignity and responsibility. Socialism derives its choice of the means of action from class struggle, a philosophy condemned in *Rerum Novarum*. Especially condemned was the idea that conflict should not be restrained by ethical or juridical considerations, or by the respect for the dignity of others. What is pursued is not the general good of society but a partisan interest, which replaces the common good and sets out to destroy whatever stands in its way.

Rerum Novarum is opposed to the state control of the means of production, which could reduce every citizen to being a "cog" in the state machine. This encyclical pointed the way to just reforms, which would restore dignity to the work and the worker. It proposed that society and the state assume responsibility for protecting the worker from unemployment by economic policies aimed at ensuring balanced growth and full employment or through unemployment insurance and retraining programs. In addition, the role of trade unions in negotiating minimum salaries and working conditions is decisive. Humane working hours and adequate free time need to be guaranteed.

The Use of "Subsidiarity" by the State to Promote Reform

The state must contribute to the achievement of these goals both directly and indirectly by the principle of subsidiarity. It must create conditions for the free exercise of economic activity, defend the weakest, place certain limits on the autonomy of the parties who determine working ~~···~~ ~~· ·~~ ~~· ensure the~~ necessary minimum support for the unem-

Private Property and the Purpose of Material Goods

The Church has always defended the right to private property, fundamental for the autonomy and development of the person. At the same time, the Church teaches that the possession of material goods is not an absolute right and that its limits are inscribed in its very nature as a human right. Each person should use his or her material possessions as common to all.

The Gift of Work and Land

God gave the earth to humanity so that it might provide sustenance for all without excluding or favoring anyone. This is the foundation of the universal destination of the earth's goods. It is through work that the individual, using intelligence and freedom, makes part of the earth his or her own, the origin of individual property. These two factors—*work* and *land*—are to be found at the beginning of every human society. In our time, the role of human work is becoming increasingly important as the productive factor both of non-material and material wealth. More than ever, work is work with others and work for others.

A new form of ownership has evolved in the form of the possession of know-how, technology, and skill. The ability to foresee both the needs of others and the combination of productive factors most adapted to satisfying those needs constitutes an important source of wealth in modern society. The role of disciplined and creative human work, initiative, and entrepreneurial ability becomes increasingly evident and decisive.

The Poor and the Modern Business Economy

The modern business economy has positive aspects. But it must also be pointed out that many people, perhaps the majority today, do not have the means which would enable them to take their place in an effective and humanly dignified way within a productive system in which work is truly central. They have no way of acquiring the basic knowledge which would enable them to express their creativity and develop their potential. If not actually exploited, they are to a great extent marginalized. Aspects of the Third World also appear in the developed countries, where the constant transformation of the methods of production and consumption devalues certain acquired skills and professional expertise. Those who fail to keep up with the times can easily be marginalized, as can the elderly, the young people who are incapable of finding their place in the life of society, and, in general, those who are weakest. In the Third World context, certain objectives stated by *Rerum Novarum* remain valid, including a sufficient wage for the support of the family, social insurance for old age and unemployment, and adequate protection for the conditions of employment.

There is a wide range of opportunities for commitment and effort in the name of justice on the part of trade unions and other workers' organizations. They defend workers' rights and enable workers to participate more fully and honorably in the life of their nation.

It is right to speak of a struggle against an economic system understood as a method of upholding the absolute predominance of capital, the possession of the means of production and of the land, in contrast to the free and personal nature of human work. In the struggle against such a system, what is being proposed is a society of free work, of enterprise, and of participation. Such a society demands that the market be appropriately controlled by the forces of society and by the state, so as to guarantee that the basic needs of the whole of society are satisfied.

The Role of Profit in Business

The Church acknowledges the legitimate role of profit as an indication that a business is functioning well. But profitability is not the only indicator of a firm's condition. It is possible for a firm's financial accounts to be in order and yet for the people—who make up the firm's most valuable asset—to be humiliated and their dignity offended. The pur-

Stronger nations must offer weaker ones opportunities for taking their place in international life. It is not right for the wealthier nations to expect payment of debts from the poorer nations when the effect would be the imposition of political choices leading to hunger and despair for entire peoples. It cannot be expected that the debts contracted should be paid at the price of unbearable sacrifices. In such cases it is necessary to find ways to lighten, defer, or even cancel the debt that is compatible with the fundamental right of peoples to subsistence and progress.

The Danger of Consumerism

Included among threats and problems emerging within the more advanced economies must be the phenomenon of consumerism. In singling out new needs and new means to meet them, one must be guided by a comprehensive picture of the human being, which respects all the dimensions of the person and subordinates material and instinctive dimensions to interior and spiritual ones. If, on the contrary, a direct appeal is made to instincts while ignoring the reality of the person as intelligent and free, then consumer attitudes and lifestyles can be created which are objectively improper and often damaging to the person's physical and spiritual health. A great deal of educational and cultural work is needed, including the education of consumers in the responsible use of their power of choice, the formation of a strong sense of responsibility among producers and among people in the mass media in particular, and the necessary intervention by public authorities.

A striking example of artificial consumption is the use of drugs. Widespread drug use is a sign of a serious malfunction in the social system; it also implies a materialistic and, in a certain sense, a destructive "reading" of human needs.

It is not wrong to want to live better; what is wrong is a style of life which is presumed to be better when it is directed toward "having" rather than "being," which wants to have more, not in order to be more but in order to spend life in enjoyment as an end in itself.

Respect for the Earth and Environment

Equally worrisome is the ecological question. In the desire to have rather than to be and to grow, humanity consumes the resources of the earth in an excessive and disordered way. Humanity believes it can make arbitrary use of the earth without regard to its original, God-given purpose. Humanity must be conscious of its duties and obligations toward future generations.

Humanity must likewise be conscious of serious destruction that takes place to the human environment. There exist serious problems in modern urbanization. Each individual is conditioned, to a certain extent, by the social structure, by education received, and by the environment. These elements can either help or hinder the individual in living in accordance with the truth.

When economic freedom becomes autonomous and the individual is seen more as a producer or consumer of goods than as a subject who produces and consumes in order to live, then economic freedom loses its necessary relationship to the human person and ends up alienating and oppressing the individual.

The Church has no models to present for an effective economic system, since these can only arise within the framework of different historical situations and from the efforts of those responsible with confronting concrete problems. But the Church can offer its social teaching as an indispensable and ideal orientation that recognizes the positive value of the market and of enterprise, but points out that at the same time these must be oriented toward the common good (30–39, 43).

State and Culture

Pope Leo XIII was aware of the need for a sound theory of the state to ensure the normal development of the human being's spiritual and temporal activities. He presented the organization of society according to the three powers: legislative, executive, and judicial, a concept commonly understood in secular government but a novelty in Church

The Development of Authentic Democracy

Authentic democracy is possible only in a state ruled by law, and on the basis of a correct conception of the human person. Those who are convinced they know the truth and firmly adhere to it are considered unreliable from a democratic point of view, since they do not accept that the majority determines truth, or that it is subject to variation according to different political trends. However, if there is no ultimate truth to guide and direct political activity, then ideas and convictions can easily be manipulated for reasons of power. History shows that a democracy without values easily turns into open or thinly disguised totalitarianism.

The Church is also aware of the dangers of fanaticism and fundamentalism when some attempt to impose in the name of an ideology their own concept of what is true and good. Christian truth is not an ideology and recognizes that human life is realized in history in conditions that are diverse and imperfect. In reaffirming the dignity of the person, the Church's method is respect for freedom. But freedom attains its full development only by accepting the truth. In a world without truth, freedom loses its foundation.

In the flowering of democratic ideals in nations formally under a totalitarian regime, it is important that recognition be given to certain explicit rights, including the right of the child to develop in the mother's womb from the moment of conception, the right to live in a united family and in a moral environment, the right to develop one's intelligence and freedom in seeking and knowing the truth, the right to share in the work which makes wise use of the earth's material resources, and the means to support one's self and family and to have and to rear children. The source of such freedoms is religious freedom, the right to live in the truth of one's faith. The contribution of the Church to the political order is its vision of the dignity of the person revealed in all the mystery of the Incarnate Word.

The Economic Activity of the State

The economic activity of the state also presupposes sure guarantees of individual freedom and private property, as well as stable currency and efficient public services. The principle task of the state is to guarantee this security, so that those who work and produce can enjoy the fruits of their labor, and feel encouraged to work efficiently and honestly.

Another task is overseeing and directing the exercise of human rights in the economic sector. The state has a duty to sustain business activities by creating job opportunities.

Care must be taken in terms of abuses in the assistance provided by the state to those who need remedies for poverty and deprivation. The principle of subsidiarity must be respected: a community of a higher order should not interfere in the internal life of a community of a lower order. By intervening directly and depriving society of its responsibility, the social assistance state leads to a loss of human energies and an inordinate increase of public agencies.

Faithful to the mission received from Christ, the Church has always been present and active among the needy, offering them material assistance in ways that neither humiliate nor reduce them to mere objects of assistance.

In order to overcome today's widespread individualistic mentality, there is required a concrete commitment to solidarity and service, beginning in the family. Evangelization also plays a role in the various nations, directed now at culture itself, so that culture is sustained in its progress toward the truth, assisting in the work of its purification and enrichment.

The Church promotes those aspects of human behavior which favor a true culture of peace, as opposed to models in which the individual is lost in the crowd, in which the role of his or her initiative and freedom is neglected (44, 46–51).

true identity of each individual is known only through faith. This social doctrine is an instrument of evangelization, proclaiming God and the mystery of salvation in Christ to every human being. Because its activity today meets with particular difficulties and obstacles, the Church devotes itself to new energies and new methods of evangelization to ensure the safeguarding of the transcendence of the human person.

Love for others and love for the poor especially is made concrete in the promotion of justice. It is not enough to draw on surplus goods for the sake of the poor, but also a change of lifestyle is needed, encouraging new models of production and consumption (53–55, 58).

For I Was Hungry and You Gave Me Food: Catholic Reflections on Food, Farmers, and Farmworkers USCCB, 2003

- **Agricultural Signs of the Time**
- **Criteria for Agricultural Policy and Advocacy**
- **Toward Commitment, Hope, and Challenge**
- **A Catholic Agenda for Action: Pursuing a More Justified Agricultural System**
- **International Trade, Aid, and Development**

To provide food for all is a Gospel imperative. It is important for the Church to reflect on the ethics of food production, land protection, agricultural structuring, compensation, and regulation for the service of the common good.

Agricultural Signs of the Time

We live at a time when many are still hungry, many family farmers are still struggling, and many have recently lost farms.

We also see an increasing focus on agricultural trade as a measure of economic vitality and increasing globalization tying our lives together.

There are fewer people making important decisions that affect more people than in the past. Large institutions and corporations can overwhelm smaller structures.

The essential starting point of Catholic social teaching is the dignity of every human life. All people have a basic right to material and spiritual support, including the right to food. As children of God, we are all brothers and sisters no matter how distant or different we might seem.

Catholic social teaching affirms the right and duty to work, right to economic initiative, right to safe working conditions, decent wages, and benefits, and right to organize and join associations to secure these rights.

Criteria for Agricultural Policy and Advocacy

The Catholic community has a responsibility to raise the ethical dimensions of issues that shape rural life and agricultural policy. Criteria that should be used in guiding agricultural policy include:

- Whether an initiative helps the most vulnerable farmers and farmworkers in the country and abroad.

- Whether it promotes safe and affordable foods and encourages sustainable, environmentally sound farming practices.

- Whether it ensures a decent life for farmers and farmworkers.

- Whether it sustains and strengthens rural communities.

- Whether it protects God's creation.

- Whether it increases participation and dialogue in the development of policies.

Toward Commitment, Hope, and Challenge

‎‎‎‎‎overcome hunger in our country and around the

Farmers must be able to

their work. Policies are needed that encourage rural development and maintain the culture and values of rural communities.

The situation of farmworkers, among the most vulnerable and exploited people, demands a response from a people of faith. Such individuals need a living wage, access to services, and mobility. Labor protection should be guaranteed in law with working conditions consistent with appropriate federal standards. A comprehensive legalization program should be initiated that would permit hard-working undocumented workers in agricultural industries to adjust to legal permanent residency.

International Trade, Aid, and Development

Greater access to local, regional, and international markets is essential for agricultural development in poor countries. U.S. and European subsidies, supports, tariffs, quotas, and other barriers that undermine market access for poorer countries should be substantially reduced.

It is important that governments of the United States and other developed countries adopt trade policies that provide special access to their markets for farmers from the world's most desperately poor nations.

In order to protect the health and well-being of all people, trade policies should provide consistent food safety standards open to public review, based on internationally accepted scientific criteria, and subject to neutral dispute resolution.

Affluent nations are encouraged to respond to requests for food aid and to focus their aid on meeting the needs of hungry people, as determined by the countries in need.

Attention is urgently needed to focus new developments in agricultural technology on reducing poverty and hunger and ensuring open discussion and participation in decision-making regarding the development and use of genetically modified products.

On Integral Human Development in Charity and Truth
(Caritas in Veritate)
Pope Benedict XVI, 2009

The problem of development links poverty closely with unemployment. What must be recognized is the essential dignity of every man and woman within their society, work freely chosen, effectively associating workers with the development of their community, and freedom from discrimination. Decent work also makes it possible for families to meet their needs and provide schooling for their children; permits workers to organize themselves and have their voices heard; provides opportunity for discovering one's roots; and guarantees a decent standard of living for those who have retired (63).

Labor unions encouraged and supported by the Church should be open to the new perspectives emerging in the world of work. There is a new complex of issues that must be addressed, including conflicts between the worker and consumer and concern for workers in underdeveloped countries (64).

Finance must return to being an instrument directed toward improved wealth creation and development. The entire economy and finance must be used in an ethical way to create suitable conditions for human development. The right intention, transparency, and the search for positive results are mutually compatible and must never be detached from one another.

The experience of micro-financing should be strengthened and encouraged, which can give practical assistance by launching new initiatives and opening new sectors for the weaker elements in society (65).

Global interconnectedness has seen the emergence of a new political power, consumers, and their associations. We are reminded that purchasing is always a moral act. The consumer has a specific social ʳ··ʳ·ʳ· ·ʳ ·ʳ· ·ʳʳʳ ʰand in hand with the social responsibility of

voice in shared decision-making. ʳʰⁱˢ ᶜᵒᵘˡᵈ ᵃˢˢⁱˢᵗ ⁱⁿ ᵃᵗᵗᵃⁱⁿⁱⁿᵍ ᵃ political, juridical, and economic order that can increase, and a direction toward international cooperation for the development of all peoples in solidarity. The integral development of peoples and international cooperation require a greater degree of international cooperation, marked by subsidiarity, for the management of globalization. This also requires a new social order that conforms to the moral order that links political, economic, and social spheres as envisioned by the Charter of the United Nations (67).

For Reflection and Dialogue

1. Does the Church have a role to play in teaching about labor relations? Why or why not?

2. How have the roles of employer and employee changed since the time of Pope Leo XIII? Does this necessitate a change in the teachings?

3. What do you believe are the advantages of labor associations for the worker? For the employer? Disadvantages for both? Has the role of associations and unions changed over the years? For better or worse?

4. Are the criteria for a just wage proposed by Pope Pius XI still workable guidelines? Why or why not?

5. What cautions should be considered by workers who would utilize work stoppages or strikes?

6. What resources could be made available at a parish, regional, or diocesan level to assist those who are presently unemployed and searching for work or in need of temporary assistance?

7. How could Pope John Paul II's vision of a "spirituality of work" be incorporated into the contemporary workforce?

8. Should "profitability" be considered the only criterion to be used as a gauge of business success? If not, what other criteria could be used?

9. What are the most serious dangers posed by consumerism to developed countries?

10. How can Christians work to change the "consumer mentality" that affects so much of society today?

11. How may Catholic social teaching concerning labor and workers be applied to farmworkers?

12. How do the teachings of Catholic social teaching about labor affect our modern trans-global economy?

6.

—

SOLIDARITY

~~own unique~~

to respect for other nations and cultures. The following summaries are taken from:

- ⊃ *Peace on Earth* (Pacem in Terris), Pope John XXIII, 1963

- ⊃ *The Challenge of Peace: God's Promise and Our Response*, National Conference of Catholic Bishops, 1983

- ⊃ *God Is Love* (Deus Caritas Est), Pope Benedict XVI, 2005

- ⊃ *Saved in Hope* (Spe Salvi), Pope Benedict XVI, 2007

- ⊃ *On Integral Human Development in Charity and Truth* (Caritas in Veritate), Pope Benedict XVI, 2009

Peace on Earth (Pacem in Terris)
Pope John XXIII, 1963

- **Order in the Universe**
- **Order between Persons**
- **Rights**
- **Duties**
- **Relations between Individuals and the Public Authorities**
- **Relations between States**
- **Relationship of People and Political Communities**
- **Pastoral Exhortations**

Order in the Universe

Peace on earth can be firmly established only if the order laid down by God can be observed by humanity. So, too, for each person there is written in the heart an order revealed by the conscience. There are laws within the nature of humanity written by God, which can help states in their relationships with each other (1, 5, 7).

Order between Persons

Every human being is a person with a nature endowed with intelligence and free will. Every human being has rights and obligations, which flow directly from personhood (9, 10).

Rights

Each person has a right to life, to bodily integrity and the means suitable for the proper development of life, primarily food, clothing, shelter, rest, medical care, and necessary social services.

There are several rights given to each person in virtue of natural law which pertain to moral and cultural values: a good reputation, freedom in searching for truth and expressing and communicating opinions, and the pursuit of art within the limits laid down by the moral order and common good. There is also the right to be informed truthfully about public events.

The natural law also provides the right to share in the benefits of culture and basic education, and the right to worship according to the dictates of one's conscience and to practice religion privately and publicly. One also has the right to choose freely the state of one's life and the right to establish a family, with equal rights and duties for men and women. Parents have the right to support and to have their children educated.

Individuals have the right to an opportunity to work and good working conditions; women have the right to working conditions consonant with their duties as wives and mothers. There exists the natural right to carry on economic activities and to earn a wage determined by the criterion of justice and in keeping with the dignity of the human person. There is also the right to private property.

From the fact that human beings are social come the rights of assembly and association. There exists the right to freedom of movement, within one's country and to emigrate when there are just reasons. There is a right to participate in political affairs and to contribute to the common good. There is also a right to juridical protection of rights according to the norm of law (11–21, 23–27).

the truth, and must function according to the norms or justice, inspired and perfected by mutual love and brought to balance in freedom.

There are three characteristics of the present day: First, working classes have gained ground in economic and public life. Second, women are taking more of a role in public life as they become more and more conscious of their Christian dignity. Third, the world human society has taken on a new appearance in the field of social and political life (28, 31, 39–42).

Relations between Individuals and the Public Authorities

Human society must have some people invested with legitimate authority to preserve its institutions and to devote themselves to care and work for the good of all. These individuals derive their authority from God. Their power to command comes from the moral order, which has God as its Creator and final end.

Civil authority must appeal to the conscience of the individual citizen. If civil authorities pass laws or command anything opposed to the moral order, and therefore contrary to the will of God, neither the laws made nor the authorizations granted can be binding on the conscience of the citizens.

Individual citizens are obliged to make their specific contribution to the common welfare. The ethnic characteristics of the various human groups are to be respected as constituent elements of the common good. The very nature of the common good requires that all members of the state be entitled to share in it, although in different ways according to one's tasks, merits, and circumstances. Those in public authority must give more attention to the less fortunate members of the community since they are less able to defend themselves. Civil authorities should promote simultaneously the spiritual and material welfare of the citizens. To safeguard the inviolable rights of the human person and to facilitate the fulfillment of each person's duties should be the chief duty of every public authority. It is necessary that the administration give wholehearted and careful attention to the social as well as to the economic progress of the citizens.

The common good requires that civil authorities maintain a careful balance between coordinating and protecting the rights of the citizens on the one hand, and promoting them on the other. It is in keeping with the innate demands of human nature that the state should take a form that embodies the three-fold division of powers.

The people of our time are becoming increasingly conscious of their dignity as human persons. It is required that government officials be chosen in conformity with constitutional procedures and perform their specific functions within the limits of law (46–48, 51, 53, 55–58, 60, 64, 65, 68, 79).

Relations between States

Nations are reciprocally subjects of rights and duties, and their relationships must also be harmonized in truth, in justice, in working solidarity, and in liberty. The same natural law that governs relations between individual human beings also serves to regulate relations of nations with one another. Authority cannot thwart the moral order, lest it sweep aside its very foundation. A fundamental factor of the common good is the acknowledgment of the moral order.

The first rule governing the relations between states is that of *truth*. All nations must be recognized to be equal in dignity. Each nation is invested with the right to existence, to self-development, to the means fitting to its attainment, and to be the one primarily responsible for its self-development. It also has the right to a good name and the respect that is its due.

Relations between nations are further regulated by *justice*. Nations are bound by the obligation to effectively guard each of their rights and to avoid actions that may jeopardize them. Disagreements between nations should be resolved by a mutual assessment of the reasons for both sides of the dispute and by a mature and objective investigation and equitable reconciliation of the differences of opinion.

intermediate societies.

It is approved and commended that every charitable effort be made to make migration of person from one country to another less painful.

Justice and right reason demands that the arms race among nations should cease and that the parties concerned should reduce the stockpile of weapons that exist in various countries equally and simultaneously. Nuclear weapons should be banned, and all should come to an agreement on a fitting program of disarmament, employing mutual and effective controls.

Relations between states should be based on freedom; no country may unjustly oppress another or unduly meddle in another's affairs. It is vitally important that the wealthier states, in providing forms of assistance to the poorer, should respect the moral values and ethnic characteristics peculiar to each and avoid any intention of political domination.

It is hoped that by meeting and negotiating, people may come to discover better the bonds that unite them together, deriving from their human nature, which indeed bind them together. It is not fear but love that should reign, expressing itself in collaboration (80, 83, 85, 86, 91–95, 97, 100, 107, 112, 120, 125, 129).

Relationship of People and Political Communities

The progress of science and technology has profoundly influenced human conduct and advanced the opportunity for cooperation and association with one another. The interdependence of world economies has grown deeper. The social progress, order, security, and peace of each country are necessarily connected with the social progress, order, security, and peace of all other countries. Individual countries cannot rightly seek their own interests and develop themselves in isolation from the rest.

Under the present circumstances of human society, no one nation or several nations can be considered adequate to promote the universal common good. The moral order would require that some form of public authority be established that would have worldwide power and be endowed with the proper means for the efficacious pursuit of its objective, the universal common good in concrete form. It must be set up by common accord and not imposed by force. This public and universal authority must have for its objective the recognition, respect, safeguarding, and promotion of the rights of the human person.

The relationships that exist between the worldwide public authority and the public authorities of individual nations must be governed by the principle of *subsidiarity*, allowing the public authorities to carry out their tasks and duties and exercise their rights with greater security.

It is hoped that the United Nations Organization, established in 1945, may become ever more equal to the magnitude and nobility of its task of maintaining and consolidating peace between peoples (130, 135, 138, 139, 141, 142, 145).

Pastoral Exhortations

Christians should endeavor, in the light of faith and with the strength of love, to ensure that the various economic, social, cultural, or political institutions facilitate human beings perfecting themselves in the natural and supernatural order.

It is necessary that human beings should live and act in their temporal lives to create a synthesis between scientific, technical, and professional elements on the one hand and spiritual values on the other.

In the temporal activity, *faith* should be present as a beacon that gives light, and *charity* should be present as a force to give life.

An integral education is needed for our young, combining religious values and moral conscience formation with the assimilation of scientific and technical knowledge.

Constant endeavors must be made to objectify the criterion of justice

in society, bringing about that p

There can be no peace among people unless there is peace in each person (146, 150, 152–155, 158, 163–165).

The Challenge of Peace: God's Promise and Our Response
National Conference of Catholic Bishops, 1983

- **Peace in the Modern World: Religious Perspectives and Principles**
- **Core of Church's Teaching on Peace**
- **Theology of Peace**
- **"Peace" in Hebrew Scripture**
- **"Peace" in Christian Scripture**
- **Defense against Aggression**
- **Proportionality and Discrimination in Targets**
- **Conscientious Objection**
- **Nuclear Arms Race**
- **Specific Steps to Reduce the Danger of War**
- **Working to Shape a Peaceful World**
- **The Work of the Church in Promoting Peace in the World**
- **Challenges to Peace: Persons and Their Roles Specifically Addressed**

Peace in the Modern World: Religious Perspectives and Principles

The threat of nuclear war is a concern of the Church, a concern which transcends all national boundaries. The Catholic tradition has offered teaching on the subject of war and peace throughout the centuries and now attempts to articulate a helpful response to an urgent concern. Catholics attempting to discern whether their moral judgments are consistent with the Gospel must give serious attention to the moral judgments given in this pastoral letter (5–7, 10).

Core of Church's Teaching on Peace

At the center of the Church's teaching on peace and at the center of Catholic social teaching are the transcendence of God and the dignity of the human person. Catholic teaching on the issue of war and peace is directed toward Catholics, assisting them in the formation of conscience, and the wider civil community, to assist in the public policy debate concerning this important issue.

Theology of Peace

A theology of peace grounds the task of peacemaking in the biblical vision of the kingdom of God and provides a message of hope. The scriptures, written over a long period of time and reflecting many social situations culturally conditioned, offer a variety of perspectives on the meaning of peace. Predominating is an understanding of peace as a right relationship with God and an eschatological sense, the full realization of God's salvation when all creation will be made whole.

"Peace" in Hebrew Scripture

The Hebrew scriptures show violence and war to be a part of the history of the people of God. One image of God that developed was as the One who would protect Israel from their enemies and provide a sense of security. This image was gradually transformed with time, and other activities of God on behalf of Israel showed different perspectives of their God.

Peace is experienced as a gift from God and the fruit of God's saving activity. True peace extends to all of creation and brings harmony and right order. Living in covenantal fidelity to God demanded that Israel put its faith in God alone and look to God for security. Because of Israel's fidelity, God's promise of salvation involving all people and all creation will be fulfilled (11, 15, 16, 25, 27, 28, 31, 32, 36).

Lord gives the gift of peace. The disciples recognize their mission to be agents of reconciliation—people who would make visible the peace that God had established through the love and unity of their own communities (39, 44, 51).

Christians are called to live the tension between the vision of the reign of God and its concrete realization in history. We are a pilgrim people in a world marked by conflict and injustice. Justice is always the foundation of peace. In the "already but not yet" of Christian existence, the members of the Church choose different paths to move toward the realization of the kingdom in history (54, 58–60, 62).

Peace is both a gift of God and a human work, constructed on the basis of core human values: truth, justice, freedom, and love. The Church's teaching on war and peace establishes a strong presumption against war, binding on all. But there are circumstances when this presumption may be overridden in the name of preserving peace, which protects human dignity and human rights.

Defense against Aggression

Christians must defend peace against aggression. The manner in which this defense takes place presents moral options, including service in the armed forces or refusing to bear arms. Catholic teaching sees these two positions as complementary, in that both seek to serve the common good.

Work to develop nonviolent means of fending off aggression and resolving conflict best reflects the call of Jesus to love and to do justice (73, 74, 78).

Saint Augustine developed what has become known as the "just war" theory. Lethal force can prevent aggression against innocent victims, the need to restrain an enemy who would injure the innocent. But first, every reasonable effort must be made to prevent war.

Catholic teaching has developed a determination as to when war is permissible:

1. *Just cause:* War is permissible only to confront a real and certain danger, that is, to protect innocent life, to preserve conditions necessary for decent human existence, and to secure basic human rights.

2. *Competent authority:* The decision to use force must be made by a competent authority charged with responsibility for the public good.

3. *Comparative justice:* A decision must be made as to whether the rights and values involved justify the taking of life. Every party to a conflict should acknowledge the limits of its "just cause" and the need to use only limited means in pursuit of its objectives.

4. *Right intention:* A just cause must be the only reason for the war and must continue to be the intention during the course of the war, avoiding unnecessary destructive acts or unreasonable conditions.

5. *Last resort:* All peaceful alternatives must have been exhausted.

6. *Probability of success:* Hopeless resistance should be avoided when the outcome will be clearly disproportionate or futile, with the recognition that at times the defense of key values even against great odds may be a proportionate witness.

7. *Proportionality:* The damage to be inflicted and the costs incurred by war must be proportionate to the good expected by taking up arms. Such consideration is not limited to the material order, but includes the moral and spiritual implications to a society as well. Also to be considered, especially in a nuclear age, is the effect of a possible war on the international community (81, 84, 86–88, 92, 93, 95, 96, 98, 99).

Proportionality and Discrimination in Targets

The way in which war is *conducted* needs to be continually scrutinized in light of the principles of *proportionality* and *discrimination*. Proportionality demands that when confronting various military options, an analysis be made of the possible harm that might be done and whether ＿＿＿ military advantage is still justified. The principle of *discrim-*

The Second Vatican Council in the *Pastoral Constitution on the Church in the Modern World* (79) called upon governments to enact laws to protect the rights of those who adopted the position of conscientious objection to all war (111, 118).

Nuclear Arms Race

The nuclear arms race highlights two elements: the destructive potential of nuclear weapons and the stringent choices posed by the nuclear age for both politics and morals. The danger and destructiveness of nuclear weapons are resisted with greater urgency and intensity. Papal teaching has consistently addressed the folly and danger of the arms race. The possibilities for placing political and moral limits on nuclear war are so minimal that the moral task must be to refuse to legitimate it. The strategy of nuclear deterrence contains serious moral issues, including the economic distortion of priorities for the nation (126, 131, 134, 136).

For the tradition that acknowledges some legitimate use of force, there are some important elements of contemporary nuclear strategies that move beyond the limits of moral justification:

➲ *Counter population warfare:* Under no circumstances may nuclear weapons or other instruments of mass slaughter be used for the purpose of destroying population centers or other predominately civilian targets. Retaliatory action (nuclear or conventional) that would indiscriminately take many innocent lives must also be condemned (147, 148).

➲ *Initiation of nuclear war:* The situation cannot be perceived in which the deliberate initiation of nuclear warfare, on however restricted a scale, can be morally justified. A serious moral obligation exists to develop non-nuclear defensive strategies as rapidly as possible (150).

➲ *Limited nuclear war:* A nuclear response to either conventional or nuclear attack can cause destruction that goes far beyond "legitimate defense." Moral perspective should be sensitive not only to the quantitative dimensions of the issue but to the psychological, human, and religious characteristics as well. The first imperative is to prevent any use of nuclear weapons with the hope that leaders will resist the notion that nuclear conflict can be limited, contained, or won in any traditional sense (160, 161).

The concept of deterrence, the dissuasion of a potential adversary from initiating an attack or conflict, often by the threat of unacceptable retaliatory damage, has become the centerpiece of the major powers' policy. Two questions particularly need to be addressed:

▪ *Targeting doctrine and strategic plans for the use of the deterrent:* It is not morally acceptable to intend to kill the innocent as part of a strategy of deterring nuclear war. The principle of proportionality would indicate that there are some actions that can be decisively judged to be disproportionate: in a nuclear age, the assertion of an intention not to strike civilians directly, or even the most honest effort to implement that intention, constitutes a policy that is not satisfactory (CP 163, 177, 178, 181).

▪ *Deterrence strategy and nuclear war-fighting capability:* Counterforce targeting, while preferable from the perspective of protecting civilians, conveys the notion that nuclear war is subject to precise rational and moral limits, a dubious premise. There is a need to rethink the deterrence policy, to reduce the possibility of nuclear war, and to move toward a more stable system of national and international security (CP 178, 181, 184, 196).

Specific Steps to Reduce the Danger of War

1. There is a need for continued work on arms control, reduction, and disarmament.

2. There must be a continued insistence on efforts to minimize the risk
    ~~of any war~~

conflict resolution.

6. Respect must be given to the role of individual conscience and legislative protection provided for the rights of conscientious objectors. The Church does not question the right of the state, in principle, to require military service of its citizens, provided the government shows it necessary (203, 209, 218, 220, 221, 232, 233).

Working to Shape a Peaceful World

Work must continue toward some properly constructed political authority with the capacity to shape our material interdependence. By a mix of political vision and moral wisdom, states are called to interpret the national interest in light of the larger global interest.

The reality of global interdependence calls us to translate our compassion into policies that will respond to international issues, especially poverty in the world.

There is a moral challenge from our interdependence to shape and develop relationships among the nations that will support our common need for security, welfare, and safety (241, 243, 263, 273).

The Work of the Church in Promoting Peace in the World

There must be educational programs and the formation of conscience to understand better the issues of war and peace. True peace calls for "reverence for life," a full awareness of the worth and dignity of every human person and the sacredness of all human life. There must be a conversion of heart and mind among all people and a prayerful union with Christ, the Prince of Peace. Conversion should lead us to penance, conforming ourselves more closely to Christ. Each Friday should be a day significantly devoted to prayer, penance, and almsgiving for peace.

Challenges to Peace: Persons and Their Roles Specifically Addressed

To priests, deacons, religious, and pastoral ministers: the cultivation of the Gospel vision of peace as a way of life for believers and as a leaven for society.

To educators: to use the framework of the Catholic teaching on war and peace toward the development of a theology of peace.

To parents: to teach their children concerning issues of justice and methods of peaceful conflict resolution.

To youth: to study carefully the teachings of the Church and the demands of the Gospel about war and peace, and to seek careful guidance in reaching decisions about civic responsibility.

To men and women in military service: to look upon themselves as the custodians of the security and freedom of their fellow citizens, contributing to the maintenance of peace.

To men and women in defense industries: to use the moral principles of this letter to help form their conscience.

To men and women of science: to continue to relate moral wisdom to political reality and to assist the Church in this effort.

To men and women of the media: to a certain extent, assist in the interpretation given by the general population in regard to the teachings of this letter.

To public officials: to lead with courage in regard to the issues of war and peace and to listen to the public debate with sensitivity.

To Catholics as citizens: to help within the context of a pluralistic democracy, to call attention to the moral dimensions of public issues (279, 285, 290, 297, 303, 304, 306, 307, 309, 318, 319, 322, 323).

God Is Love (Deus Caritas Est)
Pope Benedict XVI, 2005

- **Charity as a Responsibility of the Church**
- **Justice and Charity**

bility of each member of Christ's faithful and

nity—from the local community to the universal Church.

Love needs to be organized in order to be of service to the wider community.

Within the community of believers there can never be room for poverty that denies anyone what is necessary for a dignified life (20).

The true nature of the Church is expressed in three-fold responsibility: proclaiming the word of God, celebrating the sacraments, and exercising charity.

Charity is not an option but a part of the nature of the Church, an indispensable expression of her very being (21).

Justice and Charity
Concern for justice is always a primary concern of the state, to which the Church must add spiritual energy and rational argument (28).

The Multiple Structures of Charitable Service
Lay faithful as citizens of the state work for a just ordering of society, promoting the common good, animated by charity, and with true concern for the welfare of all.

Since modern means of mass communication make information about the needs of others instantaneously available, we are called to a new readiness to assist our neighbors in need. Modern technology also gives us the capability of using new means for responding to the plight of others.

There has been a growth in forms of cooperation between the state and Church agencies that can add to the effectiveness of charitable outreach.

The widespread involvement of the Church and other organized volunteer initiatives in serving others in need gives young people a school of life in the formation of solidarity (30).

The Distinctiveness of the Church's Charitable Activity

The Church, motivated by such examples from the Gospel as the Good Samaritan, attempts to respond to the immediate needs and specific situations of feeding the hungry, clothing the naked, caring for and healing the sick, visiting the sick, etc.

In addition to professional competence in accomplishing its mission, members of the Church, when they assist in charity, also need heartfelt concern for the humanity of each person they help, a "charity of the heart."

Love of neighbor, to those imbued with a Christian compassion, will flow from a faith that becomes active through love.

Christian charitable activity must be freed from parties and ideologies, and instead must be a way of making present here and now the love that men and women need.

Rather than appearing as a means of preserving the status quo, the Church strives to contribute to a better world from the "program" of Jesus, by acting from a "heart that sees."

The practice of charity should not aim primarily at proselytizing since love is free and is not practiced as a way of achieving other ends. However, God and Christ must not be set aside, since the deepest cause of suffering is the absence of God. Followers of Christ recognize that a pure and generous love is the best witness to the God in whom they believe, which drives them to love (31).

Those Responsible for the Church's Charitable Activity

Those who assist others in need learn humility if they follow the example of Christ, who by his radical humility took the lowest place when he came among us and took up the Cross. People who assist others learn that they receive grace to see themselves as instruments in God's hands.

Rather than become discouraged in our service, by humility we recognize that we are instruments in the Lord's hands, doing all we ~~~~~~~~~ the rest to the Lord. A living relationship with Christ is

- **The True Shape of Christian Hope**
- **Settings for Learning and Practicing Hope**

The True Shape of Christian Hope

The right state of human affairs and the well-being of the world cannot be guaranteed simply through structures alone, however good they may be. Even the best structures function only when the community is animated by convictions that are capable of motivating people to assent freely to the social order.

Since man remains free, and his freedom is fragile, the kingdom of good will never be definitively established in this world. Freedom must be constantly won over for the cause of good. If there existed structures that would irrevocably guarantee a determined good and state of the world, our freedom would be denied (24).

Every generation has the responsibility of engaging anew in the arduous search for the right way to order human affairs, and this task is never completed. Every generation must attempt to establish convincing structures of freedom and good which help succeeding generations to develop proper freedom (25).

It is not science that redeems humanity; rather humanity is redeemed by love. The human being needs unconditional love. Through Jesus we have become certain of God, a God who is not a remote "first cause" but rather a lover of humanity, redeemed by Jesus Christ (26).

Anyone who does not know God, even though they are filled with hope, is ultimately without hope, the great hope that sustains man in spite of all disappointments (27).

The great hope that sustains us is God, who bestows upon us what we ourselves cannot attain. His love alone can give us the possibility of persevering day by day, not giving up on hope, in a world which is by its nature imperfect (31).

Settings for Learning and Practicing Hope

To pray properly is to undergo inner purification, which opens us up to God and to our fellow human beings. We cannot pray against other human beings and we cannot ask for superficial and comfortable things, which are meager misplaced hopes that can lead us away from God. We must purify our hopes and desires (33).

Proper prayer includes our own personal prayer mingled with the great prayers of the Church which help us to speak to God and to be open to and prepared for service to our fellow human beings (34).

I can always continue to hope, even if my own life, or the historical periods in which I live, seem to give little reason for hope. The great certitude of hope that my own life and history, despite failures, are held firm by the power of Love can give us the power and courage to persevere (35).

We can free our life and the world from the contamination and poisons that threaten the world by opening ourselves to what is truth, to love, and to what is good (35).

The measure of humanity is essentially determined in the relationship to suffering and the sufferer. A society that is unable to accept its suffering members and incapable of helping to share their suffering through compassion is a cruel and inhuman society (38).

Love cannot exist without a painful renunciation of myself, to suffer with and for others, for the sake of truth and justice. The capacity to suffer for the sake of the truth is the measure of humanity (39).

On Integral Human Development in Charity and Truth
(Caritas in Veritate)
Pope Benedict XVI, 2009

• The Cooperation of the Human Family

When both the logic of the marketplace

agree that each will continue to exercise a monopoly over its area of influence, much is lost in the long term: solidarity in relations between citizens, participation and adherence, and actions of gratuitousness. This contrasts giving in order to acquire and giving through duty (39).

Today's international economic scene requires a profoundly new way of looking at business enterprise. There is an increasing awareness of a need for social responsibility, for example, that investments have moral as well as economic significance. What must be avoided is the use of financial resources that yield to a temptation to seek only short-term profits without regard for long-term sustainability of the enterprise and its benefit to further economic initiatives in countries in need of development (40).

Political authority involves a wide range of values that should be examined in the process of constructing a new order of economic productivity that is socially responsible and human in scale (41).

Globalization should be recognized as a growing interconnectedness made up of individuals and peoples to whom this process should offer benefits and development as they assume their respective responsibilities—singly and collectively. A sustained commitment is needed to promote a person-based and community-oriented cultural process of worldwide integration open to transcendence. We should not be victims of globalization, but rather protagonists, acting in the light of reason, guided by charity and truth. It has opened to us the possibility of unprecedented redistribution of wealth on a worldwide scale.

Globalization is a complex phenomenon capable of steering humanity toward more relational terms, of communion, and the sharing of goods (42).

The Cooperation of the Human Family

Greater solidarity at the international level is seen also in the promotion of greater access to education, including not only classroom teaching and vocational training but also the complete formation of the person. But in order to educate, it is necessary to know the nature of the human person. The prominence of a relativistic understanding of the nature of persons presents serious problems for education, especially moral education. The phenomenon of international tourism is an example of the significance of this problem. Sometimes unique opportunities are provided for the economic aspects of development, including the flow of money, a significant amount of local enterprise, and cultural aspects that include education. But in some cases international tourism has a negative educational impact both for the tourist and the local populace. This tourism sometimes follows a consumerist and hedonistic pattern as a form of escapism and is not conducive to authentic encounters between persons and cultures. We need to develop a different type of tourism that can promote mutual understanding (61).

Another aspect of integral human development is the phenomenon of migration. Policies are needed that set out close collaboration between the migrants' countries of origin and the countries of destination, accompanied by adequate international norms that coordinate different legislative systems to safeguard the needs and rights of individual migrants and their families. There is no doubt that foreign workers, despite any difficulties concerning integration, make a significant contribution to the economic development of the host country through their labor. These workers should be considered not commodities or a mere workforce but rather humans who possesses fundamental, inalienable rights that must be respected by everyone (62).

For Reflection and Dialogue

1. What do you consider to be the most important rights given to you by virtue of being a human being? Why? What are the most important rights granted to you by the state? Why?

muniues promote

5. According to the NCCB's document *The Challenge of Peace: God's Promise and Our Response*, what is the centerpiece of the Catholic Church's teaching on peace?

6. In what ways did the Hebrew people modify their understanding of God over time in relation to war and violence?

7. The US bishops describe peace as a "gift of God and a human work." Explain.

8. Do the norms against nuclear strategies proposed by the US bishops still have relevance? Why or why not?

9. How could Catholic citizens, as suggested by the bishops, within the context of a pluralistic democracy, call attention to the moral dimensions of public issues such as nuclear arms?

10. How does the Church in its three-fold responsibility of proclaiming the word of God, celebrating the sacraments, and exercising charity contribute to the concern for justice in the world today?

11. According to Pope Benedict XVI, how does the Church contribute to the making of a better world through the "program of Jesus"?

12. How is the measure of humanity determined in the relationship of suffering and the sufferer?

13. How do we become protagonists rather than antagonists of globalization?

7.

CARE FOR GOD'S

generation. We are called to live in harmony with all God's creatures. The following documents are summarized in this chapter:

- ➲ *Renewing the Earth: An Invitation to Reflection and Action on the Environment in Light of Catholic Social Teaching*, National Conference of Catholic Bishops, 1991

- ➲ *Global Climate Change: A Plea for Dialogue, Prudence, and the Common Good*, United States Conference of Catholic Bishops, 2001

- ➲ *For I Was Hungry and You Gave Me Food: Catholic Reflections on Food, Farmers, and Farmworkers*, United States Conference of Catholic Bishops, 2003

- ➲ *On Integral Human Development in Charity and Truth* (Caritas in Veritate), Pope Benedict XVI, 2009

Renewing the Earth: An Invitation to Reflection and Action on the Environment in Light of Catholic Social Teaching
National Conference of Catholic Bishops, 1991

- **Effects of Environmental Blight**
- **Religious and Ethical Dimensions of the Problem**
- **Role of Developed Nations**
- **A Christian Response**

At the core of the environmental crisis is a moral challenge: how we use and share the goods of the earth, what we pass on to future generations, and how we live in harmony with God's creation.

The effects of the crisis surround us: smog in cities, chemicals in our water and on our food, eroded topsoil, loss of valuable wetlands, radioactive and toxic waste lacking adequate disposal sites, and threats to the health of industrial and farm workers. The problems also extend beyond our borders: problems with acid rain, greenhouse gasses, and chlorofluorocarbons.

There are various opinions about the causes of environmental problems. The National Conference of Catholic Bishops adds a distinctive and constructive voice to the ecological dialogue underway, a dialogue which involves a moral and religious crisis. The goals of this statement include:

1. Highlight ethical dimensions of environmental crisis.
2. Link questions of ecology and poverty, environment and development.
3. Stand with working men and women, the poor and disadvantaged, whose lives are most often impacted by ecological abuse and tradeoffs between environment and development.
4. Promote a vision of a just and sustainable world community.
5. Invite the Catholic community and all men and women to reflect on the religious dimensions of this topic.
6. Begin a broader conversation on the potential contribution of the Church to environmental issues.

Humanity's mistreatment of the natural world diminishes our own dignity and sacredness because we are engaging in actions that contradict what it means to be human.

Effects of Environmental Blight

The whole human race suffers as a result of environmental blight. It is the poor and powerless who most directly bear the burden of current environmental carelessness. Their lands and neighborhoods are more likely to be polluted or to host toxic waste dumps, their water to be undrinkable, and their children to be harmed.

Sustainable economic policies that reduce current stresses on natural systems and are consistent with sound environmental policy must be put into effect.

Religious and Ethical Dimensions of the Problem

Catholics and all men and women of good will are invited to reflect on the moral issues raised by the environmental crisis.

Christian responsibility for the environment begins with an appreciation of the goodness of God's creation: "God looked at everything he had made, and he found it very good" (Gn 1:31). People share the earth with other creatures. But humans, made in the image and likeness of God, are called in a special way to "cultivate and care for the earth" (Gn 2:15).

To curb the abuse of the land and of fellow humans, ancient Israel set legal protections aimed at restoring the balance between land and people (Lv 25). Every seventh year the land and the people were to rest. It invited the whole community to taste the goodness of God in creation.

Jesus came proclaiming a jubilee in which humanity and all creation was to be liberated (Lk 4:16–22). Jesus is the firstborn of a new creation and gives his Spirit to renew the whole earth (Col 1:18–20; Ps 104:30).

Catholic social teaching provides a developing and distinctive perspective on environmental issues. This teaching tradition upholds a consistent respect for human life that extends to respect for all creation. It encourages a worldview affirming the ethical significance of global interdependence and the common good. It proclaims an option for the poor, giving passion to the quest for an equitable and sustainable world.

The whole world is God's dwelling. Through the created gifts of nature, men and women encounter their creator. Reverence for the creator present and active in nature can serve as the ground for environmental responsibility. Good stewardship implies that we must both care for creation according to standards that are not of our own making and at the same time be resourceful in finding ways to make the earth flourish.

By preserving natural environments, protecting endangered species, laboring to make environments compatible with local ecology, employing appropriate technology, and carefully evaluating technological innovations, we exhibit respect for creation and reverence for the creator.

Only with equitable and sustainable development can poor nations curb continuing environmental degradation and avoid the destructive effects of the kind of overdevelopment that has used natural resources irresponsibly.

In moving toward an environmentally sustainable economy, we are obligated to work for a just economic system that equitably shares the bounty of the earth and of human enterprise with all peoples. Created things belong not just to a few, but rather to the whole human family.

The ecological problem is intimately linked to justice for the poor. The option for the poor makes us aware that it is they who suffer most directly from environmental decline and have the least access to relief from their suffering.

Environmental progress cannot come at the expense of workers and their rights. Where jobs are lost, society must help in the process of economic conversion, so that not only the earth but also workers and their families are protected.

Role of Developed Nations
Regrettably, advantaged groups often seem more intent on curbing Third World births than on restraining the even more voracious consumerism of the developed world.

Consumption in developed nations remains the single greatest source of global environmental destruction. We in the developed world are obligated to address our own wasteful and destructive use of resources.

The key factor in dealing with population problems is sustainable social and economic development. Only when an economy distributes resources so as to allow the poor an equitable stake in society and some hope for the future do couples see responsible parenthood as good for their families. Such development may be the best contribution affluent societies like the United States can make in relieving ecological pressures in the less developed countries. To eliminate hunger from the ... ... reform the institutional and politi-

Our Catholic faith continues to affirm the goodness... world. A Christian love of the natural world, as St. Francis shows, can restrain grasping and wanton human behavior and help preserve and nurture all that God has made.

Scientific research and technological innovation must accompany religious and moral responses to environmental challenges.

A Christian Response

At the heart of the Christian life lies the love of neighbor. The ecological crisis challenges us to extend our love to future generations and to the flourishing of all earth's creatures. At the same time, our duties to future generations must not diminish our love for the present members of the human family, especially the poor and the disadvantaged.

Christian love forbids us from choosing between people and the planet. It urges us to work for an equitable and sustainable future in which all peoples can share in the bounty of the earth and in which the earth itself is protected from predatory use.

All in the Catholic community are called, along with others of good will, to understand and act on the moral and ethical dimensions of the environmental crisis:

- *Scientists, environmentalists, and economists* are asked to continue to help with the challenges concerning the environmental issues.

- *Teachers and educators* are invited to emphasize in their classrooms and curricula a love for God's creation.

- *Parents,* as the first and principal teachers of their children, must teach them a love of earth and nature, and the care and concern for them at the heart of environmental morality.

- *Theologians, scripture scholars, and ethicists* are called on to explore and advance the insights of the Catholic tradition and its relation to the environment and other religious perspectives on these matters.

- *Business leaders* should make protection of our common environment a central concern in their activities, and collaborate for the common good and the protection of the earth.

- *Members of the Church* are asked to examine their lifestyles, behaviors, and policies—individually and institutionally—to see how we contribute to the destruction or neglect of the environment and to see how we might assist in its protection and restoration.

- *Environmental advocates* are asked to join in building bridges between the quest for justice and the pursuit of peace.

- *Policymakers* are asked to focus more directly on the ethical dimensions of environmental policy and on its relation to development, to seek the common good, and to resist short-term pressures in order to meet our long-term responsibility to future generations.

- *Citizens* need to participate in this debate over how our nation best protects our ecological heritage, allocates environmental costs, and plans for the future.

The environmental crisis of our day is an exceptional call to conversion and a change of heart to save the planet for our children and generations yet unborn. Only when believers look to the values of the scriptures, honestly admit limitations and failings, and commit to common action on behalf of all the land and the vulnerable of the earth will we be ready to participate fully in resolving this crisis.

> ## Global Climate Change: A Plea for Dialogue, Prudence, and the Common Good
> ### United States Conference of Catholic Bishops, 2001
>
> • Scientific Knowledge and the Virtue of Prudence

God has given us the gift of creation . . .

sustains life, and fruits of the land that nourishes us. Global climate change is about the future of God's creation—protecting the human environment and the natural environment.

Scientific Knowledge and the Virtue of Prudence

The dialogue and response to the challenges that face us due to climate change must be faced with prudence. It is important that the needs of the poor, the weak, and the vulnerable be heard as issues related to climate change are debated.

The evidence of global climate change and the merging scientific consensus about the human impact upon this process have led many governments to decide to expend time, money, and political will to address the problem through collective international action.

Prudence is a thoughtful, deliberative, and rational basis for taking or avoiding action to achieve a moral good. If enough evidence demonstrates that the present course of action jeopardizes humankind's well-being, prudence dictates taking mitigating or preventative action.

The Universal Common Good

Responses to global climate should reflect humanity's interdependence and common responsibility for the future of our planet. Economic freedom, initiative, and creativity are essential to help our nation find effective ways to address the issue of climate change.

The desire to possess more material goods must not overtake our concern for the basic needs of people and the environment. Rejecting the false promises of excessive consumption and a renewed sense of sacrifice and restraint can make an essential contribution to addressing global climate change.

Population and climate change should be approached from the broader perspective of concern for protecting human life, care for the environment, respect for cultural norms, and the religious morals and faith of peoples.

Population and Authentic Development
Affluent nations, including our own, must acknowledge the impact of voracious consumerism instead of simply calling for population and emission controls for people in poorer countries.

Caring for the Poor and Issues of Equity
Historically, the industrial economies have been responsible for the highest emissions of greenhouse gasses that scientists suggest cause the warming trend.

There is a legitimate concern that as developing countries improve their economies and emit more greenhouse gasses they will need technological help to mitigate further atmospheric environmental harm. Any successful strategy must reflect the participation of those most affected and least able to bear the burden.

In solidarity and for the common good, the United States should lead developed nations in contributing to sustainable economic development of poorer nations and help them in easing climate change. Citizens should become informed participants in the public debate.

The Public Policy Debate and Future Directions
All parties should adopt an attitude of candor, conciliation, and prudence in response to the complexity of the issues related to global warming. We should all consider our lifestyle choices and how we can better conserve energy, prevent pollution, and live more simply.

> ## For I Was Hungry and You Gave Me Food: Catholic Reflections on Food, Farmers, and Farmworkers
> ### United States Conference of Catholic Bishops, 2003
>
> • Stewardship of Creation

> ## On Integral Human Development in Charity and Truth (Caritas in Veritate)
> ### Pope Benedict XVI, 2009

Development is also linked to duties that arise from our relationship to the natural environment. The environment is God's gift to everyone, and in our use of it we have a responsibility to the poor, to future generations, and to humanity. Nature expresses a design of truth and love. It is a work of the Creator with ends and criteria for its wise use. Projects for integral human development cannot ignore the coming generations but must be concerned about inter-generational justice, which includes ecology (48).

Due consideration must be given to the energy problem. Some states, power groups, and companies hoard non-renewable energy resources. Poorer countries lack the means to gain access to non-renewable energy or to finance research for new alternatives. The stockpiling of natural resources gives rise to exploitation and conflicts. The international community has an obligation to find institutional means of regulating the exploitation of non-renewable resources, involving poor countries in the process.

There is a moral need for renewed solidarity between the developing countries and the highly industrialized. The technologically advanced societies must lower domestic energy consumption while encouraging research into alternative forms of energy. Also needed is a worldwide distribution of energy resources (49).

Human beings exercise a responsible stewardship over nature in order to protect it, enjoy its fruits, and cultivate it in new ways. There is room on the earth for everyone. Competent authorities must ensure that economic and social costs of using up shared environmental resources are recognized with transparency and fully borne by those who incur them. One of the greatest challenges of the economy is to achieve the most efficient use of natural resources recognizing that "efficiency" is not always value-free (50).

The way humanity treats the environment also influences the way it treats itself, and vice versa. Contemporary society needs a serious review of its lifestyle. A new lifestyle is needed which highlights the quest for truth, beauty, goodness, and communion with others for the sake of common growth.

Many resources are squandered by wars. Peace would help provide greater protection of nature.

The Church has a responsibility toward creation, not only defending earth, water, and air as gifts of creation but above all protecting humankind from self-destruction. The decisive issue at stake is the overall tenor of society. Our duties toward the environment are intricately tied to duties toward the human person (51).

Truth and the love that it reveals can only be received as a gift; the ultimate source is not humankind but God who is himself Truth and Love (52).

One of the deepest forms of poverty is that of isolation. Man is alienated and alone when he is detached from reality, when he stops thinking and believing in a foundation. There is a need to transform the contemporary sense of being close to another, to a true communion. The true development of people takes place when we recognize that we are all part of one family working together in true communion (53).

For Reflection and Dialogue

1. Comment on the effects of the environmental crisis as seen by the US bishops in *Renewing the Earth: An Invitation to Reflection and Action on the Environment in Light of Catholic Social Teaching*. Are there additional effects that have developed during the intervening years

4. What do you believe is the single most important cause of global environmental destruction?

5. The bishops have asked members of the Church to examine their lifestyles, behaviors, and policies—individually and institutionally—in regard to ecology and the environment. What might be the results of such a review in your parish?

6. How are the needs of the poor, the weak, and vulnerable related to the issue of global climate change?

7. What is the relationship between voracious consumerism and climate change?

8. How can nations of the world better collaborate in addressing issues of energy consumption?

9. What lifestyle changes among the largest consumers of energy resources could be helpful in sustaining responsible stewardship globally?

Appendix A: Homily and Catechetical Message Guide

Dignity of the Human Person

4th Sunday in Ordinary Time-C	Jer 1:4–5, 17–19 Ps 71:1–2, 3–4, 5–6, 15+17 **1 Cor 12:31–13:13 or 13:4–13** Lk 4:21–30	*To love is the Christian lifestyle.*
7th Sunday in Ordinary Time-A	Lv 19:1–2, 17–18 **Ps 103:1–2, 3–4, 8+10, 12–13** 1 Cor 3:16–23 Mt 5:38–48	*God secures justice and upholds the rights of the oppressed.*
8th Sunday in Ordinary Time-A	Is 49:14–15 Ps 62:2–3, 6–7, 8–9 1 Cor 4:1–5 **Mt 6:24–34**	*Set your hearts first on the kingdom of God.*
8th Sunday in Ordinary Time-B	Hos 2:16b, 17b, 21–22 **Ps 103:1–2, 3–4, 8+10, 12–13** 2 Cor 3:1b–6 Mk 2:18–22	*God secures justice and upholds the rights of the oppressed.*

The Ascension of the Lord-ABC	**Acts 1:1–11** Ps 47:2–3, 6–7, 8–9 Eph 1:17–23 Mt 28:16–20 (A), Mk 16:15–20 (B), Lk 24:46–53 (C)	*The Holy Spirit provides the power needed to do the work of God.*
15th Sunday in Ordinary Time-C	Dt 30:10–14 Ps 69:14+17, 30–31, 33–34, 36a+37 or Ps 19:8, 9, 10, Col 1:15–20, 11 **Lk 10:25–37**	*The Good Samaritan is a model for the Christian lifestyle.*

The Community and the Common Good

4th Sunday in Ordinary Time-A	Zep 2:3, 3:12–13 Ps 146:6–7, 8–9a, 9b–10 1 Cor 1:26–31 **Mt 5:1–12a**	*Give your coat to that person who is in need, and be willing to walk the extra mile.*
7th Sunday in Ordinary Time-C	1 Sm 26:2, 7–9, 12–13, 22–23 Ps 103:1–2, 3–4, 8+10, 12–13 1 Cor 15:45–49 **Lk 6:27–38**	*To make peace, use nonviolence and love of enemies.*
Holy Thursday: Evening Mass of the Lord's Supper-ABC	Ex 12:1–8, 11–14 Ps 116:12–13, 15–16, 17–18 1 Cor 11:23–26 **Jn 13:1–15**	*Jesus, the Suffering Servant, washes the feet of the apostles and invites us to be of service to one another.*
2nd Sunday of Easter-B	**Acts 4:32–35** Ps 118:2–4, 13–15, 22–24 1 Jn 5:1–6 Jn 20:19–31	*We are called to live in true Christian community, concerned with others' needs.*

Pentecost Sunday, Vigil Mass-ABC	Gn 11:1–9 or Ex 19:3–8a, 16–20b or **Ez 37:1–14** or Jl 3:1–5 Ps 104:1–2, 24+35, 27–28, 29b–30 Rom 8:22–27 Jn 7:37–39	*The "dry bones" of the Church and our own communities can be renewed by the Spirit.*
Time-B	Ps 33:4–5, 18–19, 20+22 Heb 4:14–16 **Mk 10:35–45 or 10:42–45**	*necessary to be the servant of all.*

Rights and Responsibilities

3rd Sunday of Advent-A	Is 35:1–6a, 10 **Ps 146:6–7, 8–9a, 9b–10** Jas 5:7–10 Mt 11:2–11	*The Lord gives justice and liberty and invites us to provide that same justice and liberty to all.*
Sacred Heart-C	**Ez 34:11–16** Ps 23:1–3a, 3b–4, 5, 6 Rom 5:5b–11 Lk 15:3–7	*Leaders have responsibilities to ensure that rights are fostered and protected.*
9th Sunday in Ordinary Time-A	Dt 11:18, 26–28, 32 Ps 31:2–3a, 3b–4, 17+25 Rom 3:21–25, 28 Mt 7:21–27	*We are called to combine our prayer with action on behalf of others.*
13th Sunday in Ordinary Time-A	2 Kgs 4:8–11, 14–16a Ps 89:2–3, 16–17, 18–19 Rom 6:3–4, 8–11 Mt 10:37–42	*Christ invites his followers to take up their cross daily, for it is necessary to lose one's life in order to save it.*

22nd Sunday in Ordinary Time-B	Dt 4:1–2, 6–8 Ps 15:2–3a, 3b–4a, 4b–5 Jas 1:17–18, 21b–22, 27 Mk 7:1–8, 14–15, 21–23	*Be doers of the word, not only hearers.*
23rd Sunday in Ordinary Time-B	Is 35:4–7a Ps 146:7, 8–9a, 9b–10 Jas 2:1–5 Mk 7:31–37	*We must always practice what we believe and preach.*
25th Sunday in Ordinary Time-C	**Am 8:4–7** Ps 113:1–2, 4–6, 7–8 1 Tm 2:1–8 Lk 16:1–13 or 16:10–13	*The Lord decries the rich who trample upon the poor and needy.*
26th Sunday in Ordinary Time-C	Am 6:1a, 4–7 **Ps 146:7, 8–9a, 9b–10** 1 Tm 6:11–16 Lk 16:19–31	*The Lord gives justice and liberty and invites us to provide that same justice and liberty to all.*
31st Sunday in Ordinary Time-A	Mal 1:14b–2:2b, 8–10 Ps 131:1, 2, 3 1 Thes 2:7b–9, 13 **Mt 23:1–12**	*We are called to service in the name of Christ.*
31st Sunday in Ordinary Time-C	Wis 11:22–12:2 Ps 145:1–2, 8–9, 10–11, 13b–14 2 Thes 1:11–2:2 **Lk 19:1–10**	*Zacchaeus's story invites us to conversion, repentance, and restitution.*
32nd Sunday in Ordinary Time-B	1 Kgs 17:10–16 **Ps 146:7, 8–9a, 9b–10** Heb 9:24–28 Mk 12:38–44 or 12:41–44	*The Lord gives justice and liberty and invites us to provide that same justice and liberty to all.*

Option for the Poor

2nd Sunday of Advent-A	Is 11:1–10 **Ps 72:1–2, 7–8, 12–13, 17** Rom 15:4–9 Mt 3:1–12	*God liberates and defends* *the poor and those who are* *oppressed.*
	12–13 Eph 3:2–3a, 5–6 Mt 2:1–12	*oppressed.*
3rd Sunday in Ordinary Time-C	Neh 8:2–4a, 5–6, 8–10 Ps 19:8, 9, 10, 15 1 Cor 12:12–30 or 12:12– 14, 27 **Lk 1:1–4; 4:14–21**	*Jesus proclaims a mission to* *bring liberation.*
7th Sunday in Ordinary Time-B	Is 43:18–19, 21–22, 24b–25 **Ps 41:2–3, 4–5, 13–14** 2 Cor 1:18–22 Mk 2:1–12	*Show regard for the poor* *and those who are lowly.*
3rd Sunday of Lent-C	**Ex 3:1–8a, 13–15** Ps 103:1–2, 3–4, 6–7, 8+11 1 Cor 10:1–6, 10–12 Lk 13:1–9	*God is liberator and sends* *Moses to free Israel from* *oppression.*
4th Sunday of Lent-C	Jos 5:9a, 10–12 **Ps 34:2–3, 4–5, 6–7** 2 Cor 5:17–21 Lk 15:1–3, 11–32	*The Lord hears the cry of the* *poor.*

Holy Thursday, Chrism Mass-ABC	**Is 61:1–3ab, 6a, 8b–9** Ps 89:21–22, 25, 27 Rv 1:5–8 Lk 4:16–21	*Christ proclaims good news and liberation to the poor.*
Holy Thursday, Chrism Mass-ABC	Is 61:1–3ab, 6a, 8b–9 Ps 89:21–22, 25, 27 Rv 1:5–8 **Lk 4:16–21**	*Jesus proclaims a mission to bring liberation.*
13th Sunday in Ordinary Time-B	Wis 1:13–15, 2:23–24 Ps 30:2+4, 5–6, 11–12a+13b **2 Cor 8:7, 9, 13–15** Mk 5:21–43 or 5:21–24, 35–43	*We are called to share with those who are in need; Christ became poor that he might enrich us.*
19th Sunday in Ordinary Time-B	1 Kgs 19:4–8 **Ps 34:2–3, 4–5, 6–7, 8–9** Eph 4:30–5:2 Jn 6:41–51	*The Lord hears the cry of the poor.*
19th Sunday in Ordinary Time-C	Wis 18:6–9 Ps 33:1+12, 18–19, 20–22 Heb 11:1–2, 8–19 or 11:1–2, 8–12 **Lk 12:32–48 or 12:35–40**	*Jesus calls us to a special concern for the poor.*
20th Sunday in Ordinary Time-B	Prv 9:1–6 **Ps 34:2–3, 4–5, 6–7** Eph 5:15–20 Jn 6:51–58	*The Lord hears the cry of the poor.*
22nd Sunday in Ordinary Time-C	Sir 3:17–18, 20, 28–29 Ps 68:4–5, 6–7, 10–11 Heb 12:18–19, 22–24a **Lk 14:1, 7–14**	*Jesus tells a parable about the need for humility and hospitality.*

26th Sunday in Ordinary Time-C	Am 6:1a, 4–7 Ps 146:7, 8–9a, 9b–10 1 Tm 6:11–16 **Lk 16:19–31**	*The story of Lazarus and the wealthy man shows that we are called to reach out to the poor.*
28th Sunday in Ordinary	Wis 7:7–11	*The wealthy young man*

Solidarity

3rd Sunday in Ordinary Time-C	Neh 8:2–4a, 5–6, 8–10 Ps 19:8, 9, 10, 15 **1 Cor 12:12–30 or** **12:12–14, 27** Lk 1:1–4, 4:14–21	*If one suffers then all suffer.*
5th Sunday in Ordinary Time-A	**Is 58:7–10** Ps 112:4–5, 6–7, 8–9 1 Cor 2:1–5 Mt 5:13–16	*God does not desire empty worship, but a conversion of heart that produces justice, love, and mercy.*
4th Sunday of Lent-C	Jos 5:9a, 10–12 Ps 34:2–3, 4–5, 6–7 2 Cor 5:17–21 **Lk 15:1–3, 11–32**	*Christ associated himself with the outcasts of society.*
18th Sunday in Ordinary Time-C	Eccl 1:2, 2:21–23 Ps 90:3–4, 5–6, 12–14, 17 **Col 3:1–5, 9–11** Lk 12:13–21	*Eliminate all racial discrimination within the community.*

| 23rd Sunday in Ordinary Time-A | Ez 33:7–9
Ps 95:1–2, 6–7, 8–9
Rom 13:8–10
Mt 18:15–20 | *Our only debt is to have love for one another.* |
| 34th or Last Sunday in Ordinary Time, Christ the King-A | Ez 34:11–12, 15–17
Ps 23:1–3a, 3b–4, 5–6
1 Cor 15:20–26, 28
Mt 25:31–46 | *Whatever we do to our neighbor who is in need, we do to Christ.* |

APPENDIX B: SAMPLE PENANCE SERVICE

times that we have failed to respect the dignity of our brothers and sisters. May God grant you peace and friendship.

Response: **Amen.**

Celebrant:
My brothers and sisters, God calls us to a true and thorough change of heart. Let us now ask God for the grace of true repentance and a renewed heart.

(*Pause for silent prayer.*)

Almighty and merciful God, you have brought us together to bestow your mercy and grace. Open our eyes to see those times that we have failed to acknowledge the dignity and value of each human being and have ignored their needs. Forgive us for the times that we have failed in our duties to love and serve one another. Touch our hearts and return them to you. May your power heal and strengthen us, and may we be recommitted in our baptismal service to be promoters and defenders of your life within each human being. We make our prayer through Christ our Lord.

R: **Amen.**

First Reading

Isaiah 58:1–11

This, rather, is the fasting that I wish: releasing those bound unjustly. . . .

Psalm Response

Psalm 119

Happy are they who follow the law of the Lord!

R: Happy are they who follow the law of the Lord!

Happy are they whose way is blameless,

who walk in the law of the Lord.

R: Happy are they who follow the law of the Lord!

With all my heart, I seek you;

let me not stray from your commands.

Within my heart I treasure your promise,

that I may not sin against you.

R: Happy are they who follow the law of the Lord!

Blessed are you, O Lord;

teach me your statutes.

With my lips I declare

all the ordinances of your mouth.

R: Happy are they who follow the law of the Lord!

I will meditate on your precepts

and consider your ways.

In your statutes I will delight;

I will not forget your words.

R: Happy are they who follow the law of the Lord!

New Testament Reading

James 2:14–26

What use is it if someone says that he believes and does not manifest his works?

Gospel Reading

Matthew 5:1–12

When he saw the crowd, he went up to the hill and taught his disciples.

(A brief homily is given which leads the community to reflect on God's living word and on the responsibilities of living the Christian life.)

      especially the disadvantaged, been of help to my family in knowing Jesus better?

3. Do I share my possessions with others less fortunate, or do I hoard, accumulating much more than I could ever use?

4. Do I help those who are oppressed by society in any way? The poor? The marginalized? The minority?

5. Does my life reflect the mission I received in confirmation? Do I share in outreach efforts sponsored by my parish, my diocese, and other worthwhile projects and programs?

6. Have I attempted in some way to assist in the Church's mission to bring peace and justice to the world?

7. Am I concerned for the good and prosperity of the human community in which I live, or do I spend my life caring only for myself?

8. Have I done violence to another in any way? Have I been respectful of the dignity of other human beings? Do I respect life from the womb to the tomb?

9. Have I gone against my conscience out of fear or hypocrisy?

10. Have I always tried to act out of a spirit of justice and what is morally right?

Celebrant:

My brothers and sisters, we all acknowledge that we are sinners and are in need of God's mercy. We are moved to penance and look to live the new life of grace. We admit our guilt and say, "Lord, I acknowledge my sins; my offenses are always before me. Turn away your face, Lord, from my sins, and blot out all my wrongdoing. Give me back the joy of your salvation and give me a new and steadfast spirit."

We are sorry for having offended you, God, especially by our passivity and inactivity when we were called to work on behalf of your Gospel but turned aside. Be merciful and restore us to your friendship. Amen.

Now in obedience to Christ himself, let us join in prayer to the Father, asking him to forgive us as we forgive others. Our Father . . .

> Father, our source of life,
> you know our weakness.
> May we reach out with joy to grasp your hand
> and walk more readily in your ways.
> We ask this through Christ our Lord.

R: **Amen**.

(Sacramental confession may be celebrated according to the proper norms.)

Celebrant:
God and Father of us all, you have forgiven our sins and sent us your peace. Help us to forgive each other and to work together to establish peace in the world. We ask this through Christ our Lord. Amen.

Celebrant: May the Lord guide your hearts in the way of his love.

R: **Amen**.

Celebrant: May he give you strength to walk in newness of life.

R: **Amen**.

Celebrant: May Almighty God bless you, the Father, the Son, and the Holy Spirit.

R: **Amen**.

Celebrant: Go in the peace of Christ.

R: **Thanks be to God**.

Appendix C: Papal Biographies

Catholic social thought did not come from a vacuum, but rather rose

Pope Leo XIII
(1878–1903)

Gioacchino Pecci was born in Carpineto (near Rome) in 1810. He came from a family of minor nobility. Prior to his ordination to the priesthood (1837), he studied at Viterbo, the Roman College, and the Academy of Noble Ecclesiastics. He was made an archbishop and sent in 1843 as nuncio to Belgium. In 1846 he was named bishop of Perugia and made a cardinal in 1853.

During the course of his stay in Belgium as papal representative, he traveled to London, Paris, and other industrialized cities and nations, which gave him some insights into the implications of the industrial age. While in Perugia, he attempted to work toward reconciliation between modern culture and the Church, a topic which he addressed in several pastoral letters.

In 1877, Cardinal Pecci was invited to Rome by Pope Pius IX to serve as the camerlengo, the chamberlain of the Holy Roman Church, who administers the Holy See when there is a papal vacancy. After the death of Pius IX in 1878, he was elected to the papacy on the third ballot. Although he was sixty-eight years old and of seemingly frail health, he would have an energetic pontificate of twenty-five years. During his time in office, he attempted to address the many social issues that confronted the Church, especially in the area of labor and management relations and the defense of the working class. He enunciated a clear policy for workers' rights and trade unions and has been referred to as the "workers' pope." His groundbreaking encyclical was *Rerum Novarum* (Of New Things) which defended the right to private property and the obligation to pay workers a just wage, as well as the need to honor workers' rights.

Pope Pius XI
(1922–1939)

Ambrogio Damiano Achille Ratti, the son of a silk factory manager, was born in Desio, near Milan, in 1857. He was ordained a priest in 1879 and received three doctorates from the Gregorian University in Rome. He taught dogmatic theology from 1883 to 1888 at the Milan seminary. From 1888 he worked at the Ambrosian Library in Milan until he was appointed in 1911 to the Vatican Library. He was recognized for his great language fluency and was sent by Pope Benedict XV in 1918 as apostolic visitor (eventually nuncio) to Poland. Because he refused to leave the country when it was attacked in 1920 by the Bolsheviks, he was rewarded by the Polish government with the Order of the White Eagle. In 1921 he was named archbishop of Milan and later that same year was elected to the papacy following the death of Benedict XV.

Pope Pius XI took as his motto "Christ's peace in Christ's kingdom" and was a strong advocate for peace against the background of an increasingly dangerous world situation. He favored the active participation of the Church in the life of the world. He also sought to promote peaceful relations between employers and employees, continuing and expanding the social doctrine of Pope Leo XIII, particularly in his 1931 encyclical *Quadragesimo Anno* (On the Fortieth Anniversary of *Rerum Novarum*). Written in the midst of a worldwide depression, this important social teaching document, written on the occasion of the fortieth anniversary of *Rerum Novarum*, introduced the important principle of "subsidiarity," where nothing should be done by a higher agency than can be done better by a lower one.

Pope John XXIII
(1958–1963)

the war, his assignments included being named national director for the Congregation for the Propagation of the Faith. He also did historical research and writing, including work at the Ambrosian Library, where he met Achille Ratti, the future Pius XI.

Pope Pius XI appointed him to diplomatic service in Bulgaria. Under Pius XII he served in France, and in 1952 he was appointed permanent observer for the Holy See at UNESCO. On January 12, 1953, he was named cardinal and on January 15, patriarch of Venice, where he quickly became known for his great pastoral zeal. In October of 1958 he was elected to the papacy. He is particularly remembered for his calling of the Second Vatican Council, which he said was done through the inspiration of the Holy Spirit, for a new and vibrant expression of the faith. His encyclical *Mater et Magistra* (Mother and Teacher) updated the social teaching of the Church as expressed in the encyclicals of Leo XIII and Pius XI, concerning private property, the rights of workers, and the obligations of government. *Pacem in Terris* (Peace on Earth), issued in 1963, promoted respect for human rights as a necessary foundation for world peace.

Pope Paul VI
(1963–1978)

Giovanni Battista Montini, born September 26, 1897, in Concesio, near Brescia, was the son of a lawyer who was also a political writer. After his seminary courses, taken at home due to his poor health, Montini was ordained a priest in May 1920. He then began graduate studies in Rome. Much of his time

over the next several years was spent in the papal secretariat of state, involved in such areas as the Catholic Student Movement. He served briefly as an attaché in the nunciature in Warsaw in 1923. In 1937 he was appointed assistant to Cardinal Eugenio Pacelli, who was then the secretary of state. When Cardinal Pacelli became Pope Pius XII, Montini worked closely with him.

In 1954 he was appointed archbishop of Milan and spent much of his time attempting to rebuild the area which continued to suffer the devastating effects of World War II. He was especially concerned with the plight of the industrial workers.

After the death of John XXIII, he was elected pope at the papal conclave of 1963, and chose the name "Paul" to indicate his desire to reach out to the whole world as the Apostle Paul had done. He worked to complete the Second Vatican Council, which had begun under his predecessor, and then attempted to steer the reforms introduced by the Council.

Among his efforts at social justice can be included the encyclical *Populorum Progressio* (On the Progress of Peoples), which made the case for concerted efforts by the developed nations to assist those countries that were struggling in their efforts toward economic and social development.

Pope John Paul II
(1978–2005)

Karol Wojtyla was born in Wadowice, Poland, in 1920, the son of a retired army lieutenant and a devoted mother who died when he was very young. As a student in the state high school, he

after his ordination (1946) to Rome for doctoral studies. After completing his degree, he returned to Poland, where he was appointed professor of ethics at Lublin University. In 1958 he was appointed auxiliary bishop of Krakow. On December 30, 1963, he was named archbishop and in 1967 a cardinal.

He attended all four sessions of the Second Vatican Council and was influential in many of the debates, especially on religious freedom.

In October 1978 he was elected pope at the age of fifty-eight. His papacy was marked by a vigorous defense of the dignity of the human person, a theme often articulated in his encyclicals, including his first, *Redemptor Hominis* (Redeemer of Man).

Pope Benedict XVI
(2005–2013)

Joseph Ratzinger was born April 16, 1927, in Marktl am Inn, Bavaria, Germany, the son of a policeman and of a family of farmers. He spent his childhood and adolescence in Traunstein, a village near the Austrian border. His faith matured during the time of Nazi persecution. Toward the end of the war he was conscripted in an auxiliary anti-aircraft corps and trained in the German infantry. After the war, he was released from a POW camp

to attend a seminary for priesthood studies. He was ordained a priest June 29, 1951, and shortly after began teaching at the University of Bonn, later at the University of Munster, and then Tubingen.

He served as a "peritus" (expert) at the Second Vatican Council, assisting Cardinal Joseph Frings, Archbishop of Cologne. He also served as a consultant for the German Bishops' Conference and as a member of the International Theological Commission.

In collaboration with the theologians Hans Urs von Balthasar and Henri Lubac and other theologians, he began the theological journal *Communio*. His many publications include *Introduction to Christianity* (1968) consisting of university lectures on the Apostles' Creed.

Pope Paul VI, in 1977, appointed him the Archbishop of Munich and Freising. That same year he was named a cardinal of the Church.

He was named by Pope John Paul II the prefect for the Congregation of Faith in 1981. While serving in this capacity he was the president of the Preparatory Commission for the Catechism of the Catholic Church which completed its work in 1996.

He was elected to the papacy April 19, 2005. Among his works on the theme of social justice, prominence can be given to the encyclical *Caritas in Veritate* (On Integral Human Development in Charity and Truth) issued June 29, 2009, which continued many of the themes of his predecessor Pope Paul VI's encyclical *Populorum Progressio*.

Appendix D: Chart of Historic Milestones

In order to contextualize the various papal encyclicals, the following

	Kulturkampf in Prussia, 1871
	First World War, 1914–18
	Russian Revolution, 1917–18
Quadragesimo Anno May 15, 1931	Worldwide financial depression, 1929
	Adolf Hitler, German Chancellor, 1933
	Second World War, 1939–45
	UN Charter, 1945
Mater et Magistra May 15, 1961	Cold War, 1945–89
Pacem in Terris April 11, 1963	Second Vatican Council, 1962–65
	Cuban missile crisis, 1962
	John F. Kennedy assassinated, 1963
Populorum Progressio March 26, 1967	Vietnam War, 1965–73

Laborem Exercens September 14, 1981	Solidarity, labor union founded in Poland, 1980
Sollicitudo Rei Socialis December 30, 1987	Communism collapses, 1989
Centesimus Annus May 1, 1991	Persian Gulf War, 1991
Evangelium Vitae March 25, 1995	Apartheid ends in South Africa, 1993 Federal office building bombed, Oklahoma City, killing 168 people, 1995
Deus Caritas Est, December 25, 2005	Terrorist attack on multiple sites in the United States, more than 3,000 casualties, September 11, 2001 United States with other countries launches attack in Afghanistan, October 7, 2001 The United States invades Iraq, March 2003
Spes Salvi November 30, 2007	Hurricane Katrina strikes the US Gulf Coast, the costliest natural disaster and one of the deadliest hurricanes in US history, August 2005

Caritas in Veritate June 29, 2009	Fighting erupts between the Israeli government and Palestinian Hamas. After numerous airstrikes, Israel enters Gaza, December 2008
	Deepwater Horizon oil spill in the Gulf of Mexico, April–July 2010

GLOSSARY

A Place at the Table: A Catholic Recommitment to Overcome Poverty and to Respect

A pastoral reflection by the US Catholic Bishops calling Catholics to recommitment to the overcoming of poverty and for respect for the

front and combat what it called a "radical evil."

capitalism

Economic system that is characterized by the private or corporate ownership of goods with investments that are determined by private decision rather than control by the state. Prices and production are determined primarily by competition in a free market.

Caritas in Veritate (On Integral Human Development in Charity and Truth)

Encyclical issued June 29, 2009, commenting forty years after the encyclical of Pope Paul VI's *Populorum Progressio* (The Development of Peoples) on the need to continue the work of authentic development of all peoples on the basis of charity and truth.

Catholic Charities

The largest private charitable organization in the United States, raising millions of dollars to assist in meeting people's basic needs, serving 10,000,000 people annually.

Catholic social teaching	A body of teachings issued by the Church, particularly since Pope Leo XIII's encyclical *Rerum Novarum*, which seeks to apply the Gospel of Jesus Christ to society's systems and laws so that people's rights are guaranteed.
Centesimus Annus (On the Hundredth Anniversary of *Rerum Novarum*)	An encyclical issued by Pope John Paul II on May 1, 1991, to honor the centenary anniversary of the publication of *Rerum Novarum* by Pope Leo XIII. It includes teachings regarding the proper ordering of culture, politics, and economics in society, as well as reflections on the nature of "person" and "true freedom."
The Challenge of Peace: God's Promise and Our Response	Issued by the US bishops on May 3, 1983, after extensive consultation, this pastoral letter addresses several issues related to war in a nuclear age. It draws upon a long Catholic tradition regarding violence and war, including the "just war" theory, to help frame a response to the important ethical questions raised in contemporary times about the morality of nuclear war.
chlorofluorocarbons	Any of several gaseous compounds containing chlorine and fluorine used especially in aerosol propellants and refrigerants.
common good	John XXIII describes this as "the sum total of conditions of social living, whereby persons are enabled more fully and readily to achieve their own perfection" (*Mater et Magistra*, 65). Not to be confused with pursuing the greatest good for the greatest number. No one is excluded from the common good.
Constitution on the Sacred Liturgy (Sacrosanctum Concilium)	The first major document of the Second Vatican Council issued December 4, 1963, concerning reform of the Roman Catholic liturgy.

consumerism	A preoccupation toward the buying of consumer goods.
Deus Caritas Est (God Is Love)	Encyclical of Pope Benedict XVI, issued December 25, 2005, concerning the love of neighbor, grounded in the love of God

Pastoral Letter on Catholic Social Teaching and the US Economy	many sectors of American life, this pastoral letter issued by the bishops of the United States (November 18, 1986) sought to bring the Church's social teaching to the area of economics and the concrete realities and problems of the US economy, including employment and poverty issues.
encyclical	A formal pastoral letter by the pope concerning matters of morals, discipline, or doctrine, usually addressed to the universal Church.
euthanasia	The practice of killing or permitting the death of a hopelessly sick or injured individual in a relatively painless way.
Evangelium Vitae (The Gospel of Life)	Issued by Pope John Paul II on March 25, 1995, this encyclical offered an extensive teaching on various issues related to life, including abortion, euthanasia, and the "culture of death" present in today's society.

For I Was Hungry and You Gave Me Food: Catholic Reflections on Food, Farmers, and Farmworkers

A document from the US bishops that provides reflections on food, farmers, and farmworkers, issued in 2003.

Gaudium et Spes (Pastoral Constitution on the Church in the Modern World)

The last and longest document issued at the Second Vatican Council, reflecting on the nature and mission of the Church in contemporary times.

Global Climate Change: A Plea for Dialogue, Prudence, and the Common Good

A statement of the US bishops issued in 2001 concerning the appropriate response by people of good will to the challenges that face the world due to climate change.

greenhouse effect

The scientific phenomenon in which the earth's atmosphere traps solar energy.

just war theory

A theory developed by the Church that attempts to propose when a nation may ethically participate in war. This theory also offers certain limitations on the use of armed forces once a war has begun.

justice, commutative

Fairness in relations between individuals and private groups.

justice, distributive

The fair distribution of creation's goods so that basic needs are met.

Laborem Exercens (On Human Work)

An encyclical of Pope John Paul II issued September 14, 1981, to commemorate the ninetieth anniversary of the publication of *Rerum Novarum*. It provided teachings on labor in its social and spiritual dimensions.

lectionary

The book containing the scriptural readings proclaimed at the Eucharist and arranged according to a liturgical calendar.

magisterium	The teaching office and authority of the Roman Catholic Church; also the hierarchy as holding this office.
Mater et Magistra (On Christianity and Social Progress)	An encyclical letter of Pope John XXIII issued May 15, 1961, to celebrate the seventieth anniversary of the publication of P

States, empowered to make policy, subject to review by the Holy See. It was combined in 2001 with the United States Catholic Conference to form the United States Conference of Catholic Bishops.

Pacem in Terris (Peace on Earth)	An encyclical issued by Pope John XXIII on April 11, 1963, within the context of escalating tensions in international relations which had culminated in the Cuban missile crisis. It was addressed to all people of good will and offered the services of the Church in helping to relieve cold war tensions with Gospel values as a guide to promoting justice and peace.
Populorum Progressio (The Development of Peoples)	Issued March 26, 1967, by Pope Paul VI, this encyclical addressed the disparity in economic development among nations and encouraged the more developed countries of the world to assist those who were in need of greater assistance.
proportionality	The principle that requires that the damage done in a war is commensurate with the good that is expected.

Quadragesimo Anno (On the Fortieth Anniversary of *Rerum Novarum*, On Reconstructing the Social Order)	Issued by Pope Pius XI on May 15, 1931, this encyclical commemorated the fortieth anniversary of *Rerum Novarum* and addressed the mounting economic challenges caused by the Great Depression, as well as the political and philosophical issues raised by the growth of communism and fascism in Western and Central Europe. This encyclical also developed a theory concerning "subsidiarity" (q.v.).
Renewing the Earth: An Invitation to Reflection and Action on the Environment in Light of Catholic Social Teaching	A statement issued by the National Conference on Catholic Bishops in 1991, in which they attempted to present Catholic social teaching in regard to issues concerning the environment.
Rerum Novarum (On the Condition of Labor)	The groundbreaking encyclical of Leo XIII, often identified as a landmark and turning point for Catholic social teaching. Issued by Pope Leo XIII on May 15, 1891, it was written to address a myriad of social problems of the age, including questions about labor unions, the dignity of labor, and the need for better working conditions. This encyclical stressed the need for greater collaboration between employer and employee to resolve the injustices that were especially experienced by the working class.
Second Vatican Council	The twenty-first general or ecumenical council of the Church (October 11, 1962–December 8, 1965) called by Pope John XXIII to promote peace and the unity of humankind.
sensus fidelium ("the sense of the faithful")	The intuitive grasp of the truth of God by the Church as a whole, as a consensus.
shareholder	A person who holds or owns a share in property.

socialism

One of a variety of economic theories in which the government has some type of ownership and administration of goods.

Sollicitudo Rei Socialis (On Social Concern)

An encyclical issued by Pope John Paul II on December 30, 1987, the twentieth anniversary of Paul VI's *Populorum Progressio*. This ...

hope that can be found only in God which can assist the world in its perseverance in bringing about God's reign.

Statement of United States Conference of Catholic Bishops on Capital Punishment

Document issued November 1980 in an attempt to show the bishops' belief that in the conditions of contemporary society, the legitimate purposes of punishment do not justify the imposition of the death penalty.

subsidiarity

The principle that a higher unit of society should not do what a lower unit of society could do just as well by itself.

totalitarianism

A political theory that the citizen should be subject to the total control of an absolute state authority.

The Universal Declaration of Human Rights

Declaration completed by the United Nations Commission on Human Rights in June 1948, containing general definitions of civil and political rights recognized in democratic constitutions, as well as several economic, social, and cultural rights.

USCC   United States Catholic Conference, the civilly
                              incorporated service agency of the National
                              Conference of Catholic Bishops. It was com-
                              bined in 2001 with the National Conference
                              of Catholic Bishops to form the United States
                              Conference of Catholic Bishops.

SOURCES

The following sources were used for the summaries; some of the translations used did not provide a date when the translation was published.

ity and Truth (Caritas in Veritate). Ottawa: Canadian Conference of Catholic Bishops, 2009.

John XXIII. *Encyclical Letter on Christianity and Social Progress* (Mater et Magistra), in David O'Brien and Thomas Shannon, eds., *Renewing the Earth: Catholic Documents on Peace, Justice and Liberation*. Garden City, New York: Image Books/Doubleday and Company, 1961.

John XXIII. *Encyclical Letter Peace on Earth* (Pacem in Terris). Boston: Daughters of St. Paul, 1963.

John Paul II. *Encyclical Letter on Human Work* (Laborem Exercens). Ottawa: Canadian Conference of Catholic Bishops, 1981.

John Paul II. *Encyclical Letter on the Social Concern* (Sollicitudo Rei Socialis). Vatican City: Libreria Editrice Vaticana, 1987.

John Paul II. *Encyclical Letter on the Hundredth Anniversary of* Rerum Novarum (Centesimus Annus). Washington, DC: United States Catholic Conference, 1991.

John Paul II. *Encyclical Letter the Gospel of Life* (Evangelium Vitae). Ottawa: Canadian Conference of Catholic Bishops, 1995.

Leo XIII. *Encyclical Letter on the Condition of Labor* (Rerum Novarum). Boston: Daughters of St. Paul, 1891.

Paul VI. *Encyclical Letter on the Development of Peoples* (Populorum Progressio). Boston: Daughters of St. Paul, 1967.

Pius XI. *Encyclical Letter On Reconstructing the Social Order (On the Fortieth Anniversary of* Rerum Novarum*) (Quadragesimo Anno)*. Boston: Daughters of St. Paul, 1931.

Pastoral Letters and Statements of the United States Conference of Catholic Bishops

National Conference of Catholic Bishops. *The Challenge of Peace: God's Promise and Our Response*, 1983.

National Conference of Catholic Bishops. *Economic Justice for All: Pastoral Letter on Catholic Social Teaching and the US Economy*, 1986.

National Conference of Catholic Bishops—United States Catholic Conference. *Statement on Capital Punishment*, 1980.

National Conference of Catholic Bishops—United States Catholic Conference. *Renewing the Earth: An Invitation to Reflection and Action on the Environment in Light of Catholic Social Teaching*, 1991.

United States Conference of Catholic Bishops. *Pastoral Letter on Racism: Brothers and Sisters to Us*, 1979.

United States Conference of Catholic Bishops. *Global Climate Change: A Plea for Dialogue, Prudence, and the Common Good*, 2001.

United States Conference of Catholic Bishops. *A Place at the Table: A Catholic Recommitment to Overcome Poverty and to Respect the Dignity of All God's Children*, 2002.

United States Conference of Catholic Bishops. *For I Was Hungry and You Gave Me Food: Catholic Reflections on Food, Farmers, and Farmworkers*, 2003.

United States Conference of Catholic Bishops. *Socially Responsible Investment Guidelines*, 2003.

Suggested Reading and Resources

Campaign for Human Development. *Scripture Guide*. Washington, DC:

legeville, MN: Glazier/Liturgical Press, 1994.

Gremillion, Joseph. *The Gospel of Peace and Justice: Catholic Social Teaching since Pope John*. Maryknoll, NY: Orbis Books, 1975.

Haughey, John, ed. *The Faith That Does Justice*. New York: Paulist Press, 1977.

Henriot, Peter, Edward Deberri, and Michael Schultheis. *Catholic Social Teaching: Our Best Kept Secret*. Maryknoll, NY: Orbis Books, and Washington, DC: The Center of Concern, 1988.

Hollenbach, David. *Claims in Conflict: Retrieving and Renewing the Catholic Human Rights Tradition*. New York: Paulist Press, 1979.

Kammer, Fred. *Doing Faithjustice: An Introduction to Catholic Social Thought*. New York: Paulist Press, 1991.

Kelly, J. N. D. *The Oxford Dictionary of the Popes*. New York: Oxford University Press, 1986.

Machman, Edward. *God, Society and the Human Person*. New York: Alba House, 2000.

Marthaler, Bernard, ed. *Introducing the Catechism of the Catholic Church: Traditional Themes and Contemporary Issues*. New York: Paulist Press, 1994.

Massaro, Thomas. *Living Justice: Catholic Social Teachings in Action*. Franklin, WI: Sheed and Ward, 2000.

McBrien, Richard. *Lives of the Popes: The Pontiffs from St. Peter to John Paul II.* New York: Harper Collins, 1997.

Mich, Marvin Krier. *Catholic Social Teaching and Movements.* Mystic, CT: Twenty-Third Publications, 1998.

National Conference of Catholic Bishops. *Communities of Salt and Light: Reflections on the Social Mission of the Parish.* Washington, DC: United States Catholic Conference, 1994.

O'Brien, David, and Thomas Shannon, eds. *Renewing the Earth: Catholic Documents on Peace, Justice and Liberation.* Garden City, NY: Image Books/Doubleday and Company, 1977.

Pennock, Michael. *Catholic Social Teaching: Learning and Living Justice.* Notre Dame, IN: Ave Maria Press, 2007.

Pontifical Council for Justice and Peace. *Compendium of the Social Doctrine of the Church.* Washington, DC: USCCB, 2005.

United States Catholic Conference. *Sharing Catholic Social Teaching: Challenges and Directions—Reflections of the US Catholic Bishops.* Washington, DC: USCC, 1998.

United States Catholic Conference, Committee on Domestic Policy, International Policy and Education. *Leader's Guide to Sharing Catholic Social Teaching: Challenges and Directions—Reflections of the US Catholic Bishops.* Washington, DC: USCC, 1999.

Weigel, George, and Robert Royal, eds. *Building the Free Society: Democracy, Capitalism and Catholic Social Teaching.* Grand Rapids, MI: Eerdmans, 1993.

Index

Kevin E. McKenna, a priest of the Diocese of Rochester, is pastor of the Cathedral Community in the same diocese. He is past president of the Canon Law Society of America and former chancellor and canonical consultant for his diocese. McKenna's ministerial experience includes service as a parish priest, as a judge in marriage tribunals, and in a diocesan role as director of legal services. He is the author of numer-

Founded in 1865, Ave Maria Press,
a ministry of the Congregation of
Holy Cross, is a Catholic publishing
company that serves the spiritual and
formative needs of the Church and its
schools, institutions, and ministers;
Christian individuals and families; and
others seeking spiritual nourishment.

For a complete listing of titles from

Ave Maria Press

Sorin Books

Forest of Peace

Christian Classics

visit www.avemariapress.com

ave maria press® / Notre Dame, IN 46556
A Ministry of the United States Province of Holy Cross

GOAL!

JASON TOMAS

highdown

Published in 2004 by Highdown,
an imprint of Raceform Ltd
Compton, Newbury, Berkshire, RG20 6NL
Raceform Ltd is a wholly-owned subsidiary of Trinity Mirror plc

A CIP catalogue record for this book is available from the British Library.

ISBN 1-904317-72-3

Designed by Fiona Pike
Printed in Great Britain by William Clowes Ltd, Beccles, Suffolk

Dedication

To Isabella

CONTENTS

INTRODUCTION

INTRODUCTION

G oalscoring is a subject that has intrigued me for some time. But if anybody has been responsible for turning this into an insatiable hunger for knowledge about the art – and, indeed, pushing me down the road leading to this book – it is Macdonald.

As a football journalist I had the pleasure of spending a great deal of time in the former Newcastle, Arsenal and England centre-forward's company when he was manager of Fulham in the early 1980s. What made it so stimulating was that, in our conversations about strikers and how they operated, Macdonald gave deeper and more perceptive insights into the subject than any of the other scorers or ex-scorers I had spoken to.

Macdonald's first-team coach then was Ray Harford, and when Harford worked with Alan Shearer at Blackburn in the 1990s, his willingness to improve my appreciation of the secrets behind the striker's success – beyond those that were already well-known on a superficial level – was another factor which helped bring about the birth of this book.

There is, indeed, much more to consistently putting the ball in the net than often meets the eye. There are so many strands to the subject and, even now, it is difficult to escape the nagging feeling that it might take more than one book for me to rid myself of that hunger for goal knowledge for good. As I said, Malcolm Macdonald has a lot to answer for.

However, this is not meant as a textbook on the subject. Rather it is a documentary, concentrating on the contemporary game, which sets out to both inform and entertain.

In my quest to shed more light on the art of scoring, I am indebted to the 'service' I have received from a number of 'team-mates'. I am particularly indebted to the figures who were happy to give me the benefit of their expert knowledge – notably (in alphabetical order) Ade Akinbyi, John Aldridge, Steve Archibald, James Beattie, Bill Beswick, Craig Brown, Ray Clarke, Ray Clemence, Mervyn Day, Dion Dublin, Paul Elliott, Trevor Francis, David Healy, Mark McGhee, Gary Pallister, Kevin Phillips, David Pleat, Bryan 'Pop' Robson, Steve Round, Andy Roxburgh, Graeme Sharp, Alan Shearer, Gordon Smith, Gordon Strachan, Paul Sturrock, John Syer and Gordon Wallace.

My thanks, also, to Alex Norman and Jamie Jackson for their research help, to Simon Wilson at ProZone, and to Patrick Barclay, Alex Fynn, David Luxton and, of course, to my publisher Jonathan Taylor, for their moral support.

Jason Tomas
June 2004

CHAPTER ONE
BURNING UP THE FIELD

to change their normal style of play,
and usually the strikers who come
into that category are the ones
who are the quickest …
The last thing a defender wants
to see is a striker's backside.'
GARY PALLISTER

For every footballer, at any level, nothing can compare with the buzz of scoring a goal. Some have claimed that it is even better than sex. During a BBC Radio 5 Live programme on goalscoring in January 2004, Dr Mark Hamilton, Radio One's 'resident Sunday Surgery physician', was happy to expand on the analogy. 'They say that sex is broken down into three main parts, desire, stimulation [the build-up play?] and the climax at the end, which is putting the ball in the back of the net.' When strikers have done that, he added, 'they are kind of drunk on their own body's chemicals'.

But one does not need to put the ball in the net to experience this. The colleagues of the goalscorers – managers, coaches and team-mates – seem to get just as much excitement out of watching them do it. Of course, as goals are the most important aspect of the game, the whole point of the game, the same applies to the vast majority of the millions of people who follow it.

Indeed, it says much about the stimulating effect of seeing that ball nestling in the net that Fifa, the governing body of world football, cannot seem to get enough of it. Since the football laws were initially formulated in 1863, almost all of of Fifa's numerous changes to the rules, or their instructions to referees on the interpretation of them, have been designed to produce more goals. On top of the major recent amendments relating to such scoring obstacles as offside and the tackle from behind, Fifa have even attempted to make the goals bigger, on the grounds that the average heights of the men guarding them have increased since the present dimensions – eight yards by eight feet – were set in the 1800s.

How today's strikers would love to have been around before then, in the days when football and rugby were evolving in public schools and goals were all manner of different shapes and sizes. Eton's was eleven feet wide and seven feet tall; Uppingham's, though only five feet tall, ran the entire width of the pitch. In 1863, the schools and colleges reached agreement on a standard goal comprising two poles eight yards apart but with no upper limit. The standardised height of eight feet was set in 1865.

According to the head of Fifa, Sepp Blatter, the goals should be lengthened by the diameter of two balls (about 50cm) and the height by the diameter of one. But what he seemed to overlook, apart from the probability that such a change would lead to more rather than less defensive football, was the extent to which the basic tools of the players' trade – the balls and boots – have altered.

Because of the developments in the materials and design of their playing equipment, players generally can now hit shots with greater power and accuracy than ever before. In some matches the balls have seemed more like the ones one might find on a beach, the players apparently able to make them do almost everything but sing and dance. Goalkeepers might have been made to look like dummies, but the trend for the dice to be loaded in favour of attacking players generally, and goalscorers particularly, is one that Fifa and the public have welcomed.

The fact is, though, that scoring, on a regular basis over a long period, has always been an elusive art, and it always will be. If anything, it could be argued that consistent scoring has become harder. Defenders now are fitter and more athletic, and they get

change of attitude was necessary when they lost to Monaco in the 2003/04 European Championship League semi-final – after establishing a 5-2 lead – and finished fourth in La Liga.

As we saw in the European Championship in Portugal, the more important the match, the 'tighter' it is liable to be. Therefore, the more important the match, the greater the pressure on the players with the major responsibility for breaking the deadlock. 'At one time I thought about it so much beforehand that I felt knackered even before the start of a game,' Southampton's Kevin Phillips said. 'I'd analyse things to the point where by the time I was ready to take the field I had confused myself. My brain was so full of information and various thoughts about how I might score that I ended up not knowing what to do. I have spoken to a lot of strikers about this, and they have had the same experiences. I have learnt to relax more as I have got older, but after a game my mind is racing so much that no matter how physically tired I am I still have difficulty in getting to sleep. It's not so bad after a match on a Saturday – like everybody else at the weekend, you can unwind by going out and having a few drinks – but after a midweek match, when you have to be more careful about this, I usually can't get to sleep until three or four in the morning.'

Steve Archibald, the former Aberdeen, Tottenham and

Barcelona striker, added, 'All players like to score goals, but if they are not strikers, they are more or less just playing at it. It's kid's stuff compared to what the real goalscorers have to go through.' And the demand for these men exceeds the supply. Thus, the leading scorers or goal creators have tended to command the highest transfer fees; they are also the figures who tend to earn the most money and attract the most publicity. At the start of the 2003/04 season, the only defender among the ten worldwide players to have had the highest fees paid for them was Rio Ferdinand, who in 2002 cost Manchester United a British record £30 million. Ferdinand was also the only defender among the ten highest earners. Still, after the 2004 European Championship in Portugal, it seemed only a matter of time before Ferdinand would be usurped by an 18-year-old striker – Wayne Rooney, of course.

But one does not need to be in the class of Rooney, Thierry Henry, Ruud van Nistelrooy and Michael Owen – the ultimate love gods, as Dr Mark Hamilton might describe such figures – to make players in other positions jealous. Stoke City's Ade Akinbiyi, one of the less fêted members of the strikers' union, put it this way: 'Strikers are in a stronger position career-wise than most other players. Once you have established a reasonable record as a goalscorer you will always find clubs willing to take a chance on you.' So the message for the proverbial Mrs Worthington is clear: it might not be a good idea to put her daughter on the stage, but if she has a son, and he's a goalscorer, the football stage is a different matter entirely.

What are the attributes she should look for in him? What are the qualities that separate the great strikers from the good, average or comparatively impotent ones? Even for a man as knowledgeable on the subject as Andy Roxburgh, the technical director of Uefa (the European football governing body), such questions can easily cause a headache. 'It's difficult to know where to begin,' said Roxburgh, a former striker who was Scotland's coach before taking up his Uefa post. 'It's a very complex web of things. To start with, I think you have to make a distinction between a finisher – and a finisher to me is someone who literally just finishes an attacking move ... two touches – and the artist. wh~ ~ play and ~~~~ ~

~~ such as Alan
~~~~.

~~~~s, indeed, come in all shapes and sizes, and not just in their builds. Some are especially good in the air whereas others give the impression of having been influenced by that medical opinion about heading causing brain damage. On the ground, they can also be split into different categories in relation to their pace.

Generally, strikers who are exceptionally quick are the ones who can be seen bursting into the space behind opposing defences, either taking the ball into those positions themselves or chasing passes into them, while those who are relatively slow are more liable to receive the ball to their feet, with their backs to the goal. Many of the outstanding post-war scoring partnerships in England have featured both types. It is no coincidence that the players with the most pace, or more specifically an outstanding change of pace, tend best to mirror Roxburgh's point about strikers creating goals on their own. 'These are the ones who can deal with having a big space between them and the goal,' he explained. 'That is what Michael Owen is good at. Give him the ball thirty or forty yards from goal with two or three defenders in front of him, and if he has a clear run at them, they are dead.'

One of Owen's England managers, Glenn Hoddle, might have
expressed doubts about whether he was as 'natural' a finisher as
counterparts like Robbie Fowler, but even Hoddle could not help
but applaud Owen for the way he propelled himself into scoring
positions. 'I don't think I have seen many regular scorers who are
able to attack defenders with the ball like Michael does,' he once
said. 'Normally you find that in wingers like Ryan Giggs rather than
in out-and-out strikers. A lot of players are quick movers but not so
quick with the ball at their feet.' Who can ever forget the Owen goal
against Argentina in the 1998 World Cup finals in France, when he
sprinted past Jose Chamot and Roberto Ayala with the ball before
angling a right-foot shot into the left corner of the net? And who can
forget his hat-trick, and the part his pace played generally, in
England's astonishing 5–1 victory over Germany in Munich in
September 2001?

Roxburgh himself, while readily conceding that he was more of
a 'finisher' than an 'artist' (and no more than a middle-of-the-road
Scottish league finisher at that), had plenty of pace. It was certainly
helpful to him when he operated up front with Alex Ferguson at
Falkirk, with Fergie the target man and Roxburgh feeding off him.
'Generally, strikers are quicker than back-line guys, but that was
particularly the case when I was a player,' Roxburgh said. 'If it was a
straight run, I could beat most defenders – indeed, most of my goals
came from through-passes, shots on the run. I don't think I was
tough or strong enough, or had a good enough touch, to be more
than what I was. But thanks to my pace and finishing, I didn't have a
bad career.'

Among others who confirm the advantages of such attributes is
Trevor Francis. Quite apart from how they helped him to establish
an outstanding career as a striker, Francis recalled the case of one of
the players he worked with when he was Sheffield Wednesday's

manager, Paul Warhurst. Though Warhurst was a centre-half, his switch to a striking role by Francis in the 1992/93 season was so successful that, as Francis said, 'He probably made a bigger impact as a front player than any of the more natural strik... I ... I ...

... ... his impact was remarkable. I don't think he had ever operated in that role before in senior professional football, but if you hadn't known who he was you would have sworn that he was a natural centre-forward. Indeed, there was even speculation that Graham Taylor [then England manager] might pick him as a striker for the national team.'

Warhurst was particularly effective in the cup competitions, helping Wednesday reach the finals of both the League Cup and FA Cup (both lost against Arsenal) with a total of nine goals in twelve ties. Eventually he and Francis fell out, ironically over the latter's decision to switch him back to the heart of the defence for the FA Cup final and the replay, and four months later he sold Warhurst to Blackburn. 'Wednesday had paid £750,000 for Paul [from Oldham in July 1991],' said Francis, 'but because of his success with us as a striker that season, we got £2.7 million for him.'

As for what being exceptionally quick did for Francis as a striker, he'll remind you of his initial success in a struggling team at Birmingham City. Francis, who made his Birmingham debut at the age of sixteen and went on to score 128 goals for the club before Nottingham Forest made him Britain's first £1 million player in 1979, has mixed feelings about the view that his record at St Andrews would have been even more impressive in a better side. In a way, he argued, his pace made Birmingham City perfect for him. 'We were often under pressure, especially away from home, but these were the periods when I felt I had my best chance of scoring. OK, over a season I would have got more chances in a team like Liverpool than I did with Birmingham. But equally, with the opposition dominating the game and pushing forward against us, I knew that I would always get the chance to use my pace on the break.'

Some strikers are quicker than they look. Ruud van Nistelrooy has suggested that this is an aspect of his game that tends to be underestimated. In a *Sunday Times* interview in April 2003 it was revealed that the only Manchester United players faster than the Dutchman were Giggs and Mikael Silvestre. Referring to his running style, though, he said, 'You see Thierry [Henry] and it's beautiful. You see me, it's not classic. It is a little bit the same with Robert Pires: he does not pick his knees up. I've worked on it, trying to get more quickness in my feet, more power. It changes. Sometimes I see myself and I think, "Now it looks nice."'

Certainly when the jet-heeled Henry is in full flow it looks little short of awesome. During the 2003/04 season, the most vivid illustration of a striker exploiting his acceleration was Henry's 'wonder goal' in Arsenal's 5–1 European Champions League win over Inter Milan in Italy. The Italians, having had a penalty appeal rejected, were caught stretched at the back as Henry burst forward with the ball. The Inter defender Javier Zanetti, the only outfield player between Henry and the goal, did well to hold him up; indeed, with Zanetti keeping two or three yards in front of him, Henry stopped, as if caught in two minds about whether to take him on or wait for support. Few would have bet on his doing the former, given the ground he had to make up in order to beat Zanetti and the fact that other Milan players were getting into covering positions around him. But take him on he did. A marvellous double dummy by Henry was followed by an explosive burst that took him past Zanetti as if the Argentinian was wearing diving boots; and, finally, a wonderful shot into the far corner of the net

.... way in Italy and would deteriorate as a result.´ But in a football environment recognised as the hardest in the world for strikers, the Ukrainian speed machine has repeatedly been among the leading scorers. During the 2003/04 season, when he finished top of the Serie A scorers' list for the second time with 24, it was difficult to imagine any fans in the world not dreaming of seeing him in their team's line-up. His most ardent admirers included Chelsea's mega-rich new Russian owner Roman Abramovic, a close friend of Shevchenko. This was reflected by a tabloid report that Abramovic was prepared to pay the Italian club as much as £80 million for him – almost double the world-record transfer fee that Real Madrid paid Juventus for Zinedine Zidane in 2001.

It is of course more than just pace that makes the Shevchenko types such valuable commodities. Nonetheless, in any survey to find the most valuable asset for a striker, fleet-footedness would unquestionably be at the top of the list. One reason why all strikers dream of being able to cover the ground like Olympic sprinters is the dilemma it creates for opposing teams in deciding how far their defenders can push forward to compress the play and how tightly defenders can afford to mark them. Providing the strikers are able to time their runs well enough to avoid being caught offside – an art for which Gary Lineker was particularly noted – the teams facing them are always liable to be neurotic about leaving a lot of space behind their back lines. But reducing the space between the back-four players and the goalkeeper creates another potential problem, that of strikers being able to exploit the extra space in front of the defence by getting a run at them with the ball.

'The best strikers are the ones who prompt opposing defences to change their normal style of play, and usually the strikers who come into that category are the ones who are the quickest,' said Gary Pallister, the former Middlesbrough, Manchester United and England defender. 'If you are playing against a striker who is not going to outrun you, or is at his best in the air, then you push up and keep him as far from the goal as you can. It's different with the exceptionally quick strikers: generally, I would say that attempting to force them to play in front of you is a much better option than giving them the scope to get behind you. The last thing a defender wants to see is a striker's backside.'

'From a striker's point of view,' said Trevor Francis, 'a lot depends not just on the timing of his runs but also on his getting the ball played to him early. If I had been the manager of a team with someone like me in it, I would not have wanted a particularly slow build-up. It also helps to have players behind you who can see a pass and implement it. This was something I really appreciated when I played in Italy [for Sampdoria] with Ray Wilkins and then Graeme Souness. As they gained control, I would come towards the ball, with my defender following me, knowing full well that if it was "on" for the ball to be played into the space behind for me to run on to it they would immediately recognise this and act on it. But it is important to be able to vary things. If I came off the defender and he wasn't going to give me that space in behind – he was going to allow me to get the ball to my feet – well, that was a great situation for me, too. I don't

think anything was better for me than a one-against-one situation
with a defender because I could run faster with the ball than most
other players, and I could also go either side. Provided you come off
the defender properly – come off at an angle, half turned [...

... ... indeed, discussions about the
advantages for strikers in being able to run faster than their markers
immediately led him to his experiences against Romario, when the
Brazilian was playing for Barcelona, and Henry.

Pallister faced Romario during Manchester United's two
European Champions League matches in the 1994/95 season, and
he admits that the memories of them still cause him to 'cringe with
embarrassment'.

For the first match at Old Trafford, Alex Ferguson was so
concerned about Romario's pace that he left Steve Bruce, United's
captain and Pallister's central defensive partner, out of the team and
brought in Paul Parker to do a man-for-man marking job against the
striker. The change in tactics bothered Pallister, who felt that United
would have been better off sticking to the zonal defensive system to
which they were accustomed. 'Steve Bruce and I always felt this,' he
said. 'For example, whenever we played against Niall Quinn
[Sunderland], the fact that I was as tall as him would cause the gaffer
to give me the responsibility of marking him. But Steve and I felt
there were situations in which I should leave him, that it was much
more important for us to keep our defensive shape.' If any match
influenced Pallister's views on this, it was England's 2–0 defeat by

Norway in the World Cup qualifying tie in Oslo in June 1993. Pallister had been brought back into the side by manager Graham Taylor to do a man-marking job on Jostein Flo. 'I was more or less trying to track him all over the place at times and it unbalanced the whole team,' he said.

Hence the fact that, while he did not go so far as to tell Parker to ignore Ferguson's instructions for that home match against Barcelona, Pallister did suggest that he could occasionally afford to leave it to him to deal with Romario if the latter drifted into his area.

But there was some confusion between the two men when Romario broke clear onto a through-ball between Pallister and left-back Denis Irwin to make the score 1–1. Ferguson wrote in his autobiography, 'That goal angered me as my instruction had been for Parker to stay with Romario throughout. Our trouble had arisen because of the British custom of defending zones and our habit of passing the responsibility for dealing with an opposing attacker from one defender to another as the man enters a different area of the pitch. Big Gary Pallister had told Parker that he was ready to take care of Romario and then found that the Brazilian was leaving him stranded. What infuriated me was that we had spent three days adjusting our zonal defending method to incorporate man-for-man marking of Romario. I wouldn't have taken such pains if I didn't think the change was necessary.' The tie, which Ferguson felt United could and should have won, ended in a 2–2 draw. For his part, Pallister still has mixed feelings about the extent to which he might have been culpable. 'Though the gaffer gave me some stick about it [Romario's goal], I still feel that in the long run it [the zonal approach] was the better way to go about things.'

Pallister was even more uncomfortable during United's 4–0 defeat in the return tie when their defence, not helped by the gung-ho attacking boldness of some of their colleagues in front of them, was repeatedly tormented by Romario and his Bulgarian striking partner Hristo Stoichkov. 'They tore us apart with their pace and movement,' he recalled. 'I just could not live with Romario. It was the only time I have walked off the park after a defeat with no ~~~

~~~~~~ the only goal against Middlesbrough at the Riverside Stadium in November 2000. 'I would say that was probably my worst moment on a football field,' Pallister confessed. 'He is the quickest player I have ever come across. He looks sometimes as if he is just strolling through games, but when he knocks the ball past you he can make you look like the slowest player in the world. That is what happened in that match at Middlesbrough.

'It happens to all of us from time to time,' Pallister added, recalling how Des Walker – 'the quickest England defender by far when I was in the squad' – was 'blown away' by the pace of Holland's Marc Overmars in the World Cup qualifying tie at Wembley in 1993. That incident, which led to Walker bringing down Overmars in the penalty area and Holland converting the spot kick to get a 2–2 draw, signalled the end of the road for Walker as an England player. 'But he could not have felt worse than I did when Henry made me look a mug,' Pallister concluded.

There is an interesting similarity between Overmars and Henry in that both can be described as goalscoring left-wingers. Overmars, who once played with Henry at Arsenal, has always been a winger rather than a striker, whereas with Henry it has been the other way around since he joined Arsenal. Henry, a player of Caribbean parentage who was born and raised in a rundown suburb of Paris, scored plenty of goals as a boy, but because of his fleet-footedness and skill on the ball, and maybe also his slight build, the wing seemed the ideal spot for him in professional football. He was used as a left-winger or left-side attacking player at Monaco, where he was first subjected to the coaching and managerial abilities of Arsène Wenger, and it was in that position that he gained his World Cup winners' medal with France in 1998 (when he was their top scorer in the competition).

He was enjoying himself, but not after his £8 million move to Juventus in January 1999. The ultra-disciplined world of Serie A was hardly conducive to bringing out the best in a free attacking spirit like Henry. As he has said, 'We played 3–5–2 with me on the left [of the midfield group], and I had to cover the whole flank. I did my best for the team, but I had to make the choice all the time of whether to stay back and defend or go forward and attack. In the end it was too much of a problem for me. I'm not a defender and I had to leave.'

He had long wanted to join forces with Wenger again, at Arsenal. But when he finally got the chance to do so in September 1999, he did not expect Wenger to look upon him as a replacement for central striker Nicolas Anelka. 'If he had not suggested that I play through the middle I would never have thought of it,' he said. Arsenal had been forced to sell Anelka to Real Madrid because of the player's insistence on leaving the club. The blow was softened considerably by the £23 million transfer fee Real forked out for him – a remarkable return for the Gunners' original half a million investment in the Frenchman. But after Henry's opening appearances in Anelka's role, it was difficult to avoid the view that the £10.5 million Arsenal had paid for him was also well over the odds. He did not score in his opening 12 league matches, and at one point he was dropped. Looking back on those early months, in an interview with Match Magazine, Henry said, '[Playing as a striker] took a while to get used to again. When I was sixteen at Monaco I played as a striker, but when I got into the first team I had to play as a winger and started

I would shoot and it would end up by the clock at Highbury.'

Henry, struggling to adjust to the physical intensity of English football, admitted that he thought about asking Wenger to switch him back to the wing. But he didn't go through with it because of his faith in Wenger's ability to know what was best for him and the warmth and support he got from the Arsenal fans. 'When I had to come on the pitch they were always clapping me, and and when I used to miss a goal they were still singing,' he said. 'That's why I was still happy when I was not scoring. In Italy, if you miss a goal, even if you are [Gabriel] Batitusta or [Oliver] Bierhoff, they want to kill you. Here, they want to sing my name.'

This was particularly true when Henry scored his first Highbury goals in the 2–1 win over Derby County in November 1999. Arsenal had been a goal down at one stage, and Henry, whose only previous goal had been at Southampton in September, said: 'Those goals [both set up by Overmars] were my big turning point because they were typical striker's goals.' That season Henry ended up with a league total of seventeen, which put him sixth on the Premiership scoring list behind Kevin Phillips (Sunderland), Alan Shearer (Newcastle), Dwight Yorke, Andy Cole (both Manchester United) and Michael Bridges (Leeds). Since then, the only players to have finished a season ahead of him have been Jimmy Floyd Hasselbaink (Chelsea) in 2001 and van Nistelrooy in 2003. By the end of the 2003/04 season, his overall scoring record for Arsenal was 151 goals in 255 matches – just 34 short of the post-war club record established by Ian Wright over 288 matches. Some 112 of those goals had come in the Premiership, so another club record in Henry's sights was that of Cliff Bastin, the top Arsenal league scorer with 150 between 1929 and 1946.

As Bastin was also a left-winger, it is interesting to note that despite the change in Henry's job description he has continued to spend much of his time on the left flank. That has been his favourite starting position, as reflected by the number of goals he has scored with diagonal runs with the ball from that area and then shots with his right foot. All of which brings us back to Roxburgh's point about the problems speedy players can cause defences when they have plenty of running space. As Francis said, 'In effect, by coming from the left, Henry gives himself the full width of the field to work in.' This partly explains why Francis himself was initially used in a wide position, as a right-winger, when he joined Nottingham Forest. It was in that role, of course, that he scored Forest's goal in the 1–0 win over Malmö in the 1979 European Cup final.

An even better post-war comparison with Henry, perhaps, can be found in the case of George Best. Ask most people to name his role at Manchester United and they would almost certainly reply 'winger' rather than 'striker'. But look at his scoring record for United – 137 goals in 361 league matches and an overall total of 178 in 466 – and compare his goals-to-game ratio with that of United contemporaries such as Bobby Charlton and Denis Law. Charlton, who spent the early part of his United career on the left wing, was the highest scorer in the club's history with a grand total of 347 in 752 games; Law, the archetypal finisher, got 236 in 409 games.

The former Arsenal centre-half and captain Frank McLintock, one of the best defenders in England when Best was at his peak, said, 'When people ask me to name the best strikers I played against,

against Best. He glided at you like a snake, occasionally twisting and turning so much that you were almost falling on your backside. Henry is like that. Some forwards look as if they are busting a gut to get past you, but Henry – well, he makes it look so effortless, as if he has an extra gear.'

To a great extent, Best and Henry, through the areas they cover and their overall attacking flair, have transcended the guidelines by which most strikers are judged. In addition to Roxburgh's point about the distinction between 'finishers' and 'artists', this was driven home to me in my interviews with other scoring 'experts'. A number suggested that Henry belonged to a special category that almost necessitated a book of its own. One of the most common comments about the rivalry between Henry and van Nistelrooy, for example, is that the Dutchman's working area is smaller, narrower, and that he gets more close-range, straightforward goals. To many professionals, Henry is both a great scorer and a scorer of great goals (a description that can also be applied to Rooney), whereas van Nistelrooy is 'just' a great goalscorer.

On the subject of van Nistelrooy, Teddy Sheringham, among the most respected of all the Premiership strikers, has said, 'He is clinical. Chance–bang–goal. He doesn't get sloppy. When he's got two, he will put the third one in; when he's got three, he will want to get four. A lot of players get sloppy. He just wants to score goals. He is the classic striker.' Gary Pallister nodded in agreement. 'I think van Nistelrooy can punish you more. Henry can embarrass you with his pace and can get goals out of nothing, but van Nistelrooy picks up the little bits and pieces in and around the six-yard box more than he does.'

As if to emphasise his comment about the 'complexity' of the subject, Roxburgh provided further food for thought about scorers of the calibre of Henry, van Nistelrooy and Owen when he said, 'A bad player might have only one string to his bow, whereas a good player might have ten. I often liken it to the difference between the European Champions League coaches and the run-of-the mill ones. The top Champions League guys are obsessed with fine detail. It's the same with a striker. Obviously, the more options he has got, the harder he becomes to stop and the higher he can go.'

That logic is simple enough, but the extent to which strikers should broaden their abilities is a different matter altogether. Given the right team, some strikers can get away with being more 'predictable' than others. Roxburgh himself confirmed this with an anecdote about his own favourite striker, the former Real Madrid and Hungary player Ferenc Puskas. 'I once did an interview with Puskas at one of our [Uefa] coaching courses, in Budapest, and I asked him, "You were all left foot – why?" He made a joke of it. "Well," he replied, "I decided early on that you need at least one leg to stand and I decided it would be my right. There would have been no point in swinging my right foot at the ball because then I would have landed on my backside." Everybody laughed, but you could see what he was getting at. He was so good with that left foot that it wasn't necessary for him to use the right.' Roxburgh recalled that it was the same with Davie Cooper, the outside-left who played for

Clydebank when Roxburgh was a coach there and was later in Roxburgh's Scotland team. 'At Clydebank, we put him on the right flank to force him to use his right foot more. So what did he do? He just kept cutting inside and scoring with the left. H- -- 1 - -- -- 1

y ----- --- ---- ---- --y -- volley it. I had done a lot of volleying practice as a boy and was very comfortable about connecting with the ball in that way. Now, in that situation, you will hear Andy Gray say on TV, "He should have put his head in there." It's not necessarily right. It's what Andy would have done – it's the way that Andy played – but other strikers are different.'

At the same time, it is difficult to quibble with Roxburgh's view about the advantages of strikers broadening their ability when one looks at Owen. Roxburgh drew attention to the second of the two late Owen goals that enabled Liverpool to beat Arsenal 2–1 in the 2001 FA Cup final. Both were scored with his 'weaker' left foot, and the second, following a stirring run on the left, was particularly uncharacteristic. 'Contrast this with his World Cup goal against Argentina [when Owen took the ball to his right and shot with his right foot across the keeper]. That had been the typical Michael Owen goal for as long as people could remember. But I know that during Gérard Houllier's time as Liverpool manager he spent a lot of time working with Michael on his left foot, and that both of them were thrilled with those goals against Arsenal because of this. Obviously, Michael is still going to score many more goals with his right foot than the left, but the improvement on his left side has made his "armoury" that much stronger. There have been other improvements in his game. Basically, I feel he has become shrewder, cleverer as he has got older.'

It was the same with Gary Lineker, who emerged from his spell at Barcelona a considerably more complete scorer than he had been at Leicester and Everton. It was the same, too, with Trevor Francis, which helps explain why he was in his late thirties when he finally pulled down the curtain on his league playing career. 'Had I not had to combine playing with managing, I would definitely have played on past the age of forty,' he said. 'The period I spent in Italy helped me enormously, because apart from the tremendous physical conditioning methods I became much more a student of the game there. My pace, my greatest attribute, had diminished, but what had not changed was my ability to control the ball, pass, cross and shoot. So as I got older I became a better footballer, a better goalscorer. In my first few months as QPR's player-manager [when he was 34], some of the goals I scored even prompted suggestions that I should be brought back into the England team.'

Of course, having plenty of strings to that scoring bow is what Henry has going for him too. When I asked Charlton's first-team coach, Mervyn Day, about the problems the Frenchman created for opposing teams during Arsenal's unbeaten 2003/04 Premiership campaign, he replied, 'Central defenders playing against Arsenal often find that they do not have someone to mark. Dennis Bergkamp, or whoever else operates up front with Henry, drops short, while Henry likes to come down the left side. You know that Henry, with his phenomenal pace, is always liable to cut inside, on to his right foot, so in our matches against Arsenal we would be inclined to flood that area. Our right-back would be told not to go forward, not even if somebody on the other side was going down the other flank and was looking for a player to get on the end of a cross to the far post, and our right-side midfielder would probably have to hold back as well.' In the light of this, it is interesting to note that Henry scored the equaliser in the 1–1 draw between the two teams at Charlton with a free-kick, and one of the goals in Arsenal's

...p......g ..... a conventional back four, Leeds, short of midfielders, also had two central defenders, Lucas Radebe and Dominic Matteo, in front of them. But Arsenal thrashed them 5–0, Henry scoring four of the goals, including a penalty. It was the first time an Arsenal player had scored that many in a game since Ian Wright against Everton fourteen years earlier. A number of observers felt that Leeds had made it easy for Henry by defending too 'high' up the field. But then, as their assistant manager Kevin Blackwell pointed out, Henry, with his ability to take on opponents and fire the ball into the net from long range, is quite happy against deeper defensive units as well. 'That pace is only part of the Henry package,' Blackwell said. 'OK, he is exceptionally quick, but this would not count for as much as it does if he was not such an intelligent player. He has a wonderful football brain, and that is possibly his greatest asset.'

Indeed, footballing intelligence is a key factor in how almost all the other successful scoring machines work.

CHAPTER TWO
MASTERS OF DECEPTION

while the defenders are reactive.
Defenders have to work off
what the strikers do, not vice versa.'
ANDY ROXBURGH

The difference between Thierry Henry and many other strikers in the speeds with which their legs can carry them can be likened to that of a Ferrari and a Ford Escort. But, as Andy Roxburgh pointed out, 'Blistering pace is not the be all and end all. There are plenty who, while not particularly quick across the ground, have made up for it with their speed of thought.'

There can be no better illustration of this in modern-day football than Teddy Sheringham. As the vast majority of goals are scored from deep inside the penalty area, it should surprise nobody that Sheringham, physically one of the slowest of the top ten all-time Premiership scorers even when he was at his peak, is as high as fifth on the list. Sheringham has had the advantage of being able to score with headers as well as shots, of course. More important, however, is that although he has always struggled to go past opponents with the ball, he is a master at shielding it or laying it off, and then making the off-the-ball runs into the right positions for him to deliver the finishing touch.

His image as the 'thinking man's footballer' says it all, as indeed he did in an interview on the subject when he was with Manchester

United. Reminded of Terry Venables' view about the importance of a striker 'asking a defender questions', he said, 'You say to a centre-half, "If I go over here, what are you going to do about it?" or "If I go over there, what are you going to do about it?" Giggsy [Ryan Giggs] will be asking a different question: "Can you match me for pace?" If his defender can, he'll find another way because he's a clever footballer, and clever footballers find a way.

'I am sure there is a perception that I keep going so well because my game is not that taxing. Steve McClaren [then United's assistant manager] came to me a little while ago and he's got this new gimmick that tells how much a particular player runs in a game. He came to me and said, "You don't half do a lot of running." And I looked at him and said, "Don't tell me you've been sucked in by all the people who say I play an easy game?" I come off the pitch knackered after every game. Just because I don't sprint like a lot of players doesn't mean I'm standing still waiting for the ball to come.'

Whether it is outside the box or inside, the basic principles of his movement – the ability to elude markers – are the same. For all strikers, it is one of the key common denominators in the art of scoring, along with the desire to score: being able to anticipate where the ball is going and the willingness to take hard knocks, physically and psychologically.

It could be argued that the 'desire' to score applies to most outfield players, whatever their positions or roles. Even goalkeepers take delight in putting the ball in the net when given the opportunity to do so in training matches. However, for strikers, that desire is so strong that it can often be an obsession. Propelling the ball into the net – the very sight and sound of it hitting the back of the net – is like a drug to them. Some have pointed out that their need for that 'fix' is so powerful that they do not necessarily need to have beaten a goalkeeper or anybody else to get it. Ian Wright once said: 'Anybody who plays up front and says they're happy to see the team win even if they do not score is a liar. Sometimes you say that because you don't want a big-headed image, but deep in your heart, you know it

former Manchester United, Coventry and Aston Villa striker. He then mentioned a Villa match in which one of their players broke down the left wing, following a corner by the opposition, with Alan Thompson and himself charging down the middle in the hope of connecting with any cross. As the ball came over, Thompson was in a better position to put it into the net than Dublin was. 'But as far as I was concerned, it was my chance,' Dublin said. 'I had worked all week for that moment; I had run sixty or seventy yards to get on the end of that ball and nobody was going to stop me. As Alan was about to head it, I was literally screaming, "Dion's!" I was about ten yards away and I just launched myself at the ball. I caught it a peach, right in the top corner.'

John Aldridge was clearly not the type to give up a scoring chance either. 'I always wanted to be a top scorer,' he said. 'As a boy growing up in Liverpool my idol was Roger Hunt [the scorer of a record number of 245 goals for Liverpool], and I imagined myself as him when I used to practise for hours on a bit of wasteground alongside my home. You know, when I got a goal, it wasn't John Aldridge who had scored, it was Roger Hunt. For me, that love of scoring – the determination to score – was always there, although if anybody can take any credit for making it stronger it's Len Ashurst

[Newport County's manager at the start of Aldridge's professional career with the club]. I remember him saying to me, "You are scoring an average of one goal every three games at the moment, but if you want to be a top striker, it has to be one goal every two games." That advice always stuck in my mind. I spent all my career chasing that one-in-two ratio. During the spells that it dropped, even slightly, I would be panicking.'

Nobody can have loved scoring more than Aldridge, who got more goals in senior matches than any other player in the history of English football. In a career spanning nineteen years, from 1979 to 1998, he got 90 in 213 games for Newport, 90 in 141 for Oxford United, 63 in 104 for Liverpool, 40 in 75 for Real Sociedad, 174 in 287 for Tranmere and 19 in 69 for the Republic of Ireland. The grand total of 476 in 889 games put him nine ahead of Jimmy Greaves (who had the distinction of having scored all his goals in the top flight) and fourteen ahead of Arthur Rowley (who holds the British record for the highest number of league goals with his total of 434 in 619 matches for West Bromwich Albion, Fulham, Leicester and Shrewsbury between 1946 and 1965). The other particularly impressive individual scoring records in English football have been those of Dixie Dean, who scored 60 league goals in 39 First Division matches for Everton in the 1927/28 season and a total of 310 in 362 for the club at this level.

Greaves, because of his short, slight build and his brilliance on the ball in creating chances on his own, could be described as the odd man out in this group. Of the others, one similarity was that they all had outstanding anticipation inside the box. Another was that they all benefited from the service they received from the flanks. 'Losing my markers to get on the end of balls into the box from wide areas was always my forte,' Aldridge said. This was particularly important to him, and to Liverpool when they bought him from Oxford for £750,000 in January 1987. Liverpool, under the management of Kenny Dalglish, were preparing for the departure of Ian Rush to Juventus that summer and initially Aldridge, having never played in the First Division before, didn't

during the summer with the signings of Peter Beardsley, a player more comfortable in the build-up play than he was, and, most crucially, winger John Barnes. 'With Barnes on one flank and Ray Houghton [his Republic of Ireland and former Oxford team-mate] on the other, it was bingo for me.'

That had certainly been the case with Dixie Dean and Arthur Rowley. When they were giving goalkeepers sleepless nights the game was much more open and attack-orientated than it is today. Almost every team operated with wingers; indeed, the sight of such men attempting to get behind the opposing defence by taking on the opposing full-back – usually the only player they had to beat – and delivering the ball into the middle was an integral part of British football. Getting the ball into the box from wide positions is still recognised as an important aspect of goalscoring, but 'traditional' wing-play has become conspicuous by its absence. In the old days, the main aim of the wingers was to cross the ball from on or close to the goal-line so that the ball would be swinging away from defenders and into their forwards. Most defenders argue that such crosses, or pull-backs, are the most difficult for them to deal with. As for the men for whom the crosses are intended, Andy Roxburgh said, 'The easiest balls for a player to hit or head are those that come into him.' Little wonder that they were relished by Dean, a great header of the ball, and Rowley, a wonderful striker of the ball with his left foot.

However, England's World Cup win in 1966, with a 4–4–2 system in which there was no place for conventional wingers, marked a change in the styles of play of wide players throughout the game. There was a greater onus on them to defend; indeed, wingers as the likes of Dean and Rowley would have recognised them were largely replaced by wingers-cum-midfielders. This, combined with teams giving their full-backs more cover, led to a change in the positions from which crosses were delivered. Instead of teams getting the ball into the middle from on or close to the goal-line, they were more liable to fire them in from deeper areas.

At one time, most wide men wanted to emulate Stanley Matthews. Most recently, their role model has been David Beckham. 'He, more than anyone, has shown that you do not need to beat people to get in good crosses,' Roxburgh said. 'In the old days, if you received the ball on the wing, say twenty-five yards from goal, with a defender in front of you, you would have been urging him to go and dribble past him. But with people like Beckham, no. If they have a defender in front of them, they are able to provide a great scoring chance for a striker just by taking a slight touch to open up their striking angle and bending the ball around their opponent.'

One advantage of an early cross – a cross delivered with the minimum fuss and bother, without the wide player exploring his dribbling potential or taking more touches on the ball than are absolutely necessary – is that it makes it easier for a striker to 'read' it. It might not create as much panic in a defence as one of those cut-backs, but then given the right synchronisation between the player making the cross and the striker for whom it is intended, this is of little consequence. When an attack is developing down a flank, the positioning of the striker can make it increasingly difficult (and ultimately impossible) for his marker to see both him and the ball at the same time. 'He has to take his eyes off you to check where the ball is at some time,' Roxburgh pointed out. 'It might only be for a

worse when the crosses keep going behind or over the bar,' Dion Dublin added. 'That really does do your head in.'

Even at the best of times, even in teams totally dominating the opposition, being a striker is harder work than many people might think. The art of scoring is often attributed to strikers just having the knack of being in the right place at the right time. Some of the goals they score – as a result of the most glaring and uncharacteristic of defensive errors, or scruffy strikes with parts of their anatomy other than their head or feet – even suggest that they have been born under a luckier star than other players. But though intuition and good fortune do come into it, this is largely because of the footballing intelligence and mentalities of the top scorers.

One of the major differences between defenders and strikers is the way they are 'programmed'. Defenders need to perform as though they are born pessimists, whereas strikers have to approach situations like eternal optimists. For strikers, that means always expecting (or anticipating) an incident that will give them a scoring chance. For example, when a goalkeeper makes a save without being able to hold the ball, how often do we see a striker reacting more quickly to the rebound than the defenders to stick it into the net? It also means strikers being prepared to continue making runs into scoring positions no matter how many times they have done so previously without receiving the ball.

Imagine what it must have been like for strikers to play against the superbly organised defence of Arsenal when the Gunners were managed by George Graham and had that famous back-line of Lee Dixon, Tony Adams, Steve Bould (or Martin Keown) and Nigel Winterburn pushing up to squeeze the play and working the offside trap to perfection. Their defence did even better under Arsene Wenger by establishing the record for conceding the fewest goals in a Premiership season: 17 in 38 matches in the 1998/99 season. But there were even fewer chances for strikers against the 1978/79 Liverpool defence, which still holds the record for the least number of goals conceded in a season in any division: just 16 in 42 matches, and two of them were own goals.

'You can be sure that all the men who scored against Liverpool were pleased to get into a hot bath afterwards,' said Graeme Sharp, the former Everton and Scotland centre-forward. 'Really, it's the same in a lot of matches. People do not fully appreciate the work you put in. When it comes to making runs into scoring positions you are always working on the law of averages. That [the unproductive run by a striker] is the unglamorous side of being a goalscorer. It can be soul-destroying when you make run after run after run without getting a scoring chance. It's easy to think, "This is not going to be my day." But you can guarantee that the moment you switch off, the one time that you don't make the run, that will be the time the ball will go in there. That is the thought that keeps you going.'

At the height of Sharp's career in the 1980s, in an Everton team that twice won the championship and also got their hands on the FA Cup and European Cup Winners' Cup, many of the goals that were to enable him to become the club's highest post-war scorer could be attributed to his understanding with Trevor Steven on the right flank and Kevin Sheedy on the left. 'I don't think any team before or since has shown a better understanding of the 4–4–2 system than Everton did,' he claimed. 'OK, people felt we were quite a basic team, but

Nevin. They were wonderful players, don't get me wrong, but there were times when, before crossing the ball, they would want to take that extra touch or two.'

Brighton manager Mark McGhee, the former Morton, Newcastle United, Aberdeen, Hamburg and Celtic striker, recalled a similar situation. 'I went from one team who gave me the ball early [Aberdeen] to one who didn't [Hamburg]. At Aberdeen, Alex Ferguson had created a team that was good for strikers. You can make the best runs in the world, but if you don't have players who can give you the right ball at the right time then they are meaningless. We had Gordon Strachan for a start; the vast majority of my goals, indeed the majority of the team's goals, came from his passes or crosses. It's a standing joke between us that, though I thought I was making good runs, all I was doing was chasing his passes. Apart from Gordon on the right flank, we had the added bonus of Peter Weir [a conventional winger] on the left. That gave us the sort of penetration down the flanks that the great Celtic team of the 1960s had. My clearest memories of that Celtic team are of midfielders like Bobby Murdoch and Bobby Auld hitting balls with backspin right into the corners for Tommy Gemmell and Jim Craig [the attacking full-backs], and the balls being cut back hard and low from the goal-line. That is what Gordon and Peter could do. I once scored a hat-trick in a European game and all the goals were identical: balls being fired across from the goal-line, with people like me piling in to attack them with runs across the defenders.

'Aberdeen were a high-tempo team, and the idea of me joining Hamburg was sold to me partly on the basis of their being a high-tempo side as well. Well, they had been at one time, but with ageing stars such as Felix Magath they had become much more of a possession-driven team. I would work the whole line [the full width of the field] at Aberdeen – I was the type who ran the opposition into the ground – but I quickly realised it was pointless in a number of my Hamburg matches because the pace of the game was slower. Everything was being played through Magath and he was unwilling to really take any chances on possession being lost. When I did get the ball, it was usually to my feet, but because of the earlier runs I had made without getting the ball it wasn't the opposition who were liable to be knackered, it was me. Because of the delays in the ball coming to me, there were some games in which I was standing still.

'You can do that in some areas, of course. One guy who always used to fascinate me was Ruud Gullit [the former AC Milan and Holland forward]. He used to find space without moving. When the ball is on the flanks, it's natural for defenders to want to move back to protect their goal. So, if Gullit positioned himself on the edge of the penalty area, he would get the ball while standing still. He was clever – he knew what he was doing. But in most other attacking situations you have to work for your openings.'

Indeed, all the goalscoring experts I spoke to insisted that it is essential for strikers to be on the move all the time, especially in the box. Their message was: 'Movement creates space.' Once you are standing still, you are finished.

Among the British strikers noted for their intelligent movement was Gordon Wallace, the former Dundee player who is second only to Ally McCoist on the top post-war scorers list in Scotland. Wallace said, 'I think all leading scorers are born with an instinct for scoring, but you can add to it. Not being the quickest of strikers, I ...

away from the ball rather than towards it. Sometimes it might only involve a few steps: one or two in one direction, followed by a spurt in another. That is what strikers mean when they talk about 'one run for him, one for me'. Other basic movement guidelines for strikers in their battle of wits with defenders are 'run long to go short and short to go long' (when using the length of the field) and 'run in to go out, out to go in' (when using the width of the field). On top of this are the fundamental rules relating to the geometry of forward passes and forward runs: 'Straight pass, diagonal run – diagonal pass, straight run.'

It is difficult to imagine any striker having covered more ground in his attempts to elude his markers and create the right finishing angles than Alan Shearer did when he was at his physical peak. At one time, his runs to get the better of defenders would be made anywhere in the last third of the field. If an attack was developing down the right, it wasn't unusual for Shearer to start his quest to eventually get on the end of the ball by taking his marker virtually across to the other side. At times he seemed to take the principle of strikers making their first scoring runs away from the ball to the extreme.

Kevin Keegan, the Newcastle manager who signed him for the club and who had also appeared to have an inexhaustible supply of running power when he was a striker, was all for it. Less enthusiastic about it was Keegan's successor, Ruud Gullit. It is no secret that Shearer's relationship with the Dutchman was not as harmonious as it had been with his previous managers. Indeed, this was well and truly brought into the open in March 2004 when Gullit, in a News of the World interview, accused Shearer of being a 'rotten apple'. 'He thinks about himself all the time,' the Dutchman said. 'It is always about his goals and not about the team. I knew I had to change it if we were to succeed. I needed to change the way Alan Shearer played, but he did not want to change. In fact, he made it plain he did not want to play for me.' According to Gullit, his disagreements with Shearer stemmed partly from his view that the striker spent too much time outside the box. 'As the manager, I wanted him to play well and to score goals. But I wanted to use him in a different way. I asked him to move into the penalty box more, rather than keep running wide to the left and wide to the right and leaving the area empty. That's all. But after a while, he made it clear he did not want to.' Shearer declined to make any public comment on this, although to those who would argue that many of his goals came because of the distances he ran to get the better of his markers, not in spite of them, he didn't need to.

Today, at the tail-end of his career, it's a different story. As one would expect of a striker in his mid-thirties, with his list of war wounds, Shearer has had to change. In the 2003/04 season, with Newcastle possessing other attacking players to do the long-distance runs, Shearer's own runs were restricted to shorter and more central bursts inside the box. 'I think I spend a lot more time with my back to the goal [receiving the ball in central areas] than I did at Southampton and Blackburn,' he said. However, thanks to his grasp of those basic movement principles, not to mention his combativeness and determination, he still ended the campaign second only to Thierry Henry in the Premiership scoring list.

Of course, defenders are not unaware of the ways in which Shearer and other leading strikers create their shooting or heading space. But, as Roxburgh pointed out, 'The strikers will always have

enough to avoid getting into a potential scoring position too early or too late is another matter. The timing of the run into the scoring position is probably even more important than the finish itself. A shot can still go in even if you miss-hit it. Quite honestly, miss-hitting can sometimes be the best move. But if your movement is not timed properly, you are lost. Some people claim that it's down to natural instinct. There's no doubt that some people do have a natural instinct for it, but I would suggest that it also boils down to footballing intelligence, and the ability to read the game. You have to be able to anticipate things. The top strikers are so good at it that when they get the ball in the box they seem to have twice as much time as anybody else.'

No contest of football intelligence between a defender and striker can have been more absorbing than the one that the great Liverpool centre-back, Alan Hansen, conducted with Karl-Heinz Rummenigge in the 1981 European Cup semi-finals. 'He presented me with probably my biggest ever European Cup challenge,' Hansen recalled. 'He was brillliant at making diagonal runs for the ball, across me, and for a while, only my speed enabled me to stop him getting away from me. But I knew I was living on borrowed time and it was only about 20 minutes into the second leg that I was able to come up with a better solution. As the ball was about to be played through to him, I just took a step or two into the space into which he wanted to move, which put him off. But he did eventually score, so although Liverpool won, I cannot say that I overcame the challenge with flying colours.'

That there is a lot more to scoring, and especially the build-up to it, than often meets the eye quickly becomes apparent when you discuss the subject with Mark McGhee. 'A lot of strikers are instinctive players,' McGhee said. 'You can see that when they are called upon to make an instinctive finish they have no problems executing that, but when they are given a lot of time, that can be a problem to them. But they also tend to be intelligent players. I played very much off the cuff when I first started playing league football at Morton, but the more I progressed, the more I was forced to think about what I was doing. At Morton, I just ran around; my game was totally unstructured. It was the same when I stepped up into the old First Division with Newcastle, which is what worked against me there. I was playing against guys like Gordon McQueen [Leeds] and Billy Bonds [West Ham], and because of their positional sense, their footballing intelligence, they could more or less just step back and watch me. I was virtually running into them.

'The turning point for me came when I joined Aberdeen, and worked with Alex Ferguson. Up to then, though I had scored goals and created chances for others, nobody had really talked to me about the other aspects of the role – the sort of little foundation stones. I wasn't really sure what my starting points in a game were. Alex gave me lots of little targets. For example, one of the first things he said to me was, "You have to make sure that you win the first ball." That was my starting point. Then he said to me, "OK, you won the first ball, but you lost the next two." From then on I knew that I had to compete for every ball; that if a move broke down and the ball was played to the opposing full-back I had to try and stop him settling on it; and so on. So suddenly I had a list of challenges or objectives which gave me a focus I'd never had before.

'As with players in other positions, you are learning and

, ...gc., he had been studying the movement of the club's centre-forward, Neil Harris. The player, signed from the non-league club Cambridge City in March 1998 for a fee of £30,000, had quickly become one of the most respected strikers outside the Premiership. In the 1999/2000 campaign he became the first Millwall player to score 25 goals in a season since Teddy Sheringham in 1990/91, and the following season his 28 goals helped steer Millwall to promotion from the Second Division. But then he was diagnosed with testicular cancer, which put him out of action for the first half of the season.

Not surprisingly, it took time for Harris to regain his old sharpness and to adjust to the higher demands of the First Division, and he was going through a barren scoring spell when I met McGhee. 'I think he is not scoring at the moment simply because he is running out of the right positions as opposed to running into them,' McGhee explained. 'He is a very willing player, he loves to make runs, but we have just been talking to him about narrowing them, keeping himself more in the eighteen-yard box. At the moment he's making runs into the corners, and in trying to hold the ball up or beat people there not really giving himself much of a chance to get himself back in the box. A lot of it is to do with confidence. He's not the quickest of players, and in the First Division, where defenders are quicker than those in the Second, maybe he feels that he needs to put himself in areas where he is going to get a bit more time and space. I think that happens a lot with strikers who are not particularly quick. But those are not the areas in which they are going to score goals. I know that my best performances as a striker came in matches where I kept myself in the eighteen-yard box. Apart from anything else, if you are on the ball in there, defenders are always wary of committing themselves. For Neil, and other promising strikers, these sorts of things are just part of the learning process.'

By the end of the 2003/04 season, Harris's scoring record was still not as impressive as it had been in the Second Division. But, as with all strikers in teams with high-scoring midfielders, his movement in creating space for others did help Tim Cahill and Paul Ifill make up for it. Harris, indeed, was a regular member of the Millwall team that under the management of Dennis Wise reached the FA Cup final for the first time in their history.

Teddy Sheringham is among the most obvious strikers for any aspiring scorer on a learning curve to study, but when it comes to the 'tricks' of their trade, they would all benefit from some tuition from Graeme Sharp as well. Many of his opponents in the 1980s will readily confirm that he was the striker they least relished facing; and among those at the top of the Sharp Appreciation Society list is Alan Hansen. He once recalled that he was always 'twitchy' when up against opponents who attempted to turn their confrontations with him into contests of strength and aggression.

The most physically intimidating striker he faced was Billy Whitehurst, a journeyman number 9 who nonetheless was so powerful and combative that Hansen admitted he was almost scared of him. 'But,' he added, 'I would get even twitchier if the striker also had as much footballing intelligence as Graeme Sharp. He was probably the British striker for whom I had the greatest respect. If anybody had a perfect grasp of all the aspects of centre-

ability as the target for those sweeping diagonal passes from Kevin Sheedy. His movement to attack the ball was superb. The whole defence had to be on its toes when he was around. The one thing you could be sure about was that the experience of playing against him would leave you mentally drained.'

It could also leave you with some physical aches and pains as well. One of the less desirable aspects of scoring concerns the importance of strikers being prepared to go into areas where they are bound to suffer painful physical knocks – 'areas where it hurts', as they put it. Thanks to the stricter interpretation of the laws by referees, defenders can no longer dish out as much physical punishment to strikers as they once did. Even so, the conflict between the two sets of players close to goal – full of tugs, digs and pushes at the very least – quickly separates the men from the boys.

The very mention of this in Frank McLintock's sitting room was enough to cause him to become animated enough to rise from his chair to give a demonstration. 'I cannot believe it when I see some of today's central defenders,' he said. 'When the ball is on the wing, some of them – even Rio Ferdinand – can be looking for the ball [instead of the man they are marking] for five or six seconds. I know you cannot ignore the ball, but when I was a central defender I used to keep touching the striker. It would be touch-look, touch-look, touch-look. If I could not feel him I would back into him, and if he tried to connect with the ball I would block him.' At this point, McLintock showed how to stop a striker attacking the ball with a run across him by sweeping his arm into his opponent's stomach. 'As soon as he started his run, I would bloody whack him. It knocks him back a little bit – you can sometimes actually hear him catching his breath – and it also has the effect of propelling you forward. You don't mess around either when you're going for the ball in the air. You might know that you are not going to win the ball, but the main thing is that you throw yourself at the ball so that the other guy cannot get a clean contact.'

All of which makes you realise what strikers are getting at when they talk about the need not to allow themselves to be 'pushed around', and why professionals have rated Sharp so highly. 'When it came to gaining an advantage over defenders, he seemed to know everything there was to know,' said Hansen. 'One feature of his game was that when the ball was in the air he made it difficult for the defender marking him to get the ball without fouling him.' Sharp, who now employed at Everton as the club's fan liaison officer, and hosts a local radio football phone-in programme, acknowledged, 'I won a lot of free-kicks in those situations. If our team were playing a ball from the back to the front, I had a habit of jumping early and backwards. It was just one of a number of little things that you knew you could get away with.'

On the subject of strikers being able to 'look after themselves', Sharp said, 'My brother, Richard, who played a couple of games as a striker for Rangers but failed to establish himself in the top flight, was probably a better footballer than me. But he did not go further because he wasn't hard enough. My father always used to say, "Don't let anyone make a mug of you." That was his advice to me when I came to Everton as a raw teenager, because if somebody kicked me I was inclined to go into my shell a little bit. One of my first matches was against Leeds United, when they had Kenny Burns playing for

of Bob, I think about the time I first played with him in a pre-season competition in Spain. I had heard so much about him, about his not allowing defenders to take liberties with him, and I could not understand it because he was getting kicked from pillar to post in that game. I thought, "What is going on here?" But then, all of a sudden, Bob literally made his mark on the centre-half – he had to be carried off – and scored at the same time. I could not work out how he'd done it. It intrigued me.

'Then Bob left and Andy Gray came in, and I would say I learnt more about the so-called tricks of the trade from Andy than I did from anybody else. He was the one who really encouraged me to be more aggressive and not to get pushed around so much. I was never a dirty player, but if it was necessary for me to stand up for myself in that way, then so be it. Some people [defenders] will do anything to put you off and you have to be prepared to deal with it. Only the other day I had an argument with this caller on my radio show who was having a go at Alan Shearer for the way he got stuck into defenders. "He is an animal," he said. I said, "Hold on a minute. If he is up there getting kicked all over the place he has to look after himself."'

Dion Dublin nodded in agreement. 'I like the physical side of the game, getting stuck in, and the verbal side. It's a man's game, and it's all about how mentally strong you are to take all the abuse. I find it very stimulating. It's good, it's good.'

The need for mental toughness, of course, also applies to that moment when a striker, having eluded his marker to get into a scoring position, is ready to apply the finishing touch. Quite often it looks as if he should be able to score with his eyes closed, but that's assuming he hasn't thought about what the repercussions might be if he misses.

CHAPTER THREE
TARGET PRACTICE

over it. They think it's funny, but it really does my head in.'

BRYAN 'POP' ROBSON

When Malcolm Christie had a run with Derby County of fifteen matches without a goal towards the end of the 2000/01 season, the young striker was encouraged to discuss his problems with the club's sports psychologist, Bill Beswick. After Christie and other members of the coaching staff had gone through the various physical and technical aspects of his play, Beswick posed what proved to be the key question. Referring to a chance Christie had missed in the last game, he asked, 'What were you thinking about at the moment you hit the ball?'

'The boss [manager Jim Smith],' Christie replied. 'As I was about to shoot, I thought about him looking at me and saying, "For Christ's sake, Malcolm, how did you miss that?"'

So the answer was simple: Christie was clearly allowing negative thoughts to enter his mind; or, as Beswick put it, he was suffering from 'emotional static' (the 'scientific expression', he told me). As Christie's problems were all in his mind it was only to be expected that Beswick should take the lead role in helping him get rid of them. The result of this was that in the shooting practice that was organised for him, Christie had to shout a word at every moment of impact –

an action which, Beswick explained, was designed to immediately clear his mind of all thoughts outside that of hitting the ball well enough to put it in the net. 'We refer to it as the "break" or "trigger" word,' Beswick said. 'When we tried it with Ashley Ward [another Derby County striker] he preferred to use the word "net", because he told us that he loved to see the net bulge, whereas Malcolm chose "ball". The shooting practice we gave him became increasingly more difficult, and as a further test of his ability to concentrate we even ended up screaming and shouting at him to try and put him off.'

This work was followed by Derby's penultimate match of the season, against Manchester United at Old Trafford. United had already clinched the Premiership title but the view that Derby could capitalise on any mood of relaxation in the United camp was offset by the fact that the visitors were as low as seventeenth in the table, just one place above the relegation zone, and had achieved only one previous away win. But Derby beat United 1–0, and Christie, after an excellent run followed by the shout 'Ball!' and an explosive left-foot shot, scored the goal of his life. Beswick recalled, 'Shortly after the game, I asked him how it felt. "Great," he said. I then asked what was in his mind when he was about to strike the ball, and he couldn't tell me. He had concentrated so much on the finish that he could not even tell me anything about the build-up to the goal. This is common among top-class strikers. It [scoring] becomes so instinctive to them that they just cannot explain how they have done it. All Malcolm could remember was that he hit the ball with his left foot. That was it.' The following week, Christie scored another goal that brought Derby a 1–1 draw against fifth-place Ipswich Town.

Beswick, a former basketball coach whose expertise in the mind-over-matter field has also been put to use for the England youth and under-21 squads, is one of a number of sports psychologists (or 'mental coaches' as some like to call themselves) to have become involved in professional football in Britain in recent years. Two other well-known members of the breed are John Syer, who has been linked with Tottenham at various times over a period spanning some 25 years, and Willi Railla, the N———————

———— capacity. Then, when McClaren became Middlesbrough manager, he brought Beswick with him, and even appointed him assistant manager. The only other sports psychologist to have filled that sort of position at a leading professional football club in England has been the Frenchman Jacques Crevoisier. At the time of Beswick's Middlesbrough appointment, Gérard Houllier brought Crevoisier to Liverpool as his first-team coach.

The language such men use, which can come across as the application of psycho-babble to the obvious, can be irritating to the more dyed-in-the-wool members of the professional football fraternity. Also, in the macho environment of a soccer dressing room, nobody likes to think of himself as a suitable case for treatment. As one sports psychologist has remarked, 'One of the problems of dealing with some professional footballers and managers is that they confuse psychology with psychiatry.' Recalling his first few months working at Derby, Beswick said, 'The players recoiled in horror at the idea of working with a "shrink". Even Jim Smith expected some guy in a white coat.'

However, the credibility barrier they have faced has become smaller. Indeed, because of the ever-growing pressure on managers and teams to achieve success, men like Beswick could be described as essential to them rather than helpful, not least in their dealings with strikers. 'These are very vulnerable people,' Beswick pointed out. 'It is often said that a striker is never going to take all of his chances – he might only take one in six or eight – and therefore he has to be prepared to fail. He needs to have the courage to miss in order to have the courage to score. In my basketball days, I remember a prolific shooter being asked where his confidence came from, and him replying, "I decided early in my career to shoot it up and live in the streets." What he meant was that he was going to shoot at every opportunity, and if they went in, fine, he would be a hero, and if they didn't, he was quite prepared to pay the price for it. I often apply that quote to goalscorers.

'That is not to say that they are all the same. A lot of them do live a life of great peaks and troughs. They are either in sunshine or rain. But you can learn to cope with it, and I think the great strikers are able to use it to their advantage They thrive on anxiety, to the point where they actually invite it.' In that sense, Beswick agreed that the top scorers are a bit like journalists who tend to be at their best when writing to tight deadlines, 'when the pressure is really on'. He said that, in his experience, the trait of creating extra pressure and using it to one's advantage is common to many leading sportsmen and sportswomen.

As an example of another form of this, he recalled the approach of the great American sprinter Michael Johnson to the 1996 Olympic Games in Atlanta. 'In the build-up, Johnson announced to the press that he was not just going to achieve the 200- and 400-metre gold medal double [which had never been done before], but that he was also going to break the world 200 metres record. It might have seemed perverse for him to put that added pressure on himself, but in an event in which he was such a hot favourite he felt he needed it to be able to properly motivate himself.' Johnson was as good as his word, but then the work he had put into his bid for Olympic glory in training, allied to his natural talent, did much to help make this an inevitability.

In soccer, all scorers recognise the importance of ~~~~[1]

~~~~~~~~~~~~~~, the laziness of some of his strikers when he was Tranmere Rovers' manager 'drove me mad'. As a striker himself, Aldridge said he thought nothing of staying on the training ground after completing his work with the team to improve the aspects of the game particularly relevant to himself. 'I loved practising my shooting. When I was away with the Irish Republic squad, I did so much of it before games that Jack Charlton [the manager] would sometimes have to come and virtually drag me off the field. But it was different with some of the strikers I was associated with at Tranmere. Once the team training sessions had finished they just wanted to get in their cars and go home as quickly as possible.'

Some strikers do have a reasonable excuse for this. Southampton's James Beattie, referring to the high number of matches played by the leading teams in England (and possibly the amount of energy he expends during games), pointed out that strikers have to balance the requirement to hone their shooting skills against the need for them to get the right degree of rest, and to give their bodies some form of protection from unnecessary muscle strains.

However, it's not unusual for strikers to attribute an improvement in their scoring records to more shooting practice.

Certainly, in terms of that 'practice makes perfect' maxim they will have readily appreciated what the South African golfing legend Gary Player was getting at when he said, 'The more I practise, the luckier I get.'

The example set in England's rugby union squad by Jonny Wilkinson and his kicking coach Dave Alred will have been of more than merely passing interest to them as well. To say that the pair's approach to the art of scoring points from penalties and drop goals has been an obsession is putting it mildly. In their quest for perfection in mind and body, it would be virtually impossible to find any stone that they have left unturned.

In an intriguing article on Wilkinson in *The Guardian*, Richard Williams wrote, 'Together, Wilkinson and Alred practise for several hours a day, Alred standing behind the goal posts while Wilkinson kicks from every conceivable angle and range, going through his complex – and, to opponents, interminably protracted – routine before each attempt. Wilkinson finishes a session with a series of six kicks, but they all have to be perfect. If one of them misses, he starts again. He will not leave the pitch until he has sent six in a row whistling between the posts. That means stretching a session from two to three hours and sometimes beyond.' Part of that pre-kick routine, Williams pointed out, involved Wilkinson 'lowering his body into the posture of a man sitting on an invisible shooting-stick, and putting his hands together for several long seconds'. Williams continued, 'He told me that the hands are like a barrier erected against the outside world, helping him to cut out the tens of thousands of opposing fans who are likely to set up a barrage of whistles and jeers in an attempt to disturb his intense concentration.' He added, 'He [Wilkinson] imagines a jeering mouth behind the goal and attempts to send the ball down its throat. Another [psychological ploy] involves an imaginary woman called Doris who sits in a particular seat in the stand behind the goal, holding a can of Coke. As Wilkinson prepares to kick, he visualises the flight of the ball ending up in Doris's lap, knocking the drink out of her hands.'

In an interview with Jamie Jackson for the *Observer Sports*

concerning where the ball is going to go. He added, 'You've done it thousands of times on the training ground, and that's what gives you your confidence.'

This will have been music to the ears of Beswick. Donning his soccer striker's hat, he remarked, 'There is an element about the job [of scoring] that is instinctive, and some are more instinctive than others. You look at people such as Thierry Henry. When they are shooting, they can think of nothing else but the action of scoring; other thoughts such as the goalkeeper, the crowd, the tackles about to hit them are blocked out. The top scorers are the ones who get into that state the most often. But, through practice, you can train yourself to do it. The more you practise it, the more your body will take over from the brain and the more successful you will be.'

For Beswick, this is precisely why players should practise penalties. Some managers argue that it is a futile exercise on the grounds that taking spot-kicks in training cannot compare with doing so under far greater pressure in a match situation. That, it will be recalled, was the stance Glenn Hoddle adopted when he was criticised for not making penalty practice an integral part of his team's preparations before the 1998 World Cup quarter-final against Argentina (when England were beaten in a penalty shoot-out).

However, Beswick's logic is difficult to dispute, not least among the men for whom the task of putting the ball in the net (by any means) is what they are being paid to do.

Ray Clarke, one of the few British strikers to have made a big impact on the Continent, certainly sees the sense in it. Now Southampton's chief scout, Clarke looked every inch a natural scorer as a boy, but he stresses that the ability which prompted Tottenham to sign him from school was also the product of hard work. 'I could always score a lot of goals in schoolboy football, but when I was twelve or thirteen my father bought me a basic skills coaching book called *Skilful Soccer*, and it became our soccer bible. He would spend hours helping me practise the various shooting and heading tips in it in our garage and the local park. I was a right-footed player, but by the time I came to Tottenham's attention I could hit the ball equally well with the left. People just could not work out what was my natural striking foot.'

Such was his ability as a teenager that Tottenham brought him into their first-team squad when he was just sixteen. 'I came very close to putting you in the team at that age,' the manager, Bill Nicholson, once told him. However, he was never able to make further progress. This was due partly to his inability at that time to handle Nicholson's demanding, brusque nature. 'I took what he said to me as criticism rather than guidance. I became very apprehensive about my ability.' Also, Clarke suggests that his inclusion in the first-team squad might have come too early. 'I don't think I worked as hard on my game as I should have done,' he admitted.

At 21, Clarke, after just one substitute appearance for Spurs, began a downward Football League journey, first to Second Division Swindon Town where he scored two goals in fourteen matches, and then to Fourth Division Mansfield Town where he was their top scorer in his first season with 28 goals in 46 league games, thus helping them gain promotion, and again the following season with 24 in 45. All this made a rejuvenated Clarke think that he could hack it at a higher grade, but even he was taken by surprise by the fact

and had rejected the opportunity to take over at the Dutch club in favour of going to work in Saudi Arabia. All things being equal, Clarke would have preferred to join one of the English First Division clubs interested in him, but Sparta, apart from the transfer fee they were willing to pay, offered him a salary of £24,000 – more than six times what he had been getting at Mansfield.

However, as Clarke struggled to adjust to his new team, Sparta must have been cursing McGarry; despite the money he was raking in, Clarke might have been tempted to do so as well. He couldn't speak the language and he felt so much an outsider that he says he developed a siege mentality. 'I knew the players were talking about me behind my back,' he said. 'I caught one of them one day. We were in the dressing room, and the player glanced at me while making a remark in Dutch to another lad. The other lad could speak English, and when I asked what had been said he told me, "It is about time you scored some goals."' Not long afterwards Clarke ran into a member of the supporters' committee who had helped the club stump up the money for his transfer fee. 'We should send you back,' Clarke was told. 'You are no good.' Clarke added, 'The other players would wind me up about the comparatively low technical level of the game in England. It was them and me.'

It would probably have remained that way had Clarke not been forced to work harder on his finishing in training. The initiative for this came from Sparta's coach, Cor Brom, a former Ajax player whose quest to help Clarke justify Sparta's decision to sign him virtually turned into a personal crusade. 'There were only about five full-time pros at Sparta then and we trained in the afternoons,' Clarke recalled. 'But when Brom and I discussed the problems I was having, he said, "Right, as from now, you also come in every Tuesday and Thursday morning to do some training with me." Basically, for each of those mornings he set me a ninety-minute shooting and heading programme. It was all repetition work, and it was unbelievably intense. Everything was worked out in blocks of twenty, with Brom and the assistant coach standing either side of me with ten balls each, feeding them to me in quick succession. I went through every type of shot and header you can think of, from all manner of different angles, and the name of the game for me was that I had to hit the target. I don't know exactly how many shots and headers I had in each of those sessions – it must have been around three hundred – but the results were remarkable. After a while my failure rate was only about ten per cent, and as this started to be mirrored in my performances on a Saturday, it [practising scoring] became a bit like a drug. I started going in for extra finishing work even on my days off. I was happy just to get a bag of twenty balls and practise hitting them into an empty net on my own. I had started to achieve success and I had this burning urge to make sure it was maintained. I'd sometimes go in while taking my missus out shopping. I'd stop the car outside the ground and she would say, "I thought we were going shopping," and I'd say, "We are, but I need to do a bit [of shooting practice] first."'

Little wonder that Clarke became Sparta's highest scorer for fifteen years. His record in his two years there was 42 goals in 71 matches. Then came the ultimate step-up in the context of Dutch football: Brom was appointed Ajax's coach and he took Clarke with him. 'I went from being a big fish in a small pond to a small fish in a big pond,' said Clarke. Through his desire to retain that

the same success at his next ports of call. Bruges in Belgium, Brighton and Hove Albion, and finally Newcastle. However, looking back on his work behind the scenes, he is grateful for having 'seen the light' when he did. 'If I was a club manager, I would make sure that my strikers did the same as I did. I cannot possibly see how practising a particular skill would not make someone better at it.'

In most shooting practice sessions, getting into the habit of just 'hitting the target', irrespective of whether the ball goes into the net, is the most rudimentary starting point. Bryan 'Pop' Robson, the coach of Leeds United's under-18 players, said, 'It doesn't matter if there isn't a goalkeeper there; the main thing is to get into the habit of getting that ball on target.' To Robson, this is not something to be taken lightly. 'I hate it when some of the lads I work with put a shot wide, and then laugh over it. They think it's funny, but it really does my head in.'

Robson, once described by Malcolm Macdonald as one of the best strikers of the ball he had seen, is one of a seemingly endless list of experts who look upon Jimmy Greaves as the ultimate shooting role model. Greaves's most famous characteristic as a finisher was his ability almost to pass the ball into the net. That, in fact, is a hallmark of all the truly great goalscorers. Ray Clarke, recalling his experience of training with Johann Cruyff for two months at Ajax when the Dutch master returned to the club to get himself fit for his testimonial match, said, 'He taught me that you don't have to lash the ball. Sometimes you get so fired up or anxious over a scoring chance you feel you have to hit the ball as hard as you can. "Great scorers just pass it," Cruyff told me. "Just relax."' In the modern game, another striker noted for not trying to burst the ball is Arsenal's Thierry Henry. Unless it is absolutely necessary for him to do otherwise, the Frenchman's shooting emphasis is very much on accuracy rather than power.

Still, in all my conversations on this shooting-pass subject with leading English football figures, Greaves was mentioned the most. Mervyn Day, a former goalkeeper, said, 'I played against Greaves in practice matches [when the pair were at West Ham] and what struck me about the goals he scored against me was that there was no power at all in a lot of his shots. It proved to me that there were quite a few situations in which a striker only needs to pass the ball accurately to beat the keeper. For example, imagine a situation where the striker has the ball just inside the penalty area. If the keeper is six or seven yards off his line, which he usually should be, that means you are only talking about a shot over eleven or twelve yards. Why blast the ball? This was why you hardly ever saw Greaves miss the target. You think about it.'

All the technical and psychological factors involved in the art of clinical finishing, especially with a pass-shot, are perhaps best epitomised in those agonising one-against-one situations when the striker is bearing down on the goal with only the keeper to beat, or is taking a penalty. Such moments, the ultimate cases of the so-called 'battle of wits' between strikers and keepers, can easily remind one of that gunfight showdown involving Gary Cooper and his arch enemy in High Noon. In the footballing equivalent, the striker and the keeper, in trying to force each other to make the first move, can often find the time they have to think about their actions considerably more of a handicap than an advantage. As virtually all of the pressure is on the striker, these situations have tended to

there is a chance of scoring, they more than anyone should grasp it. But some strikers don't want to because the price they have to pay for missing is too high for them. I think you will find that these are the strikers who allow not scoring to get to them the most.'

But if anything, one-on-ones in open play can be even more nerve-racking, given the number of ways in which a keeper can 'out-psyche' his opponent. Ray Clarke recalled that at Ajax, the advice he was given on how to be successful in such situations made him think he was being taken into the realm of unarmed combat. A member of the coaching staff kept telling him, 'Show no mercy [to keepers].' On the eve of some away matches, Clarke would find a picture of the opposing keeper pinned above his hotel bed with the message, 'Tomorrow, you kill him.'

Maybe it would have helped him more to have had some advice from someone such as Mervyn Day. Most keepers agree that it's important for them to stay on their feet for as long as possible, and that when a striker is coming towards them with the ball they are vulnerable to shots hit early, preferably with little backlift, as they are coming out to narrow the angle. 'Generally,' Day added, 'if you are one on one and are not going to try and take the ball around the keeper, there is a point when the best shot is the one close to a keeper's feet. Then there's the one through his legs. The closer you get to a keeper, the more he will crouch to cover the goal and the wider his feet will become.' Frank McLintock said, 'The keeper will come out ten to fifteen yards when a striker is running through, but sometimes I think he is better off staying back to give himself more time to see the ball. When you get eight to ten yards from a striker and he strikes it at your feet, what chance have you got? Not much of a chance when you are facing people like Greaves. They are ice-cool, like assassins. They stroke the ball past the keeper as if to say, "Well, what else did you expect me to do?" Whereas if people like me were to get into those positions, the ball might end up ten yards over the bar.

'I would say that seventy-five per cent of Greaves's goals were sidefooted. Whenever I think of Greaves, I immediately remember a Scotland–England under-21 match at Aberdeen when he was put through our defence and I was chasing him five or eight yards behind. It was always difficult to catch him in that situation because Jimmy could run almost as quickly with the ball as he could without it, and the ball was nearly always under total control by the way. He only had the keeper to beat, and as he shaped to hit the ball to one side and the keeper moved his bodyweight accordingly, Jimmy suddenly hit it just inches the wrong side of the keeper's other foot. As the ball went in, I thought, "You lucky bastard." But that was not right because over a period of some fifteen years I saw him do it time and time again.'

Another striker singled out by McLintock as being a cut above many others in the mental battleground of one-on-ones was Leeds United's Allan Clarke. He, too, achieved remarkable precision, something which clearly gave him enormous pride when he looked back on his career in an interview with me in 1996. 'I always remember the gaffer [Leeds manager Don Revie] saying to me, "If you have only one man to beat to get in a shot, Allan, just shake your body, go past him and do it. When you get into those positions, I know I can sit back and relax."

'The thing about my shooting was that I didn't let difficult

As the keeper was moving towards me, I knew that there had to be a point at which he would have to stop, and I was quite happy to wait for that moment, even if it meant him getting quite close to me. As soon as he stopped, that was the moment I shot. Not only this, I hit the ball low and as close to the keeper as possible, knowing that he was going to struggle to get down to it quickly enough.

'Dave Harvey [the Leeds keeper] will tell you about things like that. I was only the third-choice penalty-taker at Leeds but I still used to practise taking them against Dave in training. Nine times out of ten I would hit the ball to a keeper's left if he was right-handed and vice versa. Dave was right-handed, and before I took penalties against him in training I actually told him where I was going to place the ball and he still couldn't stop them. He would then position himself increasingly further towards that post, and eventually he was so close to it that he could almost touch it. Even then I scored more than I missed.'

One obvious potential pitfall for strikers in one-on-one situations in open play concerns the difficulty of switching into the lower gear necessary to give them the right degree of composure. 'It's about accelerating to get through a defence and then suddenly decelerating to give yourself the calmness needed to stick the ball past the keeper,' said Andy Roxburgh. 'It [scoring] has to be easier if you are not trying to do it at a hundred miles an hour.' One illustration of that point, Roxburgh added, was the Ronaldo goal that brought Brazil their 1–0 win over Turkey in the 2002 World Cup semi-final. 'Of the strikers in England, Thierry Henry and Michael Owen are particularly good examples as well,' he went on. But what made that Ronaldo goal even more interesting to Roxburgh was the sudden toe-poke with which the outrageously gifted Brazilian produced as the finishing touch. It was a weak shot (if one could truly call it that), but then the nonchalant, subtle manner of the toe-ender – no more than a prod, with hardly any backlift and no follow-through – made it difficult to see how the Turkish keeper could have anticipated it.

In terms of the shooting instructions laid down in traditional football coaching manuals, the toe-poke is hardly textbook stuff, as Roxburgh pointed out. 'A lot of the old coaching books tell you that you must not toe-poke the ball. But as far as I'm concerned you can put them all in a bag and throw them in the bin.' He explained that such shots are commonplace in 'Futsal de Salon', the indoor five-a-side game that originated in South America and which has been a big factor in the development of many Brazilian stars. Roxburgh, added: 'It is easier to control the ball in futsal [than in a conventional eleven-a-side match] because the ball they use is heavier and does not bounce so much. As the ball hits you, it "dies". It's great for developing techniques such as lifting the ball over defenders and keeping it away from them with the sole of the foot. It's the same with those toe-poked shots: they just stub their toe at the ball and it flies.' Ronaldo himself attributed that goal against Turkey to his futsal experience. 'Nobody expected me to do it,' he said. 'It is a difficult technique, but it was just instinctive, and I owe it to playing a lot of futsal when I was younger.'

But there have also been some excellent demonstrations of the skill from non-futsal players. Roxburgh vividly remembers one from his days as Scotland coach, when Pat Nevin scored against the USA,

Coincidentally, the day after my conversation with Roxburgh on this aspect of forward play I found Mark McGhee encouraging his strikers to try the toe-poke technique in a Millwall training session. 'Micky Quinn [McGhee's former Newcastle colleague] was great at it. Helped by his strong ankles and calves, he toe-ended more goals than any player I have seen. In a crowded penalty box, it must be an advantage for a striker to be able to get in his shot half a second earlier.'

One would think that it must also be an advantage for any striker to have a coach attending to his needs and requirements as closely as Dave Alred does with Jonny Wilkinson. But in soccer, the idea that the striker's role is almost as much a specialist position as that of goalkeeping, and thus requires specialist coaching, has not caught on as much as one might imagine. Goalkeeping coaches have become quite common, but the number of expert coaches for the exclusive use of the men at the front end of the team – the sharp end, as they like to describe it – is limited.

The biggest name among the specialist striking coaches is Ian Rush at Liverpool, but perhaps even more interesting is the England Rugby Union-style coaching and training set-up in which Beswick is involved at Middlesbrough. Boro's manager, Steve McClaren, has not gone as far as Sir Clive Woodward, whose backroom staff for England's triumphant 2004 World Cup campaign in Australia included not only Alred but also tackling, scrummage and line-out coaches. Still, McClaren, who like Woodward is happy to explore all manner of sports science avenues to maximise his team's performances and has clearly been influenced by the departmental coaching approach in American football, does have a goalkeeping coach (Jim Barron), a defensive coach (Keith Harrison) and an attacking coach (Steve Round). Some might argue that the benefits of the latter were hard to detect in Boro's unimpressive overall scoring record in the 2003/04 season. On the other hand, though, they did not have the best of luck with injuries, and their attack – featuring Gaizka Mendieta and Boudewijn Zenden on the flanks and that Brazilian bag of tricks Juninho feeding off Joseph Desiré-Job in the middle – did help bring them the League Cup, their first ever trophy.

Steve Round is not a former striker; he was a Derby County right-back or right-side midfielder whose career was cut short by injury at the age of 22. By then he was already coaching at Derby's School of Excellence, and he was the club's reserve-team coach at the time he joined his former Pride Park colleagues McLaren and Beswick at Middlesbrough. Considering his background as a player, it seems strange that he should have been given so much responsibility for improving Boro's scoring ability, but he maintained that he has always been a keen student of the 'creative' side of the game. 'Coaching is not about showing someone how to do it [score] by demonstrating it,' he said. 'Coaching is about breaking it down and explaining it.' He admitted, however, that gaining the trust and support of the strikers in his group has not always been easy. 'Strikers are not the easiest of players to deal with,' he said. 'Dave Sexton [one of England's leading post-war coaching figures] summed it up once when he talked about the differences between defenders and forwards. He described defenders as being the game's "soldiers" in that if you say to them, "There's a big wall over there, get over it," they will reply, "How long have we got..."

...get a performance out of him, any kind of performance, was extraordinary.' But, thanks partly to the player–staff 'bonding' effect of a pre-season training camp in Spain, what Round had to offer became accepted more readily.

Boro's belief that scoring is a collective responsibility is reflected by the prominently positioned poster in their training-ground dressing room, which reminds each section of the team of the minimum goal target McClaren has set for it. Hence the insistence of Round and Beswick that it is important for them to work with all the attacking players as a group – the midfielders and strikers rather than just the strikers. 'Strikers have to integrate themselves into the team pattern, so if you are concentrating just on strikers and their finishing you're not really getting to the essence of the issue,' Round said. 'In the past there has been a coaching culture where you coach the team to defend and to win the ball, and then, when you have got it, you just go and play. We are trying to go into it a lot more deeply. So when we win the ball, how do we go and play? How do we create? How do we score? These are basically the questions we are trying to answer.'

As far as those goal targets are concerned, Round said, 'Once we have come up with criteria on how we believe they can be achieved, the next step is to have an open debate about it with the players.' When one striker was asked whether he could see any problems with what was being asked of him, he replied, 'I was seen as the star player at my previous club and was allowed to get away with whatever I wanted to. You cannot allow that to happen here – you must keep me on a tight rein.' Round said: 'That player can get sloppy in training,' Round said, 'and because of what he told me it gives me an excuse to really have a go at him. He will look at me angrily, but then I will make out that I am tightening a belt around my waist [to emphasise his need to get rid of his slackness] and off he goes, as focused as ever.'

Before the start of the 2003/04 season, each of the players in Round's group was given a 'job description' sheet outlining what Boro considered to be the most important aspects of his role. 'We try to make it as simple as possible so each player knows what is expected of him and how he is being evaluated,' Round explained. The list handed to the front men, entitled *The Requirements of a Striker*, read:

1. CHALLENGE/COURAGE
   Pressure defenders
   Take the ball
2. HOLD THE BALL
3. GET INTO THE BOX
   Skill
   Movement
   Freedom
4. CREATE A GOAL
5. SCORE A GOAL.

The last sentence stated: 'If I miss, I only think, "I will get the next one."'

The list, of course, covers all the stages often necessary for a striker to go through before he or another member of the team can

by doing all the things we expect of him [physically and mentally] he is bound to get more scoring chances. We say to the strikers, "If you win the ball thirty-five yards from the goal then you only have thirty-five yards to go to score, whereas if you win the ball a hundred yards from goal you have a hundred yards to go to score. So be our first line of defence and last line of attack."'

'They cannot score in every game,' Beswick added, 'and there are times when coming off without scoring can be very depressing to them. Strikers are noted for being a bit sensitive and requiring a lot of support. That is where the list of requirements we give them can come in handy. If you can show them the plus-points in other aspects of their game, it does help.'

But all strikers prone to 'emotional static', so when they aren't scoring, it helps them even more if they have been born with thick skins.

CHAPTER FOUR
THE WEIGHT OF EXPECTATION

without you being conscious of them.
You might think you're doing the same things
you did when you were scoring,
but that's not always the case.'

ADE AKINBIYI

THE WEIGHT OF EXPECTATION

Dion Dublin, who spent much of his time in the 2003/04 season as Aston Villa's centre-half, says that the striker role is the one he enjoys the most. Nobody will be surprised at this, given his love of scoring and his scoring record. But what is surprising is his other explanation: the fact that he finds it less stressful. 'As a central defender you are always anxious about making a mistake which might cost your team a goal,' he explained. 'You can't afford to allow your concentration to drop for a second. You are on edge virtually all the time; it's very wearing. I don't think this is as much the case if you are a striker. Your mental approach is a bit different. To get goals, you have to be relaxed.'

So do we perhaps make too much of the pressures under which strikers do their jobs at times? They certainly don't seem to affect Alan Shearer. He seems genuinely surprised when you question him on this. 'I think you have to believe that you are going to score,' he said. 'That is a lot of it – not hoping you are going to score, but expecting to do so. When you go through spells without scoring, you do think, "Well, when is the next one going to come?" But I have always felt that it cannot go on for ever, that the longer I go without scoring the closer I get to being successful again. I cannot say that I have ever been that worried about it. If you are a goalscorer, then you are a goalscorer. You will always score.'

'Great scorers, and especially ones in top teams, look upon a missed chance like a missed bus,' said Andy Roxburgh. 'Their attitude is, "Doesn't matter – there will be another one along soon." That is what makes them great strikers. As for the pressure on them to score, don't forget that almost all of them have been strikers since they were small boys, so they have become conditioned to it. For example, if you have ever been in a country like Norway and stood at the top of an Olympic ski jump, you will think, "How the hell can anyone compete in this event?" But then as you drive around the explanation is provided by the number of smaller jumps used by the youngsters. The Olympic guys have built themselves up for the big jumps since they were boys. I think the same applies to goalscorers. Obviously, strikers can lose confidence. But they don't allow it to drop easily. Their confidence is not as fragile as you might think. It can't be.'

Indeed, signs of a striker not being as confident as he should be can often be detected only by an expert. 'One thing strikers do when they are confident is that they shoot when they cannot see all the goal,' Mark McGhee pointed out. 'The ball is in the box, they quickly get it under control, and even though they might have defenders in front of them, whoosh, they have a shot. It's amazing how many times the ball goes straight through [past the keeper and into the net]. When they are less confident they are inclined to want to take an extra touch so they can see more of the target, which is something you cannot do in league football because as soon as you take that extra touch the gap has closed completely. We are only talking about split seconds, which means that if that happens, the crowd are likely to think that the chance was not good enough, but quite often it was.'

Players generally and strikers particularly do not often admit publicly to being affected by nerves. Strikers believe it is essential to

the Brazilian icon, bearing the hopes of millions on his shoulders and suffering from injuries which had looked like ruling him out of the match, was on the verge of a nervous breakdown.

According to Clarkson, a member of the Brazilian squad revealed that Ronaldo 'was shaking with fear' during the build-up to the game. 'Ronaldo was sleeping in his hotel room [eight hours before the nine pm kick-off],' Clarkson wrote. 'His room-mate Roberto Carlos was listening to his Walkman when, he later claimed, he was disturbed by the muffled sound of Ronaldo apparently having some kind of fit. Ronaldo turned pale, began sweating profusely and then suffered convulsions, with his arms flexed and his hands misshapen by the nervous tension.'

Certainly Ronaldo, who had scored four goals in his previous World Cup matches in France, looked a pale shadow of his old self in that final. However, if the pressure really did get to him – the only other explanation was that he might have been suffering a reaction from the drugs he had been prescribed to ease his injuries – he presented a far different picture of himself with the way in which he got over the experience. He, of course, was the star of Brazil's 2002 World Cup triumph, scoring both goals in the 2–0 win over Germany in the final to bring his total for the competition in Japan and Korea to eight. Apart from being the top scorer in that tournament, his aggregate World Cup record of twelve goals put him level with his Brazilian idol, Pele.

In another book, *Full Time* by Tony Cascarino and Paul Kimmage, Cascarino gave arguably the most remarkable of all insights into the self-doubts that can affect strikers. To many of his colleagues, the former Aston Villa, Celtic, Chelsea and Republic of Ireland centre-forward was the life and soul of any party. But in a breathtakingly honest account of his career, Cascarino admitted that when he was on the field he was repeatedly haunted by an 'irritating voice' in his head reminding him of his faults and all the reasons that could prevent him from scoring. 'Think positive?' he wrote. 'Not me. I think negative. I have always been a negative person. I have always thought negative thoughts. For as long as I can remember, there has been a little voice in my head that highlights my weaknesses and undermines my confidence. When it comes to the art of shooting oneself in the foot, I am world class. I think too much during the games. Most players analyse their performance after a game. Not me; I do it all the wrong way: I think of how I am playing as I play. Three bad passes and I'm glancing at the touchline [looking for the signal for him to be substituted]. I've scored and played brilliantly one week, and gone out and been awful the next, purely because some negative thought has hijacked me.'

In terms of missed chances, it's difficult to think of any striker who has fluffed more in one match than Plymouth Argyle's Marino Keith did during his team's shock 2–1 FA Cup fourth-round replay defeat at Dagenham and Redbridge in the 2001/02 season. It was possibly one of the most embarrassing performances by a striker in recent seasons, although Paul Sturrock, who had made Keith one of his first signings as Plymouth manager, saw no reason why he should feel uncomfortable about the decision. Sturrock, who had seen his fellow Scot in action at his previous clubs, Dundee United, Falkirk and Livingston, told me: 'I knew that a lot of teams would come to Plymouth to defend, pack a lot of men in or around our penalty box, so I needed a striker who could operate effectively in that area

generally put teams under greater pressure, he was a striker I felt I could take a chance on.'

On the nightmare that Keith and Plymouth experienced at Dagenham and Redbridge – where he missed enough chances for two or three games, let alone one – Sturrock continued, 'I'm not sure that his self-belief was really up to what it usually is. Confidence is a big factor in scoring, a very big factor, and to varying degrees all strikers go through low-confidence spells. When they get a chance you can sense their minds telling them to take extra care, whereas in normal circumstances they don't think about it, they just do it. The difference can be very subtle. Sometimes, this can happen to them without their really being conscious of it, and I think it can be dangerous to even mention it to them. It is something I rarely do because I am always wary of making the psychological barrier bigger. If a striker has a run of matches when he is missing chances, it can be amazing how easily he can get back on to the right track. Just one goal, any type of goal, will do, and Marino is one of those strikers whom you would never bet against getting that turning point. Though he goes through spells when he cannot hit a barn door, any slight drop in his finishing confidence does not mean he will give up.

'In that match at Dagenham and Redbridge I think he missed something like nine chances. Most of his misses were in the first half, and even now people ask me, "Why did you not take him off?" It was simple: he was the only player creating chances. They were all dropping to him and I thought that sooner or later he was bound to stick one or two of them in.' Just as he did in a subsequent match at Queens Park Rangers, where he scored Plymouth's goal in a rare 3–1 defeat with a tremendous shot into the far corner of the net from the left. 'About five minutes before, he missed a good chance with a header – he didn't even hit the target – and then he struck a shot which I think hit the corner flag,' Sturrock continued. 'But there he was, trying his luck again from the same position. Sometimes you think, "What is he shooting from there for?" and then it's "Oh my God, what a goal!" That's the kind of striker he is.'

Apart from his mentality, Keith has possibly also been helped by the fact that his club and the level at which he has operated do not attract much media coverage. The newspaper and TV spotlight on his mistakes is nowhere near as broad and intense as it is on those of his counterparts in the Premiership or in international football. It is certainly nothing like the spotlight that fell on Gordon Smith after the Scot's miss for Brighton and Hove Albion in the 1983 FA Cup final against Manchester United – arguably the most famous of all the goal misses in English football.

When Smith was presented with his chance in the last minute of extra time, with his unfancied team holding United at 2–2, he was perhaps the last player one would have expected to make a mess of it. After all, Smith had played in six Scottish Cup finals for Rangers, and he had even scored the winner for them against Celtic in the 1978 Scottish League Cup final. He had also opened the scoring for Brighton at Wembley, with a header. Thus, when Brighton's centre-forward Mick Robinson burst through the United defence and laid off the ball to an unmarked Smith ten yards out, the BBC Radio 2 match commentator, Peter Jones, had no hesitation in stating, 'And Smith must score!' Smith thought the same, with only the keeper Gary Bailey to beat, especially when Bailey dived to his left, leaving

..., of course, was not Smith's fault. But had Brighton won the FA Cup, and thus qualified for the European Cup-Winners Cup, maybe some of the problems that followed their Wembley disappointment – especially the financial ones – might have been avoided. Inevitably, it was particularly difficult for them to wipe out the memory of that disappointment in the 1983/84 season, when their erratic results caused them to finish ninth.

This was not a good season for Smith at Brighton either. He made only eleven full and four substitute appearances for them in the league the following season, scoring just four goals (including two penalties). But then Billy McNeill signed him for Manchester City for £35,000, and he went on to get fifteen goals in 49 appearances for them. He ended his career in England with Oldham Athletic and played in Austria and Switzerland before retiring as a player and becoming assistant manager at St Mirren in 1988.

Smith, now working in Scotland as a financial consultant and a TV and radio pundit, has never been allowed to forget his Wembley nightmare. Those Jones words, 'And Smith must score!' – which became the title of the Brighton fanzine – are almost as famous as the Kenneth Wolstenholme BBC TV commentary ('They think it's all over – it is now') that accompanied Geoff Hurst clinching his World

Cup final hat-trick in 1966. Smith recalled a Manchester City club tour of Malaysia the following year, when a Chinese boy approached him for his autograph while he was soaking up the sun by the hotel swimming pool. 'You Gordon Smith?' the boy asked. 'How you miss that sitter in final?' 'It is all people ever want to talk to me about,' Smith said. 'I could make a cottage industry out of telling the story of what happened with me that day. Even now, hardly a day goes by without somebody mentioning that miss to me.'

However, his memories of it do go down well in his after-dinner speeches, and it is clear that the miss has not left him with any emotional scars. One reason, he explained, is that he wasn't really a striker. 'A lot of people have tended to overlook this. I remember an article in which Jimmy Case [his Brighton team-mate] recalled a Brighton fan bemoaning the fact that the FA Cup final chance had fallen to me, and Jimmy telling him, "Look, of all the players I have played with here, Gordon is the one I would have backed the most to score in that situation." I was quite chuffed by that because I was a midfield player. I only played up front in the cup final because we were short of strikers: Andy Ritchie had been transferred to Leeds in a part-exchange deal involving Terry Connor, and Connor couldn't play at Wembley because he was cup-tied. I was not a recognised striker at Manchester City either, even in the season when I was their joint top scorer [1984/85]. I was actually operating as a wide left midfielder.

'The miss might have had an adverse effect on me if I had been a young, inexperienced player, but I was twenty-eight then; I had a good understanding of what I was all about as a player and a person and I was mature enough to be able to put my experiences in football, the good and the bad, into their proper perspective. Obviously I was disappointed over the miss, for myself, the team and the supporters. But I cannot honestly say that I went to pieces over it.'

Smith's point about being more of a midfielder than a striker could also be used in defence of Geoff Thomas. He, too, is famous for missing a chance most believed he should have taken with his eyes shut, and it happened in his one and only England ~~~~~~~

~~~~~~~ Brazilian defender heading the ball straight to his feet by blasting it over an open goal. England were a goal down at the time, and that's the way it remained. The possibility that Astle might have been suffering from 'emotional static' seemed to be lost on the England players as they debated the incident around their hotel swimming pool the following day. 'How was it possible for Jeff to miss a chance like that?' Alan Ball asked. As it happened, Ball should have known the answer because Astle had earlier provided him with a good chance by getting his head to a high cross, only for Ball to waste it.

The England striker who has suffered the biggest credibilty problems in recent seasons is Emile Heskey. Few international strikers have been subjected to greater media criticism than Heskey, whose struggle to assert himself as a scorer for Liverpool as well as Sven-Goran Eriksson's team led to his being transferred to Birmingham in May 2004. Among those who have also found it difficult to shine under the microscope of an entire country is John Aldridge. He said that the Republic of Ireland team he played for was the only one in which he suffered what he described as 'a mental scoring block'. He did not score in any of his first nineteen international matches – by far the longest non-scoring run of his entire career and one that coincided, strangely, with his emergence as a top-class player with Liverpool. Aldridge reckons it was partly due to the Republic of Ireland's tactics under Jack Charlton. He put a big emphasis on turning opposing defenders with passes hit deep into the space behind their full-backs – the 'corners', as coaches describe it, and Aldridge says: 'In that system, I was a runner not a goalscorer. I would be the one chasing the ball into the corners.' He admits, though, that he might have taken Charlton's instructions too far at times and that the longer he went without scoring the bigger that mental block became. 'When I did get chances, I was hitting the woodwork, they were getting cleared off the line – I was missing sitters, really. I didn't want to admit it publicly at the time, but deep down I knew I wasn't as confident as I was at club level. Had I been an England player, I don't think I would have lasted very long: the media would have hounded me out after five or six games. I have a lot to thank Jack for, because he kept faith in me. He felt I was pivotal to the system he wanted to play, so the more the Irish media said he shouldn't play me the more he dug his heels in.'

Aldridge eventually broke his duck in the 4–0 win over Tunisia in Dublin in October 1989. He got the last goal thanks to the spirit of generosity in Ray Houghton, who passed up a scoring opportunity for himself to lay one on a plate for Aldridge. 'I think he probably felt sorry for me,' Aldridge said. Not long afterwards he moved to Real Sociedad in Spain where his experience of being used as a lone striker against teams using man-for-man marking systems, not to mention his exposure to a more disciplined lifestyle, helped take his game on to a different level. 'The Real Sociedad system rotated around me and was mostly about manipulating teams into certain positions in order to give me the final ball. My spell in Spain taught me a lot about when to run the corners and when not to.'

Aldridge ended his international career with a total of nineteen goals from 69 matches. It put him joint second on their list of all-time international scorers with Don Givens, just one goal behind Frank Stapleton.

In all the time it had taken him to get off the mark, the

1,298 minutes – was particularly agonising to their Preston striker David Healy. True, Northern Ireland are the weakest of the four national United Kingdom teams, and Healy often found himself toiling up front on his own. However, he was recognised as their best striker and he did get some good chances in that depressing run, notably during the 1–0 defeat in Armenia in March 2003, when sympathy for him over the tremendous shot the keeper managed to touch on to the woodwork was offset by disappointment with his failure to get in a close-range header with the goal at his mercy.

All this seemed difficult to understand when one looked at the start of Healy's international career. He had just been loaned to Port Vale by Manchester United when he made his international debut against Luxembourg in February 2000, and in fact had made only one appearance in senior football up to that point (for United in a League Cup tie at Aston Villa four months earlier). Nonetheless, he scored twice in a 3–1 Irish victory, and over the rest of his spell at Port Vale he took his international goal ratio to three in three matches. It became five in seven after his return to Old Trafford, and following his transfer to Preston in December 2000 (initially on loan) it was extended to a highly respectable eight in fifteen matches.

He had made a good start at Preston, too, with ten goals in his

26 matches in the 2000/01 season, thus summing up why the club had paid £1.5 million for him in January. But the season ultimately produced disappointment for Preston: they were beaten in the First Division promotion play-off final by Bolton, and Healy's star seemed on the wane the following season. At the time of his eighth Northern Ireland goal in the 1–0 win over Malta in October 2001, Healy's record for his club was one in twelve games, and he was able to add only nine more (including a hat-trick against Stockport County) in his remaining 37 matches.

It seemed clear that Healy, in his early twenties, had begun to suffer a mental and physical backlash from the excitement of his early successes. Indeed, a few weeks before the end of the season, with Kelham O'Hanlon installed as Preston's caretaker-manager following the departure of David Moyes to Everton, Healy was displaced in the starting line-up by Clyde Wijnhard. 'Clyde is a big striker,' Healy said, 'and Kelham opted for a style of play that was more direct. It didn't really suit me – I prefer the ball into feet – but I couldn't really complain about it because Clyde did quite well and I was low on confidence anyway.'

Healy's anxiety that another Preston manager might not rate him as highly as Moyes had done seemed to be borne out when Craig Brown, appointed Moyes's successor at the end of the season, opted for Ricardo Fuller (his summer signing from Hearts) and Richard Cresswell as his first-choice strikers. Even after Fuller's serious injury that October, Healy was kept largely on the periphery of the first-team action.

But Northern Ireland, woefully short of striking options, continued to play him – which was part of his problem in that non-scoring run. 'I was thankful to Sammy McIlroy [the manager] for sticking by me, but maybe that was the wrong thing to do because when you are short of confidence at club level you are bound to take it on to the international stage,' Healy argued. 'My early success probably hindered me a bit. Initially, everything is new: teams don't know much about you and you are full of adrenalin. But then people start expecting you to score in every game, which is difficult for a [illegible] football, I know I did. In terms of giving me a competitive edge, I wasn't getting as much out of it as I needed. In international football, there are games in which you might only get six touches of the ball and only one half chance – a twenty-yard shot or something like that. So you have to be in that zone.'

Healy was able to get back into it with Preston in the 2003/04 season following a less than spectacular loan spell at Norwich City, because of a slight change in roles. Brown told me, 'I like my mainline striker to have a lot of pace, and I'm not sure that David is quick enough for that. Unlike people such as Fuller, he cannot outrun defenders. But he can beat them with trickery, and he is an excellent striker of the ball, so we have played him off the main striker. Being deeper means he gets a bit more attacking freedom. He tends to come forward mainly from the right, because whenever the opposition win the ball it's his job to shuttle across and cut off their left-back. His attacking ability from that sort of area is excellent.'

Brown has certainly been impressed with Healy's shooting. 'He is possibly the finest striker of a ball I have worked with,' he said. 'I love the way he clips the ball. With such a short backlift, he surprises you with the power he gets into his shots. Our players marvel at some of the goals he gets in training and matches.' Brown's favourite was Healy's winning goal in Preston's 2–1 victory at West Ham in January 2004. 'He was about fourteen yards out when the ball was cut back to him from a corner, and he hit the ball first-time, without appearing to really set up his body shape for it. He actually put spin on it, and the ball went under David James's body.'

But it was with his head that Healy ended his Northern Ireland nightmare, against Norway at Windsor Park the month following that West Ham tie. With McIlroy having resigned as manager to join Stockport County (how was that for an indictment on the state of his national team?) and having been replaced by Lawrie Sanchez, the Irish suffered another humiliating defeat. However, you could understand why the dismay over the four goals they conceded was cast aside to some extent by Healey's fifty-sixth-minute headed goal from Keith Gillespie's cross. It was his first Northern Ireland goal in fifteen matches, and what made it doubly exciting for him was that his international total of nine put him level in the all-time scorers' list with two Irish soccer legends, George Best and Norman Whiteside, and only four behind Colin Clarke at the top.

It was a breakthrough that could have been anticipated in the light of the change in his fortunes at Preston. He hadn't scored in any of their opening eleven matches, but by the time he faced Norway he had got ten in eighteen. The upsurge in his confidence was again seen in Northern Ireland's next match, against Estonia in Tallinn at the end of March, when he scored his most spectacular goal at international level with a wonderful strike from twenty yards. And he should have got another in that game: he reacted quickly to the rebound from a blocked shot by Jeff Whitley but fired the ball over the bar from six yards. But he was easily forgiven by the Irish faithful because the chance he did take meant their team won 1–0 – their first victory in sixteen games.

It also happened to be quite a good season for Stoke City's much-travelled and much-maligned Ade Akinbiyi. It's difficult to think of any striker who has received the amount of stick from fans that he has. It's also difficult to think of any striker who can provide

why they have been attracted to him. The Nigerian, big, strong and exceptionally quick, cuts a dynamic figure in the athletic sense. Indeed, as a schoolboy growing up in Hackney, east London, he could easily have joined Arsenal, but as his parents wanted to move to Norfolk he plumped for Norwich City. Although he struggled to establish himself there, he went on to make an increasingly big name for himself at Gillingham (28 league goals in 68 matches), Bristol City (21 in 47) and Wolves (16 in 37). Indeed, his progress was reflected by the transfer fees handed out for him: Gillingham had only paid Norwich £25,000 for him, but Bristol City signed him for a club-record £1.2 million, Wolves for a club-record £3 million, and then Leicester brought him on to the Premiership stage for a club-record £5 million. So much for the rise of Akinbiyi. The fall was illustrated by Leicester selling him to Crystal Palace for £2.2 million and then Stoke taking him off Palace's hands on a free transfer.

It was at Leicester, where Akinbiyi looked ill at ease in the Premiership and the pressure on him to save his team from relegation, that his image took its biggest battering. He managed only eleven goals in 58 league matches, and he was in no position to complain about not having had enough chances. Leicester fans still wince over the memory of his hatful of glaring misses during the televised 4–1 home defeat by Liverpool in October 2001, especially the one where his attempt to head the ball in from a few yards out ended with it hitting him on the shoulder and going wide.

Shortly afterwards, Opta, the Premiership's official statisticians, revealed that as many as 83 per cent of Akinbiyi's shots that season had been off target. This was highlighted by the *Sun* newspaper, which ran a prominent story describing Akinbiyi as 'the worst striker in the league'. Mark Irwin, the writer, suggested that Peter Taylor, the manager who had signed him from Leicester and who had subsequently been replaced by Dave Bassett, might have lost his job because of the striker's wayward finishing. 'Leicester fans are wondering why their club forked out £5 million for a guy who cannot hit a cow's backside with a banjo,' he wrote. By this stage the Leicester fans had turned against Akinbiyi – to the point where a Leicester supporters' spokesman admitted that the striker's fallibility had become an 'obsession' with them. Micky Adams, then Leicester's assistant manager, said, 'We just have to relax him more. I have told him that whatever is troubling him, let me worry about it during a match. It's not easy when 22,000 fans are booing, but he needs to clear his mind.'

But the tag of being the worst striker in the game continued to prove a heavy psychological millstone around his neck, even when he moved back to the Nationwide League to join Crystal Palace. It seemed a big compliment to Akinbiyi that he was signed for Palace by a former striker as accomplished as Trevor Francis. But Palace's fans, brainwashed by Akinbiyi's Leicester image, did not give him much of a chance to show them it was justified. Akinbiyi, not helped at Palace by his injury problems either, attracted negative vibes even when Steve Kember, Francis's successor as manager, froze him out of the first-team picture and put him up for sale. Reports indicated that, though other clubs were interested in him, they were put off by

Akinbiyi's unwillingness to accept a drop – or at least a major one – in the salary Palace were paying him. The inference to be drawn from all this was that Akinbiyi was putting money before professional

getting stick from the media, but when you are on the pitch as a professional footballer and can hear supporters from both sides laughing at you – that's what was happening to him. He is a smashing fellow. He was very well liked by the other Palace players and he worked tremendously hard, yet our own supporters were laughing at everything he attempted to do, ridiculing him. I have always said to my players that I will back them as long as they give me a hundred per cent. That's what the supporters expect as well, so I found it rather strange that Ade, who could not be faulted in his general effort at all, was subjected to that sort of stick. It's cruel.'

Francis can easily understand why Leicester signed him. 'He is very pacey and he is constantly looking to get in behind defenders,' he explained. 'He's a good player to have in any team because he turns opponents and stretches defences. The downside is that he is not a particularly clinical finisher. If you had come to watch some of his training sessions at Palace, you probably would have thought, "How has this player scored the goals that he has?" He's not what I would call a clean striker of the ball; he can often be a very scruffy striker of the ball. But I think this is offset by his ability to get into scoring positions.' Echoing the point that Paul Sturrock made about Marino Keith, Francis continued, 'It is essential for strikers to be able to anticipate where the ball is going to go. Not all of them do. Occasionally, when I'm watching what a striker does when the ball comes across the box or is played through, I'm thinking, "Why hasn't he reacted to that?" Usually the reason is that he hasn't a good enough understanding of the game; he hasn't been able to anticipate the situation. He just does not see it. It is different with Akinbiyi – that's what he's really good at. OK, he might miss more chances than other strikers, but then this is possibly because he gets into the positions to miss more often than them.'

Francis's assertion that Akinbiyi did not deserve to be treated so harshly by the Leicester and Crystal Palace fans is quickly underlined when you meet him. He seems smaller than he looks on the field, and is surprisingly reserved and quietly spoken. Initially he comes across almost as shy, but then as the publicity he has been given has caused him to think twice about granting media interview requests it's tempting to put that down to caution.

How else has the criticism affected him?

'I'm a Christian, which I think helps a lot,' Akinbiyi told me, 'and I have had a lot of support from my family and friends. I have my own little world, and the people in it are the only ones who really matter to me. I don't go any further than that. The other thing that has kept me going is that I love football. I came from nowhere to be a professional footballer; in fact, for some time when I was a boy I wasn't that keen on playing football. I was very much into athletics at school and, if anything, I wanted to be an athlete. Then, all of a sudden, my teacher sort of bullied me into playing football and it all mushroomed from there. So every time I'm on a downer, I think, "Look how far you have come."'

I tell him about Francis's comments concerning his anticipation.

'There are a lot of things to it,' he said. 'Some of it is gambling.

If a centre-half looks like he's going to get the ball, you have to think that he's going to miss it. That's what I was taught as a youngster – you have to gamble. As a kid, you tend to run about just for the sake

created by that left foot of his. But generally, there is a frustrating side to it in that a lot of the runs you make go unnoticed by the crowd. You can spend the whole ninety minutes running around, getting into positions to receive the ball, but it's usually only when you score that they notice.'

And also when you miss?

'That's right. One problem for me [with finishing] is that because I'm naturally quick I want to do everything quick. I admit that sometimes I rush things unnecessarily. The manager says to me, "When you get there [into a scoring situation], that's when you need to relax and shut out everything." But occasionally it's difficult for someone like me to get into that state, especially in one-against-one situations where you have so much time. Then you fail to score, and the crowd are thinking, "He gets tons of money and he has missed an opportunity like that," as if it was something you meant to do. All that has happened is that it has not gone right for you, which happens to everybody in every walk of life.

'When you aren't scoring, it's amazing the little faults that creep into your game without you being conscious of them. You might think you're doing the same things you did when you were scoring, but that's not always the case. I keep a lot of videos and DVDs of my matches, and as I was watching one the other day I saw something which surprised me a bit. When the ball was played up to me, and I laid it off, I noticed that I had had more time to turn with the ball than I had thought. I got kidded by the defender, who had touched me on the back as the ball was being played to me to make me think that I wasn't going to be able to turn with the ball, and then dropped back five yards. I hadn't been aware of that at the time.'

Now, he can also see why he didn't do better at Leicester. Referring to his lack of experience of playing in high-pressure matches in front of big crowds, he said, 'I probably didn't spend long enough at Wolves. It was only ten months, but if I could turn back the clock I would have wanted it to be two or three years. It's a big club, and staying there would have helped me develop more. But I cannot really have any excuses for what happened to me at Leicester. I blame myself because I took too much for granted and relied too much on people pushing me. The standard in the Premiership is so much higher than it is in the Nationwide, and you cannot expect to adjust just like that. I worked exceptionally hard at Gillingham and Bristol City: I did a lot of extra training at both clubs, and also at Wolves. But when I got to Leicester I found that there was no one to do extra training with. I should have said, "OK, you will have to take the initiative and do it yourself." But for some reason – maybe because I was in the Premiership and felt that I had arrived – I did not have the motivation. That's the habit I got into. Peter Taylor did eventually try and rectify this, but by that time I think I had lost it.

'Generally, the crowd at Leicester didn't bother me that much. Even the article in the *Sun* didn't really upset me. The first I knew about it was when my brother telephoned me that morning and said, "Don't get the *Sun*." Well, I did, and I had a right giggle over it. It appeared the day before the match against Sunderland, when I scored my first league goal of the season [to give Leicester a 1–0 win]. They were saying, "The worst striker in England scored." You had to see the funny side of it.

me. I challenged him about it the next day. "You were shouting abuse at me," I said. "Yeah," he said, "but I'd had too much to drink." Which was no excuse as far as I was concerned. From that day onwards I took extra care in deciding who my friends were. It made me better, stronger.'

But he still needed his colleagues to show faith in him. 'The crowd might have been on my back at Leicester, but the good thing for me was that all the boys [the other Leicester players] stuck by me. All players give each other stick in training and the dressing room, but when I was going through my worst periods, they were like my family.' And he certainly needed the public backing he was given by Peter Taylor and Trevor Francis. 'The support of the manager is the main thing,' Akinbiyi said. 'When you are going through a bad time, it's great to have a manager who will stand up for you and say, "I know this boy, I know what he can do." No matter how mentally strong they are, I think all strikers would agree that this is important to them.'

No manager has shown as much faith in Akinbiyi as Stoke City's Tony Pulis, who was also the manager who signed him for Gillingham and Bristol City. Such is the rapport they have established it seems unlikely that Akinbiyi would have been able to adopt a laid-back attitude to improving his game at Leicester had Pulis been there. As Akinbiyi said, 'He is a manager who is in your face. He even likes to know what you eat, what you do at home, things like that. It can be irritating, but I don't mind because he wants you to do well.' Pulis nodded in agreement. 'You have to keep on at him and push him,' he said. 'He's a lad who needs attention and I probably spend more time talking to him than I do with a lot of the other players. Some players need a little bit of tender care more than others – we are all different, aren't we? – and Ade is probably one of them. But it's not all about kisses and cuddles. He does react to people who are straight and honest with him, so the occasional kick up the backside, at the right time, is OK with him as well.

'If there is one thing that I have kept on at him about, it's the importance of him concentrating on his strengths. Some managers and coaches have a strange attitude to goalscorers as far as I'm concerned: they're inclined to talk to them more about what they can't do than what they can do. Ade is not a ball-player. His greatest attributes are his pace, power and anticipation, so getting the best out of him is all about simplifying things for him and getting him to get right up on to the shoulders of opposing defenders and find scoring positions. I get annoyed with him sometimes when he moves deep and plays in front of defenders. When we were at Gillingham, it prompted me to give him the biggest rollicking he has ever had from me. In the first half he was pussyfooting around like you would not believe. I really tore into him at half-time, so much so that his neck puffed up and his eyes were glaring at me as if he was about to throttle me. In the second half he scored two fantastic goals. "I meant what I said," I told him. "You are not a pussyfooting player, you are a dynamic player, and you will only score goals by exploiting that." Maybe this aspect of his game was lost at Leicester. Most Premiership players are skilful on the ball, and maybe Ade felt that he had to be the same as them. I don't know. All we have really done here is to encourage him to concentrate on his strengths and show him that we value him.'

Pulis initially signed Akinbiyi on loan at the end of March 2003, in the First Division. He scored his

up at Brighton's expense, whereas a victory at Grimsby would have meant the reverse.

Stoke seemed to have the tougher task because although Reading had already clinched promotion they had one of the best defensive records in the country and their manager, Alan Pardew, was a close friend of his Brighton counterpart, Steve Coppell. Though he wasn't aware of it, Akinbiyi took a leaf from the psychological 'creative visualisation' book on his car journey to the Stoke ground. He recalled, 'As I was driving through Stoke, I put the radio on. It's something I don't usually do before a game, but I was so excited about this match. It was amazing because I immediately heard a guy talking about the match and saying something like, "Wouldn't it be a great boost for Akinbiyi if he were to score the winning goal?" It gave me a good feeling, and I kept visualising it.'

As it happened, a winning goal for Stoke didn't matter because Brighton were beaten 2–1. But the Stoke fans could not have known that when, after 55 minutes' play, Akinbiyi gleefully dispatched a Lewis Neal cross into the net with a header.

Zero to hero? Akinbiyi, who was signed by Stoke permanently

that summer, hardly had a scoring record in the Henry category in the 2003/04 season (ten goals in 23 league matches). However, in view of that goal against Reading, few Stoke fans were quibbling with the fact that the number 10 jersey – famous in other countries as the one donned by a team's star player – had been allocated to him. One Stoke supporter even initiated a website in honour of Akinbiyi. His introductory message reads: 'As an avid Stoke supporter, I can safely say that my favourite player is Ade Akinbiyi. This is a site to show the world that Ade Akinbiyi is no longer a joke and all those negative connotations he has carried with him are well and truly in the past. He has quickly become a cult hero among Stoke supporters and this site is a sign of our appreciation of a player I can well and truly call a Stoke City hero. For all those Leicester and Crystal Palace fans reading this, you must have had bad managers because Ade is certainly The Man here at Stoke.'

CHAPTER FIVE
LORDS OF THE MANOR

STEVE ARCHIBALL

Arsenal manager Arsène Wenger has mixed feelings about the age-old view that goalscorers need to be selfish and greedy. To Wenger, the best strikers play for their teams, not themselves. Despite the importance of their jobs, they have no problem with helping colleagues in other departments do theirs; and when they get a scoring chance, they are quite happy to set up someone else for a goal if he happens to be in a better position. As Wenger said, this point is perfectly illustrated by Arsenal's Thierry Henry.

In helping his defence, Henry is not quite in the same class as Ian Rush, whose willingness to do a lot of running off the ball up front just to make it difficult for opposing defenders to start attacking moves led to the view that he was Liverpool's best defender, let alone goalscorer. But Henry still does his bit at Arsenal. He is no strolling player. In addition to his high number of goals, he also happens to have one of the best Premiership records for goal-assists.

After Henry's performance in setting up the Robert Pires and Freddie Ljungberg goals that gave Arsenal their 2–0 European Champions League win over Lokomotiv Moscow in December

2003, putting the Gunners through to the last sixteen of the competition, Wenger said, 'Lokomotiv were organised to give him no room at all, yet he found the space to make others score. That is an area where he has improved a lot. Football suffers from selfishness in front of goal. For me the complete player is the player who gives the ball when it has to be given in the final third. People are too forgiving of players who want to score goals to the point where it is an obsession. Those players try to score from all manner of angles and, because of their persistence, they finally get one. But they have killed ten chances on the way. Those players will say, "The team lost 2–1, but at least I scored." However, I do not think that is something to be proud of. I have as much respect for the player who plays the final ball as I have for the goalscorer.'

But, as Wenger added, Henry is arguably the most gifted all-round forward in the world. The terms of reference for most other strikers have to be narrower.

The extent to which they should be expected to concentrate on their basic responsibility has always been something of a grey area. Graeme Sharp recalled, 'When Howard Kendall [his manager at Everton] pointed out to me that I hadn't been scoring, I would say, "But my general play is OK – I'm making chances for other players." But his reaction was, "Yeah, your general play is good, but at the end of the day people judge you on your scoring record." I must admit that there were times when I allowed all the compliments about my play as a target man to go to my head. I started believing my own publicity and probably did not get into scoring positions as much as I could and should have done. But unselfishness was looked upon as one of my strengths.'

To varying degrees, all strikers argue that it is important for them to remain mentally and physically sharp to be able to apply the finishing touches to attacking moves and that this cannot be achieved if they are devoting too much energy to other aspects of the game. But with teams being forced to become more fluid tactically, in terms of outfield players interchanging positions and being able to do different jobs, and the game as a whole becoming so geared to

ment of strikers only needing to

than

were always immaculate. In the last minute

most of the other players were tired, he was as fresh as a daisy. He scored a lot of goals towards the end of games, but the days when strikers could isolate themselves from the other aspects of the game have gone.'

Those who have been perceived as having done so include Jimmy Greaves, the greatest of all scorers in top-flight football in England since the war. But Greaves's image as just a brilliant finisher – a so-called 'goal-poacher' who was generally hardly seen in the build-up – hardly does him justice. He created the opportunities for a number of his goals virtually on his own, occasionally with mazy dribbles through a defence from the halfway line. He scored one such goal on his Chelsea debut at Tottenham, at the age of seventeen. In the famous photograph of it, taken from behind the Tottenham goal, was best summed up by the expression of bewilderment on the face of one of the Tottenham defenders who had been left on their backsides in their attempts to stop him taking the ball past them. The experience of seeing that goal is one of my most cherished football memories as a schoolboy. Another personal favourite was a similarly individualistic Greaves goal for Spurs against Leicester

City, when he just managed to stop a long clearance from the Spurs keeper, Pat Jennings, from going out of play on the right touchline, then beat three Leicester defenders and finally the Leicester keeper, Peter Shilton, before slipping the ball into an empty net.

Greaves, though, did personify the unwillingness of outstanding scorers to do a lot of running off the ball in general play – a characteristic that ultimately rebounded against him in the 1966 World Cup finals. The fact that a scoring genius such as Greaves, having lost his England place for the quarter-final against Argentina through injury, wasn't able to get back into the side at the expense of his replacement Geoff Hurst or Roger Hunt provided as good an example as any of the demand for strikers to broaden their contribution to teams. Sir Alf Ramsey's belief that Hurst and Hunt would be better suited to his 4–4–2 system was proved right by England's 4–2 win and, of course, Hurst's achievement in becoming the first player ever to score a World Cup final hat-trick. Even so, his decision to leave Greaves out was one he never fully lived down. Even now it tends to be viewed among Greaves's admirers as some kind of insult against the little maestro and the extraordinary scoring standards he represented.

Of all the top-class strikers of the modern era who could be described as singing from a different hymn sheet to that of their colleagues, Gerd Müller, the Bayern Munich and West Germany star of the 1970s, must be at or close to the top of the list. 'Der Bomber', as he was called, did not need to do much more than apply the finishing touch to his team-mates' work, mainly because the other nine outfield players had more than enough ability to dominate the opposition. And that was just as well, because Müller, who did not cut the most impressive of athletic figures with his short, stocky build, and whose basic ball skills were comparatively limited, would almost certainly have been a liability to them had he been asked to do more.

Looking nothing like a great footballer was a cross Müller had to bear from the very start of his career at the top. Legend has it that when he moved to Bayern in 1963, their coach, 'Tshik' Cajkovski, told the club president, 'I'm not putting this bear among our

chances inside the penalty box,

over England in the World Cup quarter

When England centre-half Brian Labone attempted to reach a ball that had been headed back across his goal, Müller, sensing that he was going to miss it, resisted the temptation to challenge him in favour of getting into the space where he felt the ball might drop. Even then he didn't have the easiest of shots because the ball wasn't directly in front of him. However, he was able to twist his thick-set body quickly enough to get a shot on target, and past the England keeper, Peter Bonetti.

Another goal for which he is well remembered was his last at international level, when that uncanny knack of finding space in the box was followed by the quick turn and the close-range shot that brought West Germany their 2–1 win over Holland in the 1974 World Cup final.

During a career spanning fifteen years, his predatory instincts, which he always struggled to articulate, resulted in his scoring 365 goals in 427 matches for Bayern. For West Germany, it was 68 goals in 62 matches, a record that has never been surpassed. His goals-to-game ratio was even better than that of Pele, the scorer of 77 goals in 92 matches for Brazil, and Ferenc Puskas, who got 83 in 84 games for Hungary. More recently, the outstanding scorer in international football has been Gabriel Batistuta, who scored 56 goals in 78 matches for Argentina.

Batistuta and Müller could hardly be more different. If Müller was at the bottom end of the overall-contribution scale, Batistuta, with his tremendous pace, stamina and ball-playing ability, has been at the other. Many managers hold up the Argentinian as the perfect role model for their strikers. Craig Brown says that whenever he hears strikers 'moaning' that the general work demanded of them is detracting from their scoring potential, he tells them, 'Look at Batistuta.'

Brown's insistence that no striker can be a law unto himself also comes across in his negative attitude to such men getting bonuses for scoring. It is not unheard of for the contracts of strikers to include clauses relating to extra payments linked to their scoring records. This was the case with some of Preston's strikers when Brown became manager of the club in April 2002, but Brown has gradually put an end to it. 'It's dangerous,' he said, arguing that though all strikers need to be single-minded about scoring, club bonuses for doing so would lead to the situation Wenger highlighted when discussing strikers being too greedy to score for the good of their teams, and could easily have an adverse effect on team unity.

It is a question of balance, of course, but for the strikers who have the ability to get the most goals and bring their teams the most victories, the right balance is never easy to achieve. While taking into account the ways in which the game has changed, some believe that a number of today's strikers are not single-minded enough about scoring and tend to be too subservient in their relationships with their colleagues. Even Thierry Henry, for all his brilliance, can invoke mixed feelings about his sense of priorities. Gary Pallister, admitted that he has never been able to get his brain around the sight of Henry taking corners. 'I see him doing it week in, week out and I cannot understand it,' he said. 'How can you, as a scorer, be out there taking corners when there might be a great scoring chance to be had in the middle? If you were to ask somebody like Alan Shearer to do that he'll tell you to get lost.'

be a scorer at the start of his career, even after ___ had signed him as an apprentice, had decided he was too small and weak physically to make it as a striker and switched him to right-back. 'It was difficult for me to accept,' he said. 'As a kid, I was scoring sixty to seventy goals a season, and I found the right-back role, just defending and giving the ball to the attacking players, quite boring. When I saw the lads up front scoring, I thought, "I want to be doing that." I wanted the limelight.' When Southampton released him, Phillips, at the age of eighteen, drifted into non-league football with the Hertfordshire club Baldock Town, where he was moved back to the striker role and where the experience of playing in a highly physical league, with and against players considerably older and more aggressive than himself, had a 'toughening-up' effect.

The next stage of his development came at Watford, through the coaching and encouragement of their manager, Glenn Roeder. Then, in the summer of 1997, it was on to Sunderland (in the Nationwide League First Division) and a striking partnership with Niall Quinn that was to make him the most prolific scorer in the game. It was the Little and Large show, the 6ft 4in Quinn doing most of the spadework, driving himself towards the long balls or crosses, and the 5ft 5in Phillips – quick, razor sharp and a superb striker of the ball – feeding off him. Phillips recalled, 'I have lost count of the number of goals I scored by latching on to Niall's headed flick-ons. A lot of strikers are happy just to get their heads to a high ball, but Niall was able to sort of hang in mid-air and direct the ball exactly where he wanted to. His headers to me were passes.'

In those days, Phillips was little more than a finisher. But Sunderland were not complaining. In his first season, Phillips broke Brian Clough's post-war scoring record for the club with 35, which included scoring in nine successive home matches – another record. The next season, the 1998/99 campaign, he scored 25, despite being out of action for four months through injury, to help steer Sunderland to promotion. In his first season in the Premiership he was the top league scorer with 35, a total that was also good enough to bring him the distinction of becoming the first Englishman to win the European Golden Boot award.

Since then, though, Phillips has not come anywhere near matching that achievement. In the league, his goal total dropped to fourteen in 2000/01, eleven in 2001/02 and six in 2002/03 – his last Sunderland season, when the team's misery over being relegated was compounded by their losing every one of their last fifteen league matches. 'I was coming off the pitch without having had one chance,' Phillips recalled. 'The team had changed, and I didn't want to be there to be honest, which didn't help.' Perhaps the major problem for him was the decline of Quinn. Troubled by a back problem, the veteran had finally been forced to retire in November 2002 at the age of 36. However, the dearth of goals also stemmed from Phillips's desire to become a better all-round player.

He put it this way: 'It was towards the end of my Sunderland career that I started dropping deeper and got more involved in matches. When I look back on it now, part of me says that perhaps I should not have done that. But although my first three seasons at Sunderland had been fantastic for me, goal-wise, there were many times when I walked off the pitch at the end not completely happy with my game. Even if I had scored two or three goals, I wasn't totally content. I suppose I became spoilt. Goals were no longer

runs in behind [into the space]

but as I had previously been making those runs for some time without getting the ball, I'd thought, "Why should I keep doing this?" As I was developing other aspects of my game, it was difficult to change.'

Scoring still means a lot to him, if only because of his determination to show that his partnership with Quinn was helpful but not essential to him. As he said to me shortly after his transfer to Southampton during 2003, 'Everyone associates me with Niall. It makes me hungry to show that I can get along without him.' Even so, it was only after Christmas that he truly got back into the scoring habit, and his final league total for the Saints for 2003/04 was twelve.

For all his good work in other aspects of the game, Phillips's recent scoring record will have been viewed with some disdain by a striker as focused as Brian Clough was. Not for nothing did Clough achieve the best post-war goal ratio of any striker in English football, albeit mainly in the old Second Division. His record for Middlesbrough and Sunderland, from 1953 to 1961, was 267 goals in 296 games. At Middlesbrough, his manager, Bob Dennison, once told Clough about a complaint he had received about him from another member of the team. Dennison explained, 'The player says that every time he has the ball close to goal, you shout, "Give it to me," even when he has a good chance of a shot. Why do you do that?'

Clough just shrugged. 'Because I am better at it than he is,' he replied.

'I was king of the castle, king of the castle,' he has said. 'I used to stick it through their bloody legs and say, "Now pick that out."'

Among those whom Clough will surely have recognised as kindred spirits were Malcolm Macdonald and Steve Archibald. They were poles apart as people: Macdonald was gregarious and uninhibited, very much the public showman, while Archibald came across as introverted and uncommunicative. But both men, as knowledgeable and articulate on the art of scoring as any ex-strikers one could find, had similar scoring mentalities. Neither was a shrinking violet in recognising that consistently putting the ball in the net had to be their main priority, or, equally importantly, in pushing for set-ups conducive to their chances of doing this. 'Squeezing the lemon' is how Archibald described it. 'You could say I was a tad demanding,' he said. 'I would think that any striker worth his salt has to be.' It seems difficult to dispute that the single-mindedness with which Archibald and Macdonald pursued this concept, combined with the depth of their thinking about their jobs, was one of the main reasons for their excellent scoring records and, in turn, the success of their teams.

Of all the football figures I have met, Archibald, now living in Spain where he is a football transfer market 'broker' and is also involved in the fields of property acquisition and business development, has struck me as being the closest equivalent to the former England goalkeeping legend Peter Shilton. It was not enough for Shilton to be widely recognised as the number one keeper in the world just through his dedication to training, his off-the-field professional habits and his performances; it was also important to him to look the part, to portray the image one might expect of someone in that lofty position, through the house he lived in, his car and clothes, and the money his clubs paid him. In making managers ... of the importance of having a keeper with his ability, Shilton

got too close to me. I want ...

with can see you, get to know you, too much. It just isn't me.'

No player can have had a stronger personality than Shilton. This certainly came in handy in his attempts to persuade the players immediately in front of him that instead of him adapting his approach to the game to suit theirs, it had to be the other way around. He once recalled an England training session during which manager Ron Greenwood organised an exercise involving himself and three other players to give the latter 'third man running' and shooting practice. The three men positioned themselves just outside the penalty area and the object of the exercise was for one player to pass to another, then run forward to receive the final pass from the third player inside the box and have a shot. 'Shots were coming in from between the penalty spot and the edge of the box,' said Shilton, 'and as I was only two or three yards off my line I was having to react to them. I thought, "This isn't right – you're allowing them to dictate to you." So what I did was move further off my line, before the final pass was made, so I was now dictating to them. It could be argued that I ruined the session for the other players, but then I see no reason to apologise for doing my job as a goalkeeper.'

Archibald, seemingly as dogged about the importance of goalscorers to a team as Shilton was about that of goalkeepers, can appreciate where he was coming from. When I first raised the subject of Shilton's desire to build up his image with Archibald some years ago, at a time when his career as a player was drawing to a close at Hibernian, he said, 'I hope you will be careful how you write this – I would hate to give people the wrong impression of me – but I have been similar. While I would never openly describe myself as a star, I do try and live the part in some ways. I was the same even in my early days. Some people might think it's being flash, but it isn't. I honestly feel it had a beneficial psychological effect on me as a player.'

More recently, when we touched on the subject again in an interview for this book, he added, 'When I joined Tottenham [from Aberdeen], I remember the club secretary Peter Day telling me, "The biggest adjustment you will have to make here will not be on the football side, it will be on the financial side. You will have a problem knowing what to do with the extra money you will be earning." It was a good point because I was only a young lad. But earning a lot more money did not affect my hunger for success – it was the opposite. When you come down [to England] as an established striker, you have to act like one. The whole package [the ability and the image] has to be right. The extra money enabled me to maintain my lifestyle and that, among a number of other factors, helped me keep my edge.'

One man at Tottenham who found Archibald's mentality particularly enlightening was John Syer, the club's sports psychologist. 'Steve was wonderful to work with,' Syer said. 'He had an amazing mind.' In one 'creative visualisation' session, Archibald summed up his attitude to scoring by telling Syer that when he had a scoring opportunity he felt like 'a hungry bear suddenly let out of a

cage'. Equally telling was his response to Syer's question about what
he felt like when he had scored. 'I am the Lord of the Manor,'
Archibald told him.

Archibald smiles over the memory. 'He told you about that, did
he? All players are important to a team, obviously, but I think that

Obviously, the

can depend a great deal on the nature of your club. For example,
Aberdeen are a small, tightly knit club, which was reflected by the
attitudes and mentalities of the players I worked with there. It was
like being in a close family. It was different at clubs like Tottenham
and Barcelona. Having so-called 'stars' – players with egos, if you
want to put it that way – was part of their culture. When you go
home, you are a different person, but when you have that "main
man" image you have to take it with you into the dressing room and
on to the field, in both training and matches. You are The Man, and
everybody expects you to be The Man. You have to deliver.'

Lord of the Manor? Archibald, an exceptionally ambitious
person, will have had no qualms about taking on that guise (and all
the pressure that goes with it) right from the very start of his career
in Scotland, when he combined an apprenticeship as a Rolls-Royce
motor mechanic with playing as a part-time professional for Clyde.
Craig Brown was Clyde's manager then, and Archibald was able to
develop his noted overall ability there by filling every position for
the club, including that of goalkeeper. Such was his ability to read
the game that, in those days, he felt his best position was that of

sweeper. It was at Aberdeen, where he worked under Billy McNeill and then Alex Ferguson and progressed from midfield to a front-line role, that the notion of becoming one of Britain's most respected post-war scorers started to take root. As Ferguson, a former centre-forward, was cast in the same aggressive mould as Archibald, it wasn't unusual for the two men to be in conflict. In fact, they had so many arguments in Fergie's Pittodrie office that the manager named the chair his striker sat in 'Archibald's Chair'. It says much about Ferguson's respect for Archibald, however, that the Old Trafford supremo has since gone on record describing him as one of his all-time favourite players.

The more Archibald progressed up the soccer ladder, the more strong-willed and assertive he seemed to become. 'It was due to the experience I had gained, the knowledge that what I had been doing had worked,' he explained. One wonders what might have happened to him had this not been the case at Barcelona. He was virtually unknown in Spain when Terry Venables brought him to the club. In those days, clubs in that country were allowed to sign only two foreign players, and Archibald's attempts to gain credibility among his highly skilled fellow players and the ultra-critical Nou Camp fans were not helped by the fact that the star he effectively replaced was Diego Maradona. 'You have to give them [team mates] the confidence to think they can work with you,' Archibald said. 'Quite apart from showing them that you are on the same wavelength in technical ability, it's also a question of proving that you have the necessary mental strength.' In that respect, Archibald 'threw down the gauntlet' on his very first day of training at the club. Having been given Maradona's old locker, he promptly asked a club official to replace the Argentinian's name on it with his.

Those who felt that Archibald was 'difficult' might well argue that Tottenham's captain when he joined the club, Steve Perryman, had a lot to answer for. According to Archibald, it was Perryman who did the most to cause him to look upon himself as a 'natural' goalscorer, as opposed to a forward. He explained, 'Soon after I joined Spurs, Steve came up to me and said, "I'm convinced that we are going to be successful now we have signed a natural goalscorer

point for me.'

A turning point that inevitably led Archibald to become more sensitive than ever about strikers getting the right service. For example, during our conversation, I struck a chord with him by mentioning the advice Southampton's James Beattie had been given once by his then club manager Gordon Strachan. In addition to encouraging Beattie to reprimand any team-mate who had not given him the type of pass or cross he needed to score, Strachan told him, 'Don't wait until half-time or after the game to do it. Do it at the time.' This was not something Archibald needed to be told, and when he did deem it necessary to express his displeasure with a colleague over not getting the ball at the right time or in the right way, he admitted that he did not believe in diplomacy. 'You have to adopt an aggressive or angry manner in these situations – that's what I would tell any striker. A lot of times, this really is the most effective way of getting the message across.'

Archibald recognises that he was fortunate to operate with men as skilful on the ball as Strachan (at Aberdeen), Ossie Ardiles and Glenn Hoddle (Tottenham) and Bernt Schuster (Barcelona). Nonetheless, even with these figures, Archibald says that he occasionally felt the need to impose himself. 'Sometimes, the ability that these sort of players have can create problems for a front man because when they play the ball to you they often want it back; they can play a ball to you in a way in which they are basically only lending it to you. I feel that a number of strikers in that situation do not truly understand what is happening and how it might be detracting from their potential as scorers. When they're repeatedly being used as a "wall" they will get a certain amount of satisfaction out of not losing possession etc. But it seems to me that being forced into this role can become so much of a habit that, while they might have a vague feeling that something isn't quite right, they struggle to really pinpoint the problem.

'All strikers like that should watch Ronaldo, especially when he is playing with David Beckham [for Real Madrid]. If you watch his matches, you will notice that he doesn't come deep to link the play. He realises that, because of his past injury problems, he can no longer cope with opponents hacking at his legs from behind, so when Beckham is on the ball you will see him right on the shoulder of the defender, looking for a pass into the space behind him. He will dictate where he wants the ball to go just through his body language and his positioning. Others have to do it differently, and I'm all in favour of it. When it comes to getting the right service, you have to demand certain things and you cannot be afraid to have showdowns with people.'

For Archibald, this also applied to the question of his involvement in his teams' defensive work. Once described by his highly respected former Hibernian manager Alex Miller as the best attacking 'technician' he had ever worked with, Archibald was no slouch in broadening his outlook and helping his teams in other aspects of the game. He was one of the most complete strikers of his generation and, as indicated by the versatility he showed at Clyde, did not look out of place in most areas of the field. At the same time, he was always conscious of the need to know where to draw the line.

'I understood that I couldn't concentrate just on scoring,' he said. 'If a manager told me to drop back to the halfway line when we lost the ball, or shuttle across to stop the full-back breaking forward

relationship between Burkinshaw and Archibald, two of the proudest and most stubborn figures one could find in the game, was always difficult. The most famous explosion point arose from an incident in a match against Coventry during the 1983/84 season when Archibald signalled to the bench that he had sustained an injury and needed to be substituted. Burkinshaw, who felt that Archibald had made too much of the injury, was quoted in the media accusing him of 'cheating', which prompted Archibald to refuse to talk to him. The situation continued even after the manager had made a private apology to him, because of Archibald's insistence that it had to be a public one. This was never forthcoming, but it was typical of Archibald that he scored his highest number of goals for Spurs that season (33) and helped them win the Uefa Cup.

Another row between Burkinshaw and Archibald took place during a training match because of Burkinshaw's persistent attempts to instruct the striker to operate as a defensive marker when Spurs were facing free-kicks and corners. 'I have never been in such a confrontational situation in my life,' Archibald recalled. 'Whenever we conceded a free-kick or corner I had to come back to mark someone, while Crooksey [Garth Crooks, his striking partner] was left up the field. I didn't mind that, but after doing it time after time I thought Crooksey should share the job. That's what all strikers do. Burkinshaw called me back again when we had to face another corner, and as I was walking towards him I said, "Hang on a minute, why can't Crooksey come back this time?" Burkinshaw said, "No, you come back. You are better marking at corners than he is." True, I was taller than him, but I felt he could jump as high as I could; I couldn't see how having him challenging for a ball in the air instead of me was going to cause a problem. Burkinshaw, though, would not have any of it, so I said, "No, I'm not going to do it," and walked back to the middle of the field. The atmosphere was unbelievable. But finally, Crooksey said, "I'll go back," and that was it.'

Does Archibald have any regrets about digging his heels in so firmly?

'Well, it was unfortunate that it came to that, but I couldn't have backed down because had I done so, what would the other players have been thinking about me? You have to take into account the numerous little psychological factors involved in the game. Had I backed down, they would have taken the view that I had bottled it. This would surely have had an adverse effect on what I was asking of them on the Saturday.'

Malcolm Macdonald could easily have anticipated how Burkinshaw's football philosophy would affect his relationship with Archibald because Supermac also had big rows with the manager, for the same reason, when the pair were at Newcastle United. 'Keith [then Newcastle's coach] was forever on to me about helping out the defence,' Macdonald has told me. 'He wanted me to chase back and harass opponents when we lost the ball, things like that. But I couldn't see the point. As a striker, I relied on sudden, explosive bursts and felt I would quickly get knackered if I couldn't take the

A left-footed snap-shot from the master fin

Diego Maradona weaves another magic spell and cuts through the English back line once more during that epic match in the 1986 World Cup quarter-finals

Alan Shearer has been English football's mo...

...e past decade

Brazilian Ronaldo's electrifying speed and upper body strength are guaranteed to cause problems for even the tightest of defensive formations

A trademark Michael Owen finish, tucked away beyond the keeper's reach

Adrian Dennis/AFP/Getty Images

For such a short man, Paul Scholes' aerial ability is legendary. His goal-scoring record goes to prove what can be achieved from a world-class midfield operator

Thierry Henry's wonderful athletici
to become the most potent atta

bis club –
'ship

Ruud van Nistelrooy's all-round scoring prowess and insatiable appetite for goals have catapulted him into the very top bracket of world-class poachers

necessary recovery time. We used to have the most incredible rows over this.'

At Arsenal, Macdonald also crossed swords with coach Don Howe, especially during a training session during which he was called upon to go into wide positions to create scoring space for a team-mate bursting through from deep positions. Macdonald recalled 'I told Don, "Why do you want me out here, when I can

wouldn't let it go

Macdonald suggested that the belligerence with which he rejected appeals to address himself to other aspects of the game was something of a defence mechanism. Referring to the shortage of strings to his bow outside his scoring ability, he said, 'I couldn't "play". Coaches found me difficult to handle because I always had this protective barrier up. "Don't ask me to do that, I don't want to do it," I would say. What I was really saying was that I couldn't do it because I wasn't good enough.' This, he added, helps explain his apparent scoring bravado. 'I was a great believer in publicly projecting my strengths. In media interviews before a match, I would be quite happy to be quoted as saying that I would score. People used to say, "You bighead – I don't know how you have the front to do it." But I knew what I was doing. You know, while the attitude of coaches like Burkinshaw and Howe was that I should try to improve my weak points, mine was, "Blow your weaknesses – build up your strengths to the point where they could hide a million bloody weaknesses."'

As a consequence, Macdonald was a striker for whom the words 'selfish' and 'greedy' could have been invented. This, for example, is what he once told me about his attitude to shooting: 'I shot from anywhere and everywhere. Players used to throw their arms up and say, "I don't believe it. What are you doing?" I'd say sorry, but I wasn't sorry at all. I knew what I was doing. If you don't buy a ticket, you can't win the Lottery, can you? Also, I had to find out whether I could score from certain positions. At Luton, I even used to shoot from corners – honestly I did. I'd take them from the right, with my left foot, and if I saw the keeper slightly off his line I'd try to curl the ball into the net. Usually the ball would sail over the bar or go straight over to the other side of the field for a throw-in. The other players would say to Jimmy Andrews [Luton's coach], "Get him off corners, Jimmy. He's useless." They didn't appreciate I was trying to score from them. They just thought I was a bad corner-taker. The more goals I scored, the more single-minded – all right, arrogant – I became. I must have been unbearable to live with at times.'

This was also reflected by his reaction to the principle of strikers 'hunting' in pairs. 'The way I looked at it was that strikers play in pairs; they do not hunt in pairs. When it came to strikers sharing the scoring responsibility, I think I was probably too selfish to hunt with anybody.' His most democratic partnership was the one with Frank Stapleton at Arsenal in the late 1970s, but at the start of it, when Stapleton was eighteen and Macdonald 26, Supermac recalled, 'I dominated him. Some of the best partnerships are those in which one striker does all or most of the spadework and the other puts the ball in the net. In those days, however, I took advantage of my seniority by making him run about all over the place. All I did was look to get on the end of the final ball and stick it into the net. I remember him saying to me, "Why is it that I keep making all your goals and you never make me any?" I told him that I had been expected to do what he did when I was his age. As it happened, the big difference between Frank and myself was that I didn't do it, but of course I didn't tell Frank that.'

Of the clubs Macdonald played for, Newcastle United seemed ~ ~h~ most appropriate home for him. Newcastle have a ~l~corers, especially top-scoring ~ f^+~d by

his career there Newcastle and England centre-forward c~ was then working in the city as a football journalist. Macdonald fondest memory of the late Milburn concerns the way in which the old star put his mind at rest over what was expected of him at a club of Newcastle's stature. Macdonald, having never been in the top flight before, asked, 'What do I need to do to win over the fans?' Milburn replied, simply, 'Just score goals. Do that, and the fans will love you.'

Today, another centre-forward in the traditional British mould has established a similar love affair with the Geordie public. He can seem to get quite tetchy when you raise the subject of Supermac with him – the result of his sensitivity over one or two of Macdonald's criticisms of his performances in the media, and perhaps Macdonald's apparent brashness. When I interviewed him, and suggested that one of his comments about scoring ('You must never be afraid to miss') was virtually a carbon copy of what Macdonald had once written in a book, he muttered, 'I certainly didn't get it from him.' However, Macdonald would be the first to concede that

CHAPTER SIX
STRENGTH IN ADVERSITY

The footballers w... those who keep reminding us of the ... gets tough, the tough get going'. Strength in adversity is a maj... success factor in all football-playing countries, but it has long been associated mainly with British teams, and more specifically with British players; and it is often the men at the front end of those teams who have done the most to provide the lead. These strikers have usually been tall, powerfully built centre-forwards with styles of play that have mirrored the renowned physical power and competitiveness of British football. Quite apart from their goals, they have represented the heart and soul of their teams.

Among the most famous members of the breed is Nat Lofthouse, the Bolton and England centre-forward of the 1950s. To this day, Lofthouse is still known as the 'Lion of Vienna', the nickname he was given for his stirring two-goal performance during England's 3–2 win over Austria in May 1952. The match was billed as the 'unofficial championship of Europe', and also as a clash between the 'new' and 'old' ways of playing the game. England seemed stuck in a tactical time-warp, as Hungary were to emphasise the following year with their 6–3 hiding of England at Wembley. But on this occasion, with Lofthouse leading England's forward line, it didn't matter. His winning goal eight minutes from the end encapsulated all that foreign teams have always admired about their British counterparts. Having received a pass from Tom Finney, Lofthouse showed tremendous will-power as he ran 45 yards with the ball with a pack of defenders snapping at his heels. As he produced his decisive shot, he was knocked unconscious in a collision with the Austrian keeper, and was thus probably the only person in the stadium who did not see the ball roll over the line. Lofthouse was carried off but, though still dazed, insisted on returning to the action for the last five minutes. Not content to just try and help England preserve their lead, he struck a shot against a post in the closing moments.

In recent years, no striker has highlighted this bulldog spirit as impressively and in as many different ways as Alan Shearer – the striker who can teach us the most about the secrets of being an outstanding scorer in English football. He is the highest Premiership scorer in the league's history; he became the youngest player ever to score a hat-trick at the top level in England (against Arsenal on his full league debut for Southampton at the age of seventeen in April 1988); he was the first player to reach the 100-goal and 200-goal milestones in the Premiership; with Newcastle's Andy Cole, he holds the record for the highest number of Premiership goals in one season (34 for Blackburn in 1994/95), not to mention the record for the highest number of goals in one game (five for Newcastle against Chelsea in 1999); and in the 1995/96 campaign, when his Blackburn team were at their lowest ebb, he became the first player to score 30 goals or more in the top flight in three successive seasons. By the end of the 2003/04 season, his overall Premiership total, including penalties, was 243 in 381 matches; if one includes all his senior club matches at the top level, for Southampton as well as for Blackburn and Newcastle, the figure is 346 goals in 650 games. For England, he got 30 in 63 matches. What makes all this particularly impressive is that Shearer has never been in an outstanding club team, and is not ¹ ⌐ most gifted of players. Little wonder that most managers and ˙ ⌐˙ the ultimate striker role model.

⌐⌐⌐hological, physical and

˙h⌐t '

fondest memory of tne ˙⌐⌐⌐
first-team place at the start of the 2000/ ˙⌐
assistant manager, said, 'With Mark Viduka having joined tne ˙⌐⌐ from Celtic, and Michael Bridges emerging as our top scorer the previous season, it looked as if Alan would struggle to get a place in our starting line-up. David O'Leary [then the Leeds manager] asked me to have a word with Alan about this, and as I was doing so, on the pitch before a friendly match at Huddersfield, David came on to the field to join us. Alan, with no trace of anger or resentment, told him, "I think I am a better player than Viduka and Bridges put together, and I am going to prove it to you." People have knocked Alan because of his hot-headedness and his poor disciplinary record, but that incident told another story about him. Instead of throwing his dummy out of the pram, as a lot of highly acclaimed young strikers might have done, Alan looked upon the situation as a challenge that could bring the best out of him.' That season, Smith, in partnership with Viduka, led Leeds to the European Champions League semi-final.

Henrik Larsson was confronted with a challenge of a different and more agonising kind in October 1999, when his achievement in clinching the Celtic record for getting 50 league goals for the club in the shortest period was quickly followed by his fracturing both his tibia and fibula. The following season, Larsson was the top scorer in Europe.

Ruud van Nistelrooy showed similar strength of character by fighting back from his cruciate ligament injury prior to his move to Manchester United. When asked once to pinpoint the secrets of his success, van Nistelrooy said, 'I feel you are always striving to prove a point to people, a point to yourself in a way, that you can score goals on a consistent basis. I have a good awareness and a pretty good turn of speed, but it's the hunger and determination that sets you apart from other players. When I came to England, I had a pretty good record in Holland, but after the knee injury I think people wondered whether I would be the same player. I have always had tremendous faith in my ability and I have always had supportive people around me. And if you want something enough, no matter how hard you have to work, if you are prepared to give everything, you can climb mountains.'

Shearer, who has also overcome serious injuries, has thrived on all manner of battles against the odds. Being between a rock and a hard place has never bothered him. In fact, it's when he's in that situation that he has often been at his best. Hence the willingness of his teams to put their trust in him, as Blackburn did when they made him the focal point of their side and he responded by leading them to the Premiership title, at the expense of more talented teams, in 1995.

One of the many ways in which Shearer's exemplary temperament has been illustrated is through his record of scoring on his debuts for all his teams. He even did it for England against France at Wembley in February 1992, despite the pressure on him as a result of the exclusion of Gary Lineker from the starting line-up.

At a time when England were struggling to cause any major problems for the French defence, it was Shearer who broke the deadlock. Then Lineker came on to replace David Hirst, and it was Shearer who set him up for the second England goal in a 2–0 win. Perhaps his biggest scoring challenge came at Euro 96. Before the _____ment, his run of twelve matches without an _____ ell during which he had _____

This characte_____

start of his career, and it needed to be. He sc_____ schoolboy, but Newcastle, his home-city club, allowed him to sup out of their net because he lacked the flair of others available to them. Some felt that Shearer was too 'one-paced', slightly built and limited in his work on the ball to establish an outstanding career. But Shearer did not let that get to him. He told me, 'Providing they are not personal, the opinions of other people [about his shortcomings as a footballer] do not bother me. I have always had belief in myself and gone my way rather than anyone else's. If it goes wrong, then I know I only have myself to blame. I like it that way.'

No less confident about Shearer's ability to reach the top was Jack Hixon, the scout who recommended Shearer to Southampton when the player was fourteen. 'What attracted me to Alan,' Hixon recalled, 'was that he had a good football brain and what I would call the three essential fundamentals: attitude, application, character. He struck me as being a lad who would always make the most of what he had got. When I first saw him, I was struck by his positive, aggressive running and his "bottle". To be successful as a striker, you have to be prepared to go into positions where you know you are going to get hurt, and he stood out like a beacon in that way. He just came across as a lad with remarkable strength of character and maturity, and in my experience, if you have these things, you are two thirds of the way there.'

Even so, Southampton, having signed Shearer as a schoolboy, took their time in deciding whether or not to sign him as a trainee professional. The club's youth development officer at that time, Bob Higgins, has been quoted as saying that a few months before Shearer was due to leave school at sixteen he felt the player still 'had a little bit more to do' to convince him he was worth taking on. This, of course, gave Shearer – who was getting somewhat 'edgy' about the situation, according to Hixon – the perfect opportunity to show his mental toughness again. Higgins, in order to make a final assessment of Southampton's schoolboy players and triallists, arranged for them to be put through their paces together at a teacher-training centre in Hampshire during the 1986 Easter period. The training sessions were followed by a full-scale final trial match in which Shearer outshone everybody else by scoring five goals. As the fifth one went in, Shearer, understandably high on the adrenalin of clearing what he perceived to be the last obstacle to a Southampton apprenticeship, looked across at Higgins and showed him the five fingers of his hand.

At this point, a member of the Southampton coaching staff who had been watching the match alongside Hixon remarked, 'We will be taking Alan.'

'Thought so,' Hixon replied, wryly.

Having got his foot in the door at Southampton, Shearer did not find himself short of other admirers. Jimmy Case, the former Liverpool and England midfielder who was Southampton's captain as Shearer progressed through the ranks there, recalled, 'The first description that came into my mind when I saw Alan was "power player". From an early age I thought he showed tremendous power in holding off defenders, getting past them, and I was also impressed by his shooting power. I would stay behind after training to help

:- Rofe [the Southampton coach] in giving players any extra

᠇ ᠆᠋᠁ was necessary, and Alan was one of the

᠁᠁᠁᠁petite for learning his

᠁᠁ the

come a᠁᠁ ᠁

 Shearer's biggest 11a᠁ ᠁
Nicholl, Southampton's manager for four ᠁᠁ ᠁᠁
there as a full-time professional, was once quoted as saying ᠁᠁᠁
initially the centre-forward 'couldn't trap a bag of cement'.
However, while most people felt that Shearer was at his best when
he was facing the opposing goal and the ball was played in front of
him, this did not stop Nicholl (and Shearer) striving for the
improvement in his ball skills that would enable him to add another
dimension to his game. 'I saw no reason why he could not operate as
a target man [as a striker who could receive the ball to his feet, with
his back to the goal],' Nicholl said, 'for the simple reason that, like
strikers such as Kenny Dalglish and Mark Hughes, he did have a big
backside and big, powerful thighs. The first priority for a target man
is to be able to "protect" the ball, and the way Alan was built made
him ideal for this as far as I was concerned. Dalglish's build was one
of the reasons why I found him the most difficult player to mark
when I was playing [as a centre-half]. It was the way he used his
backside and hips to keep you away from the ball. In fact, not only
did he stop you from getting to the ball, often you couldn't even see

it. You thought you might be able to get a touch, but then bang, his hips and leg would come across and would be shoved into you. After a match against Dalglish, my thighs would be covered in bruises. Physically, Alan had the same things going for him, and we felt this was a great foundation for us to work on. In training, we would keep hitting the ball to him and it would keep breaking away from him. We had him out for extra practice on this almost every day; I lost count of the number of hours I spent just throwing balls at him from every angle. But he would never give up. He was determined to learn his trade.'

During his Southampton career, Shearer scored ten goals in eleven England under-21 matches and two in three senior international matches. Strange as it might seem, though, his goal total from his 118 Southampton league appearances was just 23. It was only in his last season there, when Ian Branfoot had succeeded Nicholl as manager, that he emerged as the club's leading scorer. Even then, his record of thirteen goals in 41 matches, while more than reasonable in the light of his team's struggle against relegation, was hardly earth-shattering. One explanation is that, despite Shearer's remarkable hat-trick against Arsenal in his first full league match, Nicholl, in common with many other managers with exciting young players, had been sensitive about exposing him to the pressures of regular first-team football too early. He preferred to make Shearer's development a gradual process.

Under Nicholl, Southampton usually operated with only one recognised central striker. Their most effective combination turned out to be Shearer at centre-forward with the exceptionally quick and mobile Rod Wallace on the right and the extravagantly gifted Matthew Le Tissier on the left. Shearer was very much the focal point for attacks, with the two others feeding off him. It did seem to make sense because, although being virtually the workhorse detracted from Shearer's own scoring ability, his finishing could be somewhat erratic, anyway. Wallace and Le Tissier, both older and more experienced than he was, were more clinical.

But there was no doubt that Shearer's attitude was a key element in the team. Southampton's full-back, Jason Dodd, recalled, ~~~t for me to have someone like him at centre-forward

l- -^l I could just bang the ball

he wasn t playing

dog in scoring – Matt and Rod were – ...
respect from the rest of the lads as they did.'

Jimmy Case, reflecting on the new lease of life he experienced as a Southampton player in his thirties, said, 'I had been spoilt by playing behind Kenny Dalglish at Liverpool. In addition to Kenny's ability on the ball, his vision was amazing. Whenever he got the ball, he seemed to know where everybody was. I lost count of the number of times at Liverpool that I would go on a forward run after giving him the ball and then get it back from him in a position in which I didn't think he had seen me. Alan didn't have that, but he was great for me in other ways. He was what you would call a very straightforward type of striker, so that in itself made him an easy person to play with because you could read him. The runs he made [to receive the ball] were great. At that stage in my career, the last thing I wanted was to have nothing on when I was in possession and have to hold the ball and fight people off before making a pass, because that's more tiring than anything. But Alan was always moving for you. The point is that he would invite me to play the pass which was easy for me; he would not take up a position which would have needed a Pele or Maradona to find him. Also, once you played the ball in front of him, you knew that even if it was only a 50/50 ball for him, the first thing in his mind would be to end up with a shooting chance from it.'

Among others who were to capitalise on this ability was the late Ray Harford, who first came into contact with Shearer when he combined his duties as Wimbledon manager with those of being the head coach of the England under-21 team for the Toulon International Tournament in France in the summer of 1991. Harford, no more than an average Football League centre-half during his own playing career with Charlton, Exeter, Lincoln, Mansfield, Port Vale and Colchester, was inevitably a great believer in teams getting the ball into the opposing danger area as quickly as possible, as opposed to playing what he was fond of describing as 'pretty' football. With a centre-forward like Shearer, whom he looked upon as a kindred spirit in terms of the striker's pragmatic 'working-class' approach to the game, Harford had the perfect excuse to implement his philosophy in the England under-21 set-up.

Harford knew exactly how to fully exploit Shearer's ability and much of his work on the training field was devoted to this. One aspect of it concerned the confusion between the England under-21 central defender Carl Tiler and Shearer in the opening match, when the former came forward with the ball and the latter came towards him with the aim of suddenly spinning off the man marking him to take the ball behind him. Tiler, though, played the ball to his feet, and Shearer, taken by surprise, was easily dispossessed; then, when Shearer wanted the ball to his feet, Tiler played it long for him.

In these situations, the onus is usually on the striker to give the man in possession a clear indication of the sort of pass he wants. Some strikers do it with subtle hand signals. Jimmy Case recalled that when he played with Rod Wallace, Wallace would do it with his eyes. 'If they were screwed up, it meant that he didn't think there was anything on for him and I should just knock the ball to his feet; if he opened them wide, he just went whoosh. All I had to do was play the ball in behind the defence and he was gone.' In Shearer's

told him that if he wanted the latter he should shout

Sexton [the former Chelsea and

told

with Alan. Alan

In that Toulon tournament, Shearer, captain by Harford, was the top scorer with seven goals in four matches. These included the only goal in the semi-final against Russia and in the final against France. Harford described him as the English version of the outstanding West German centre-forward Karl-Heinz Rummenigge. 'I fell in love with him,' Harford recalled. 'Absolutely fell in love with him.'

By that stage Southampton and Nicholl had parted company, and Harford was being widely tipped to take over from him. That did not materialise, but before Harford and Shearer did work together again, at Blackburn, Shearer cannot have been disappointed at the way his development was maintained by his new Southampton boss, Ian Branfoot, even though Southampton continued to struggle in the lower half of the table. Branfoot himself became arguably the most unpopular manager in their history among the fans. So much so that a Southampton fanzine even went to the outrageous step of a front-page headline portraying the message that they wished he was dead. Apart from Southampton's results, such hostility also had its roots in the fact that Branfoot didn't have the personality and charisma of his predecessors, and the style of play of his team seemed to emphasise this.

But as that style meant Southampton repeatedly 'hitting' Shearer early and playing lots of 'channel' balls (passes through the gaps between central defenders and full-backs), it suited the centre-forward perfectly. So, too, did the fact that the sale of Rod Wallace to Leeds United was followed by Branfoot giving him a proper central striking partner (initially Paul Rideout, then Iain Dowie). As Shearer said at the time, 'It used to be a case of getting the ball out to Rod or Matt, but now Paul Rideout and I will have a bigger role. While I don't dislike being the target man, having another striker to share the responsibility is bound to help me. I have always said that it suited me playing alongside a central striker, and I do like the direct style of play that the boss is favouring.' Jason Dodd recalled, 'We did a lot of channel-ball practice in training. It wasn't a question of just hitting the ball forward in behind opposing defenders; we were given specific areas to aim for. When you say "You have to get the ball in the area between the right or left touchline and the edge of the eighteen-yard box" it sounds simple, doesn't it? But there is an art to it. If you play too far to one side, then it's liable to run through to the goalkeeper; if you play it too far to the other side, it will run out of play. You also need to play the ball early enough to give the player for whom it is intended a reasonable chance of gaining possession without being caught offside. I thought we did it as well as anyone when Branfoot was the manager. It definitely worked well for Alan.'

Indeed, Shearer's league goal total of thirteen that season was misleading because he had enough chances to have achieved a much higher figure. Branfoot has said, 'He had lots and lots of chances that he failed to put away, so many that instead of finishing sixteenth in the table we should have been in the top six. I don't think any of us could work it out. In the end we just put it down to Alan's inexperience. I was convinced he would just get better and better. He absorbed things very quickly. With some players, you might have to tell them something two or three times before it sticks, but with Alan you only had to tell him once. His general approach to the game

the one

played it across to the other hand, well and chased him almost to the halfway line. When you put this together with his goals – well, despite the chances he missed in the season I worked with him, we all came away thinking, "Yeah, he's smashing. He's got everything. He can't go wrong."'

Shearer had good cause to feel the same way in the 1992 close season when Blackburn Rovers, rolling in money as a result of Jack Walker's lavish patronage of the club, bought him for a then British record transfer fee of £3.5 million. Many accused him of being too money-conscious; surely, they argued, it would have made more sense for him professionally to hold out for a move to Manchester United (who wanted him but were not prepared to pay the transfer fee and wages Blackburn were willing to fork out). Against that, of course, was the challenge Blackburn, as Premiership newcomers, presented for Shearer; and, of course, the fact that Harford was at Blackburn by this time, having formed a managerial partnership there with the great Kenny Dalglish.

Southampton badly missed Shearer, as did Branfoot, who was

sacked two seasons later. Branfoot, stressing that he had been powerless to stop the transfer, said, 'You have to be a manager to fully appreciate the feeling that goes through the dressing room when a great striker has left a club. If I could have paid Shearer four times what the other players were getting – which I couldn't – I don't think it would have bothered them too much. If anything, I think they would have been more bothered about Matthew Le Tissier [probably the most popular player in the club's history among the fans] getting four times more than them.'

The point was emphasised by what Shearer's colleagues at Blackburn thought about him. Harford, who spent five years at Blackburn, once said that his relationship with Shearer during the club's rise to the championship helped make it 'the football adventure of my life'. If anything, Harford, who used to argue that managers or coaches who were once central defenders can often teach centre-forwards more than ex-number 9s can, probably helped Shearer push himself further than even Dalglish did.

In common with a lot of other football geniuses, Dalglish, unlike Harford, was not a particularly good coach in the sense of organising training sessions and team tactics to bring the best out of lesser players. Mike Newell, one of Shearer's striking partners at Blackburn, commented, 'Kenny just wanted to pick his team and let them get on with it. Obviously, he would give advice – he was very astute – but he tended to focus on you as an individual, on your individual ability, whereas Ray dealt with the collective side of things more.' This is where Dalglish and Harford, two men from opposite ends of the football tracks, complemented each other perfectly. They got on well together, both professionally and socially.

Nonetheless, their different ideas on how the game should be played did occasionally bring them into conflict. To Dalglish, Harford's approach at Blackburn was too disciplined and regimented and did not allow players enough scope to express their individuality; to Harford, Dalglish was inclined to lose sight of the fact that precious few players were capable of the skills he and his team-mates at Liverpool had been able to produce, and that attempts to get Blackburn to adhere to exactly the same principles would be tantamount to the team leaving too much to chance. The two men would often have long debates on the subject, but neither

But we had a system in which everybody knew his job and was good at it. What we lacked in individual flair we made up for in our work-rate, organisation and commitment.'

Dalglish's view of all this was summed up at the start of the 1994/95 season when he remarked to Harford that he felt Blackburn were too predictable. 'Kenny told me that he was bored with the way the team were playing,' Harford said. 'I said, "I'm bored with it too, Kenny, but if we try to change it now we are liable to fall apart."' To his credit, Dalglish allowed Harford to have his way – and that season, of course, Blackburn went on to win the championship for the first time in 81 years.

As far as Harford's work with Shearer was concerned, one Dalglish criticism concerned Harford's insistence that when the striker invited a pass to his feet, a ball delivered to him from the right should be directed to his right foot and one played to him from the left would need to be directed to his left. Harford felt that Shearer could look a limited player in these situations ('He doesn't really have any tricks to beat you,' he explained). He felt that his passing 'rule' would help offset this. Through his specialist knowledge of the marking habits of defenders, he reasoned that it would usually mean Shearer getting the ball on the side that the opponent breathing down his neck had left 'open'. For his part, Dalglish suggested that in going into such fine detail about the service to Shearer, Harford might have been underestimating the striker's ability and overestimating that of the men who were playing against him. The chances Shearer created suggested otherwise.

Harford also felt that the players then at his disposal were better equipped to hit the opposition on the break than to force the play themselves, and who better than Shearer to make it work for them? He did not have the explosive pace of a Thierry Henry or Michael Owen – Harford viewed him as a strong footballer rather than a particularly quick one – but his intelligence in knowing when and how to break free of defenders, and his determination and physical power in holding them off, made him the most difficult of strikers to stop. Hence Harford's insistence on repeatedly getting Shearer, and the team, 'turned around'. In practice matches, Shearer, on receiving a clearance from his defence, was not allowed to play the ball back. 'He had to turn with it and go forward,' Harford said. 'So the only way you could get a return pass from him would be to move forward into a position alongside him or beyond him. That helped Alan, because having team-mates bursting through, as well as himself, unsettled opposing central defenders.'

Another aspect of Harford's bid to exploit Shearer's ability was Blackburn's work on crosses. Shearer himself saw no reason why, when Blackburn were developing an attack down the flank, one of the wide players should not attempt to 'hit' him with the ball once they got within 30 yards of the goal. Given that Shearer was at his best when facing the goal, Harford insisted on crosses being made from what he described as the 'magic square': the space either side of the eighteen-yard box. 'Give him the right ball from that area and you could almost take it for granted that he would put it in the net,' Harford commented.

When you suggest to Shearer that the style of play Harford initiated and developed was ideally suited to him, he quickly stresses, 'It was designed to get the best out of all the players, not just me.'

When I relayed to Harford Jason Dodd's recollection about Shearer not expecting the service to him to be spot on, he immediately provided a similar anecdote. He recalled a Blackburn training session at the start of Shearer's Ewood Park career, part of which was devoted to Shearer making diagonal runs from the middle on to passes behind the opposing full-back. The player responsible for playing the ball was having a bad day, giving Shearer an impossible task by hitting the ball too long or too short. Harford stopped the session, but before he could say anything, Shearer, recognising the problems his colleague was creating for himself through striving for slide-rule accuracy, shouted to the player, 'Look, you don't have to give the perfect ball. As long as you just get it into the right general area, it's up to me to do something with it.' Harford pointed out, 'Some players in Shearer's position would have tried to be smart or had a go at the fellow, but his reaction was to take all the pressure off the player.'

The obvious danger in this was that it almost invited Shearer's team-mates to give him below-par service, which Dalglish found particularly difficult to accept in connection with some of the crosses he was given. But being forced to stretch himself was a situation Shearer relished. His willingness to bust a gut in striving to adjust to different situations and circumstances has been an integral part of his game throughout his career.

Take his relationship with his striking partners. When Blackburn landed the title, his sidekick was Chris Sutton. But Shearer's number-one choice would have been Newell, who was his closest friend at the club and who is still described by Shearer as probably the striker he has most enjoyed playing with at club level. Newell, whom Dalglish had signed in November 1991 and who was Shearer's regular partner until Sutton came along, enjoyed involving himself in the build-up play and got as much enjoyment out of setting up chances for others as he did from scoring himself. Because of his work in deeper areas, Harford described him as a 'half' centre-forward. He was the ideal foil for Shearer – a 'full' centre-forward. It was the same with Teddy Sheringham (like Newell, a 'half' centre-forward) when he and Shearer played together in the England team.

'Centre-halves want to have people to mark,' Newell observed, 'and with Alan right up there and me dropping off him into a deeper position, they had problems straight away. They were so scared of Alan that instead of one of the two central defenders pushing forward on to me they would both stay in there. At times, I couldn't believe the space I was getting and it was good for Alan too, because strange as it might seem, it can be easier to create space for yourself when it's one against two than when there are two of you up front and you are being marked man for man. Ray [Harford] was very keen on me dropping off Alan because when we were defending it gave us another man who could pinch the ball. When the attack broke down, it was amazing the number of times the ball broke into my area. I could have the ball played into me, and turn with it, and that is when the two central defenders were in trouble because Alan would just make a run off them and you would put the ball in for him.

'We could both play, but the big thing was that we knew our strengths. When Blackburn started in the Premiership, a lot of the matches were real physical battles. If we were in trouble away from

and myself. We were great friends off the field as well as on it. We looked upon ourselves as a team within a team. It would be wrong to say that Chris didn't try to help Alan. I wouldn't call him a selfish player – he did his bit. But if you think you're being asked to do something which is going to detract from what you believe you are good at, then you're not going to be totally effective. It's the same in any walk of life.'

Harford agreed. 'I always felt that someone like Newell was better for Shearer than a player like Sutton,' he said, 'for the simple reason that Sutton was more focused on scoring. I am not saying that Chris didn't make any chances for Alan – he did. But the problem was that both players were number nines and their natural instincts were to get as far up the pitch as they could. They didn't provide enough depth.' Harford, in fact, disagreed with Dalglish's decision to sign Sutton from Norwich City, for a club-record fee of £5 million, in the 1994 close season. He felt that Sutton, who could also play at centre-half, was more effective in that position. However, he had to concede that there was a lot to be said for Dalglish building up competition for first-team places and increasing his selection options; and Newell, having undergone a knee operation in the summer, was ruled out of action for the start of the championship-winning season anyway.

Though Sutton seemed uneasy about the high expectations that his price tag had created for him, he and Shearer scored thirteen and seventeen goals respectively in Blackburn's first 21 league matches. But Sutton found it difficult to maintain his form: in the second half of the season, Shearer again scored seventeen times, but his partner could manage only two. 'Chris seemed to lose a bit of confidence,' Newell recalled. 'He wasn't going past people and creating chances as he did before, and he was no real help to Alan because of it. Before, it didn't matter if he wasn't going deeper because he was creating chances for Alan in other ways: through his shots or headers that were rebounding to Alan, for example, and his knock-downs.' With the team struggling as well, it seemed almost perverse that Sutton continued to keep Newell out of the starting line-up. But, thanks to Shearer, Blackburn still managed to scrape out results good enough to bring them the league title.

Also at Blackburn then was another striker who has emphasised the strength-through-adversity message, James Beattie. A local lad, born and raised in Darwen, Beattie started his career at Ewood Park but was very much a peripheral figure during his four seasons there as a full-time professional. He made a total of only four league appearances (including three as a substitute), and in the summer of 1998 Blackburn transferred him to Southampton in a part-exchange deal involving Kevin Davies.

In a Southampton team haunted by relegation fears, he marked his first season there with just five goals in 35 matches. But Beattie did get into the England under-21 team, and Southampton's fans, recognising the ways in which he unsettled opposing defences, voted him their Player of the Year. The next season, during which Glenn Hoddle replaced Dave Jones as manager, was virtually a write-off for him, partly because of injury problems.

Then, at the start of the 2000/01 season, Hoddle attempted to sell him to Crystal Palace. 'He got me in his office and said, "I am thinking of selling you to Crystal Palace,"' the striker recalled. 'I

he justified Hoddle's willingness to give him a reasonable crack of the whip shortly afterwards with a burst of ten goals in as many matches.

Since then, Beattie has been among the leading Premiership scorers and got into the England team. But then, how could it have been otherwise with a striker who has been described as 'Shearer Mark Two', or 'The Chief', as his ex-Southampton boss Gordon Strachan referred to him? It could easily have been Shearer talking when Beattie told me, 'I have always had faith in my ability. You do take knocks, but you can't allow them to set you back. You have to turn them into something positive. You can always find a positive side, no matter what. I was only twenty when Blackburn released me; they did it with one telephone call to me, and my whole family were really upset. I don't know why Blackburn took that decision, but my attitude [to joining Southampton] was, "OK, this is an opportunity for you to prove them wrong." It was the same when Glenn Hoddle wanted to sell me to Crystal Palace. I always used to say that if I kept injury-free and had a decent first-team run I would score at least fifteen goals a season. But in the last two seasons my expectations of myself have got higher. Before a match, I look at the opposing centre-half in the tunnel and think, "There's no way you are going to stop me." That's not being arrogant in any way; it's just the frame of mind I have got into. People might say that I put too much pressure on myself, but I don't see it like that. I enjoy it. It spurs me on.'

Still, there is only one Alan Shearer, as Beattie found out in his struggle to maintain his success.

CHAPTER SEVEN
METHODS OF ATTACK

F formula. Maintaining it, or ma~~~~ ~
effective, can present even bigger headaches. That is why, during
Southampton's home League Cup tie against their arch south-coast
rivals Portsmouth on 2 December 2003, the Saints' demonstrative
manager Gordon Strachan seemed particularly agitated when
James Beattie received the ball with his back to the goal. Strachan
thought the world of Beattie. At the same time, he knew that
Beattie's first touch could be erratic, so if there wasn't much space
for him to manoeuvre the ball it was always on the cards that the
flow of the move would be disrupted. On this occasion, Beattie's
failure to make the ball instantly obey him was clearly too much for
Strachan to bear. Standing on the edge of the technical zone, the
manager signalled his frustration by throwing his hands forward
from behind his head. He then walked back to the dug-out, shaking
his head and muttering. He must have felt like hugging and kissing
Beattie later, after the striker had scored the goals that brought
Southampton a 2–0 win. But though this was by no means a rare
occurrence, it had become increasingly clear that the technical

rough edges to Beattie's game, previously hidden because of his physical qualities and scoring success, had started to rebound on him and his team. Indeed, Beattie's experiences epitomised Andy Roxburgh's point about the need for strikers, and the team-mates responsible for creating their scoring chances, to add greater variation to their play.

Even the most successful teams need to keep changing their scoring methods to stay ahead, and this is obviously easier for clubs such as Arsenal, Manchester United and Chelsea – the ones with the money and stature to attract the best players – than it is for the rest. Indeed, over the years, there have been countless examples of teams at the top adding a new dimension to their attacking play with the signing of new strikers, and of the strikers themselves getting better as well.

When Don Revie was Leeds United's manager, their transformation from a dour, somewhat negative team to an exciting, attacking one stemmed partly from the signing of Allan Clarke from Leicester in June 1969 for a then British record fee of £165,000. Leicester, who had reached the FA Cup final the previous season but had been relegated, could no longer offer Clarke the platform he required to keep improving. That Leeds did so was very much to the benefit of both parties. Leeds, who had won the championship for the first time in 1969, largely because of their defence, became more forceful, ingenious and potent at the other end than many can have anticipated.

'I had the time of my life,' Clarke has said. 'I was with great players. I was with winners. I was also confident about my technical ability, but I can honestly say that I worked ten times harder at Leeds than I did at my previous clubs. It wasn't that I didn't want to do this at Leicester and Fulham, but as I was a sort of big fish in a small pond, nobody really challenged me about my approach to the game there. At Leeds, all the players demanded that I pull my weight on behalf of the team. Playing in Europe had a lot to do with my development there as well. But the biggest thing was the way Leeds dominated teams and the number of chances they created. Look, I don't want to make it seem as if goalscoring is easy – it isn't – but at Leeds it was a piece of cake compared with what it had been like at ---- ---- clubs. I go back to the number of great players they had.

instruction I got from --
Leeds." That's all he really ever said to me.'

It is difficult to imagine Leicester ever being able to take Clarke as far as Leeds did. The same could be said of most other clubs. It is rare for a small-town club to have the financial resources that Blackburn had when Alan Shearer fired them to the Premiership title, a crown worn in all the other seasons by Manchester United or Arsenal. Moreover, Blackburn did it when the Premiership was in only its third season and the number of foreign stars bringing greater individual technical expertise to teams was minuscule compared to what it is today. In 1994/95, Blackburn were a typically British team playing in a typically British competition. The bottom line in the Premiership is that money is very much the name of the game, more so than it has ever been at the top level, and 75 per cent of the teams, being more or less in the same financial boat, are effectively playing just for survival. There is so little to choose between them that a team that might have finished at the top of the group in one season, thus creating expectations and hopes of getting into the elite category, can easily find itself struggling to avoid relegation the next.

In his quest to better himself and keep improving, who could blame Shearer for his moves from Southampton to Blackburn and then to Newcastle? The season after Blackburn's championship triumph – Shearer's last at the club – he again scored more than 30 goals. But Blackburn, having curtailed their money-no-object transfer-market shopping policy, could only finish seventh. The feeling that they had previously over-achieved and that it was time for Shearer to move on to a bigger stage was endorsed by the continuation of their slide. By 1999 they were back in the First Division, following a season in which their total number of league goals amounted to just 38.

One wonders what would have happened to Southampton – one of the lowest-scoring teams in the Premiership in recent seasons – if they hadn't had James Beattie. Strachan himself acknowledges that in rehabilitating himself as a manager at Southampton, after being sacked by Coventry, he owed a considerable debt to his centre-forward. 'Instead of the coaching staff motivating him, he motivates us,' he said. 'You can argue that he could be better at this or that, but there comes a point when there is no way you can say anything to him about it because he has worked himself to a standstill.'

When Strachan became manager in October 2001, Southampton were in the relegation zone. Strachan's first step to pull them out of trouble was to make them fitter, which led to their finishing eleventh. Beattie, despite missing three months because of injury, scored twelve league goals that season, just two fewer than the club's leading scorer Marian Pahars. Then, with Pahars forced out of action for almost all of the 2002/03 season, Beattie reached the twenty-goal mark for the first time in his career. His league haul of 23 made him the Premiership's third highest scorer behind Ruud van Nistelrooy and Thierry Henry. With Southampton's second highest scorer, Brett Ormerod, finding the net no more than five times, the team total stood at just 46, but thanks to their excellent defence it was enough to enable them to end up in eighth place – their best-ever Premiership achievement. An even bigger feather in Strachan's cap, of course, was that Southampton's ability to scrape out good results, through their organisation and energy more than ⎯ ⎯ ⎯ to the FA Cup final against Arsenal.

⎯ and

Why? Part of the answer ⎯ approach to the game (which ultimately led to Strachan leaving him out of the starting line-up for a while to give him a rest). Beattie, 6ft 1in and thirteen stone, has always been noted for his athleticism, fitness and willingness to stretch himself. Recalling his schooldays, and his emergence as a top junior 100-metre freestyle swimmer, he recalled, 'I was able to train on my own for long periods – it was just me and the pool. I was ranked second in the country at one stage, but I wanted to be at the top of the podium and that's what drove me on. In training, I was doing something like 50,000 metres a week, which is quite a lot for a twelve- or thirteen-year-old.' It has been the same story in his football career.

All players need to work hard; but depending on their level of ball skills and the nature of their teams, some have to work harder than others. In Beattie's case, his image as a powerful rather than skilful striker has been a sensitive subject for him, especially with regard to his limited opportunities to make his mark in the England set-up. His five England appearances were all in largely low-key friendlies (against Australia, Serbia and Montenegro, Croatia, Liechtenstein and Denmark); and because of the manager Sven-Goran Eriksson's policy of using all the players in his squad in such games, Beattie wasn't given much time on the field to really show what he could do. Some observers have suggested that Beattie might also have suffered through some of the other England players having doubts about him being on their technical wavelength.

Certainly, after Beattie's last England match, the 3–2 defeat by Denmark on 16 November 2003, the argument that he had not been given the help he needed came over loud and clear in the report of the game on Southampton's official website. Under the headline 'Beattie Shut Out', Dave Hilley wrote, 'James Beattie learnt a valuable lesson about looking after number one. The Saints striker came off the bench at half-time but was seriously starved of service. He rarely received a pass or cross, as for some reason the other England players appeared to cut him out of the game. That was best highlighted on 71 minutes, when Frank Lampard elected to shoot from a tight angle to the right when a pull-back would have left Beattie with a simple finish.' Some contrast to the unselfishness Beattie showed near the end when he spurned a good shooting chance to set up Danny Murphy for a strike that drifted wide. 'It probably went largely unnoticed,' Hilley continued, 'but there was a key moment around the hour mark when Beattie peeled away from his man, making an intelligent run into the box as Joe Cole picked up the ball in the centre of midfield. It was crying out for the sort of telling ball he is supposed to favour and yet he [Cole] chose to go sideways and the moment was lost. That was the story of the game for Beattie.'

Not surprisingly, when I mentioned all this to Beattie he was unwilling to be drawn on the issue. 'I am well aware of it [the report],' he said, 'but I don't want to go into it. Yeah, there were a few times when I felt I should have received the ball, but there's nothing you can do about it.' At club level, though – and particularly in a team like Southampton – Beattie's approach to the game has been welcomed more warmly. 'When Beattie is doing the running he is capable of, it has the effect of wearing defenders down mentally and physically,' Strachan explained. 'That is what he has to do [in order to score goals], he has to grind people down. I think it suits his

statistical details of his performances available to Southampton through their use of the high-tech ProZone computer match analysis system. The system, which has become an integral part of the coaching and match preparation work at a number of leading clubs, comprises a video of games with a tracking set-up involving the use of eight to twelve highly placed sensors around the stadium. This provides every bit of information one could possibly wish to know about the movement of every player on the pitch for the entire game. In Beattie's case, the reports he receives about his physical output – incorporating data on his number of 'low-fatigue, moderate-fatigue and high-fatigue' accelerations and decelerations, the amount of ground he covers with 'high-intensity' runs (at three-quarter pace or higher), the overall distances he covers in games and his running speeds – are not in the easy-reading category. To Southampton, however, the overall message is simple.

Take the club report on Beattie in February 2004, comparing his physical output in the first half of the 2003/04 season, when his scoring touch seemed to have deserted him, with that in the same period the previous season, when he achieved his best scoring record. It revealed drops in his average number of accelerations and decelerations (from 117 to 168); the average distances he had covered with high-intensity runs (956.5 metres to 838 metres); and his average total running distances (from 10.57 kilometres to 10.14 kilometres). In some matches, it was pointed out to him, his high-intensity runs had dropped to around the 400-metre mark. The report commented, 'Even though you are performing in the upper limits of the medium to high categories for your position, your average from last season suggests there is more to come from you. It has been noted that when the manager asks for a response from you physically, you respond to great effect. All you can do to improve your scores is to gain more consistency from game to game.' In the section relating to Beattie's speed, it stated, 'Your performances have been slightly below the standard you set last year. We measure your speed during games for two reasons: one, simply to get a picture of how fast you are; and two, to get an idea of your fatigue state on the day of a game. In aspects such as endurance you can push your body through the work, but a tired body simply won't be able to reach the same top speed as a fresh one. As a side, when we work hard we tend to play better, so it is important to maintain a high level in every game.'

To get the best out of Beattie's physical ability, Southampton, inevitably lacking the individual quality that is a feature of the top teams, concentrated on hitting balls into space for him, as opposed to hitting them at him. This might not have helped other members of the team to give him greater scoring support, but as long as he was getting goals regularly, what did it matter? But once the goals dried up, because of a combination of Beattie's tiredness and opponents becoming more competent in countering Southampton's style of play, it was a different story. 'Your methods of attack, of creating chances, depend mainly on the type of strikers you have,' Strachan observed. 'The top strikers know they are judged on their goal records, so their first thought is to get behind a defence – that must be their main aim. But if that isn't on, then OK, they are able to come short to take it to their feet and join in the build-up. If a striker ... how are you going to keep the move going

'Opposing teams are making ... Beattie the service we want to give him. When they lose the ball deep in our half, they push up on our back men and force us to play through them. James likes to be the furthest man up the park, to take on the last man, but in order to get the ball he is having to come towards it, to the point where sometimes he is virtually on top of it. That's where any problems he might have with his touch and close control can come to the fore. At Coventry we used to force Niall Quinn to do that [in matches against Sunderland]. Instead of hitting the ball straight up to him, they would have to pass it through us. All Quinn could do when he came deep was play it wide, and even then the chances of his being able to get on the end of a cross in the box were minimal.

'James's hold-up play has improved in the time I have been with him at Southampton, and it will continue to do so. He is a wonderful player for a manager or coach to work with. I have given him bollockings, but he's all right with that – he accepts criticism. He is also an intelligent lad, which is probably even more important. He absorbs everything you tell him, and that's why I think he will surprise a lot of people over the next few years. At this stage, though, a lot depends on his fitness. I would say that when he's fit and running well, his technical level goes up to seven or seven and a half out of ten, whereas when he's tired it drops to about four out ten.'

Before the start of the 2003/04 season, Strachan had gone at least some of the way towards varying Southampton's attacking approach and thus increasing their scoring potential with the signing of Kevin Phillips from Sunderland for £3.25 million. Strachan reasoned that Phillips's control and vision in tight areas and his ability to orchestrate Southampton's play in the last third of the field would enable them to become less 'one-dimensional'. Nobody could argue with that logic. However, in the ebb and flow of a game there were bound to be times when the areas in which Phillips excelled would be filled by Beattie. Moreover, Phillips needed the defenders and midfielders to be as comfortable on the ball as he was to be able to properly prove his worth – a situation that was bound to take Southampton time to achieve, if only because of the extent to which the team's previous footballing habits had been ingrained. Sure enough, as Southampton's performances and results became ever more erratic, Strachan was forced to revert to the approach they knew best.

To watch some of Strachan's work behind the scenes at Southampton was to provoke the thought that getting more goals from a team outside the Arsenal–Manchester United–Chelsea axis is often even harder work for the managers and coaches than it is for the players. Their planning for matches is almost like a military operation, with much time being spent analysing the strengths and weaknesses of the opposition through videos and scouting reports and working on ways to deal with them on the training ground. To managers and coaches, the strategic aspect of matches can resemble a game of chess; and what makes it all the more complicated is that many don't have all the pieces.

One example of Strachan's problems in that department was Southampton's home match against Blackburn in October 2003. Southampton had scored only once in their previous six matches, in the 1–1 draw against Steaua Bucharest at home in the first leg of their ... Steaua beat them 1–0 in the return leg, and ...

August; Leandre Griml, a nineteen- ... been signed on a Bosman free in the summer but had yet to make his senior debut; and Agustin Delgado, the Ecuador star who had been on the injured list for so long since his move to Southampton in the summer of 2002 that the fans and local media had dubbed him 'The Invisible Man'.

As expected, Strachan opted to work mainly with Beattie and Tessem in his tactical preparations for the game. Pondering his options in his office at Southampton's training ground, he said, 'Not being able to play Kevin is probably the biggest headache. Neither Brett nor Joe have his ability to receive the ball to their feet and play. Joe is reasonably good technically, but he is not strong. So any thoughts we might have of playing the beautiful game on Saturday will have to go out of the window. Our build-up play will have to be more basic.' Strachan then moved over to the 'players' on the magnetic board on his office wall to give some visual examples of how he felt Beattie and Tessem, and the team, could best overcome Phillips's absence. Moving both 'Beattie' and 'Tessem' into central positions, in which they were in close contact with each other, he said, 'When we are attacking, we have to keep the strikers narrow.' He then showed why by moving the discs representing Blackburn defenders towards the pair, and showing the space this created for Beattie and Tessem to run into.

For a while, it seemed that this was going to work only up to a point; Blackburn, with their back four protected by a five-man midfield unit, were able to keep Beattie and Tessem at arm's length. Beattie did get one great chance, a free header, but failed to take it. But three minutes later, with the pressure on Southampton escalating, Beattie had no hesitation in pushing himself forward to take a direct free-kick 25 yards out, and further underlined his tremendous temperament by firing the ball into the net. Beattie, not known as a creator of chances for others, also made the defence-splitting pass from which Griffit, brought on as a substitute for Tessem, made it 2–0.

Despite that victory, Southampton continued to blow hot and cold in attack. Strachan's feeling that he needed to go back to the drawing board became particularly strong after the 1–0 defeat at Aston Villa in November. It was perhaps only to be expected that, as a result of Southampton's attempts to string more passes together than they had the previous season, their number of shots and headers would decline. But after the Villa game Strachan found it impossible to ignore the fact that the home team, despite having made fewer passes than any of Southampton's other Premiership opponents, had created the most chances.

It was at that point that he elected to revert to what he termed 'reality football'. Recalling his experiences in Leeds United's highly successful if not technically sophisticated teams under the management of Howard Wilkinson, he argued, 'You cannot really knock any style of play if it's creating chances. I was brought up in good passing teams [at Aberdeen and Manchester United], but there are times when you have to say that this side of the game – the importance that people attach to it – can be termed propaganda. I'm sure there are plenty of good passing teams who have been relegated. As a manager, my attitude is, "You can pass as much as you want, but if it's not hurting me, what does it matter?"'

All of which took Strachan into which many will have

Hughes, as director

followed his lead to the point where statistics, especially with regard to the brand of football most likely to produce goals, provided the foundation for the FA's coaching strategies. These are the men who are viewed as having the most to answer on the preoccupation of a high number of teams, both at home and abroad, with the so-called 'long-ball' game, a style of play that has always caused football's most skilful performers to wince.

For Reep, it had all started in the 1950s when he went to watch a match at Swindon and, having logged the number of times they had been in possession of the ball, wondered why it was that they had scored only two goals. He became obsessed with the subject, and embarked on a massive research programme which over the course of some 30 years emphasised two statistical points to him. The first was that the highest number of goals were scored in an area of the field which he described as the PoMO (Position of Maximum Opportunity) sector. As if this was not enough to get teams tuned in to the idea of getting the ball from one end of the field to the other as quickly as possible – not wasting too much energy on weaving pretty patterns with it in order to make sure they retained possession – his other finding was that the smaller the number of passes in an attacking move, the greater its chances of success.

One manager who acted on such information was Stan Cullis, whose Wolves team emerged as one of the most successful in England in the 1950s as a consequence. Another was Graham Taylor, who handed Reep a contract as an adviser during the early part of his career at Watford in the 1980s. Taylor was once quoted as saying, 'Some things [in Reep's teachings] are dangerous. But here is a man who has recorded how goals are scored over more than thirty years. When he throws that number of goals at you, and when you watch it yourself, you say to yourself, "Hey, that fellow's right."' Indeed, under Taylor, Watford burst from the old Fourth Division to the First in five years, and reached the FA Cup final. Wimbledon, using similar methods, rose from non-league football to the First Division in nine years and provided one of the greatest boosts of all time for teams of their indifferent individual technical ability by sensationally beating Liverpool in the 1988 FA Cup final.

For all the criticism directed at managers who have applied the match analysis findings in their purest form – for instance John Beck when he was at Cambridge – most can see the sense of them with teams that have comparatively ordinary or average players. Less easy to accept is the view that the tactics are no less valid for even the most talented of sides. Reep once wrote, 'The time will come when the choice of the manager for the England team will have to be confined to those very few who have a clear understanding of random chance in soccer and who have exploited it successfully.' When I once interviewed Hughes, he pointed out that even in matches involving the top teams, the vast majority of goals came from no more than five passes, usually from counter-attacks stemming from possession regained in the last third of the field. His message was that even in a World Cup final a team getting the ball forward as quickly as possible and pushing up to compress the play would have the best chance of victory. He saw no reason why this should not form the main part of player coaching sessions. Referring to the development of schoolboy players, he said, 'They need not just more practice, but more practice on the things that will pay the

Strachan was never liable to go that far. Nonetheless, in his attempts to halt Southampton's slide you could appreciate why he saw no reason to be embarrassed about getting back to basics. In a club website interview, he said, 'I was looking for a bit more variation in our play this season, but I was possibly asking them [the players] to do things they were not comfortable with. Maybe some of them aren't ready to take that step forward. At this stage, we are brilliant at being ordinary and playing from the heart, and through that comes our ability. We are now going back to what we were. We will still work on the other things in training, so when the time is right we can introduce them gradually. But for now, we will stick with what works for us.'

Portsmouth, in their League Cup tie at Southampton, became the first team to feel the full force of this. Strachan, as he showed when Beattie was on the ball, still fretted about his side's inability to retain possession. But the other side of the coin was the way in which Portsmouth were undermined by his centre-forward's power and determination. After 33 minutes, Ormerod suddenly put Portsmouth in difficulty by taking the ball off a defender and putting Chris Marsden clear down the left. Marsden crossed hard and low, and Beattie, attacking the ball as if his life depended on getting to it, put it in the net. In injury time, Beattie's will to score was seen again as he forced himself in between two defenders. The only way one of them, Arjan De Zeeuw, was able to stop him was to bring him down, a foul that led to the big Dutchman being sent off and Beattie converting the penalty.

So there were no prizes for guessing the name of the Southampton player that Charlton, the Saints' next opponents, thought about the most in their preparations for the game. When I visited their training ground three days before the match, Charlton's coach, Mervyn Day, and the manager, Alan Curbishley, were discussing Beattie's performance against Portsmouth as they were walking on to the pitch with their squad. There hadn't seemed anything especially riveting about Beattie's opening goal; after all, it was from close in and he did have virtually an unguarded target. Curbishley, though, referring to the way in which Beattie attacked the ball, was struck by his apparent hunger to score. 'You could almost see it in his eyes,' he said.

Later, Day expressed his admiration for Phillips as well. 'We wanted him desperately [when Sunderland agreed to sell him in the summer] and he badly wanted to come here,' he said. 'But at that time we just couldn't raise the money. Phillips and Niall Quinn complemented each other perfectly at Sunderland, and Phillips and Beattie also complement each other at Southampton. You often find good striking duos like those, where the two strikers are total opposites. You rarely get two the same. That's not to say that you don't want both to score, but as long as one is getting a lot of goals, it doesn't matter. I do like striking partnerships like this.'

Phillips hadn't played against Portsmouth because of tonsillitis, but Day and Curbishley both felt he would be back in the starting line-up for Charlton's visit to St Mary's Stadium. This became particularly clear as Day, who takes on most of the responsibility for organising Charlton's defence, supervised the customary training match involving the first-team keeper and back-four players against a group of attacking players replicating the styles of play of those at

[illegible text obscured]

Powell was on the right flank because Powell is a natural left-footed player, the same as Southampton's French right-side midfielder Fabrice Fernandes, whose balls into the box (with his left foot) had proved one of Southampton's most effective attacking assets. Also included in that training session were the sort of long throw-ins propelled into opposing goal areas by The Saints' Rory Delap.

Because of Beattie's ability in the air, especially when the ball is played to the far post, it was no less interesting to note the positional changes among Charlton's back four. In normal cirumstances, their line-up would have been Radostin Kishishev at right-back, Chris Perry and Mark Fish at the heart of the defence, and Hermann Hreidarsson at left-back. The plan against Southampton was for Perry and Fish to swap sides. Why? Day explained that in the usual set-up, the positions on the right side of Charlton's defence were filled by the smallest of the defenders. 'So if I was manager or coach of Southampton,' he added, 'I would be telling our team to keep getting the ball to Fernandes and I would tell Beattie to keep getting in between Kishishev and Perry [for the far-post cross].' The positional changes meant that the line-up in terms of height changed from 5ft 11in–5ft 9in–6ft 4in–6ft 3in to 5ft 11in–6ft 3in–5ft 9in–6ft 4in. 'Obviously their main scoring threat at the moment is Beattie,' Day continued, 'and we have concentrated on that threat. When Southampton are in the final third they put a lot of crosses into the box and he attacks them very well. Today has been about getting our back four in the right positions – hopefully the right positions! – to deal with it. Beattie is a strong runner, he can get behind you, but the main priority is to nullify his ability in the air. That means defending higher up the pitch when the ball is in crossing areas. When Fernandes checks back and crosses the ball with his left foot, you want the back four holding the line; the last thing you want is for them to drop back to the six-yard box. You have to force him to head the ball from sixteen or seventeen yards out, as opposed to six or eight yards out.

'I think you will find that if they are going to play into feet, they are going to play into Phillips's feet, not Beattie's. They will play down the sides for Beattie [hit direct passes into space for him so that he can run with it towards the goal]. If the ball is played up to him, he's not the type who finds it natural to turn with it, so you can afford to get quite tight on him and pressurise his first touch. If he gets turned and is running at you, then it's important to shove him on to his left foot and force him away from the goal. Above all, we have to work hard enough to cut out a lot of the service to him.'

This led Day on to the subject of Strachan's comment about 'passing propaganda'. Day, once Strachan's team-mate at Leeds, said, 'People said Leeds were a long-ball team, which they were. But what was wrong was the stigma attached to this. A long ball does not necessarily mean a crude whack up the field. A quality fifty-yard ball is better than a quality ten-yard ball because the fifty-yard one takes you forty yards further up the field. When it comes to creating scoring chances, it must be an advantage to get into the last third of the field quicker.

'As you get higher in the league, you need better players [to provide greater variation]. You cannot stand still. I do sometimes think that you can make existing players better just through a change of system, but I can see where Gordon is coming from. The ways you

inexperienced Jonathan Fortune. Also, Beattie again lined up alongside Ormerod and not Phillips, and Fernandes had to make way for Pahars. The changes seemed to make Southampton stronger than ever. Having established a 2–0 lead and then been pulled back to 2–2 through two outstanding shots from Scott Parker, they finally won 3–2. Perhaps the most surprising aspect of the victory was that Beattie didn't score (Rory Delap got the first goal with a deflected shot and Ormerod the other two). It was the first home match Southampton had won without any goals from him for fourteen months.

However, Beattie did do much to undermine Charlton in other ways. One of his best moments came just before half-time when his tenacity in chasing an apparently over-hit pass from David Prutton through the inside-right channel enabled him to just keep it in play. Then, as if to disprove the notion that he is not the best at setting up chances for others, he pulled the ball back for Ormerod to score Southampton's second goal. He was also involved in the Saints' third goal, taking advantage of Charlton's failure to properly clear a Jason

Dodd corner with a headed pass that led to Michael Svensson giving Ormerod the opportunity to get the winner. 'Today was the first time this season that we have been a threat every time we have got the ball,' Strachan said. 'In defence, which we don't practise that much, we have been nine out of ten, but attacking-wise, we have only been five out of ten. Today, I think we were up to nine out of ten.'

There were other Southampton performances for Strachan to savour before his departure from the club in March 2004 (a parting of the ways arising from the decision by Strachan himself not to remain there beyond the end of the season). But with the physical strain on Beattie having caught up with him, and his team still inconsistent, it seemed that Southampton had run into a brick wall.

Strachan and Southampton had come a long way together. No doubt, in addition to his feeling that he needed to take a break from the pressures of management, his reluctance to sign the new contract that had been offered to him also stemmed from doubts about whether it was possible to take the club further under their exisiting financial structure. It was tempting to suggest that in order to make the step from being a middle-of-the-table team to a good top-half one Southampton needed to loosen their purse strings in the transfer market. At the same time, in view of the horrendous financial problems Leeds have experienced, one could understand why the Saints' chairman Rupert Lowe, in common with many of his counterparts, was sensitive about the dangers of his club trying to live beyond its financial means.

Perhaps one consoling thought for Southampton, and all the other teams striving to improve their scoring ability, was that even Arsenal did not have everything. Even during a season in which the Gunners became the first top-level team in modern times (and only the second in the history of English football) to go through the season with no league defeats, some professional observers felt that they occasionally missed not having a conventional centre-forward. Their argument was that a big, strong number 9 who was good in the air and could create problems for the opposition in the physical sense, would have provided an invaluable extra dimension to their build-up play in periods when their close-passing and dribbling skills were not working.

Who could have given them that option? One of the names put

CHAPTER EIGHT
SHARING THE LOAD

maybe leaving it to the front two.

PAUL STURROCK

team. In recent seasons, the advantages of this have been borne out particularly spectacularly by David Beckham's free-kick goals and, at the less skilful end of the English football scale, Plymouth Argyle's achievement in becoming the highest-scoring team in the country.

Who can ever forget the 30-yard Beckham free-kick in the last minute of England's World Cup qualifying tie against Greece, which gave England a 2–2 draw and an automatic place in the 2002 finals? Getting the ball in the net from outside the penalty area (not just from free-kicks but also in open play) was also Peter 'Hot Shot' Lorimer's speciality during his Leeds United career. The right winger or right-side midfielder who was Leeds' record post-war league scorer might not have been able to bend it like Beckham, but the power and accuracy of his long-range shots was awesome. He once said, 'It was a great thing to have in your attacking armoury. Your team could be in trouble, but suddenly they'd get a free-kick and – bang. They were level or ahead, and you were a hero.

'In those days, it [the art of converting free-kicks] was mostly about power. You could not make the ball bend and dip – the balls were heavier than the ones used now when the conditions were wet and muddy – but this was no handicap to me. Sometimes I would blast the ball straight at the keeper, and other players would pick up goals from the rebounds. We knew it was unlikely that the keeper would be able to hold the ball, so when I hit it we would have two or three players in specific areas around him to pick up the pieces. Most of the goals I scored in open play came from long range. Like Eddie Gray [Leeds' left winger], I used to pick the ball up deep and go at people. Once I was over the halfway line, maybe thirty to forty yards from goal, I would start thinking, "Goal here." It was quite funny sometimes because just as people were starting to give you stick for not passing to them – and it usually came from the strikers – the ball would be flying into the top corner of the net. So then it would be OK.'

Plymouth did not have a Lorimer or a Beckham when they won the Second Division title in the 2003/04 season. But this wasn't of much consolation to the defences they faced because they had all the other elements necessary to get plenty of goals from non-strikers. Managed for the most part by Paul Sturrock, who was to become Gordon Strachan's replacement at Southampton, Plymouth (unlike Southampton) had an outstanding target-man centre-forward in Micky Evans; and the vast majority of Plymouth's work in training was based on getting defenders and midfielders into scoring positions.

Of course, there is a world of difference between the Second Division of the Nationwide League and the Premiership. But it was interesting to note that while Southampton's league goal haul was 44 in 38 matches, Plymouth, with Evans the top scorer among their central strikers on just twelve, got 85 goals in 46 matches. During

Sturrock's time there, they never relied as heavily on one player, and especially a striker, to get their goals as Southampton had on Beattie. In their 2001/02 Third Division championship-winning season, Plymouth's most prolific scorer was their central defender Graham Coughlan, with eleven; the only front man able to present a serious challenge to him was Marino Keith, who was in second place on nine. Keith did manage to regain some of his self-respect by being

1978 World Cup-winning team. Passarella was the defender who scored the highest number of goals in the Argentinian League and Italy's Serie A. It was the same story at international level, where his record was 22 in 70 matches. Although he was only 5ft 9in, Passarella, strong and athletic, scored a high number of goals with his head.

The most obvious way in which central defenders can get in on the scoring act is through set-piece moves. Almost all of them are good in the air, and the routines managers and coaches come up with to bring them into the picture at indirect free-kicks and corners are many and varied. Central defenders can also find the net in open play, of course, especially if they are in the mould of Colin Hendry (the former Blackburn and Scotland centre-half who seemed to perform at times as if hypnotised into believing he was the centre-forward); and, most importantly, they can time their runs into scoring positions properly.

It is in the latter respect that attacking midfielders come into their own as scorers. As Sturrock said, 'I have always found that the late runs into the box are the hardest for teams to defend against.' In the past, midfielders running off their markers and taking advantage of the attention of opposing defenders being focused on the strikers has been particularly well illustrated by the remarkable scoring records of men such as Martin Peters at Tottenham and West Ham in the 1960s and 1970s, and John Wark at Ipswich and Liverpool in the 1970s and 1980s.

Peters, nicknamed 'The Ghost' because of his ability to sneak virtually unnoticed into finishing positions, was probably the first player in England to truly bring this facet of the game to the fore. There wasn't much that Peters could not do on a football field. Indeed, the footballing intelligence and wide range of skills that enabled him to fill a multitude of different positions or roles at West Ham prompted his England manager, Sir Alf Ramsey, to come out with that famous comment about Peters being 'ten years ahead of his time'. Ramsey meant it as the ultimate compliment. It stemmed from the manager's vision of teams of the future being packed with players interchanging positions, the sort of players for which Ajax were to become renowned when their 'total' football swept them to three successive European Cup triumphs at the start of the 1970s. For his part, though, Peters was initially touchy about the comment because at that time he viewed his versatility as a handicap. In his 1975 autobiography, aptly titled *Goals from Nowhere*, he wrote that he 'detested' being described in his early days at West Ham as a 'utility' player. 'Do you know where the term "utility man" comes from?' he complained. 'It's an old theatrical term which, my dictionary explains, means "an actor employed to play unimportant parts, when required".'

His turning point came when he was left out of the West Ham team for their 1965 European Cup Winners' Cup final win over Munich 1860, and demanded to the manager, Ron Greenwood, that he be given a more clearly defined role. Greenwood eventually gave him the job of hunting for goals from the 'hole' just behind the strikers. Even then it bothered Peters that the subtlety with which he did his job – the fact that much of his work boiled down to intelligent but largely unnoticed runs off the ball – caused him to be underrated by the general public. As for that comment by Ramsey, he said, 'It looked at first to be the sort of thing someone says about you before

his scoring record. Quite apart from the part he played in England's 1966 World Cup triumph, his new role at West Ham brought him 100 goals in 364 matches, including a career-best total of 24 in 48 in the 1967/68 season.

John Wark, initially a centre-half, did not have Peters' talent, but through his strength and power, and his scoring instincts, his record as a midfielder-striker was even more impressive. Wark is best remembered for his amazing exploits in the 1980/81 season, when he scored 36 goals, including fourteen (then a record) in the Uefa Cup. More recently, the most highly-rated Premiership scorer among those not filling conventional central striking roles has been Manchester United's Paul Scholes.

In taking some of the scoring pressure off the strikers, men such as Peters, Wark and Scholes have done much to mirror the changes in the basic playing 'shapes' or systems of teams. The earliest of these basic patterns, in the 1880s, was the 2–2–6 formation. These days, the most common line-up, certainly at the top levels, is 4–5–1 or

4–4–1–1. How did we get to this? In the tactical 'numbers game' played by managers and coaches, 2–2–6 was followed by 2–3–5 and then the WM formation, which could be said to be basically 3–2–2–3. The extra man at the back arose as a result of the 1925 change in the offside law, which meant that to remain onside a striker in the most advanced attacking position needed to have only one outfield opponent in front of him, not two, when he received the ball. With most teams still using only two men as their last line of defence (they were ostensibly full-backs), with the centre-half further forward alongside two 'wing-halves', the change inevitably led to a higher number of goals.

Ironically, the decision by teams to increase the number of players at the back, by moving the centre-half there, has been attributed partly to the Sunderland and Arsenal forward Charlie Buchan. Newcastle, one leading team that did take up the idea of a three-man defence and became recognised as the masters of the offside game as a result, beat Arsenal 7–0, and legend has it that Buchan was so incensed about it that he persuaded the Gunners' manager, Herbert Chapman, to follow Newcastle's example. It was therefore Arsenal, as a result of their emergence in the 1930s as the most dominant team in England, who did the most to make this defensive line-up so common.

The writing on the wall for the WM shape, indeed for any system in which players do not adjust, became particularly clear when England suffered their first-ever home defeat against Hungary at Wembley in 1953. As the Hungarians adopted a 4–2–4 structure, England's three-man defence was often outnumbered and it conceded six goals. Not only this, Hungary's centre-forward Nandor Hidegkuti did not operate in the way England's centre-half Billy Wright had come to expect of number 9s. In today's parlance, Hidegkuti seemed more like an attacking midfielder than a striker.

Some years later, Wright wrote, 'He was the one who really won it for Hungary. Others, like Puskas [who scored a hat-trick], got more credit, but it was Nandor who pulled us all over the place and opened up the gaps. No one had put the centre-forward as deep as that before. Don Revie did the same thing later with Manchester City. It made a big difference to the English game. No longer was it relevant to take much notice of the numbers on players' shirts.' So

Arsenal or Chelsea, your 3–5–2 is inclined to be more like 5–5–2 (or even 5–5–0 if you are a poor team!). In the space of 90 minutes the shape of a team can alter so many times that most spectators trying to work out what is going on could easily end up reaching frantically for the aspirin bottle. However, the way in which the team systems have evolved does show that strikers getting help from other members of the team has become increasingly important.

One explanation for teams cutting the number of men in their front line, and increasing the number in the midfield zone, is that it increases their chances of retaining possession and controlling the play, and makes it more difficult for the opposition to penetrate them. These factors are viewed as being of paramount importance in matches involving the most skilful and accomplished teams. No less pertinent is the fact that teams, conscious of the uneasiness of defenders when they don't have anybody specifically to mark, have become increasingly attached to the idea of having potential scorers in areas in which their goal threat is less apparent.

In his book '*Flat Back Four: Tactics of Football*', Andy Gray, looking at the pros and cons of 4–3–3, 4–4–2 and 4–5–1 from a striker's point of view, wrote, 'Three up front is harder to work as a front man [than two up front] because you have to be more disciplined. You are much more limited as to where you can go. When you just have two, you are always interchanging; it is less regimented and harder for defenders to work out what you are doing. In modern-day football, the hardest thing about playing as a [conventional] striker is finding space. Defences are so well organised that trying to break them down can be like banging your head against a brick wall, which is why a lot of teams play with one up and one off [in the space just behind]. One thing that defenders hate above all is players who run at them with the ball, and that's what the player in the "hole" does.'

As Gray said, some lone strikers are more isolated than others, which goes some way towards explaining the difference between 4–5–1 and 4–4–1–1. For example, Eric Cantona was looked upon as a 'hole' player when he was with Manchester United, but as Gray pointed out, even when United were in possession the Frenchman spent much of his time 'scurrying around near the centre circle'. But, on the general principle of a striker being up front on his own, Gray argued that it was essential for his team to be able to play through the midfield and have team-mates in deeper positions quickly supporting him. 'There is no point in knocking endless long balls to a player on his own up front. It's too big a job for him to protect the ball. It's a strange role for a striker, because he becomes more of a creator around the box than a finisher.'

The job clearly created problems for Alan Shearer when Terry Venables subjected him to the lone-striker role, as part of his 'Christmas Tree' 4–5–1 system, with the England team in the mid-1990s. Venables said, 'David Platt and Peter Beardsley [the most attack-minded of England's midfield five] are essentially functioning as forwards so I don't think Shearer is left isolated up front any more than Ian Rush was for Liverpool when they were at their best, or any more than Shearer is with Blackburn. Obviously it's a great advantage for attackers to come into the box from deeper positions because they arrive facing the goal, which creates more options for them and for the man who is already there.' Outside the arguments

that England nearly reached the World Cup final playing with two strikers. The truth is, Peter Beardsley has never been a genuine front man and he was more a link between midfield and me up front.' He added, 'There is no questioning the Blackburn goal machine's [Shearer's] commitment or, indeed, his talent, but the forward's function in this England team requires more thought than effort. In the white shirt of England, Shearer continues to make the runs into wide areas that he does for his club. He does this with total honesty, believing he is helping his team. Without the support of a fellow striker, what he is in fact doing is distancing himself from his team-mates. The build-up should be through the team, with Shearer staying central and attached to his team, enabling him to be used like a wall to bounce the ball off. His runs directly towards goal should only be made when the teams are well into the opposing half.'

In Shearer's defence, Ray Harford told me, 'It goes against the grain for Alan to curtail his running. He likes to play to his physical limits, and I think it's important to him to be seen to be doing that.

Also, the more isolated you are up front, the more you need to have good acceleration. There are times when you have to virtually stand still, and then suddenly go to quick and then lightning quick. He doesn't have that change of pace, and the only way he can compensate for it is to keep on the move and maintain the highest momentum he can.'

It might also have gone against the grain for Shearer to sacrifice some of his scoring instincts, although the view that the odds are heavily stacked against lone strikers getting a lot of goals hardly seemed to stand up in the case of Ruud van Nistelrooy when he was the Champions League's top scorer in the 2002/03 season. And it certainly didn't in the case of Clive Allen at Tottenham in the 1986/87 season.

That was David Pleat's first season as Spurs manager, and in addition to Allen the other attacking players at his disposal included Glenn Hoddle, Ossie Ardiles and Chris Waddle. If Pleat's decision to opt for a 4–5–1 framework was meant to get the best out of any one player, it was Hoddle. The extravagantly gifted England midfielder had always maintained that he needed a free attacking role, one without too many defensive responsibilities, and giving him the support of an extra midfielder seemed the ideal way to grant his wish. The midfield five were in a diamond shape, with Ardiles at the top point – the one closest to the defence – and Hoddle at the bottom point (closest to Allen). Pleat recalled, 'Ardiles would be the one to start off attacks and Hoddle was like the second striker. He did not get a lot of goals himself, but because of his superb passing ability he became the supplier and provider. When people made forward runs from midfield he would often be the one to put them in.'

But it was Allen, very much a goal-poacher – a penalty-box 'ferret', as Pleat described him – who benefited the most. Of course, Allen, too, didn't have to get involved in too much defensive work.

Moreover, apart from having the likes of Hoddle to take the attention of opposing defenders away from him, he didn't have to worry about another striker limiting his positional options. As Pleat explained, 'We gave him the full width of the penalty box – 44 yards across – to work in. We did not want him running into corners, we wanted him to poach. The system gave opposing central defenders a problem. The number 5 would mark Allen, but the number 6 would

into double figures. That season, Spurs finished third in the First Division, reached the FA Cup final and were League Cup semi-finalists.

As it happens, Paul Sturrock also gave an excellent account of himself as a lone striker in a number of European matches for Dundee United. Thanks to the outstanding knowledge and coaching skills of their manager, Jim McLean, that club – traditionally not even the biggest in Dundee let alone Scotland – repeatedly belied their limited financial resources; and what Sturrock learnt there as one of McLean's leading 'protegés' clearly came in handy at Plymouth.

When I talked to Sturrock about Plymouth's impressive scoring record, before his move to Southampton in March 2004, he said that the starting point for it had come at the end of the 2002/03 season when a review of the club's training schedules prompted him to put a greater emphasis on full-sided training games. Previously, Plymouth had put on a lot of small-sided matches, on half the pitch, to help improve the players' control and close-passing skills, but Sturrock felt that this had been taken to the extreme and had caused his team to become too narrow-minded. 'In the context of the sort of football that is played in the Second Division, the full-sided matches gave us more game-related situations,' Sturrock told me. 'I thought we badly needed to open up our play more.' He deemed it even more important for Plymouth to get in more crosses. 'If there is one thing I know [about the art of teams scoring a lot of goals] it's that crosses into the box are the be all and end all,' he said. 'That's how most goals are scored, and it's something we work exceptionally hard on in training.'

As he pointed out, it was not merely coincidental that Manchester United were looked upon as being at their attacking best when they had David Beckham, arguably the best crosser of the ball in the world, on their right flank – notably in the 1999/2000 season when United, with Ryan Giggs on the other wing and a potential scorers' list that included Paul Scholes, Andy Cole, Dwight Yorke, Ole Gunnar Solskjaer and Teddy Sheringham, established their Premiership scoring record of 98 goals. In that particular season, the breakdowns of United's goals revealed that Beckham had set up almost 40 per cent of them.

One of Sturrock's main priorities before the start of the season was to find players who could make Plymouth as dangerous on the left as they had been on the right. This was achieved with the signings of Peter Gilbert on loan from Birmingham and Tony Capaldi on a free transfer from the Midlands club. 'We were very much a right-sided team before,' Sturrock said. 'Although Martin Phillips is a left-footed player, I have preferred to use him on the right because he seems to put in better crosses from there. He's a bit like Fabrice Fernandes [at Southampton]. I ended up playing David Norris [a right-footed player] on the left, and he did quite well for me considering that he was totally out of position. But I just felt we got nothing from that side. The signings of Gilbert and Capaldi changed that. We are much better balanced than we were last season. We are getting in loads of crosses from both sides.'

This was not reflected by the scoring records of Plymouth's strikers – a list that comprised Keith and Evans (Sturrock's first-choice front men), Stonebridge, Lowndes and Sturrock's son, Blair.

Second Division this season,' Sturrock said. 'His scoring ability has improved. Micky was a poor mover in the box before. If the ball was about to be crossed, he would just sort of position himself by the back post and wait for it. You needed radar to find him. Now he's on the move all the time – back post, front post – and he's reaping the benefit. But that is only part of the story with him this season. Just as important to us is that he can hold the ball up and see a pass. When we need him to do that, it doesn't mean he cannot score: if he knocks the ball wide there's no reason why he cannot get into the box and be on the end of the cross. But the main thing is that he has helped to take us forward and given others the scope to put the ball in the net, if not himself. The way Micky has linked our play has been superb. You can bang the ball up to him from the back knowing that it will rarely come back. We work on statistics, and these show that as much as 68 per cent of all the passes that have been played up to our front men have been held. I would say that Micky has been mainly responsible for that.'

To put it another way, it was Evans who could take much of the credit for Plymouth repeatedly being able to bring their wide men into play and, in turn, the midfielders being able to start thinking about making those runs to get on the end of their crosses. 'David Friio created the biggest headaches for defences because he could leave it so late,' Sturrock said. The most stunning example of Plymouth's overall scoring power was the 7–0 win over struggling Chesterfield – their biggest home victory since 1936. Sturrock ranked Plymouth's first-half display, when they scored five goals in the opening seventeen minutes and six by the interval, as the best by any team he had managed. The other reason why the match stood out in his memory was that all but two of the goals came from midfielders. Friio, with two headers from corners and a shot from a headed knockdown by Evans, became the first Plymouth player to get a hat-trick in more than three years. Lee Hodges and Tony Capaldi also found the net.

Upon joining Southampton, Sturrock said: 'Players [non-strikers] have got to have the confidence to go and score goals. They need to go out on the pitch believing they can score and ready to take responsibility rather than maybe leaving it to the front two. Maybe not enough players go out looking to score. They have to have that mindset, and that is something we will work on.' Prior to his arrival, only two goals had come from players in the Saints' midfield section, but on 27 March, in Sturrock's third match as manager, it became three with the extraordinary overhead kick by Rory Delap that brought the new boss his first Southampton win, 1–0 over Tottenham.

Delap, signed for a club-record fee of £4 million from Derby County in the 2002 close season, is noted for his versatility. He filled every outfield position at Derby, including that of striker, and was even their leading scorer at one point. So why was it that his goal against Spurs was his first of the season, and only his third in some 80 matches for the club? Part of the reason was that Southampton often used him at left-back. Moreover, Sturrock suggested that as a midfielder he tended to try to take on too many responsibilities. The manager liked to think that he helped Delap get on the scoresheet by giving the club's eighteen-year-old French player Yoann Folly his first-team debut in a midfield anchor role, thus providing Delap with

Sturrock pointed out. 'He may as well wear a duck on his head because he is never normally on the end of things. He has to appreciate that he is not just there to drag opponents out of position to give others a scoring chance; that he has to try and score himself. I have been chipping away at him over the last couple of weeks, and he has responded in the right way.'

Of course, Delap and Lundekvam still have a long way to go to match David Friio and Paul Wotton. Still, in taking some of the scoring pressure off Southampton's strikers, at least they started moving in the right direction.

CHAPTER NINE
PROVING THE TALENT-SPOTTERS WRONG

achieved, I don't want to be
mollycoddled.'
DION DUBLIN

common occurence nowadays) the transfers of these players represent their best chance of getting out of it. So the importance of the men responsible for bringing them to the clubs in the first place, notably the managers and the chief scouts, cannot be overstated.

One would think that the job should be relatively straight-forward, given the obvious guidelines to the ability of strikers provided by their scoring records. But the competition to sign them is more intense than it is for players in other positions; and the demands of their roles as they go higher on the football ladder mean many other assessment factors have to be taken into account. For strikers, the development process embodies all manner of potential banana skins, and in overcoming them, some have made professional observers appear the biggest of mugs. Indeed, football is littered with many cases of strikers who one way or another have proved clubs wrong; and, of course, that in itself is a pretty powerful reason for all strikers to keep believing that they can earn decent livings from the game.

Because of the traditional physical nature of the British game, clubs searching for schoolboy strikers to sign have always believed in including the builds and physical strength of the players among their key terms of reference. One of the most famous instances of this backfiring was Aberdeen's mistake in the mid-1950s in not signing a striker who went on to prove arguably the greatest player ever to be born and raised in their area – Denis Law. Aberdeen are hardly in one of the traditional football 'hot-beds' and their scouting network in those days was not as rigorous as it was to become when Alex Ferguson took over as manager in 1978. Even so, not giving Law the chance to start his career there was a boob they have never totally lived down.

In truth, many clubs would have found Law an easy player to overlook. As a boy, he gave the impression that he could easily be blown over by a puff of wind. In addition to his frail-looking build, he wore glasses – the uncool, obtrusive National Health type – to correct a squint. He was only able to play for his school team on the basis of a letter from his mother giving permission for him to take them off.

Law was fourteen when he was brought to Huddersfield Town's attention, thanks to their manager, Andy Beattie, who had been born and raised in Aberdeenshire and had a brother who did some scouting for him there. Beattie once said that his first reaction on meeting Law was that his brother was trying to play a practical joke on him. However, the more he saw Law in action, the more he appreciated how deceptive appearances can be. To Beattie, Law's physique could easily be worked on and improved. In the meantime, Law, with his fiery, combative personality, was not the type to allow defenders to walk all over him; on top of this came his hunger for success and those razor-sharp scoring instincts.

Bill Shankly, Huddersfield's assistant manager when Law was

signed by the club, was also enthusiastic about his potential. So much so that Shankly's appointment as Beattie's successor led to Law being given his league debut at the age of just sixteen, a club record. Two years later, Law became the youngest player to be capped by Scotland. For Aberdeen, the agony continued with Law's transfers – all for record fees – to Manchester City, Manchester ... Such was his impact at United that to this day he

did well in his first two ... problem for him was that he was torn between football and golf. He devoted so much time to the latter that it took the edge off his sharpness in goalscoring situations.

Robson became so 'slow off the mark' that Newcastle were considering putting him on the transfer list. But Robson then came into contact with a man called Len Heppell, a local nightclub owner, a former professional dancing champion and an expert on body movement and balance in relation to sport. Heppell worked with a number of top players, including Peter Shilton and Bobby Moore, but he paid particular attention to Robson. After all, Robson was dating Heppell's daughter, Maureen, one of the top table-tennis players in the country who was to become the striker's wife. So for his father-in-law-to-be, the quest to make Robson quicker became virtually a personal crusade.

Throughout the close season, Robson was subjected to an intensive programme of exercises designed to change his posture, running gait and step patterns. 'When I went to his house, I had to practise running up the stairs lightly,' he recalled. 'I had to do it lightly enough for him not to hear me. It was a bit nerve-racking – he had two big Alsatians at the time.' Another aspect of his training under Heppell was that he had to play table tennis for two to three hours each day. The results of this were plain for all to see the following season, not to mention the rest of Robson's 21-year career as a player. The legendary ex-Newcastle striker Jackie Milburn summed it up when he approached Heppell and asked, 'What has happened to Pop? He looks like a sprinter who has had lead taken out of his boots.'

Even then, many would-be buyers would have been tempted to put him under the microscope to see if they could find anything else that might be wrong with him. To varying degrees, all signings are gambles, but it is those involving strikers that often provoke the most procrastination. As Gordon Strachan said, 'You really can tie yourself in knots when you are assessing a striker. It's good to not want to make a mistake, to do your homework properly, but I think you can take this to the extreme. Obviously, the closer you study him, the more likely it will be that you will see him do something wrong or have a bad game. You can easily take it out of context.'

'The number of goals he averages per season has to be the starting point,' Mark McGhee said. 'Some people score a lot of goals and others can't and never will. I sometimes forget this when I am organising a team to defend free-kicks and corners. They [the opposition] might have two tall guys who get involved in set-pieces, and I am telling our lads, "Right, you mark him, you mark him." Then, suddenly, I think, "Why are you doing this? They hardly ever score." As far as strikers are concerned, you will find that some play on the periphery and that these tend to be the ones who get, say, ten goals a season as opposed to twenty or twenty-five goals a season.' Still, as McGhee went on to point out, such bare statistics do not show the service the strikers have received, the standard and styles of play of their teams and the number of chances they have missed. Thus, though scoring records do not lie, they can be misleading. 'It [the terms of reference in the assessment of potential striker signings] is not easy to simplify,' McGhee added. 'What sort of striker do you need? A target man? A runner? Are you going to be able to play in a way that will bring the best out of him? If he is

club chairman] to watch Pontus Kamark [the Swedish full-back playing for IFK Gothenburg]. Early in the game he hit a pass of great quality from one side of the field to the other, and I said to Martin, "Let's go. I've seen enough." You see one small thing and that's it. It can be the same with strikers. One I wanted to sign for Millwall was Brett Ormerod [who was bought by Gordon Strachan for Southampton from Blackpool]. We had watched him a couple of times and I felt that his work-rate, enthusiasm and pace were bound to bring him goals at our level. Although his touch wasn't great, he had too many other things going for him for us to be unwilling to take a chance on him.'

If any club at Football League level have benefited from their willingness to take chances on strikers, to rely on their ability to unearth rough diamonds and polish them, it's Bristol Rovers. In recent years, the strikers they have picked up, mainly from schoolboy and non-league football, and then sold on for a profit have included Marcus Stewart, Barry Hayles, Bobby Zamora, Jamie

Cureton, Jason Roberts and Nathan Ellington. The money they paid for these six amounted to a couple of hundred thousand pounds; the money they received for them totalled more than £6.5 million. Though Rovers needed the cash to ease their financial problems, and the players inevitably wanted to move on to bigger stages, it's easy to see why their fans have had mixed feelings about the situation. After Rovers had narrowly failed to reach the Second Division promotion play-offs in 2000, Zamora, Cureton and Roberts were sold to Brighton, Reading and West Bromwich Albion respectively. The following season, Rovers were relegated; the season after that (during which they eventually sold Ellington to Wigan), they came close to losing their league status. The success of Zamora at Brighton will have been particularly painful to Rovers followers. His goals were the main reason why Brighton were able to climb from the Third Division to the First in successive seasons.

The progress of those strikers at Rovers reflected enormous credit on the hard work and expertise of their manager at the time, Ian Holloway, and his coaches Gary Penrice and Garry Thompson, especially as, according to Thompson, the trio's opinions about the players' potential was not widely endorsed by some figures at boardroom level.

In some cases, they were in good company. Take Jason Roberts, who started his career at Wolves and was signed on a free transfer by Rovers at the age of twenty, without having made any league appearances for the Molineux club. Thompson, the former Aston Villa and West Bromwich Albion centre-forward, said, 'I was with Northampton when I first saw him. He had been loaned to Torquay, and in his match against us he caused absolute havoc in our defence. He was big, strong and quick, and though he was very raw, he just struck me as a lad who was willing to learn. I asked someone who had worked with Jason for his views about him, and he said, "Oh, he's effing hopeless." The guy was particularly critical of his ability to hold the ball with his back to the goal and bring other people into the game. "He keeps falling over," he said. Well, OK, I could see where he was coming from. But I knew this aspect of his game could be improved. One thing I noticed about Jason was that he tended to receive the ball square on. If you do that, and the centre-half pushes you in the back, then unless you have the strength and the build of

have the happiest of times there, but his fortunes rose again after Wigan signed him for £1.8 million in the 2003/04 season. His partnership with Nathan Ellington was one of the most effective in the First Division; but for Roberts' suspension at the tail-end of the season it could easily have propelled Wigan into the Premiership.

On the subject of rough diamonds, Southampton's Ray Clarke, the only ex-striker filling a chief scout role in the Premiership, recalled his spell at Coventry and the club's signing of the young Belgian centre-forward Cedric Roussel from Gent. 'People said that he wasn't good enough for the Premiership because he wasn't the quickest or most polished of strikers,' Clarke said. 'I don't think that his scoring record for us – about eleven goals in 31 matches – was bad. In any case, we bought him for other reasons. He was a big lad and we felt that he would be able to hold the ball up for us and give us the greater physical presence we needed to help bring out the best in players like Robbie Keane. Our most impressive performance with Cedric in the side was a 3–2 home win over Arsenal. He caused all sorts of problems for Arsenal's central defenders Tony Adams and Martin Keown. In fact, a couple of days later I got a call about it from Arsenal's chief scout. "Where did you get the boy Roussel from?" he asked. "He really battered our two central defenders and there aren't many strikers who have done that."

'Cedric wasn't with Coventry for very long, just a season. Unfortunately, apart from injuries, he had some personal problems. But he did do a job for us, and though some people felt that we ended up paying too much for him [£900,000], we did get more than £1.5 million for him when we sold him to Wolves.' What a great piece of business that proved for Coventry. Roussel failed to make an impact with Wolves, whose determination not to lose more money on him than was absolutely necessary when offloading him led to the striker taking his case to Fifa. He was eventually transferred back to Racing Genk for an 'undisclosed' fee.

Generally, it is foreign strikers who represent the biggest transfer-market gambles. In addition to the problems for them in Britain caused by the language barrier and cultural differences, Clarke pointed out, 'Teams in England tend to "hit" their front men earlier than they do in other countries. The game here is not as studious and technical. It's quicker and more competitive, and I think players have to work harder. The pressure is relentless.' Indeed, for every Henry or van Nistelrooy there are plenty of other foreign strikers who have not fared as well in England as their obvious talent promised. And in some cases, that's putting it mildly.

Southampton themselves saw that side of the coin through the extent to which Ecuador's 2002 World Cup star Agustin Delgado (effectively brought to the club by the chairman, Rupert Lowe) became conspicuous by his first-team absence. So, too, did Blackburn after buying Corrado Grabbi for £6.7 million; Middlesbrough after signing Massimo Maccarone for a club-record

£8.15 million; Aston Villa after they also broke their transfer-market spending record by splashing out £9.5 million on Juan Pablo Angel; and Liverpool following their £10 million purchase of El Hadji Diouf. At least Angel, who was signed by John Gregory, then banished to the sidelines by Gregory's successor Graham Taylor, but who finally found an ally in Taylor's successor David O'Leary, came good eventually. In the 2003/04 season, his third in English football,

star's poor performances were a factor in Liverpool parting company with the manager.

Of course, British strikers have also had mixed fortunes abroad. Even scorers in the class of Jimmy Greaves and Ian Rush found it an uphill struggle when they moved to Italy. Greaves lasted only four months at AC Milan, and Rush spent just a season with Juventus, where he got seven goals in 29 matches in 1987/88 before returning to his spiritual home of Liverpool.

It has been suggested that the big clubs in other countries tend to be less conservative in their transfer-market shopping for overseas players than their English counterparts. One wonders what they would make of the thoroughness with which Clarke assesses potential signings for Southampton. Clarke has initiated a system whereby every time he or one of the Southampton scouts under his jurisdiction runs the rule over a player, he has to log his evaluation of his performance on a four-page document. The one Clarke has formulated for strikers comprises eight sections, each of which is broken down into around eight aspects of their game. Alongside every one is an 'Excellent, Very Good, Good, Average, Poor' ticking box. It seems to go against McGhee's point about 'gut feeling', but, Clarke said, 'While that does come into it – it has to – I don't think you can have too much data about a player, especially if you are a Premiership club. The Premiership is a different world compared with, say, the Nationwide League. You have to be as discerning as you can because the standard is so high. As far as strikers are concerned, it's one thing to get X number of goals in the Nationwide League, quite another to get the same number in the Premiership, where defenders don't make as many mistakes.'

During the 2003/04 season, the Nationwide striker who impressed him the most was Jonathan Stead. Clarke was one of a number of Premiership scouts attracted to the 21-year-old as he emerged as one of the leading scorers in the Third Division with Huddersfield. Having been with the club since leaving school, Stead had established himself in their first team only the previous season and his scoring record then was just six goals in 42 matches. Clarke found that difficult to believe when confronted with the assessment reports he had gathered on the player's 2003/04 performances. One that was particularly complimentary to Stead concerned his performance against Doncaster Rovers in January 2004. Stead was assessed as 'very good' or 'good' on all but one of the points in his evaluation document for that game. The exception concerned his movement, for which he was deemed to have been 'excellent'. On top of this, he received a mark of eight out of ten for his overall performance and nine out of ten for his potential. As for 'gut feeling', Clarke said, 'Whenever I saw him, he always looked dangerous. I liked the fact that he was always looking to play on the shoulder of defenders – I don't like to see strikers go too short when they have the chance to get in behind defenders – and he also impressed me with his football intelligence and composure. I remember a great goal he scored against Mansfield. When the ball was crossed from the right, the odds on him reaching it before the keeper could only have been 60/40, if that. But he had the presence of mind to dummy it and, with the keeper having sold himself, the finish was just a formality for him. OK, it was the Third Division, but I thought,

Southampton

were unwilling to match Southampton included, preferred to play a waiting game.

The issue, which came to a head in March, created something of a dilemma for Southampton, because of Gordon Strachan's decision not to remain their manager. Rupert Lowe, who has the final say on all transfer deals at the club, was sensitive about the possibility that, while Strachan might like Stead, his successor would take a different view of the signing. Moreover, Lowe's debate with other members of the training and coaching staff over Stead didn't produce any overwhelming conclusions about his ability one way or the other.

On top of all the usual pros and cons involved in assessments of young players in the lower divisions, Stead didn't immediately strike one as having the athleticism required of a Premiership player. At 6ft 3in and just over twelve stone, he has a gangling build that can give the impression of his lacking the power to hold off opponents and get away from them. Clarke said, 'I had an argument over this with a friend of mine who had seen him play. He asked whether I thought

Stead was quick enough for the Premiership, and I said, "Well, he's not greased lightning, but I think he's quick enough, and if he isn't quick enough now, I'm sure he will be." The way I looked at it was that he had yet to fulfil his physical and mental potential. I felt he could get stronger with the right training, and through that he would get quicker as well.

'To be honest, if it had been down to me I would probably have taken a chance on him,' Clarke admitted. 'But I wasn't about to throw my dummy out of the pram [when Blackburn bought him]. While I have confidence in my ability to judge players, I have long learnt that you cannot be too dogmatic about these things. It's all about opinions, and sometimes, what might have seemed the wrong opinion in hindsight might still have been the right one at the time. Yes, I think Stead has the potential to be a good Premiership player, but with respect to him, we aren't talking about an Henry or a van Nistelrooy. I am quite aware of how I could be proved wrong about him.'

Blackburn, of course, needed to take that Stead gamble more than Southampton did. They were in danger of being relegated at the time, and with Grabbi having failed to adjust to English football and Andrew Cole and Dwight Yorke not performing as they had at Manchester United, they badly needed some fresh firepower to get them out of trouble. Stead responded to the challenge impressively, scoring five goals in his opening ten matches – goals that directly brought them thirteen points from those games – and prompted increasingly flattering public comments about his performances from Blackburn manager Graeme Souness. After Stead's second goal in as many matches in the 1–1 draw against Newcastle, Souness said, 'The way he took it was reminiscent of Alan Shearer. It was a really aggressive finish. Jon was going to make sure that the ball was only going to finish up in one place – in the back of the net. He pleased me in other ways. He embarrasses people with the amount of honest running he does for himself and the team, and if you do that you have a chance of being a player.' After his tenth goal, in the 1–0 win at Everton, Souness added, 'Every week I try to play down Jon's contribution, ' ... I'm going to have to tell the truth.' Perhaps one ... referring to Stead's part in

well initially. He s p..., what happens when that burst of exc... opposing teams have become more aware of what he has to o... How is he going to handle the pressure of people expecting him to do well as opposed to hoping he will do so? I would say that strikers – goalscorers – tend to experience the biggest problems in these areas. You look at the attention Wayne Rooney has attracted. For all his brilliance, it's going to be difficult for him to cope with all the expectations that have been heaped on him.'

Still, Stead, in his bid to keep progressing, has no shortage of role models. One to have made it as a top Premiership striker after initially catching the eye at the bottom of the Football League ladder is Dion Dublin. After being released by Norwich City (without making any first-team appearances) and then going into non-league football with King's Lynn, Dublin was a member of the Cambridge United team that rose from the old Fourth Division to the Second in successive seasons in the early 1990s. He became a top-flight player with Manchester United, and maintained his status with Coventry (where he gained his England caps) and, most recently, Aston Villa.

'I have never been the quickest player in the world,' he said, 'but I was always good in the air, my touch was good and I had a hunger for goals.' Cambridge, under the management of John Beck, were hardly among the most stylish of teams. Dublin, referring to Beck's adherence to a no-frills long-ball game, admitted, 'In a way, I was possibly a better player than I might have looked there. We were a young team, and we knew we could play, but it [Cambridge's pragmatic style] was working, so who were we to argue with the manager? Also, I was learning all the time. In training, John Beck and Chris Turner [his assistant] gave me countless coaching tips in connection with my movement in the box and things like that, and I just got better and better. I also had some great advice from people like Brian Kidd at Manchester United and Gordon Strachan at Coventry.

'The fact is that I have always been able to take all the coaching tips on board and never ever felt that I had nothing more to learn. I think the real secret of being able to adjust to different levels is having a good football brain. The higher you go, the more important it becomes for you to be able to think one or two moves ahead. It's also important to be able to accept criticism. I look upon myself as an "old-school" striker because, no matter how much success I might have achieved, I don't want to be mollycoddled. Obviously I don't want my manager or coach to be rude or disrespectful to me, but I like to be told if I haven't done something well or not had a good game, and I like him to explain why.'

It probably goes without saying that, to Clarke, even better role models for Stead (and any other young striker on the way up) are Shearer, Henry and van Nistelrooy. Clarke is particularly enamoured with the latter. Having long felt a particular affinity with Dutch football through his background as a player in Holland and his contacts in the country, Clarke was among the first English football figures to recognise that van Nistelrooy could become an outstanding player. Clarke had started keeping tabs on the Dutchman at the end of the 1996/97 season, when the player was just twenty and playing mainly as an attacking midfielder for Den ˙ ˙ ᵗʰᵉ Dutch Second Division. Clarke was Southampton's ⁻ⁿᵈ with his team's fixtures completed, ˙ ˙ʰ ꜱome matches there. ⁻ʰᵗ ᵗₒ

Heeᵣₑₙ..

doubts Clarke might have ₙₐ₋ get to the top were finally dispelled when nₑ w₋. debut as a substitute for Holland's under-21 team, and then ꜱₑₑ₋ twice for Heerenveen in 4–2 win over Utrecht the following Saturday. Clarke recalled, 'I said to Gordon, "This guy is going to be a top player." Alex Miller [Coventry's assistant manager] then went to watch him, and finally Gordon did so as well. I'm not sure if either was as excited about him as I was – don't forget, I had watched him a number of times – but both agreed that he had a lot of potential.'

That Coventry did not take their interest in van Nistelrooy further was due partly to the fact that Heerenveen, who had paid only £400,000 for van Nistelrooy, said that they wanted at least £4 million for him (his eventual transfer fee when he moved to PSV Eindhoven in 1998 was £4.2 million, a record deal between Dutch clubs). Moreover, it coincided with Coventry's existing first-choice strikers, Dublin and Darren Huckerby, coming to the fore and establishing one of the hottest scoring partnerships in the Premiership. 'Coventry were not a club who could afford to pay that sort of money for any player and put him on the bench,' Clarke said.

'You also had to take into account that van Nistelrooy had reached a stage in his career where he was looking beyond clubs such as Coventry. PSV Eindhoven are one of the biggest and most successful clubs in Holland, but Coventry, despite being in the Premiership, were not one of the biggest and most successful clubs in England.

'Because of my connections with Dutch football, I started receiving calls from friends of mine at other clubs asking for advice on him,' he added. 'There was a feeling that he did not work hard enough and was a bit of a prima donna. However, as Coventry weren't going to try and sign him I saw no reason not to tell them exactly what I felt about him. I just said, "Go and get him."'

This became increasingly a case of stating the obvious. In his first season with Eindhoven, van Nistelrooy was the top scorer in the Dutch League with 31 goals in 34 matches, which put him in second place in the European Golden Boot rankings, and was voted the country's Player of the Year by his fellow professionals. The following season it was 29 goals in 23 matches. No club needed convincing that he was a special talent by this stage, least of all Manchester United. Their first attempt to sign him, for £19 million towards the end of the 1999/2000 season, floundered because of medical worries concerning a previous knee injury. But even after those fears had been brought into sharp focus shortly afterwards by the torn cruciate ligament that was to force him out of action for the best part of a year, United were unwilling to give up on him.

In his first season at Old Trafford, he became the first player in United's history to score in seven successive matches (a sequence that was stretched to eight matches), and his eventual total of 36 in all competitions was the best by a United player for fourteen years. He again pushed Henry into second place the following season, with 44. It was a different story in the 2003/04 campaign, although fans of van Nistelrooy will be quick to point out that he was playing in a revamped, comparatively unsettled team.

In September 2003, Ron Atkinson, in his column in the ⸱ ⸱ ⸱ wrote, 'There has been a change in the way Manchester ⸱ ⸱ ⸱ ⸱d Beckham and Juan Sebastian Veron left. ⸱ ⸱ ⸱me invention in their passing, ⸱ ⸱ ⸱ holes is injured. ⸱ ⸱ ⸱ng

With Dᴄᴄ marker and spring on ᴛᴏ ⸱ the passing tends to be safe bread-aɴᴅ a lot of possession to feet with his back to the goaʟ. ⸱ record was still good enough to put him in the number two spoᴛ ᴄ the Premiership's scoring list; and of course unlike Henry, he was among the leading European Championship scorers. Indeed, he is more than Manchester United's top scorer. He is also their most saleable playing asset.

Is there anything van Nistelrooy lacks as a striker? 'My only criticism of him would be that he is not physical enough,' Clarke said. 'With the greatest of respect, though he is a big lad [6ft 2in, 12st 13lb], he doesn't use his physical power as much as I feel he could.' Then he smiled, and added, 'But maybe he doesn't need to because he has so much.'

CHAPTER TEN
THE GREATEST GOALS

TREVOR FRANCIS

Goals are generally remembered ... match have been forgotten. But of all the sh... that have found the net in top-level football since the war, and especially those seen by big television audiences, which have been the best?

Such questions can always be relied upon to spark a long, animated debate among followers of the game. There are, of course, a number of ways in which the merits of various goals can be assessed, as Trevor Francis acknowledged when we discussed the ones that have tended to be featured prominently in books and videos on the subject. 'You have to be very specific in your criteria,' Francis pointed out, 'and even then it can be extremely subjective. I have lost count of the number of goals that have excited me and I would find it very difficult to narrow them down to what I would consider to be my biggest favourites. Where do you draw the line?'

A goal doesn't necessarily need to come across as technically spectacular to stand out in the memory. If one is talking about important goals, there are, for example, those scored by Adrian Heath and Mark Robins for Everton and Manchester United respectively. Both were typical 'bread-and-butter' striker goals, apparently simple, straightforward efforts that illustrated some of the fundamental requirements of the front man's job rather than outstanding individualism. However, those goals will always be recognised as major defining moments in the histories of the two clubs.

Heath's strike came during Everton's fifth-round League Cup tie against Oxford United at the Manor Ground in January 1984, at a time when Everton were near the bottom of the First Division and there was much speculation about the future of their manager, Howard Kendall. Having been appointed in 1981, Kendall had struggled to improve the team's fortunes and it was widely believed that defeat against Oxford, then at the top of the Third Division, would signal his departure. Few would have bet against that defeat occurring after Bobby McDonald gave the home team the lead. But nine minutes from the end Heath got the equaliser. There didn't look to be much for Oxford's fans to worry about when defender Kevin Brock gained possession and, under pressure from Peter Reid, elected to play the ball back to his keeper. But the pass was under-hit, and because of Heath's anticipation and predatory instincts, Oxford were unable to get away with it. Heath, clean through with only the keeper to beat, was the epitome of coolness as he applied the finishing touch. From that day on, Kendall and Everton went from strength to strength. Everton beat Oxford 4–1 in the replay and went on to reach the final, where they lost to Liverpool. They also reached the FA Cup final, this time ending up victorious (against Watford), and finished seventh in the league. Over the next three seasons they won the championship twice, the European Cup Winners' Cup, and reached another two FA Cup finals.

Robins' goal, in a 1–0 FA Cup third-round win at Nottingham Forest in January 1990, was an even more famous turning point in football, for Alex Ferguson at Manchester United. As with Kendall at Everton, Ferguson had been at United for three years and had failed to produce the results and performances expected of him. United had slipped since the heady days of their European Cup ⋯ 1968 (the last time they had qualified for the competition ⋯ their decline was such that in 1990 ⋯ Edwards, had come ⋯

though a lean ⋯ goals in that period. A few mon⋯ 5–1 at Manchester City; and when they were bea⋯ Crystal Palace in December 1989, on the third anniversary of Ferguson's arrival from Aberdeen, a banner unfurled at Old Trafford's Scoreboard End read: 'Three years of excuses and it's still crap. Ta-ra Fergie.'

In the week of the Forest match, the consensus of media opinion about Fergie's position was that he was living on borrowed time and that an early exit from the FA Cup – by that stage the only competition he could win – would mean time-up for him at Old Trafford.

As for Robins, he was only twenty and was making only his third full first-team appearance. Ferguson had described him as 'the best finisher at the club', which was borne out to some extent by Robins' scoring record for the reserves, but the manager felt that he had a long way to go to become a serious contender for a regular place in the side at the expense of Hughes or McClair. Apart from his comparative lack of experience, there were also reservations about Robins on the grounds of his limited overall contribution to his teams. He himself drew attention to this after he had left United when he was asked to comment on United's signing of Andy Cole, a striker who seemed no less focused than Robins had been on getting on the end of attacking moves. 'I'm quite happy now to be talked of in those terms, and I'm sure Andy Cole is too,' Robins said. 'People say, "All he does is score goals," but that seems a pretty good label to me. My all-round game has actually improved a lot. At Norwich [his second club] I concentrated more on my contribution outside the box, which affected my goal ratio but made me a better team man. Now [at Leicester] I want to get back to what I'm good at.'

The chance to do what he was good at for United against Forest stemmed mainly from the injuries that rendered a number of their key players unavailable for selection. Among them was the club captain, Bryan Robson, whose place in midfield was filled by McClair, with Robins brought in to fill the latter's role as Hughes's partner up front. In a tight, scrappy match, Hughes and Robins combined to bring United the only goal after 55 minutes. The move began with United's Lee Martin dispossessing Thorvaldur Orlygsson near the left touchline; he just managed to stop the ball going out of play and then played a short pass to Hughes. The Forest defence was caught square as Hughes curled the ball into the goalmouth with the outside of his right foot, and Robins, having made a cleverly timed run to get in front of the last defender, Stuart Pearce, did the rest. It was hardly a 'Roy of the Rovers' type of goal; the ball bounced up invitingly as Robins got the better of the Forest and England left-back, and he was able to find the net with a gentle stooping header. But thanks to missed chances by Forest's striker Nigel Jemson, United held on to that lead – and Ferguson held on to his job.

It proved, of course, to be the launching pad for United to win the FA Cup that season – their first trophy for five years – for Ferguson to establish himself as the most successful manager in

British football history, and for Manchester United to become the
world's richest club. Robins' fate was rather different. Though he
scored decisive goals in other FA Cup rounds that season, against
˙ ˙ˑ the fifth round and Oldham in the semi-final replay, he
ˑˑꞁ for both United's matches against
˙ ꞁ ˖ Norwich two years later
ˑʳts about his

[1]

remained ɑ ˑ
Manchester United. Even ˑˑ
a United fan, anywhere, he is liable ᴛᴏ ˑˑ
suspects that in the company of a United follower he ᴡˑ
to buy a drink.

And imagine the celebrity status Robins would have achieved
had that goal against Forest been in the class of the ones that can be
seen in most of those 'Great Goal' videos, the sort that immediately
spring to mind when one thinks of the truly great players: Puskas,
Pele, Carlos Alberto, Maradona, Van Basten, Beckham . . .

It's a potentially endless subject, but how's this for a short-list
to sate the appetites of all goal gluttons?

**FERENC PUSKAS: Hungary's third goal in the 6–3 win over
England at Wembley in November 1953.**

England captain Billy Wright can never have had a more
embarrassing experience throughout his 105-match international
career than the one Puskas inflicted upon him when a cross landed
at the roly-poly Hungarian's feet on the edge of the six-yard box.

That was more than enough to give Puskas a great scoring chance, but he made it even better as Wright attempted a last-ditch sliding tackle. Wright was left tackling thin air because as he lunged in, Puskas pulled the ball away from him with the sole of his left foot. It was a drag-back par excellence, and the next step – a searing shot past the keeper, also with that magic wand of a left foot – was a formality. 'What struck me about this goal,' said Trevor Francis, 'apart from the dexterity with which Puskas beat Wright, was the extent to which he wanted to use his left foot. Most players who favour one side as much as he did can be described as being too predictable. But the only thing predictable about this goal was that it was predictably brilliant. A lot of players would have felt they had a reasonable chance of scoring without having to do that trick. Puskas did not have a bad shooting angle for a finish with the right foot when the ball came over to him; one touch, if that, and a sidefoot might have done it. But Puskas clearly had it in mind to get a lot of power into the shot, on the premise that even if the keeper got to the ball he would be unlikely to keep it out, and for him, getting the ball on to that left foot was the best way to achieve this. When Wright put him under pressure, Puskas's quickness of thought, confidence and composure were tremendous.'

PELE: Brazil's third goal in the 5–2 win over Sweden in the 1958 World Cup final.

What a way for the then seventeen-year-old Pele to mark his arrival on the World Cup stage. He had already scored the only goal in the 1–0 win over Wales in the quarter-final – on his debut – and a hat-trick in the 5–2 victory against France in the semi-final. He got two more against Sweden, one with a leap for a cross and a header that made it difficult to believe that, at 5ft 8in, he was considerably shorter than the defenders he beat. But his other goal, his first, was the one that made the biggest impact. From a Nilton Santos pass, Pele edged the ball past one defender with his ˹ then, most memorably, he coolly hooked the ball over ⋯ touch was to despatch it into the net ˹odge the importance ˹˹˹

made the ˹˹˹ the ground, controlled the ˹˹˹ his chest. Players need to be very well balanc˹ mastery of the ball that Pele showed in that situation. It set him up perfectly for what was to follow. Apart from anything else, that goal also showed the determination and single-mindedness that scorers need. He was actually fouled by the next defender he beat: the player caught him at the top of his thigh, and Pele could easily have gone down and got a penalty. But there was only one thing on his mind: to keep going and put the ball in the net.'

CARLOS ALBERTO: Brazil's fourth goal in the 4–1 victory against Italy in the 1970 World Cup final.

As with Real Madrid at club level, Brazil are the national team that has traditionally put the biggest emphasis on open, attacking football. Their reputation for playing without inhibitions, with all players expressing their creative talents and making themselves potential scorers no matter what their positions, was summed up perfectly by that Alberto goal. The wonderful build-up to it started just outside the Brazil penalty area and comprised eight passes and a mazy Clodoaldo dribble through four Italian defenders. For the last phase of the move, Rivelino, on the left flank, hit the ball down the line to Jairzinho, who moved inside and squared it to the feet of Pele in the middle. Pele's path to goal was blocked by Italy's captain and sweeper Giacinto Facchetti, who also had a team-mate covering him. But Pele knew that he would not have to wait very long for support. Within seconds, Alberto, making a late run into the area to Pele's right, was alongside him. Pele knocked a simple pass into his path, and the Brazil right-back and captain did the rest with a thunderous low shot across the keeper. 'This was what I would describe as the best "team" goal I have seen,' said Francis. 'One of the things it highlighted was Pele's ability to involve himself in the general play. Quite apart from the way he set up Alberto, he was involved in the early build-up deep inside his own half. The fact that he then had to get to the other end of the field as quickly as possible was no problem to him. Among the most common aspects of successful teams is that all the players want the ball – nobody hides – and that the communication among them is good. Looking at the video of this goal, I am 99.9 per cent sure that Pele got a call from Alberto as the defender was coming through behind him. It was a response to what he heard, not what he could see; and in that respect, the pass that Pele gave him is also worthy of special mention. People might say, "Oh, what was so great about a simple pass like that?" It was great because it was absolutely perfectly weighted: Alberto did not have to break stride to make the most of it. As for the finish, Alberto did what managers and coaches advise all strikers to do in that position: shoot across the keeper. Any striker in the world would be proud to produce a shot like that.'

DIEGO MARADONA: Argentina's second goal in the 2–1 win over England in the 1986 World Cup quarter-final.

... ~~the~~ greatest ever solo goal? From deep within his own half,
~~wi~~th the England team with the ball before
~~...~~ range. It began with a drag-
~~...~~ ~~Reid~~ and Peter

wake. Final,
steering the ball wide
Argentinian's shooting angle and supr
imperiously nonchalant prod as Butcher, tearing ...
second opportunity to stop him, was poised to get in a tackle. Earlier,
of course, Maradona had greatly undermined his image, and that of
the game, through the blatant cheating with which he put Argentina
ahead with that 'Hand of God' goal. But the second was
unquestionably thrilling enough to at least partly make up for it.
'Other memorable goals in this mould have included the one that
John Barnes scored for England [in the June 1984 friendly against
Brazil in Rio] and Ryan Giggs's goal for Manchester United [in the
April 1999 FA Cup semi-final replay against Arsenal at Villa Park],'
pointed out Francis. 'They were fantastic; from a technical
viewpoint, both can be compared with Maradona's effort. But,
rightly or wrongly, I always base my assessment of goals partly on the
sort of matches in which they were scored, so I have to put
Maradona's at the top of the list for that reason alone. Also, I don't
think I have ever seen a player keep the ball under such close control
while running with it at such high speed. The ball seemed to be tied
to him. It was almost as if it was part of his body. The awareness he

showed with his finish, in terms of his decision to take the ball past Shilton and the fact that Butcher was probably no more than a split-second away from getting in a decisive tackle, was spot on too.'

MARCO VAN BASTEN: Holland's second goal in the 2–0 win over the USSR in the 1988 European Championship final.

Volleys are the most difficult shots to execute, which is why the superb one with which Zinedine Zidane gave Real Madrid their 2–1 victory over Bayer Leverkusen in the 2002 Champions League final has gone down as one of the best finishes in the competition's history. But even that effort was not as eye-catching as the volleyed goal scored by Van Basten, the greatest centre-forward of his generation, which helped bring Holland their only major trophy. It came from a great left-wing cross by Arnold Muhren that cleared the USSR defence and picked out Van Basten on the far side of the penalty area. Even then, the USSR could not have envisaged what was to follow because Van Basten, with his marker still only a yard or two away from him, had the most difficult of shooting angles. However, as the ball dropped, Van Basten elected to hit it first time, and propelled it into the far top corner of the net. Not for nothing was Van Basten the boyhood idol of Ruud van Nistelrooy. The latter was only twelve when he saw his hero score that goal (Van Basten's twelfth of the competition). 'It was one of my most inspiring experiences,' he has said. 'I was at that match,' said Francis, 'and the goal made a big impression on me as well. I have never seen a goal quite like that; for me, only a world-class striker with an abundance of confidence in his ability would have even dreamt of trying such a shot. The fact that he pulled away from his marker as the ball came across made the shot even more difficult. He was about twenty yards from goal and the shooting angle looked virtually impossible. The defender opposing him had every right to think that he would have to bring the ball down and take him on. The keeper wasn't in a bad position, but because of the power and accuracy of the shot, no ' - world would have got to it.'

attention. It ca...
coasting and happy just to re...
receiving the ball some 55 yards from the w...
noting that their keeper Neil Sullivan was off his line, had other ideas. Like a golfer playing a shot from the fairway to the green, he chipped the ball over Sullivan's head and into the net. Beckham did what even the great Pele had failed to do in the 1970 World Cup finals, when from just inside his own half, the Brazilian produced a similarly outrageous chip over the Czechoslovakian keeper, but the ball bounced narrowly wide. 'This might seem a strange thing to say,' said Francis, 'but not all professional players have enough strength in their quadriceps, or the necessary technique, to be able to hit the ball that far, never mind do so with any degree of accuracy. I sometimes watch a light-hearted Saturday-morning television programme called Soccer AM in which they invite players to attempt to chip balls against the crossbar from the halfway line. Very few players are able to do it; generally, their attempts are dreadful. OK, you could argue that hitting the ball on to the bar is more difficult than getting the ball into the net. But even if you were to ask them to do what Beckham did, without a goalkeeper there,

the percentage of players not being able to manage it would be considerably higher than you might think. You would certainly have to look long and hard to find any prepared to try it in a match. For me, his goal was typical of someone not just with his ability but also his inexperience. Quite often it's the younger players, the players who are relatively free of inhibitions, who are the most adventurous.'

The latest and most vivid example, of course, is Wayne Rooney, England's star in the European Championship in Portugal. 'In terms of performing without fear, he played like Michael Owen played in the 1998 World Cup finals,' Francis said. 'But in another sense, he also played as if he had been a top player for 10 years. What i find so remarkable about Rooney is that his individualism is combined with an excellent understanding of the game. He does the right thing at the right times, which is unusual for a lad of his age.' Rooney's image as a player who can score the sort of goals that a lot of other forwards can only dream about was born publicly in October 2002, when the Everton teenager, five days before his 17th birthday, was brought on as a substitute at home against Arsenal. It was only his tenth Everton appearance but with the highlights of the match shown on ITV that night, Rooney made it one for millions to remember by running the Gunners' defence ragged and finally producing a superb last-minute lob over keeper David Seaman from 35 yards to give Everton a 2-1 win.

Great goals were very much a feature of Francis's performances when he was a teenager. Quite apart from the ones he got with long-range shots, Francis – like Rooney a first team league player when he was only 16 – recalled: 'There were a number where I collected the ball on the half-way line and dribbled past three or four defenders before scoring.'

I did not have the courage to ask Francis whether he viewed such experiences as being better than sex; publicly, it is not known whether the likes of Adrian Heath, Mark Robins, Ferenc Puskas, Pele, Carlos Alberto, Diego Maradona, Marco Van Basten and Beckham have ever subscribed to that view. But if the answer is yes, 1d blame them?

INDEX

INDEX

LAW & ETHICS
for Pharmacy Technicians

Second Edition

LAW & ETHICS

for Pharmacy Technicians

Jahangir Moini, MD, MPH, CPhT

Professor and Former Director
Allied Health Sciences

Pharmacy Technician Program
Everest University
Melbourne, Florida

Adjunct Professor of Science
Brevard Community College
Palm Bay, Florida

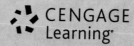

CENGAGE
Learning

Australia • Brazil • Mexico • Singapore • United Kingdom • United States

**Law & Ethics for Pharmacy Technicians,
2nd Edition**
Jahangir Moini

Vice President, General Manager for Skills &
Product Planning: Dawn Gerrain

Product Director: Stephen Helba

Senior Acquisitions Editor: Tari Broderick

Director, Development-Career and
Computing: Marah Bellegarde

Product Development Manager: Juliet Steiner

Product Assistant: Nicole Manikas

Executive Brand Manager: Wendy Mapstone

Associate Market Development Manager:
Jonathan Sheehan

Senior Production Director: Wendy Troeger

Production Manager: Andrew Crouth

Content Project Management and
Art Direction: PreMediaGlobal

Media Developer: William Overocker

Cover Image: © Orla/shutterstock

Library of Congress Control Number: 2013933572

ISBN-13: 978-1-285-08206-6

Cengage Learning
200 First Stamford Place, 4th Floor
Stamford CT 06902
USA

Cengage Learning is a leading provider of customized learning solutions
with office locations around the globe, including Singapore, the United
Kingdom, Australia, Mexico, Brazil, and Japan. Locate your local office at
www.cengage.com/global

Cengage Learning products are represented in Canada by
Nelson Education, Ltd.

To learn more about Cengage Learning, visit **www.cengage.com**

Purchase any of our products at your local college store or at our preferred
online store **www.cengagebrain.com**

Printed in the United States of America
2 3 4 5 6 7 17 16 15 14

Dedication

This book is dedicated

to my granddaughters,

Laila Jade and Anabelle Jasmin Mabry

Contents

Acknowledgements

Corporate Director of Pharmacy,
Health First,
Melbourne, Florida

Norman Tomaka, CRPh, LHCRM,
Former President and Chairman of the Executive Board,
Florida Pharmacy Association, and Pharmacist Consultant,
Melbourne, Florida

Sincere thanks go to the following Cengage Learning staff for their considerable efforts:

Tari Broderick,
Acquisition Editor

Juliet Steiner,
Product Development Manager

Nicole Manikas,
Editorial Assistant

Jim Zayicek,
Senior Content Project Manager

Additional thanks go to Greg Vadimsky, assistant to the author, for his help.

The author also would like to thank the following reviewers:

Paula Lambert, M.Ed., CPhT
Pharmacy Technology Instructor
North Idaho College
Coeur d'Alene, ID

Martin Mathis, CPhT
Lead Instructor Pharmacy Technician Program
Remington College-Cleveland West
North Olmstead, OH

Laurisa McKissack, RPhT, CPhT
Pharmacy Technician Instructor
Virginia College Pensacola Campus
Pensacola, FL

Preface

lations that affect pharmacy technicians, pharmacists, and other pharmacy employees. Special attention is paid to the Controlled Substances Act and the resultant activities of the Food and Drug Administration (FDA) and the Drug Enforcement Administration (DEA). The text emphasizes the importance of ensuring that each patient receives the highest quality care possible. It is the responsibility of all pharmacy staff members to assist the pharmacist in respecting the rights of every patient and in providing services that strictly adhere to federal and state laws, as well as to the ethical standards of the industry.

ORGANIZATION OF CONTENT

This book consists of two parts: General Introduction and Appendices. Part I is divided into three sections, and further divided into nine chapters that focus on the foundation of law and ethics, federal laws, and state laws affecting pharmacy practice. Part II contains eight appendices, a glossary, and an index. The appendices cover diverse topics, including medication errors, pharmacy technician duties and tasks, state qualifications for pharmacy technicians, state boards of pharmacy, professional organizations, and the United States Pharmacopoeial Foundation/National Formulary.

This second edition of *Law & Ethics for Pharmacy Technicians* contains a new chapter (Chapter 2), which is entitled

"Principles of Liability." Also, in this edition, information about the Joint Commission is addressed in Chapter 9. This edition has been fully updated to cover new federal pharmacy legislation in Chapter 4.

FEATURES

Each chapter contains an outline of the key topics, a list of key terms (which are **bolded** in the chapter text), and objectives that the student must be able to meet upon completion of the reading. Following this is a scenario relevant to each chapter, entitled "Setting the Scene," which includes critical thinking questions to encourage deeper understanding of real-life situations. The answers to these questions are provided near the end of each chapter.

Overviews serve to introduce the student to the key concepts of each chapter. "Focus On" features highlight interesting key points of knowledge. "What Would You Do?" and "You Be The Judge" scenarios add further realism to the text by providing actual case studies to consider. Suggested responses to these scenarios are provided in Appendix A. Accurate tables focus on legal and ethical information that must be fully understood in order for the student to master each chapter's content. Certain chapters contain figures that show legal forms and other paperwork. Chapter summaries serve to reinforce the chapter content, and focus on key ideas from the text.

At the end of each chapter, review questions are given that help students to test the knowledge they have gained from their reading. The questions are given in a variety of formats

TEACHING PACKAGE TO ACCOMPANY THE SECOND EDITION

A teaching package has been created for this text to aid instructors as they cover material.

Instructor Companion Website

ISBN-13: 978-1-285-08208-0

This book is accompanied by an instructor companion website with additional free resources for instructors who adopt this text for their class. Resources include the following:

- PowerPoint presentations for each chapter.

- An instructor's manual that features lecture outlines, teaching strategies, lists of legal cases, and sources for these cases.

- A question bank of additional questions for the creation of tests and quizzes.

About the Author

pharmacy technicians in 2000 at EU's Melbourne, Florida campus. For five years, he was the director of the pharmacy technician program. He also established several other new allied health programs for EU. Based on his 35 years of experience as a physician and instructor, he believes that pharmacy technicians should be skillful in various types of compounding, and be confident in the performance of their duties and responsibilities in order to prevent medication errors. Pharmacists and pharmacy technicians must obey state and federal laws, and remain up-to-date on new legislation. Therefore, he stresses the importance of law and ethics in the pharmacy to all of his students.

Dr. Moini is actively involved in teaching and helping students to prepare for service in various health professions, as pharmacy technicians, medical assistants, and nurses. He worked with the Brevard County Health Department as an epidemiologist and health educator consultant for 18 years, offering continuing education courses and keeping nurses up-to-date on the latest developments related to pharmacology, medication errors, immunizations, and other important topics. He has been an internationally published author of various allied health books since 1999. He is now an adjunct professor at Everest University and at Brevard Community College, teaching various subjects for allied health.

SECTION I

Introduction to Law

1. Explain why knowledge of the law is important.
2. Differentiate between private law and public law.
3. Explain the role of law and ethics in pharmacy practice.
4. Differentiate between criminal law and civil law.
5. Explain tort law.
6. Describe the U.S. court system.
7. Define the terms *felony, malpractice,* and *negligence*.
8. List differences between federal law and state law.

KEY TERMS

Administrative law—The body of law governing the administrative agencies (e.g., Occupational Safety and Health Administration or Department of Public Health) that have been created by Congress or by state legislatures.

Appeals—Legal proceedings in which cases are brought to higher courts to review decisions of lower courts.

Contract law—A system of law that pertains to agreements between two or more parties.

Criminal law—The body of law that defines offenses against the public.

Felony—An offense punishable by death or by imprisonment in a state or federal prison for more than one year.

Jurisdiction—The power and authority given to a court to hear a case and to make a judgment.

Law—A rule of conduct or procedure established by custom, agreement, or authority.

Malpractice—Professional misconduct or demonstration of an unreasonable lack of skill, with the result of injury, loss, or damage to a patient.

Misdemeanors—Crimes punishable by fine or by imprisonment in a facility other than a prison for less than one year.

Negligence—A type of unintentional tort alleged when one may have performed or failed to perform an act that a reasonable person would or would not have done, respectively, in similar circumstances.

Private law—The type of law that governs conflicts between private parties.

Public law—The type of law that governs conflicts between private parties and the government.

Tort—A private wrong or injury, other than a breach of contract, for which the court will provide a remedy.

SETTING THE SCENE

A patient brought a prescription to a pharmacy for a sulfa drug that was prescribed by her physician. The patient is allergic to sulfa drugs, a fact that was noted in the handwritten medical record located in the physician's office. However, the medical records assistant did not transcribe the allergy note into the computerized patient record. The pharmacy technician dispensed the drug because there was no information about the patient's sulfa drug allergy included in the computerized patient record. The technician did not ask the patient if she had any drug allergies. The pharmacist signed off on the prescription and approved the dispensing of the drug. After taking one dose of the sulfa drug, the patient had a severe allergic reaction that ultimately led to her death. The patient's family filed a civil suit against both the pharmacist and the physician for negligence.

Critical Thinking

- What should the pharmacy technician have done to best benefit the patient in this situation?

- Was it appropriate for the patient's family to sue the pharmacist?

- If criminal charges were filed, what possible outcomes might affect the pharmacist, the physician, and the pharmacy technician?

OVERVIEW

As the field of pharmacy becomes more complex, understanding of pharmacy law becomes more important. The effect of state and federal government regulations and lawsuits in the field of pharmacy is greater than ever before. Pharmacy has a distinct vocabulary and a set of professional standards and regulations. Once you become familiar with the vocabulary, rules, and regulations, the ideas, concepts, and structure of the job become understandable. Pharmacists and pharmacy technicians need to have a clear understanding of the laws and regulations related to their field of practice. If these laws and regulations are not understood or not followed, the consequences to the consumer of pharmaceutical products could be life-threatening.

ROLE OF LAW

Law is generally defined as a system of principles and processes that is devised by organized society to deal with problems and disputes without the use of force. Standards for human behavior are established by law. The law is used by indi-

zens. Law provides guidelines for resolution of disputes in a safe manner.

Although based on solid and long-held beliefs, customs, and principles, the law is always growing and evolving to meet the changes, challenges, and constantly occurring shifts of society. This can be evidenced by the history of drug laws in the United States. In the 1800s and early 1900s, there was no regulation or control over medicinal products. Any substance or product could be claimed to have health benefits or medicinal effects. As a result, contamination of products occurred, leading to injury to consumers, and potentially addictive products were distributed.

In response to these circumstances, laws such as the Pure Food and Drug Act (enacted to ensure accurate labeling and the purity of marketed foods and drugs) were passed. Some of these laws, such as the Food, Drug, and Cosmetic Act of 1938, resulted in the establishment of agencies such as the U.S. Food and Drug Administration (FDA), which regulates food and drugs along with the labeling of their contents. As time went on, deficiencies in existing legislation were identified and additional legislation was enacted to continue to improve pharmacological products in the United States. For instance, laws were enacted to make certain substances illegal for public use or to limit how they could be used. Fine-tuning of laws continues today as the need arises.

Focus On...

Divisions of Law

In the United States, the legal system divides laws into three categories: criminal law, civil law, and **administrative law**. Administrative law focuses on the regulations set forth and enforced by governmental administrative agencies.

PUBLIC LAW

Public law governs conflicts between private parties and the government. Sometimes, the difference between private and public law is difficult to ascertain, since certain behaviors can violate both types of law. To help understand the differences more fully, see Table 1-1.

Public law defines appropriate behaviors between individuals, organizations, and the government. The primary sources of public law are written constitutions, regulations, statutes, and decisions of administrative and judicial bodies.

Criminal Law

Criminal law is concerned with acts against society that are violations of criminal statutes or codes. It is one form of public law. Criminal laws are enforced by representatives of the state against persons or corporations. State or federal governments may impose monetary fines, imprisonment, or even death in certain circumstances for violations of criminal law. **Misdemeanors** are lesser crimes, usually punishable by fines and/or imprisonment for less than one year (for example, traffic violations, thefts under a certain dollar amount, or attempted burglary). **Felonies** are punishable by much larger fines and imprisonment for more than one year, and in some jurisdictions, certain felonies are punishable

TABLE 1-1 Private and Public Law

Public Law	Private Law
Administrative Law	Agency
Civil, Criminal, and Appellate Procedure	Commercial Paper
Constitutional Law	Contract Law
Criminal Law	Corporation Law
• Substantive	Intellectual Property Law
• Procedural	Partnerships
Evidence	Personal Property
Taxation	Real Property
	Sales
	Torts
	Trusts and Wills

by death. Examples of felonies are rape, murder, robbery, domestic violence, and child abuse. A *robbery* is defined as the forcible stealing of property during which a victim is physically injured, is threatened, or is put in fear of bodily injury. Many states hold that certain felony convictions are grounds for revoking licenses to practice in the healthcare ~~field. Practicing without a license,~~ falsifying information when obtaining

liability, and specific punishments. ~~Specific offenses~~ felonies and misdemeanors.

- Procedural law focuses on the steps through which a criminal case passes, from initial investigation of a crime to trial, sentencing, and the eventual release of the criminal offender.

Focus On...

Criminal Law

Criminal law involves crimes against the state.

Another segment of public law consists of constitutional provisions, regulations, and statutes. It requires governmental entities and private parties to follow specific courses of action. Government regulations in this area are designed to secure compliance with the goals of law, rather than to punish offenders. Areas of criminal law include administrative, antitrust, constitutional, environmental, labor, and securities law.

What Would You Do?

Brian has had three traffic violations in the past three months. He has also been charged with domestic violence against his girlfriend. You are the pharmacist for whom Brian works, and you are aware of some of these events. One day, you hear him harassing another worker until an argument breaks out. Brian becomes very agitated. Knowing his background, what would you do in this situation?

Table 1-2 explains the differences between criminal and civil law cases.

TABLE 1-2 Criminal and Civil Law Case Differences

Criminal Law	Civil Law
Parties: Plaintiff is state, county or federal government (always).	Parties: Plaintiff and defendant may be the government, corporations, or individual persons.
Punishment: Fine and/or imprisonment.	Punishment: The party who loses cannot be imprisoned even if unable to pay damages assessed by the court.
Source: State or federal statutes.	Source: State or federal statutes and court decisions.
Jury decision: Must be unanimous.	Jury decision: Varies from state to state; certain state courts require a majority vote by a jury in order to issue a decision, while others require a unanimous jury decision. Federal courts require a unanimous jury decision.
Burden of proof: Beyond a reasonable doubt.	Burden of proof: Preponderance of the evidence (defined as "more likely than not").
Appeals: Only the defendant may appeal a guilty verdict.	Appeals: Either party may appeal the decision
Decision: The defendant is either guilty or not guilty— there is no "partial fault."	Decision: The plaintiff and defendant may both be found partially right and partially at fault.

PRIVATE LAW

Private law governs conflicts between private parties. Private law is legally referred to as *civil law* since it focuses on private rights and remedies. *Civil law* is a term that may be understood more definitively however, since it is more distinctly compared to criminal law. The primary source of private law comes from court decisions, which can later be modified by regulations or statutes.

Civil Law

In civil law, a plaintiff (injured party) may bring suit against an alleged defendant (wrongdoer). Most civil law cases concern either contract law or tort law. Civil wrongs are often called torts. A **tort** is a physical or non-physical injury to a person by another person. The person causing the injury is legally responsible for his or her actions. The injury may be intentional or unintentional.

Most civil law cases against healthcare workers are for **malpractice** (professional misconduct or **negligence**). *Malpractice* is defined as improper discharge of professional duties or failure to meet the *standard of care* of a professional person. *Negligence* is defined as a failure to exercise reasonable care, and is further defined as the omission or commission of an act that a reasonably prudent person would or would not do under given circumstances. *Gross negligence* is the reckless and wanton disregard for the standard of care and interest of others, and is a criminal offense. Negligence and malpractice are discussed in detail in Chapter 2.

Penalties in civil law are almost completely monetary in nature,

Tort is a French word meaning "wrong." Torts include assault (in general, the threat of violence); battery (contact in a manner that may cause bodily harm); fraud; libel; negligence; medical malpractice; slander; defamation, theft; trespassing; invasion of privacy; and wrongful death. *Assault* is further defined as an intentional act that causes another person to experience the apprehension of being touched in an offensive manner, or of physical harm. When assault results in physical contact, it is called *battery*. *Defamation* is defined as a false statement of fact that causes damage to a person's reputation. *Libel* is written defamation, while *slander* is spoken defamation. *Theft* is the taking of property without consent of the owner.

Tort law often results in civil lawsuits, with the injured party suing the injurer (*tortfeasor*). It is also concerned with duties and rights between parties that exist independent of contracts. Legal issues related to the control and storage of electronic health information fall under a form of civil law called *intellectual property law*.

Intentional torts are those that are committed willfully against a person or property. The offender must intend to commit the act. The injured party may seek a civil case against the person who committed the tort against him or her. Intentional torts include assault, battery, false imprisonment, fraud, libel, slander, trespassing, and invasion of privacy. Some intentional torts may also be prosecuted as crimes in separate court cases. Tort liability may be based on intent, negligence, or *strict liability*, which is the responsibility of a product manufacturer or seller for any defect that unduly threatens personal safety. For intentional torts, legal action requires a legal duty between a plaintiff and defendant, a breach of that duty, and injury that occurs as a result of the breach. Defenses that are available against accusations of intentional torts include consent, privilege, self-defense, the defense of others, and error.

Unintentional torts are those that are committed accidentally. For example, when a pharmacy technician fails to verify accurate information, and a patient receives a medication that is less effective than intended, an unintentional tort has occurred. Negligence, malpractice, and product liability are examples of unintentional torts. In negligence, injury to a patient occurs because a healthcare provider has failed to exercise the degree of care required to perform an otherwise permissible action. Civil complaints are designed to "make the victim whole" by restoring whatever was his or her original position before the injury or loss.

Contract Law

Contract law pertains to agreements between two or more parties. In a contract, each of the concerned parties agrees to do (or not do) certain things. Contracts are legally binding exchanges of promises. The term "contract law" is based on the Latin phrase "*pacta sunt servanda,*" which means "pacts must be kept." In contract law, an agreement (contract) sets forth promises to act (or not act) in specific ways, documents the agreement of both parties to act (or not act), and describes what each party receives from the other for performing the contractual obligations. Contracts may be oral or written, and must follow applicable state and federal regulations and statutes. If the terms of the contract are not fulfilled, a breach of contract occurs. The *aggrieved* party may sue to seek compensation or to force performance of the terms of the contract.

You Be the Judge

Mark has been working in a retail pharmacy for 17 years. He is a senior technician, and a reliable person at work. About a year ago, his wife died, causing him to become very depressed. Last week, he made a mistake while he was compounding two medications. The pharmacist found out about his failure to exercise reasonable care while working. He told Mark that this was a case of negligence and that legal action could be brought based on his error. Mark responded rudely and even pushed the pharmacist.

In your judgment, what would be the possible consequences for Mark, taking his entire situation into account? What could he be accused of for being physically violent with the pharmacist?

THE U.S. COURT SYSTEM

There are several levels of courts in each state. Local courts usually deal with civil and criminal cases whose penalties do not exceed certain dollar amounts that are established by the legislature. The next level is a state court with general jurisdiction. This includes any major trial court that has broad powers. Often, cases of negligence, malpractice, elder abuse, and other civil wrongs are tried at this level. Major crimes are also prosecuted in these courts.

A court must have **jurisdiction** over any case that it tries, whether *in personam* (over the person) or *in rem* (over the thing or property). Ma-

~~jurisdiction is based~~ on county lines or similar divisions

~~ing on all lower courts~~

The top court of a state is usually called its *supreme court*, with the only recourse after that being the *United States Supreme Court*. However, the U.S. Supreme Court chooses to hear only a few cases per term, as determined by vote of at least four justices. The cases chosen are usually the most important and consequential cases that have been presented to it. Once the Supreme Court makes its decision and tries a case, the decision is binding on all state and federal courts.

Focus On...

The Supreme Court

Supreme Court justices are appointed by the president of the United States and approved by the Senate. An appointment to the Supreme Court is a lifetime appointment.

Some cases may be tried in a federal district court. These courts hear cases that raise issues of federal law, or those involving parties from different states with an amount in controversy that exceeds $75,000.

THE DIFFERENCES BETWEEN FEDERAL LAW AND STATE LAW

Neither federal nor state courts are completely independent of each other. Many federal and state laws interact. Federal courts handle crimes under statutes that have been enacted by Congress. Table 1-3 outlines the types of cases related to pharmacy that are handled in federal and state courts.

Individual states have the authority to enact legislation in any area in which Congress has enacted legislation as long as no conflicts between state and federal laws are created as a result. If a conflict exists, federal law

TABLE 1-3 Courts Handling Specific Pharmacy-Related Cases

Federal	State	Both
Interstate and international trade/commerce cases	Cases involving state laws or regulations	Crimes that can be punished under federal or state law
Bankruptcy cases	Most private contract disputes	Class action cases
Disputes between individual states	Most trade or professional regulation cases	Environmental regulation cases
	Most professional malpractice cases	
	Most business law cases	
	Most personal injury cases	
	Most worker injury cases	

Adapted from www.uscourts.gov

outweighs state law and must be enforced. A conflict may exist if a state law is less strict then the federal law and following the state law would be in violation of the federal law. If, however, the state law is stricter than the federal law, no conflict with the federal law exists and the state law may be followed without causing a violation of the federal law.

SUMMARY

The practice of dispensing drugs is subject to many laws and regulations. Both state and federal laws affect the profession and practice of pharmacy. Often, a felony conviction results in revocation of the defendant's license to practice. Pharmacy technicians must be familiar with terminology, concepts, and the structure of their jobs; this includes knowledge of the legal issues surrounding pharmacy. A pharmacy technician should understand criminal and civil law, as well as the court system of the United States. Laws that are broken in this profession are punishable by monetary fines and imprisonment.

SETTING THE SCENE

The following discussion and responses relate to the opening "Setting the Scene" scenario:

- The pharmacy technician should have double-checked with the patient to find if she had any allergies to sulfa drugs.

- It was appropriate for the patient's family to sue the pharmacist, since he has supreme responsibility for the welfare of every patient to whom he dispenses.

- If the patient's family wins this case, the pharmacist and the physician may be at risk for additional administrative or criminal actions resulting in fines, imprisonment, and/or the loss of their

1. Which of the following is a type of punishment for a felony?

   A. imprisonment for more than one year
   B. large fines
   C. death
   D. all of the above

2. Which of the following types of court cases do local courts usually deal with?

   A. civil law
   B. criminal law
   C. both A and B
   D. none of the above

3. Which of the following chooses to hear very few cases?

   A. local court
   B. state court
   C. court of general jurisdiction
   D. U.S. Supreme Court

4. After a trial is completed or a case is final in a court, the case may be

   A. stopped.
   B. waived.
   C. appealed.
   D. none of the above.

5. Which of the following is a crime that may result in criminal prosecution?

   A. practicing without a license
   B. falsifying information when obtaining a license
   C. failure to provide reasonable care
   D. all of the above

6. Which of the following levels of courts try cases of negligence, malpractice, and elder abuse?

   A. appeals court
   B. general jurisdiction court
   C. state supreme court
   D. U.S. Supreme Court

7. Supreme Court justices are appointed by the

   A. president of the United States.
   B. Congress.
   C. Senate.
   D. all of the above.

8. A system of principles that is devised by organized society to deal with problems and disputes without the use of force is known as

   A. morality.
   B. law.
   C. ethics.
   D. jurisdiction .

9. Conflicts between private parties and the government are collectively known as

   A. contract law.
   B. private law.
   C. tort law.
   D. public law.

10. Criminal law is actually a form of which of the following types of law?

   A. public
   B. private
   C. tort
   D. contract

11. Which of the following types of crimes are punishable by imprisonment for less than one year?

    A. felony
    B. mitigation
    C. misdemeanor
    D. arbitration

    A. It is a voluntary agreement.
    B. It involves a specific promise that is made.
    C. It involves two or more parties.
    D. All of the above are correct concerning contracts.

14. All of the following are intentional torts, except

    A. battery.
    B. assault.
    C. negligence.
    D. slander.

15. The term "tort" actually means

    A. libel.
    B. wrong.
    C. fraud.
    D. crime.

Matching

    A. felony

    B. public law

    C. criminal law

    D. negligence

    E. misdemeanor

_____ **1.** governs conflicts between private parties and the government

_____ **2.** a failure to exercise reasonable care

_____ **3.** a lesser crime usually punishable by fines and imprisonment of less than one year

_____ **4.** punishable by much larger fines and imprisonment for more than one year

_____ **5.** concerned with violations against society

Fill in the Blank

1. Legal proceedings in which cases are brought to higher courts to review decisions of lower courts are called _____.

2. The power and authority given to a court to hear a case and to make a judgment is referred to as _____.

3. Professional misconduct involving an unreasonable lack of skill with the result of injury or damage to the patient is called _____.

4. A private wrong or injury, other than a breach of contract, for which the court will provide a remedy is known as a _____.

5. _____ law is the type of law that governs conflicts between private parties and the government.

6. _____ is a type of unintentional tort alleged when one may have performed (or failed to perform) an act that a reasonable person would (or would not) perform in similar circumstances.

7. _____ law is the type of law that governs conflicts between private parties.

8.   _____ law is the body of law that defines criminal offenses against the public.

9.   The top court in a state is usually called its _____.

10. Assault and battery or false imprisonment is an example of a/an

medication instead of phenobarbital. Because the pharmacist was so busy, he decided not to check the medication or consult with the mother. She gave the medication to her child for about one month to prevent seizures. Because of the incorrect medication, the infant had a serious brain injury that caused a permanent disability.

1.   Who is mostly responsible for this medication error?

2.   What would be the consequences of severe seizures in this premature infant?

3.   If a lawsuit claiming malpractice results, who may lose their jobs?

RELATED INTERNET SITES

http://biotech.law.lsu.edu

http://www.aspl.org

http://www.druglibrary.org Click on "Schaffer Library."

http://www.fda.gov Search for "Laws FDA enforces."

http://www.resource4pharmacymalpractice.com

http://www.rxtrek.net Click on "Enter RxTrek" and then "Certified Pharmacy *Technicians/Technologists (CPhT)*"; shows the number of certified pharmacy technicians across the United States.

http://www.uscourts.gov

REFERENCES

Abood, R. (2010). *Pharmacy Practice and the Law* (6th ed.). Burlington, MA: Jones and Bartlett.

Flight, M. (2011). *Law, Liability, & Ethics* (5th ed.). Clifton Park, NY: Cengage Learning.

Jackson, J. A. (2007). *Ethics, Legal Issues, and Professionalism in Surgical Technology.* Clifton Park, NY: Cengage Learning.

McWay, D.C. (2010). *Legal and Ethical Aspects of Health Information Management* (3rd ed.). Clifton Park, NY: Cengage Learning.

Miller, R. D. (2006). *Problems in Health Care Law* (9th ed.). Burlington, MA: Jones and Bartlett.

Reiss, B. S., & Hall, G. D. (2006). *Guide to Federal Pharmacy Law* (7th ed.). Boynton Beach, FL: Apothecary Press.

Walston-Dunham, B. (2011). *Introduction to Law* (6th ed.). Clifton Park, NY: Cengage Learning.

Principles of Liability

1. Explain the theories of liability.
2. List the four elements necessary to prove negligence and explain them.
3. Explain unintentional negligence.
4. Define malpractice as it relates to pharmacy technicians.
5. Identify reasons for the high cost of malpractice insurance.
6. Differentiate between vicarious liability and corporate negligence.
7. Compare breach of confidentiality and invasion of privacy.
8. Explain the statute of limitations.

KEY TERMS

Contributory negligence—Conduct by a plaintiff that is below the standard to which he or she is legally required to conform for his or her own protection.

Damages—The sum of money that may be recovered in court as financial reparation for any injury or wrong suffered because of a breach of contract, tort, negligence, or medical malpractice. Damages are divided into three types: nominal, actual, and punitive.

Duty of care—An obligation to conform to a particular standard of conduct toward another.

Malfeasance—The execution of an unlawful or improper act.

Medical malpractice—Medical professional misconduct, which differs from negligence because the tortfeasor is a licensed medical professional.

Misfeasance—The improper performance of an act.

Nonfeasance—The failure to act as a reasonably prudent person would in similar circumstances when there is a duty to act.

Product liability—A tort that makes a manufacturer liable for compensation to anyone using its product if damages or injuries occur from defects in that product.

Proximate cause—An action or event that produces injury in a natural, continuous sequence that is unbroken by any intervening cause.

Statute of limitations—That period of time established by state law during which a lawsuit or criminal proceeding may be filed.

SETTING THE SCENE

Kelly, a pharmacy technician, dispensed medication to an HIV-positive patient who is her neighbor. When she went home after work, she told her boyfriend that their neighbor was HIV positive. A few days later, while mowing the lawn, the boyfriend asked the neighbor how he was feeling. The neighbor asked, "What do you mean?" The boyfriend explained that he just wanted to know his health status, since the neighbor had AIDS. The neighbor was furious that Kelly had told her boyfriend about his health status.

Critical Thinking

- What is the legal term for Kelly's action?

- Kelly's action is classified as what type of tort?

- Kelly's action violates which federal acts?

OVERVIEW

It is important to understand the principles of liability as they relate to the field of pharmacy. Injuries to patients that may give rise to liability include physical harm, as well as damage to the rights, reputation, or property of individuals or groups. Lawsuits may occur as the result of many liability issues, including improper disclosure of health information. Once the nature of the relationships from which liability can arise is understood, related legal theories and defenses can be studied.

THEORIES OF LIABILITY

In the field of pharmacy and other areas of healthcare, theories of liability are divided into three types: breach of contract, intentional torts, and nonintentional torts. As discussed in Chapter 1, *intentional torts* are committed with the intent to do something that is wrong. *Nonintentional torts* are committed without this intention. Table 2-1 lists some theories of liability as they relate to both types of torts. Most **medical malpractice** lawsuits in the United States are related to nonintentional torts.

TABLE 2-1 Some Theories of Liability Related to Torts

Intentional Torts	Nonintentional Torts
Assault and battery	Breach of confidentiality
Defamation	Corporate negligence

NEGLIGENCE

Negligence is defined as delivery of care that is below the expected standard. The unintentional tort of negligence is the most common type of liability in medicine. It usually means any deviation from the accepted medical standard of care that causes patient injury. Though similar to *medical malpractice*, it is actually a separate legal theory. The *standard of care* is the level of care that a reasonably prudent healthcare professional would have rendered in the same or similar circumstances.

All medical professional liability claims are classified as one of the following:

- **Malfeasance**—The performance of a totally wrongful and unlawful act, such as the prescribing of medications by a person who is not licensed to do so.

- **Misfeasance**—The performance of a lawful act in an illegal or improper manner, with damage resulting; an example is not using sterile technique when preparing an IV, and therefore causing an infection.

- **Nonfeasance**—The failure to act when one should, such as failing to scan a bar code on a package.

There are four elements that must be established to prove a healthcare professional guilty of negligence. The "four Ds of negligence" are the following:

- **Duty of care**—The healthcare professional owed a duty of care to the accuser. (Caregivers are obligated to conform to particular standards of conduct towards their clients.)

- Dereliction—The healthcare professional breached the duty of care to the patient.

- Direct cause—The breach of care was a direct cause of the patient's injury.
- **Damages**—There is a legally recognizable injury to the patient.

For each of these elements, the burden of proof is on the plaintiff. This means the patient's attorney must present evidence of the four Ds of negligence.

You Be the Judge

Pamela is a pharmacy technician who recently prepared eyedrops for a patient with glaucoma. The patient used the eyedrops per the enclosed instructions, but experienced no positive effects, and, after one week, was still experiencing minor but continuing visual impairment. The patient went back to her physician and complained about the eyedrops she had used. He checked the eyedrops, and found out that they were long past their expiration date. In your judgment, what would the possible consequences be for Pamela since she did not check the expiration date before the medication was dispensed by the pharmacist? In addition, what would happen to the pharmacist because of this error?

MALPRACTICE

When a patient is treated in a manner that is improper or negligent, the pharmacist or pharmacy technician may be sued for malpractice. Negligent behavior that results in injury, damage, loss, or death is referred to as *malpractice.* It is important to understand that malpractice also governs unethical practices. Malpractice lawsuits have increased dramatically. Malpractice insurance covers a wide variety of health care practitioners, including doctors, nurses, pharmacists, and even pharmacy technicians. In medical malpractice, the core of every negligence claim is the allegation of a breach of duty of care. This means that the medical professional has failed to maintain a certain standard of care.

Professional liability insurance protects against suits being brought against pharmacists or pharmacy technicians for malpractice. Though amounts of coverage vary, plans are available (for example, for pharmacists and technicians) that pay $1 million per claim for up to three claims per year. These policies are able to cover property loss or damage, personal injury, death, and even legal costs.

Having schooling, certification, licensure, registration, and insurance coverage that are adequate according to the requirements of state law will help protect against legal action. Pharmacists and pharmacy technicians may take specific steps that help to protect against errors and other acts that could lead to legal action against them. These steps are as follows:

- Always communicate effectively, accurately, and correctly. Always ʰᵉ straightforward, honest, and descriptive in communications; ᵈ ᵗʰ ᵘⁿderstanding of what you have

- Being cᴏⁿᶜᴵˢᵉ anything not focused on the patients health aⁿᵈ ᶜ versation or documents; wordiness and restating of information are not necessary, and the patient record should not include information unnecessary to patient care.

- Verbal and written communication must be consistently handled; behaviors and patterns of communication must remain relatively the same for all patients so that the focus on good patient care may be uniform and be maintained for all patients.

- All spoken or written information must be cautiously worded, avoiding terms that may be confused or may misrepresent the intentions of the pharmacy staff. Suggestions for future patient care may be made, but should not be phrased as demands or warnings; considerations that may be required, as well as suggestions regarding care, should be indicated in a positive manner.

During a medical malpractice trial, the prosecuting attorney will attempt to show that the defendant deviated from the appropriate standard of care. General standards contained in state laws and regulations will be introduced into evidence. General standards of care can also be found in written materials from sources such as professional associations, accrediting organizations, and textbooks. Healthcare facility policies and procedures, including medical staff bylaws and manuals, may also be used. Often, an institution's polices and procedures may actually establish a higher standard of care than is found in other sources. Expert testimony during a trial may also be used to establish a breach of the standard of care.

After establishing that the standard of care was breached, the prosecuting attorney must establish that the breach actually caused the injury to the patient. This causal connection is sometimes referred to as *causation*, and is difficult to prove. *Foreseeability* is examined here. If the medical professional anticipated that the intervening force would occur, then the injury is considered foreseeable. Therefore, the medical professional would be held liable.

Once medical malpractice is proven, the patient is entitled to damages, which may consist of nominal, actual, or punitive damages. *Nominal damages* are small amounts of money awarded to vindicate a right when minimal injury is proven. They are awarded as recognition of a technical invasion of a person's rights. Nominal damages are not awarded if other types of damages are proved. *Actual damages* (compensatory damages) are awarded to "make the plaintiff whole." They are designed to restore the patient's position prior to the injury, and compensate for actual loss. They include (but are not limited to) the value of past and future medical expenses. They also include but are not limited to past and future loss of income. *Punitive damages* (exemplary damages) are awarded above and beyond actual damages. There must be proof of malicious, outrageous, or intentional conduct. They are designed to punish wrongdoers, or to make an example of them.

Focus On...

Punitive Damages

Punitive damages are not usually requested in medical malpractice cases because most cases are based on negligence as opposed to intentional harm.

Another type of negligence theory is *res ipsa loquitur*, which means "the thing speaks for itself." This is a rare scenario that only applies when a plaintiff cannot prove negligence with the available direct evidence. The plaintiff must prove that injury occurred as a consequence of negligence, which creates a presumption of negligence. To succeed in this type of case, the plaintiff must prove three points:

- The injury would not ordinarily occur without someone's negligence.

- The healthcare professional had exclusive control and management over the instrument or cause of the injury.

- The injury could not have occurred as a result of any action by the patient.

Focus On...

Punitive Damage Cases

In some states, the plaintiff is also required to prove that the healthcare professional had superior knowledge of the cause of the injury.

Civil Malpractice Lawsuits

A civil malpractice lawsuit requires the patient to prove the following, in this order:

- There was a healthcare provider–patient relationship.

~~~~~~~~~~~~~~~ by the healthcare provider

patients injury.

The *relationship* between healthcare provider and patient is established by contract law. Injury to a patient does not require the healthcare provider to have made an error.

Malpractice Insurance

The cost of medical insurance has increased astronomically in comparison with many other types of insurance. This is, in part, because litigation is expensive, and the amount of damages awarded to successful plaintiffs is also rising. In certain areas of medicine, individuals who work under the supervision of others may be required to carry their own malpractice insurance, even though their supervising entity has its own. In the pharmacy, pharmacy technicians are generally insured under the malpractice insurance of their employer.

Focus On...

Malpractice Insurance

Malpractice insurance is required for all professionals who practice in any field of medicine.

VICARIOUS LIABILITY

The term *respondeat superior* refers to *vicarious liability*, which makes a healthcare organization, such as a pharmacy, responsible for any negligent act by one of its employees. Since the individual is responsible for negligence, so too are his or her supervisors. However, the individual employee must be found legally negligent in order for the superiors or company also to be found legally negligent. The court will examine who hired the employee, who pays the employee, who has the power to fire the employee, and who controls the details of the employee's work.

CORPORATE NEGLIGENCE

Corporate negligence differs from vicarious liability because it focuses on the responsibility of the healthcare organization as a whole to provide proper patient services, and not its individual employees. This responsibility cannot be delegated to employees. The organization must adhere to its own bylaws and any applicable state statutes concerning its credentials.

FAILURE TO WARN (FAILURE TO PROTECT)

Failure to warn (or *failure to protect*) applies when a healthcare professional determines that there is a likelihood of patient harm, and then fails to warn the patient. The duty to warn patients is a legal as well as an ethical duty. Also, failure to warn is a theory that may support a lawsuit involving a patient's danger to a third party. Primarily, failure to warn is used in reference to psychiatric patients, but it may relate to pharmacy because pharmacists fill prescriptions for psychoactive medications.

BREACH OF CONFIDENTIALITY

Breach of confidentiality is a nonintentional tort defined as the unauthorized acquisition, access, use, or disclosure of protected health information that compromises the security or privacy of such information, except where an unauthorized individual to whom this information is disclosed would not reasonably have been able to retain it. Should the confidentiality of a patient's health information be breached, the patient must be notified by the healthcare provider within 60 days after the breach is discovered, unless the patient cannot be contacted within this time. The Secretary of Health and Human Services must then be notified of the breach. Table 2-2 lists the items contained in a Notice of Breach of Confidentiality.

Another name for a breach of confidentiality is "improper or wrongful disclosure of individually identifiable health information." Acts that address this include the Health Information Technology for Economic and Clinical Health (HITECH) Act and the Health Insurance Portability and Accountability Act (HIPAA). Intentional disclosure of individually identifiable health information to another person, which

TABLE 2-2 Notice of Breach of Confidentiality Contents

NOTICE OF BREACH OF CONFIDENTIALITY MUST INCLUDE THE FOLLOWING, REGARDLESS OF THE METHOD USED TO PROVIDE IT.
A brief description of the breach, including its date, and the date of discovery of the breach (if known)

violates HIPAA, is a federal offense. It is punishable by fines, imprisonment, or both. If the offense is committed under false pretenses, or with intent to steal, transfer, or use the information for commercial advantage, personal gain, or malicious harm, the penalties gradually increase.

> **You Be the Judge**
>
> Greg, a pharmacy technician, was asked to fill a prescription by a man who entered the pharmacy. However, the prescription was, according to the man, for his girlfriend who was too ill to bring it herself. The man asked Greg what the medication was intended to treat. Greg told him it was used to treat sexually transmitted diseases. Which laws were violated by Greg's response? Could Greg be legally liable for a breach of confidentiality?

INVASION OF PRIVACY

Invasion of privacy is defined as dissemination of information about another person's private, personal matters. To prove invasion of privacy, the following points must be shown:

- There was an unwarranted appropriation or exploitation of the individual's personality.

- There was a publication of the individual's private affairs that would cause embarrassment.

- There was a wrongful intrusion upon the individual's private concerns or activities.

- There was some form of publicity that portrayed the individual falsely.

An example of an invasion of privacy case is the use, without consent, of a patient's image as part of medical instruction, such as in "before and after" studies. Improper disclosure of patient health information may also be deemed an invasion of privacy.

INFORMED CONSENT

Informed consent is very important in today's medicine. Patients must be informed of a variety of information in order for them to give informed consent to the use of medications, procedures, and equipment. Examples of areas of information that must be provided to patients include adverse drug reactions, adverse treatment outcomes, alternative forms of treatment, and explanations of terminology. Each patient must understand the risks of his or her treatment. For example, cancer patients must be fully informed about their prognoses, as well as the adverse effects of the medications and other treatments available that may cure their conditions.

INTENTIONAL INFLICTION OF EMOTIONAL DISTRESS

The intentional infliction of emotional distress upon a patient is explained as follows:

- The healthcare professional's conduct is so extreme and outrageous that it causes the patient to experience severe emotional distress.

- The healthcare professional intended to cause emotional distress to the patient.

Cases of this type must prove that the conduct was so extreme and outrageous that it was indecent and intolerable according to community standards of behavior. The distress suffered must be of a type that a reasonable person would not be expected to endure. Some states require this distress to be so severe that it requires medical attention.

STATUTE OF LIMITATIONS

The **statute of limitations** is the period of time established by state law during which a lawsuit or criminal proceeding may be filed. The statute of limitations varies by state and by the type of legal claim. Pharmacy technicians must understand the specific laws and statutes of their state. In filing professional negligence suits, the statute of limitations is generally from one to eight years, with two years being most common.

Therefore, patients cannot file negligence lawsuits against physicians if this designated length of time has expired. Specific statutory time limits may be found in state codes, online, and in most libraries.

The following are the most common occurrences used to mark the beginning of a statutory period:

ttable immunity. This defense was permitted so that assets intended for charitable purposes could not be used for improper reasons (such as paying damage awards). *Governmental immunity* keeps a plaintiff from suing a governmental entity unless that entity consents to the lawsuit. Governmental immunity has been abandoned in most jurisdictions. However, the federal government can only be sued if it consents to the lawsuit.

Good Samaritan laws protect caregivers from civil liability as a result of their attempts to render emergency care. They do not prevail if the caregiver acted in a willful, reckless, or wanton manner in providing emergency treatment. These laws exist in all 50 states. They mostly apply in nontraditional settings, such as when someone provides emergency care on the roadway following an automobile accident.

Focus On...

Statutes of Limitation

Statutory time limits apply to many legal actions, including collections, wrongful death claims, and medical malpractice.

Contributory negligence is a term referring to conduct of a patient that contributes to his or her own injury. In many jurisdictions, if this is found, there is no form of recovery possible. For example, if a pharmacist provides a patient with a medication that has clear instructions to take "one tablet per day," and the patient takes three tablets per day, the pharmacist cannot be held liable for the negligence of the patient in ignoring the dosing regimen. *Comparative negligence* means that where the patient is shown to have contributed to the negligence that caused harm to him- or herself, and the pharmacist was also negligent, the amount of recovery of damages may be reduced because of the patient's actions. In other words, though damages may be awarded to the patient because of something the pharmacist did wrong, the patient's own actions reduce the amount that can be recovered. Adequate documentation of all health information may be the only way to support defense of either contributory or comparative negligence cases.

Assumption of risk is a method used to limit liability, either partly or completely. If a plaintiff exposes himself or herself to a known, appreciated danger, damages may not be recovered for injury caused by that danger. The defendant must therefore prove that the plaintiff knew of the risk, assumed the risk voluntarily, and was not coerced. Many healthcare professionals have avoided more lengthy and costly litigation by simply admitting mistakes that caused patient injury. They may offer a full apology, which admits responsibility as well as expressing sympathy, or a partial apology, which only expresses sympathy for the patient.

PRODUCT LIABILITY

Product liability concerns negligence of manufacturers, distributors, or other suppliers in providing safe, effective products to patients. Medications, equipment, supplies, and lack of proper instructions may all be involved in product liability cases. Examples of product liability cases have involved pacemakers, tampons, prosthetics, and anti-aging creams. Procedures that have given rise to product liability include blood transfusions and insertion of breast implants. Medications involved in product liability cases have included Tylenol®, antidepressants, Celebrex®, ephedra, and Vioxx®. In the pharmacy, it is the job of the pharmacist to ensure that each patient understands how medications are to be used, including what other substances they cannot be taken with.

SUMMARY

Negligence occurs when a person hurts another without intent. When negligence involves injury by a professional, it is called malpractice. The difference is the standard of care required of the party who injured the other party. This difference is important when legal action is taken in liability cases. Medical organizations such as pharmacies may be held liable for the actions of their employees. Patients must be provided with enough information about their healthcare that they can give informed consent concerning decisions to be made. Defenses that are available against malpractice claims include the statute of limitations, contributory negligence, comparative negligence, assumption of risk, and emergency. Medical malpractice insurance is very expensive, but is available for defense costs as well as awards against the defendant.

SETTING THE SCENE

The following discussion and responses relate to the opening "Setting the Scene" scenario:

- Kelly's discussion of her neighbor's HIV status with her boyfriend constitutes *breach of confidentiality*.

- Breach of confidentiality is classified as an unintentional tort.

- Breach of confidentiality violates the HITECH Act and HIPAA.

REVIEW QUESTIONS

    C. malpractice.

    D. remedy.

2. Professional negligence is also called

    A. malpractice.

    B. malfunction.

    C. arbitration.

    D. felony.

3. The statute of limitations is generally from one year to

    A. two years.

    B. four years.

    C. six years.

    D. eight years.

4. The "four Ds of negligence" include each of the following except

    A. direct cause.

    B. depth of cause.

    C. dereliction.

    D. damages.

5. The failure to act when one should is termed

    A. nonfeasance.

    B. noninvasive.

    C. misfeasance.

    D. malfeasance.

6. Professional liability insurance protects pharmacy technicians against which of the following?

    A. constitutional law

    B. common law

    C. tort law

    D. lawsuits

7. Good Samaritan laws

    A. encourage physicians to render emergency first aid.

    B. protect caregivers against liability for negligence in certain circumstances.

    C. deal with the treatment of accident victims.

    D. apply to all of the above.

8. Individuals are guaranteed certain fundamental freedoms by the Bill of Rights, including

    A. freedom of speech.

    B. equal protection.

    C. due process.

    D. all of the above.

9. The term "liable" is defined as

    A. false, defamatory writing.

    B. accountable under law.

    C. without legal force or effect.

    D. a moral code.

10. The relationship between the healthcare provider and patient is established by

    A. contract law.

    B. criminal law.

    C. case law.

    D. common law.

11. The term "respondeat superior" refers to

    A. corporate negligence.

    B. failure to protect.

    C. product liability.

    D. vicarious liability.

12. If a breach of confidentiality occurs, the patient must be notified by the healthcare provider within how many days?

    A. 7
    B. 15
    C. 45
    D. 60

sent, except

    A. explanations of terminology.
    B. adverse drug reactions.
    C. examination of the status of insurance.
    D. adverse treatment outcomes.

15. Which of the following is defined as the unauthorized acquisition of protected health information?

    A. informed consent
    B. failure to protect
    C. vicarious liability
    D. breach of confidentiality

Matching

    A. dereliction

    B. malfeasance

    C. statute of limitations

    D. misfeasance

    E. nonfeasance

_____ **1.** the performance of a lawful act in an illegal manner

_____ **2.** the failure to act when one should do so

_____ **3.** the execution of an unlawful or improper act

_____ **4.** the period of time established by state law in which a lawsuit may be filed

_____ **5.** the breach of the duty of care to a patient

Fill in the Blank

1. Negligent behavior that results in injury or loss is referred to as

    _____.

2. Professional liability insurance protects against _____
    _____ being brought against pharmacy
    technicians.

3. Having adequate certification, licensure, and insurance cover-
    age are the requirements of _____ law.

4. Actual damages are also referred to as _____
    _____ damages.

5. *Res ipsa loquitur* means "the thing _____
    for itself."

6. The relationship between the healthcare provider and patient is
    established by _____ law.

7. Corporate negligence differs from _____
    liability because it focuses on the responsibility of the health-
    care organization as a whole, and not its individual employees.

8. The statute of limitations _____ from
    state to state and by the type of legal claim.

9. _____ negligence means that a patient
    may have contributed to the negligence that caused him to be
    harmed.

10. _____ of risk is a method used to limit
    liability.

CASE STUDY

A 30-year-old test pilot for a watercraft manufacturer suffered severe
leg injuries that required surgery after several wrecks during the testing
procedure. He was prescribed methadone for pain, and his physician also
ordered an off-label, experimental form of ketamine tablets that required
special compounding. This required a prescription order form to be filled
out correctly prior to the compounding and dispensing. The patient,
whose pain was not sufficiently relieved by the methadone, readily agreed
to take this additional medication in the hope that complete pain relief
would be achieved. The experimental medication had warnings against
concurrent use with other pain medications. The patient was later found

dead and an autopsy confirmed that the combination of the two drugs proved to be lethal.

1. Since the ketamine was in an experimental tablet form, what should the pharmacist have done prior to filling the prescription?

http://www.ama-assn.org

http://www.hpso.com

http://www.medlaw.com

http://www.peoplespharmacy.com

http://www.pharmacytimes.com

http://www.proliability.com

http://www.resource4pharmacymalpractice.com

http://www.uspharmacist.com

REFERENCES

Abood, R. R. (2010). *Pharmacy Practice and the Law* (6th ed.). Burlington, MA: Jones and Bartlett.

Beardsley, R. S., Kimberlin, C., & Tindall, W. N. (2011). *Communication Skills in Pharmacy Practice: A Practical Guide for Students and Practitioners* (6th ed.). Philadelphia: Lippincott, Williams, & Wilkins.

Flight, M. (2011). *Law, Liability, & Ethics* (5th ed.). Clifton Park, NY: Cengage Learning.

Hepler, C. D., & Segal. R. (2003). *Preventing Medication Errors and Improving Drug Therapy Outcomes: A Management Systems Approach.* Boca Raton, FL: CRC Press.

Jackson, J. A. (2007). *Ethics, Legal Issues, and Professionalism in Surgical Technology.* Clifton Park, NY: Cengage Learning.

Delmar (author). (2010). Virtual Pharmacy Externship for Technicians (CD-ROM). Clifton Park, NY: Cengage Learning.

McWay, D. C. (2010). *Legal and Ethical Aspects of Health Information Management* (3rd ed.). Clifton Park, NY: Cengage Learning.

Roach, W. H., Jr. (2006). *Medical Records and the Law* (4th ed.). Burlington, MA: Jones and Bartlett.

Singer, P.A., & Viens, A.M. (eds.). (2008). *The Cambridge Textbook of Bioethics.* New York, NY: Cambridge University Press.

Ethics in Pharmacy Practice

1. Distinguish the differences between morals and ethics.
2. Define what is meant by the terms "legal" and "ethical."
3. Explain professional ethics.
4. Define moral rights versus legal rights.
5. List three examples of how healthcare professionals may deal with mistakes.
6. Discuss the process used for making an ethical decision.
7. Explain why confidentiality is an ethical issue.
8. List the major points in the codes of ethics for pharmacists and pharmacy technicians.

KEY TERMS

Autonomy—The ability or tendency to function independently.

Beneficence—Acting to benefit others.

Bioethics— It is concerned with how ethics apply to biological research and applications.

Code of ethics—Standards developed to affect quality and ensure the highest ethical and professional behavior.

Confidentiality—The obligation of the healthcare provider to maintain patient information in a way that will not allow dissemination beyond the healthcare provider.

Deontology—Also known as formalism or duty orientation; a concept that asserts that ethical decision making is based on moral rules and unchanging principles, which are derived from reason and can be applied universally.

Ethics—The study of values, or morals and morality; it includes concepts such as right, wrong, good, evil, and responsibility.

Loyalty—A faithfulness or allegiance to a cause, ideal, custom, institution, or product.

Morals—Motivations based on ideas of right and wrong.

Nonmaleficence—An ethical principle that asserts an obligation not to inflict harm intentionally; it is sometimes combined with beneficence to form a single principle.

OUTLINE

Patient rights—The recognition that patients are entitled to determine for themselves the extent to which they will receive (or not receive) care and treatment.

Privacy—The right to be left alone, or the right to control personal information.

Professional ethics—Moral standards and principles of conduct that guide professionals in the performance of their functions.

Utilitarianism—Also known as consequentialism; a concept that proposes that persons, organizations, and society in general should make choices that promote the greatest balance of good over harm for all.

Values—Desirable standards or qualities.

SETTING THE SCENE

A patient who is always very worried about her prescription medications arrives at the pharmacy with a prescription for metoprolol. The pharmacy technician knows this patient well and knows that she has high blood pressure, but often stops her medications because she is nervous about the side effects they sometimes cause. He fills her prescription but does not include the patient printout describing potential side effects and adverse reactions because he hopes she will take the medication and not worry so much. The pharmacist instructs her on properly taking metoprolol and she leaves.

Critical Thinking

- What should the pharmacy technician have done to best benefit the patient in this situation?

- Is it legal for the technician to avoid including the patient printout that describes potential side effects and adverse reactions because he knows the patient well?

- Using the Internet, research and list five major adverse effects of metoprolol.

OVERVIEW

The study of ethics is related to the study of law, but is distinct from it. Ethics is the study of moral choices that conform to professional standards of conduct. It is very important for pharmacy technicians to follow ethical standards of pharmacy practice, as well as to exhibit professional behaviors that are of strong moral character. Technicians must always remember the value of the pharmacy profession, and how society and their own community trust in them.

Various pharmaceutical codes of ethics in the United States have been adopted and revised since 1848. The **code of ethics** established by the American Pharmaceutical Association was intended to publicly state the principles forming the fundamental basis of the roles and responsibilities of pharmacists. Likewise, the code of ethics for pharmacy technicians (as set forth by the American Association of Pharmacy Technicians) applies to pharmacy

systems of moral values. People commonly adopt ethics as part of a formal system of rules. Abstract thoughts or ideas dealing with ethics are called *ethical concepts.* They aid in decision making, and include the concepts of **autonomy, beneficence** or **nonmaleficence**, the *best-interest standard*, fidelity, justice, rights, and veracity (see Table 3-1). The *double-effect*

TABLE 3-1 Concepts of Ethics

Concept	Definition	Example
Autonomy	Freedom, independence, or self-determination	Informed consent
Beneficence	Charity, kindness, and mercy	Hippocratic Oath
Best-interest standard	A way of determining what is the best interest of another who cannot determine it for himself or herself	Decision making for impaired individuals
Fidelity	Devotion to one's obligations, faithfulness, and loyalty	Operating within acceptable constraints of practice
Justice	Fairness to all people; *comparative justice* refers to balancing competing interests of individuals and groups against one another, with no independent standard used for this comparison; *distributive justice* refers to fair distribution of burdens and benefits using an independent standard	Access to healthcare services
Nonmaleficence	Prohibition against doing harm	Hippocratic Oath
Rights	"Just" claims or entitlements that others must respect; *patient rights* are often addressed in terms of confidentiality and privacy	Confidentiality and privacy
Veracity	Habitual honesty and truthfulness	Patient–provider relationship

principle recognizes that ethical choices may result in adverse outcomes. *Ethical theories* refer to systematic plans or statements of principles used to deal with ethical dilemmas, and include **utilitarianism** and **deontology**.

Morals are good principles or rules of conduct. They are more important socially than values. Morals are recognized as principles of good or "right" conduct that take into account virtues such as courage, balance, fairness, and wisdom. *Immoral* behavior is in conflict with morals. When behavior does not take moral principles into consideration, it is referred to as *amoral*. In the pharmacy, moral issues are often related to topics such as the use of the *morning-after pill*, which provides emergency contraception after unprotected sex.

Values are desirable standards or qualities. They may also be defined as rules about right and wrong. Values are often not thought of until a conflict arises. Together ethics, morals, and values provide for rules of behavior upon which good character standards are established. In today's pharmacy (and other healthcare settings), ethics often involve a personal understanding of right and wrong, as well as appropriate behaviors. *Etiquette* refers to how human beings relate to each other under specific circumstances, and is a social code of customs and rituals. Examples of etiquette include courtesy, politeness, and proper dress. Table 3-2 compares ethics and related terms.

The study of **bioethics** is concerned with how ethics apply to biological research and applications. In medicine, this is referred to as *medical ethics*. Bioethics refers to ethical issues that affect life and death,

TABLE 3-2 Ethics and Related Terms

Definition	Basis	Summary
ETHICS—The formal study of moral choices that conform to standards of conduct	Philosophy	Judgments of right and wrong
MORALS—Principles or fundamental standards of "right" conduct that are internalized by each individual	Traditional religious beliefs and personal choices	Right-conduct standards
ETIQUETTE—Principles of human interrelationships under certain circumstances	Society	Social code
LAW—A body of rules of action or conduct that are prescribed by a controlling authority and have a binding legal force	Controlling authorities such as legislatures	Rules with legal force
VALUES—Concepts that give meaning to life and serve as a framework for decision making	Society, religion, and family	Life's meaning

TABLE 3-3 Some Bioethics Issues

Issue	Explanation	Occurrence
Abortion	Termination of pregnancy before viability of fetus	Beginning of life
Organ transplantation	Transfer of tissue or an organ from one body to another, or from one individual to another	
End-of-life planning	Planning in advance for the level of medical care to be received at end of life	Death and dying
Euthanasia	Causing death painlessly with the goal to end suffering	
Withholding or withdrawing life support	Decisions of patients, their families, or legal guardians to refrain from giving permission for treatment or care	

as well as the implications of applying biological research. It is linked to technological and scientific advances in medicine, biology, and related sciences. Bioethical issues are increasing with the rapid advances in science and technology. Some current bioethics issues are listed in Table 3-3.

You Be the Judge

Phil is a pharmacy technician who is asked by a customer about Plan B®, a medication intended for use as a morning-after pill. Because Phil believes that the use of a morning-after medication to prevent conception is wrong, he describes all sorts of serious adverse effects and states that they happen to most of the people who take the drug. As a result, the patient calls her doctor, who later calls the pharmacy and speaks with the pharmacist, telling him what Phil said and asking for an explanation. In your judgment, was Phil ethically correct in his actions? What sorts of legal repercussions do you think could await Phil as a result of his misstatements about Plan B?

Focus On...

Ethics

Ethics refers to standards of behavior developed as a result of society's concept of right and wrong.

Focus On...

Moral Values

Moral values consist of one's personal concept of right and wrong, formed through the influence of family, culture, and society.

THE RELATIONSHIP BETWEEN ETHICS AND THE LAW

In comparing ethics and law, it is important to understand the purposes, standards, and penalties that relate to each. Law is designed to protect society and help it to function efficiently by imposing civil or criminal penalties if laws are violated. In medicine, the law is designed to protect the rights of all individuals, be they patients, practitioners, or employees. Laws are enforced by penalties that may include fines, imprisonment, or both. Ethics are designed to assure adherence to standards while also serving to raise competence levels and to build values. In the United States, the Medicare system was established with the intention of providing fair and ethical medical treatment for the elderly and the disabled. Ethical penalties include suspension from medical societies, a sanction imposed by one's own medical peers.

Distinguishing between legal and ethical issues is difficult, but may be somewhat simplified by considering potential consequences. While breaking ethical codes results in disapproval from societal segments such as professionals in various organizations, breaking laws results in enforced penalties. If the focus of a choice of action is external, it relates to law. If the focus of a choice of action is internal (based on conscience), it relates to ethics. Usually, ethics are taken into account when the following occur:

- There is no obvious right or wrong.
- Justice will not likely be brought about by enforcement of law.
- A "right" behavior is likely to bring about a "wrong" effect.
- Personal sacrifice will result from following ideals.

PROFESSIONAL ETHICS

The term **professional ethics** is used to denote "the profession's interpretation of the will of society for the conduct of the members of that profession augmented by the special knowledge that only the members of the profession possess." Professional ethics are concerned primarily with moral issues and responsibilities. Professionals must make informed decisions based on specialized training. They must act in the proper manner when their action is required to help or save the life of another. The medical profession and each of its separate areas have special codes of professional ethics that must be followed. The characteristics of a professional consist of a set of specific attitudes, which are essential for establishing professional ethics.

Guidelines for professional ethics are based on *principalism*, which is the application of four distinct moral principles. These principles func-

Also, veracity (truthfulness) is important; healthcare providers should be truthful to patients and families. The four principles are applied to actions and decision making, constituting the foundation for professional ethics.

CODE OF ETHICS FOR PHARMACISTS

The American Pharmaceutical Association authored the Code of Ethics for Pharmacists. This code of ethics is based on moral obligations and designed to establish guidelines for professional ethical behavior. Codes of ethics include theories based on actions, agents, and situations. The central themes of the Code of Ethics for Pharmacists are as follows:

- Pharmacists must respect the trust that their patients put in them.

- They must always focus on the patient's well-being and comfort.

- The dignity and **privacy** of the patient must always be respected. Each patient's health is private information. The pharmacist should counsel patients so that they can make proper decisions about their own health.

- Pharmacists must always be truthful and non-discriminatory.

- They must continually keep aware of new advances in the field of pharmacy.

- The values of other professional colleagues must always be respected whenever they must be consulted.

- Though pharmacists focus on one patient at a time, the overall good of the community and society in general must always remain in their thoughts.

- Fair and equitable distribution of health resources must be maintained between patients and within society.

The Patient–Pharmacist Relationship

The relationship between patient and pharmacist is one of the most critical in the medical field. A pharmacist must keep complete records on each patient in order to avoid medication errors or interactions that may result in harm. Some of the information that the pharmacist must manage is lists of all medications that a patient is taking, including prescription, non-prescription, and herbal medications. It is important that the pharmacist establish a trusting relationship wherein the patient feels completely comfortable in discussing his or her health concerns with the pharmacist.

The patient's complete medical history is vital in helping the pharmacist to understand his or her overall health picture, and to determine if any previous health issues may be related to his or her current condition. A patient's allergies are one of the most critical points of discussion, and patients must be instructed just how important their allergy information is in determining the correct medications to take. Any previous problems with medications should be noted, including unexpected reactions. Patients must be able to tell their pharmacist about previous, current, or planned pregnancies. They must be honest about their use of alcohol, tobacco, and recreational drugs if their health is to be maintained. These substances can and do interact with many different medications, and it is the continued job of the pharmacist to educate patients about how important the sharing of this information is.

Any time a pharmacist dispenses a new medication, be it to an existing patient or a new one, the patient should be counseled about the medication's effects. If anything is changed concerning the use of a medication (including dose, route of administration, or strength), the pharmacist and patient should communicate. The pharmacist must place patient counseling high on his or her priority list. Effective counseling establishes a solid patient–pharmacist relationship that can avoid misunderstandings that lead to medication errors. Strong, effective communication between the patient and pharmacist helps to achieve the optimum outcome in treatment and care.

Patient Advocacy

Many healthcare providers are required to represent patients while helping them to obtain healthcare services and information. These patient advocates—healthcare providers and pharmacists concerned with the cause and best interest of their patients—can assist in many different areas, including the choice of healthcare, getting needed information in order to make good healthcare decisions, addressing how treatment will affect livelihood, discussing treatment with family members of the patient, watching for adverse effects, determining

must be allowed to decide on their own medical care without being unduly influenced by healthcare providers. Healthcare providers must give the patient proper information in order to make an informed decision, but cannot actually decide for the patient. *Informed consent* is the term used to describe the patient's decision making related to his or her own health. It can only be given after proper information has been given to the patient. Informed consent requires a patient to be competent to make decisions about his or her health. The decisions must be voluntary, based on recommended strategies from qualified healthcare providers.

Patients must fully understand all of their options, and have had all information about their condition disclosed to them before deciding. Once the patient's decision has been made, he or she must give authorization to his or her healthcare providers to proceed with whatever treatments the patient has decided upon. The American healthcare system is fundamentally based upon ensuring the rights of patients. **Patient rights** recognize that patients are entitled to determine the extent to which they will receive (or not receive) care and treatment. To respect patient autonomy, no action may violate patient confidentiality. The patient must consent to every action, and must be informed of alternatives and possible complications.

What Would You Do?

It is a busy afternoon, and the pharmacy has only one pharmacy technician on duty. The pharmacist does not consult with two patients because of all his other responsibilities, and they leave the pharmacy. If you were the pharmacist in this situation, what should you have done?

Professional Competence

Professional competence is achieved over time, with continued learning and development. It is important to seek out continuing education and keep abreast of new technologies, developments, and the latest medical publications. Competency-based education, which has increased in popularity in the medical community, measures student competence with specialized testing. This testing includes written exams, reviews by peers, and even self-assessment. Continuing education credits are required every few years. The goal of increasing competence is to deliver the best healthcare possible to protect the public from disease. The pharmacist is ultimately liable for the actions of the pharmacy technician, so extremely rigorous levels of competence are required.

Pharmacy technicians must be able to balance busy daily activities with a strict adherence to detail. They must triple-check every drug that they dispense, all labeling, and the instructions provided by the physician as well as the pharmacist. As their job description evolves, pharmacy technicians are responsible for more duties than ever before, some of which used to be the sole responsibility of licensed pharmacists. It is important that pharmacy technicians alert supervising pharmacists to any discrepancies in information. The competence of a pharmacy technician is vitally important in today's pharmacy. Incompetent actions may result in legal action against the pharmacy technician, the pharmacist, and the company they work for.

Good communication skills, the ability to share information clearly and accurately, and the ability to keep information confidential are all required. Understanding of and empathy for others are important elements for quality pharmacy practice. Technical skills are also vital. These may include the following:

- Computer literacy
- Proficiency in English, science, and mathematics
- A willingness to learn new skills and techniques
- An ability to document well

Respect for Other Colleagues

It is important to always treat colleagues with respect. Staff members must work together for the good of their patients. Discrimination of any kind against a colleague has no positive results, especially with colleagues alongside whom the pharmacist works on a regular basis. However, it is wise to challenge colleagues when they behave in less-than-professional ways. Criticism of their work should always be kept aboveboard and never be unfair or cruel. Being honest, on time, trustworthy, and a team player shows respect for colleagues. Any unethical behavior shows a lack of respect for other colleagues, as it reflects on the workplace as a whole and may tarnish colleagues' reputations as well as that of the pharmacist.

Pharmacy technicians must be willing to perform duties outside of their formal job descriptions when they are needed to help in other areas of the pharmacy. They must respect other healthcare professionals and work as a team with them. Verbal and non-verbal communication ~~important to the establishment~~ of respect for other healthcare profes-

Unacceptable behaviors include theft, rudeness, lying, ~~blaming~~, complaining.

Focus On...

Respect

You must treat each person, whether patient or coworker, the way you wish to be treated.

Serving the Community

Pharmacists are respected professionals on whom both patients and physicians rely. They are key allied health professionals who are trusted to provide safe and appropriate medications to the public. They serve their community by educating patients and consulting with them to prevent medication errors. Today, technology has changed greatly, and the role of pharmacists is more important than ever before.

Equitable Treatment

The term *equity* refers to attempting to distribute equally to all who are in need. Pharmacists must always be ethical and moral. They cannot discriminate against patients for any reason (race, religion, color, financial status, etc.), and they must provide fair and equitable treatment. They must always follow their code of ethics to treat patients equally.

CODE OF ETHICS FOR PHARMACY TECHNICIANS

Pharmacy technicians, like pharmacists, should strive to make the care of every patient their utmost concern. They should always treat patients respectfully, responsibly, and honestly. Pharmacy technicians should use their best professional judgment at all times, and ask their pharmacist for advice if unsure about anything that occurs. They should encourage patients to speak directly with the pharmacist about any concerns. Professional competence must be continually maintained so that they can deliver the best healthcare service.

The American Association of Pharmacy Technicians (AAPT) drafted its own version of a code of ethics distinct from that of pharmacists. The code of ethics for pharmacy technicians includes the following points:

- Delivering competent, safe, and appropriate pharmacy and related services

- Recognizing limitations of practice and providing services only when qualified and authorized by a supervising pharmacist; furthermore, these services must be consistent with applicable laws and regulations

- Maintaining and respecting **confidentiality** of sensitive information obtained during all activities, as directed by the supervising pharmacist, and consistent with legal requirements, unless legally directed to release such information

- Using credentials properly, and providing truthful, accurate representations concerning education, experience, competency, and performance of services

- Providing truthful, accurate representations to the public and employers

- Following appropriate health and safety procedures

- Protecting the public, employers, and employees from conditions where injury and damage are reasonably foreseeable

- Disclosing to patients or employers significant circumstances that may involve conflicts of interest or appearances of impropriety

- Avoiding conduct that could cause conflicts of interest with patients or employers

- Assuring that real or perceived conflicts of interest do not compromise legitimate interests of patients or employers, and do not influence or interfere with work-related judgments

Maintaining Health and Safety

Pharmacy technicians are responsible for maintaining their own health so that they can be well enough to serve both pharmacists and customers. When a technician is physically or mentally ill, his or her health can interfere with the ability to provide good care to patients, or to safely execute professional pharmacy activities or decision making. Pharmacy technicians must be cautious and careful in the practice of pharmacy. They must strive to avoid exposure to chemical substances in order to maintain both health and safety. In the workplace, safety is of the utmost importance to keep in mind. Maintaining good health for themselves and others is essential. To

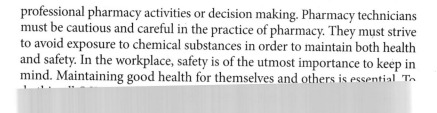

...What may be the consequences of this type of behavior?

Honesty and Integrity

Pharmacy technicians must always be honest, even when mistakes occur. Errors should be reported to supervisors immediately. All topics must be discussed factually, without exaggerations or distortions. The patient deserves to know the "straight truth," even if it is difficult to hear. Patient dignity is of utmost importance, and it can only be preserved by honesty and integrity in communications with patients.

Privileged Communication

Information that passes between individuals that cannot be submitted into evidence into a court of law because of the legal relationship of the individuals is referred to as *privileged communication*. Communication between various types of healthcare providers and patients is legally recognized as *privileged*. Therefore, these providers cannot reveal confidential patient information in court unless the patient voluntarily gives up (waives) his or her privilege against disclosure. The law regulates the revealing of private information since both confidentiality and privacy are regulated. When ethics are followed regardless of the law, there are regulations about confidentiality that determine the correct legal outcome.

What Would You Do?

Sheila, a pharmacy technician, dropped a few capsules on the pharmacy floor while dispensing medications. Nobody else saw this happen. Quickly, she picked the capsules off the floor and put them back onto the tray, after which she included them in the container of dispensed medication. If you were Sheila, what would you do in this situation? If you were another pharmacy worker who saw this happen, what would you do?

Focus On...

Errors

Taking responsibility for your errors shows true integrity and character, and allows the mistake to be corrected.

Assist and Support the Pharmacist

The pharmacy technician assists the pharmacist with all tasks that he or she is allowed to perform by state law. The pharmacist must be supported in all activities so that he or she may perform his or her duties without distraction. The combination of a qualified and professional pharmacy technician with an equally competent pharmacist results in accurate and ethical healthcare that is as free of errors as possible. It is vital that the pharmacy technician support the pharmacist's activities and adheres to instructions, bearing in mind all legal and ethical matters.

Maintaining Confidentiality

Confidentiality—maintaining a patient's private information so that it does not become accessible to anyone who should not have access to it—is important. Sharing private information with anyone who is not supposed to know it is a breach of ethics and may have legal ramifications. Those who do not respect and maintain confidentiality may be fired. Patient information, be it written, computerized, or even verbal, is not to be shared with anyone except approved healthcare professionals. The Health Insurance Portability and Accountability Act (HIPAA) governs the disclosure of confidential information. Patients are usually required to read and sign a document that addresses to whom and under what circumstances their private medical information may be disclosed (see Chapter 6).

Observing Quality and Legal Standards

Pharmacy technicians must have knowledge of many techniques and principles, including related legal and ethical issues. Ethical standards are usually more severe and demanding than the standards required by law. Pharmacy technicians must also acquire a working knowledge of, and tolerance for, human nature and its individual characteristics. Daily contact with a wide variety of individuals with different problems and concerns is an important part of a pharmacy technician's duties. Courtesy, compassion, and common sense are vital to the success of the pharmacy technician.

Focus On...

Standards

A violation of either a legal or ethical standard can mean the loss of a technician's reputation.

Maintenance of Professional Standards

The pharmacy technician who works to improve his or her professional approach in the workplace will be a great asset to an employer. This ability will help them to be promoted to positions of more responsibil-

ployees are interested in only what the employer can provide for them. This is an immature way to approach a job. When a technician is employed by a pharmacy, his or her skills are exchanged for different types of compensation, benefitting both the technician and the employer. Often, pharmacy technicians forget that experience is a great benefit that they get from work. Supporting the employer with loyalty is important. Likewise, the pharmacy should loyally support its employees, including its pharmacy technicians.

The relationship between pharmacists and pharmacy technicians must be one of mutual respect and professionalism. Pharmacists have ultimate responsibility for all of the actions of their pharmacy technicians. Clear communication between them is essential because any errors or negligence committed by the pharmacy technician will ultimately have to be answered for by the pharmacist. The pharmacist must check the accuracy of all of the pharmacy technician's actions.

What Would You Do?

Mr. Johnson, who has been coming to your pharmacy for many years, approaches you. You know that his wife died the previous year, and that he is taking medications to treat depression as well as cancer. When he arrives with a new prescription, he asks about the prescribed medication and comments, "I sure wouldn't want to take too much of this stuff. How much of this do you think would kill me if I wasn't careful?" Do you think Mr. Johnson may be contemplating suicide? What should you do first in this situation?

MAKING ETHICAL DECISIONS

An individual's life experience and values come into play when making good ethical decisions, which will occur on a daily basis. The effects their decisions can have on other individuals must be considered. Both long-term and short-term consequences must be taken into account.

7. A student pharmacy technician asks his uncle, a pharmacist, "Why did my advisor recommend an ethics class for me?" Which of the following is the best response by the pharmacist?

   A. "Ethics must be learned in order to obey the law."
   B. "You may find studying ethics interesting."
   C. "It is the responsibility of pharmacy technicians to recognize ethical dilemmas in the workplace."
   D. "You must have misunderstood because pharmacy technicians do not have to study ethics."

8. Which of the following organizations approved the Code of Ethics for Pharmacy Technicians?

   A. the NAPT
   B. the AMA
   C. the APA
   D. the AAPT

9. A patient's self-governance, privacy, and right to liberty comprise:

   A. maintaining confidentiality.
   B. professional competence.
   C. patient autonomy .
   D. legal standards.

10. The patient's complete medical history is important in assisting the pharmacist to understand and determine

    A. his or her previous health issues.
    B. his or her overall health picture.
    C. his or her allergy information.
    D. all of the above

11. The pharmacist's actions of supporting and pushing for improvements in patient healthcare issues are referred to as

    A. patient advocacy.
    B. patient confidentiality.
    C. quality of medications.
    D. professional competence.

12. The profession's interpretation of the will of society for the conduct of the members of the profession is referred to as

    A. professional network.
    B. professional ethics.
    C. professional organization.
    D. professional liability.

13. The exchange of gifts or money exemplifies serious

    A. professional issues.
    B. pharmaceutical issues.
    C. medical issues.

15. Motivations based on ideas of right and wrong

    A. duties.
    B. action plans.
    C. morals.
    D. needs.

Matching

    A. Values

    B. Nonmaleficence

    C. Ethics

    D. Code of ethics

    E. Morals

_____ **1.** An obligation not to inflict harm intentionally

_____ **2.** Desirable standards or qualities

_____ **3.** Motivations based on right and wrong

_____ **4.** The study of value, or morals and morality

_____ **5.** Standards that affect quality and ensure ethical and professional behavior

Fill in the Blank

1. The characteristics of a professional consist of a set of specific _____.

2. Each patient's health is _____ information.

3. The pharmacist must place patient counseling high on his or her _____ list.

4. The ability to function independently is called _____.

5. Pharmacy technicians must _____ check every drug that they dispense.

6. A good attitude should be demonstrated _____, and patients and customers should be greeted with a _____.

7. A pharmacy technician must have a strong knowledge of ethical issues that might relate to his or her _____.

8. The goals of increased competence are focused on delivering the best healthcare possible to protect the public from _____.

9. The Code of Ethics for Pharmacists was established by the American _____.

10. Professional competence must be continually maintained so that healthcare professionals can deliver the best _____ services.

CASE STUDY

A celebrity who is spending time in the United States asks his doctor back home in England to prescribe some painkillers and antidepressants. The doctor complies according to the standards of his country, and the celebrity goes to a pharmacy in the United States to have the prescriptions filled. Because the pharmacy technician recognizes the celebrity, he begins dispensing the prescriptions. Meanwhile, the pharmacist also recognizes the celebrity, and begins to talk to him, asking what he is doing in the United States. He notices that the prescriptions originated in England, not the United States.

1. What is the pharmacist's first responsibility regarding filling these foreign prescriptions?

2. Do you think that the pharmacist and pharmacy technician can fill these prescriptions under any circumstances?

3. Assuming that the celebrity received these prescriptions, and took them to commit suicide, who would be responsible for his death?

RELATED INTERNET SITES

http://changingminds.org Click on "values" under the explanations

http://www.op.nysed.gov Search for "pharmacy"

http://www.pharmacist.com Search for "code of ethics for pharmacists."

REFERENCES

Buerki, R. A., & Vottero, L. D. (2002). *Ethical Responsibility in Pharmacy Practice* (2nd ed.). Madison, WI: American Institute of the History of Pharmacy.

Burkhardt, M. A., & Nathaniel, A. K. (2007). *Ethics and Issues in Contemporary Nursing* (3rd ed.). Clifton Park, NY: Cengage Learning.

Guido, G. W. (2009). *Legal and Ethical Issues in Nursing* (5th ed.). Upper Saddle River, NJ: Prentice Hall.

Harris, D. M. (2007). *Contemporary Issues in Healthcare Law and Ethics* (3rd ed.). Chicago: Health Administration Press.

Judson, K., & Harrison, C. (2009). *Law & Ethics for Medical Careers* (5th ed.). New York: McGraw-Hill Higher Education.

Rickles, N. M., Wertheimer, A. I., & Smith, M. C. (2009). *Social and Behavioral Aspects of Pharmaceutical Care.* (2nd ed.). Burlington, MA: Jones and Bartlett.

Veatch, R., & Haddad, A. (2008). *Case Studies in Pharmacy Ethics* (2nd ed.). New York: Oxford University Press USA.

White, B. D. (2007). *Drugs, Ethics, and Quality of Life: Cases and Materials on Ethical, Legal, and Public Policy Dilemmas in Medicine and Pharmacy Practice.* London: Pharmaceutical Products Press.

SECTION II

Federal Regulation of Drug Products

Upon completion of this chapter, the reader should be able to:

1. Describe the purpose of the Pure Food and Drug Act.
2. Identify the reason that Congress adopted the Harrison Narcotics Tax Act.
3. Briefly explain the sulfanilamide tragedy.
4. Identify the concept of the Durham-Humphrey Amendment.
5. Explain the thalidomide tragedy.
6. Describe the purpose of the Kefauver-Harris Amendment.
7. Define OBRA-90 and explain its basic framework.
8. Describe the purpose of OSHA.
9. Explain the Drug Regulation Reform Act.
10. Describe the codes of the Drug Listing Act.

KEY TERMS

Adulteration—Tampering with or contaminating a product or substance.

Fraud—The intentional use of deceit to deprive another person of his or her money, property, or rights.

Fraudulent—Deceitful; intending to deceive.

Investigational—Drugs used to provide detailed inquiry or systematic examination of their effects.

Legend drug—Prescription drug.

Misbranding—Fraudulent or misleading labeling or marking.

National Drug Code (NDC)—The federal code that identifies a drug's manufacturer or distributor, its formulation, and the size and type of its packaging.

Orphan drug—Drugs used to treat diseases that affect fewer than 200,000 people in the United States.

Over-the-counter (OTC) drug—Non-prescription drug.

Phocomelia—A severe birth defect, also known as "seal limbs," involving the malformation or non-formation of arms and legs; it is caused by the drug thalidomide.

Teratogenic—Causing genetic defects.

SETTING THE SCENE

A pharmacy technician dispensed a prescription in a non-child-resistant container. Her supervisor checked the medication and approved it. The patient left the pharmacy, only to return three days later. His grandson had opened the container and taken 15 pills. His physician had told him that this situation was the fault of the pharmacy.

Critical Thinking

- What did the pharmacy technician do wrong?

- What law was ignored? Explain this law.

- Who is responsible for this error and what may the consequences be?

OVERVIEW

The federal government enacts and interprets laws for the general population. State and local governments are responsible for determining the specifics of certain laws within their jurisdictions.

Regulatory agencies are government-based departments that create specific rules about what is and is not legal within a specific field or area of expertise. The regulatory agencies for the practice of pharmacy are the individual state boards of pharmacy. The U.S. Food and Drug Administration (FDA), which is a branch of the U.S. Department of Health and Human Services, regulates all drugs with the exception of illegal drugs. All federal legislation pertaining to drug administration is initiated, implemented, and enforced by the FDA. The FDA is responsible for the approval of drugs, over-the-counter (OTC) and prescription drug labeling, and standards for drug manufacturing.

Many laws and amendments that have shaped the current Food, Drug, and Cosmetic Act were enacted over the past 100 years. In most cases, they represent attempts on the part of lawmakers to protect the American public.

PURE FOOD AND DRUG ACT OF 1906

The Pure Food and Drug Act of 1906 prohibited the interstate distribution or sale of *adulterated* (made impure with other ingredients) and *misbranded* (improperly labeled) food and drugs.

Almost 30 years after its enactment, the law was found to be inadequate for the following reasons:

1. It did not include cosmetics.

2. It did not provide authority to ban unsafe drugs.

What Led to the Legislation?

The Pure Food and Drug Act came into being because many products, including meats, patent medicines, and substances that contained cocaine, were sold to an unsuspecting public with labels that did not adequately describe the contents or the safety of consuming them. Many public figures, including those in politics and journalism, complained about unsanitary and hazardous conditions that existed in the packaging process of foods and drugs. These advocates were opposed by many manufacturers who thought the proposed legislation would destroy their livelihoods.

Key Points of the Legislation

This act prevented the manufacture, sale, or transportation of impure (due to additives), misbranded, poisonous, or harmful drugs, foods, liquors, and medicines. It also controlled the traffic in these substances.

HARRISON NARCOTICS TAX ACT OF 1914

The Harrison Narcotics Tax Act of 1914 was implemented to regulate and tax the distribution, importation, and production of opiates. These substances included opium and coca products (which were used to manufacture cocaine). At this time, the distribution, sale, and use of cocaine were still legal for both companies and individuals. It is ironic that use of opiates and cocaine actually increased following the implementation of this act.

Throughout the 1800s, opiates and cocaine were mostly unregulated. Many people were addicted to these substances, and as many as 1 in 400 U.S. citizens were addicted to opium itself. As time went on, an increasing number of crimes were linked to the use of opiates and cocaine. Public opinion began to sway toward prohibition—a ban on alcohol and drugs.

Points of the Legislation

The legislation was intended to control commerce in these drugs. It required drug manufacturers, sellers, distributors, importers, compounders, and dispensers to register with the Internal Revenue Service (IRS). The use of opium and coca leaves was closely monitored from then on, and only permitted for limited medical and scientific purposes. The term "narcotics" was used in the act's title to encompass opiates as well as cocaine, although cocaine is not actually a narcotic but instead is a central nervous system stimulant.

SULFANILAMIDE TRAGEDY OF 1937

In 1937, the Massengill Company introduced Elixir Sulfanilamide into the market. The elixir contained a solution that included diethylene glycol as a solvent. Sulfanilamide was a sulfa drug used to treat hemolytic streptococcal infections. Toxicity tests of the product were not conducted, and very little was known about the inherent toxicity of diethylene glycol (a deadly poison now used as a type of permanent antifreeze in automobiles). More than 100 patients died from ingesting Elixir Sulfanilamide before the FDA removed it from the market under a technical labeling violation of the 1906 Act; this became known as the sulfanilamide tragedy of 1937.

FOOD, DRUG, AND COSMETIC ACT OF 1938

The 1937 sulfanilamide tragedy propelled the passage of the Federal Food, Drug, and Cosmetic Act of 1938. Under this act, pharmaceutical manufacturers were required to file new drug applications with the FDA. Manufacturers had to ensure the purity, strength, safety, and packaging of drugs. Foods and cosmetics were also regulated. Under this act, the FDA has the power to approve or deny new drug applications and even to conduct inspections to ensure compliance. Pursuant to this act, the FDA approves the **investigational** use of drugs on humans and ensures that approved drugs are safe and effective.

This act remains the basis of today's law. The Food, Drug, and Cosmetic Act requires anyone who wishes to introduce a drug product to prove its safety to the FDA before it can be marketed. This act was the beginning of the "pre-market approval process" for drugs in the United States, which requires the submission of a New Drug Application (NDA). For those interested, the entire act may be found online at http://www.gpo.gov.

What Led to the Legislation?

The sulfanilamide tragedy of 1937 was of primary importance to the development of the Food, Drug, and Cosmetic Act of 1938. Because of the lack of testing, diethylene glycol was included in Elixir Sulfanilamide

could now be better enforced because of this acts requir... strengthened the FDA's ability to enforce the standards that it set forth.

DURHAM-HUMPHREY AMENDMENT OF 1951

During the 1940s, the FDA began to use internal regulations to create classifications of prescription (**legend drugs**), and non-prescription (**over-the-counter [OTC]**) drugs. This process did not work very well. Therefore, in 1951, Senator Hubert Humphrey, a pharmacist from Minnesota, and Congressman Carl Durham, a pharmacist from North Carolina, supported legislation to establish clear criteria for such decisions. The Durham-Humphrey Amendment of 1951 prohibits dispensing of legend drugs without a prescription. Non-legend OTC drugs were not restricted to sale and use under medical supervision.

This act created an exemption for drugs that could not be labeled safely for use by the public. Drugs marketed under this exemption could not be dispensed without prescriptions, but specific drugs were not indicated. A prescription that did not have refills indicated on its labeling when issued could still be refilled if the prescriber was contacted at a later date.

Focus On...

The Durham-Humphrey Amendment

The Durham-Humphrey Amendment allowed verbal prescriptions to be transmitted over the phone and also allowed refills to be called in from a physician's office.

What Led to the Legislation?

This legislation came about primarily because the FDA could not approve many important new drugs, such as antibiotics, under the existing law, because they could not be safely labeled without a physician's intervention. Before this law was passed, there was little legal distinction between the use of many non-prescription and legend drugs. Manufacturers regularly marketed directly to consumers without considering potential effects of the misuse of their products.

Key Points of the Legislation

This amendment required that drugs intended for use by humans that were not safe to use without medical supervision be dispensed only by prescription and bear the legend "Rx." Drugs marketed as "by prescription only" were generally considered to be misbranded if dispensed without a prescription. This amendment also required that legend drugs be labeled "Caution: Federal law prohibits dispensing without prescription." The use of the "Rx" symbol alone instead of this legend was the result of the later FDA Modernization Act (in 1997).

You Be the Judge

A pharmacy technician is working on a Saturday morning. His pharmacist decides to take a break since there are no customers in the pharmacy. During the pharmacist's break, a friend of the pharmacy technician enters the pharmacy and asks if he can have a few Percocet tablets because of back pain. The pharmacy technician gives his friend six Percocet tablets out of a container in the pharmacy. His friend takes these tablets and leaves. What do you think the pharmacy technician did wrong in this situation? If the pharmacist finds out about this, what do you think the consequences will be? What possible legal action could ensue against this pharmacy technician?

THALIDOMIDE TRAGEDY OF 1962

In 1961, the "thalidomide tragedy" began to unfold. Thalidomide was initially marketed in 1958 and was sold without prescription as a tranquilizer in West Germany until April 1961, when the drug was recognized as causing polyneuritis in adults. In November 1961, the drug was first linked with **phocomelia** (seal limbs), a severe birth defect. Thousands of infants had, by that time, been born in West Germany without one or both arms or legs, or with only partially formed limbs. The manufacturer withdrew the drug from the West German market on November 26, 1961.

Many drug firms had obtained licenses to market thalidomide on a worldwide basis. In the United States, the William S. Merrell Company had distributed the drug experimentally in 1960 under the trade name "Kevadon," but the FDA did not give final approval to the NDA that the company had submitted.

The FDA's timely action in withholding Kevadon approval was attributed to an FDA medical officer who refused approval while seeking data on further proof of safety. Even so, 29,413 patients in the United States had been involved in the human clinical trial testing of Kevadon. When the evidence that thalidomide was **teratogenic** (able to cause

Thalidomide

The lesson of the thalidomide tragedy is that serious adverse effects can be caused by certain new drugs, as well as by new uses for older drugs. These adverse effects may not be discovered until very wide clinical use has occurred and after some damage has taken place.

KEFAUVER-HARRIS AMENDMENT OF 1963

The Federal Food, Drug, and Cosmetic Act was amended again with the Kefauver-Harris Amendment of 1963 to require that drug products, both prescription and non-prescription, be pure, effective, and safe. Prescription drug advertising was placed under FDA supervision and qualifications of drug investigators were subjected to review. These amendments provided for registration of manufacturers and inspection of manufacturing sites, and required an unprecedented level of accountability from manufacturers.

What Led to the Legislation?

Senator Kefauver's ongoing study of trade practices within the drug industry, including the marketing of worthless and potentially dangerous drugs, led to the Kefauver-Harris Amendment. It was clear that the federal government needed further regulations in order to keep drug manufacturers from making worthless or dangerous drugs available to the public.

Key Points of the Legislation

This amendment required that all drug manufacturers prove the efficacy of the drugs to the FDA before marketing them. This meant that thorough and rigorous controlled studies had to be conducted. It specified that all drugs brought to market since the 1938 Food, Drug, and Cosmetic Act would have to meet the same requirements. Manufacturers had to report all adverse effects as well as benefits to the FDA, and include such information in advertisements. Patients testing new drugs had to provide "informed consent," meaning that they had to be thoroughly educated about the possible medical risks of the drug they were testing.

Focus On...

The Drug Efficacy Study Implementation

The Drug Efficacy Study Implementation (DESI) program was implemented by the FDA after the Kefauver-Harris Amendment. It was intended to classify all pre-1962 drugs that were already on the market as effective, ineffective, or needing further study. By 1984, the FDA had evaluated more than 3,000 separate products as well as more than 16,000 therapeutic claims. An early effect of this program was the development of the Abbreviated New Drug Application.

COMPREHENSIVE DRUG ABUSE PREVENTION AND CONTROL ACT OF 1970

The Comprehensive Drug Abuse Prevention and Control Act of 1970 requires the pharmaceutical industry to maintain physical security and strict record keeping for many types of drugs. Its main achievement was to divide controlled substances into five categories called "schedules." Substances in Schedule I have the highest potential for abuse, while those in Schedule V have the least. Title II of this act is known as the Controlled Substances Act (CSA), and it is discussed in greater detail in Chapter 5. Drugs may be added or deleted from the schedules, or be moved to a different schedule, based on Drug Enforcement Agency (DEA) or Department of Health and Human Services (HHS) actions. Individuals and companies may also petition the DEA to add, delete, or change a drug's scheduling. The most important factor in placing a drug into a specific drug schedule is its potential for abuse. Any person who handles or intends to handle controlled substances must obtain a DEA registration. The DEA limits the amount of Schedule I and II substances that may be manufactured within the United States in a given one-year period. Anyone manufacturing, distributing, or dispensing controlled substances in an unlawful manner is liable for prosecution under the rules of the CSA. A complete listing of drugs of abuse may be found at http://www.usdoj.gov (click on "DEA Home Page"> "Publications"> "Drugs of Abuse"> "Drugs of Abuse Chart"). This act is discussed in greater detail in Chapter 5.

What Led to the Legislation?

There were many laws and regulations in existence that dealt with dangerous drugs. However, punishments for the use and sale of various

tion of illegal drugs were given harsh penalties. The act also established standards to deal with drug abuse.

POISON PREVENTION PACKAGING ACT OF 1970

The Poison Prevention Packaging Act authorized the Consumer Product Safety Commission to create standards for child-resistant packaging. Its "special packaging" terminology signifies containers made to be very difficult for young children to open. This act requires that a few OTC drugs, and nearly all legend drugs, be packaged in child-resistant containers that cannot be opened by 80 percent of children younger than five, but can be opened by 90 percent of adults (see Figure 4-1). It

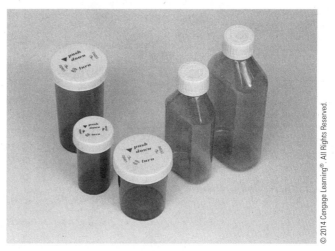

Figure 4-1 Child-resistant safety caps.

requires pharmacists to dispense certain drugs in child-resistant containers. Drugs dispensed for use by patients in hospitals or nursing homes are usually not required to be packaged in child-resistant containers because children usually do not have access to them in these environments. However, assisted-living environments are considered "households," and child-resistant containers are usually required. Stock bottles of medications do not usually require special packaging because they are intended to be used by pharmacists for repackaging of drugs prior to dispensing. It is important that pharmacy technicians also understand that many "blister packs" (such as the Z-Pak) are considered child-resistant under the provisions of this act.

If a prescriber authorizes non-child-resistant containers, they may be provided by the pharmacist. Also, if a patient (for example, an elderly or handicapped patient) requests non-child-resistant containers, they may likewise be provided by the pharmacist. Non-child-resistant containers are commonly labeled "Package Not Child Resistant" or "This Package for Households Without Young Children." It is important that pharmacy personnel ascertain, prior to dispensing medications in non-child-resistant containers, that there are no young children who might potentially come in contact with the medication containers. A signed release form confirming the patient's request should be placed into the patient record. Legally, the patient must sign the back of the original prescription requesting a non-child-resistant container. Pharmacy technicians should also check the box on the patient profile indicating the patient's preference for non-child-resistant containers.

"Reminder" packaging (commonly referred to as "Bingo cards" or "Medisets") are not compliant with this act, so a request must be obtained from the patient in order to approve these non-child-resistant types of containers. Medications that do not need to be placed in a child-resistant container include the following, though these often have specific dosage requirements that apply:

- Betamethasone, prednisone, mebendazole, and methylprednisolone tablets
- Chewable isosorbide dinitrate
- Erythromycin ethylsuccinate granules, suspension, and tablets
- Potassium supplements
- Powdered anhydrous cholestyramine and colestipol
- Sodium fluoride and pancrelipase preparations
- Sublingual nitroglycerin and isosorbide dinitrate

Focus On...

An Additional Poison Prevention Method

Another method of avoiding potential poisonings is the use of tamper-resistant prescription pads. These are designed so that anyone using them fraudulently will be caught due to hidden components that the pads

Stock medication bottles should include the following information: name of the medication; reasons for use; directions for use, including route of administration, dosage instructions, possible side effects and adverse reactions; warnings or conditions under which it is inadvisable to administer the medication; and expiration date.

What Led to the Legislation?

Many young children ingested poisonous or toxic substances before this law was enacted. Aspirin was the first substance that had to be packaged with childproof lids because of this act. Included under this act's provisions are corrosive, irritative, and toxic substances.

Key Points of the Legislation

The Poison Prevention Packaging Act requires that the types of substances referenced above be packaged in a way that makes it difficult for children younger than five years old to open them. It provides that the same packaging should be easy for most adults to open. Regarding medications, nearly all prescription medications, with a few exceptions (such as nitroglycerin), must be packaged in this manner, and some OTC medications must be similarly packaged. Adult patients who may have trouble opening their medications (because of conditions such as arthritis) may decline to receive child-resistant packaging, though they must sign a release form to document their request.

OCCUPATIONAL SAFETY AND HEALTH ACT (OSHA) OF 1970

In 1970, Congress passed the Occupational Safety and Health Act to prevent workplace disease and injuries. This statute applies to virtually every U.S. employer. The general purpose of the act is to require all employers to ensure employee safety and health.

The Occupational Safety and Health Act includes regulations for physical workplaces, machinery and equipment, first aid, and job-related materials. It was intended to require employers to provide safe and healthy working conditions. It ensures that workplaces must be free of recognized hazards. These may include dangerous machinery, excessive noise, extreme temperatures, toxic chemicals, or unsanitary conditions. The Occupational Safety and Health Administration (also called OSHA) was established by this act. This administration is discussed in detail in Chapter 7.

What Led to the Legislation?

For many years, workers were at the mercy of their employers in regard to the safety and healthfulness of their work environments. After the advent of mechanized production equipment, injuries at the workplace became more common. After World War II, workplace-related deaths peaked at approximately 14,000 per year. Until the enactment of this law, and the founding of OSHA, there was little government regulation concerning the safety and health of employees.

Key Points of the Legislation

OSHA was established to protect the health and safety of workers in the private sector as well as in government jobs. Its key points are the protection of workers from chemicals, lack of sanitation, machinery, noise, and extreme temperatures. The act also created the Occupational Health and Safety Review Commission to ensure proper enforcement of its standards.

DRUG LISTING ACT OF 1972

Under the Drug Listing Act, each new drug is assigned a unique and permanent drug code. This code is known as a **National Drug Code (NDC)** and identifies the manufacturer or distributor, the drug formulation, and the size and type of packaging. The FDA uses this code to maintain a database of drugs by use, manufacturer, and active ingredients, and of newly marketed, discontinued, and remarketed drugs. Each drug is assigned an 11-digit NDC number. The first five digits identify the manufacturer. The next four digits represent the drug product, and the last two digits determine the package size or type of packaging. An example of an NDC number is 00135-0315-52. The first segment is the labeler code, assigned by the FDA; the second segment is the product code; and the third segment identifies the package size. Pharmacy technicians should understand that accurate tracking of NDC numbers is the key to avoiding audit problems regarding Medicaid and Medicare. If an insurance claim is filed using the wrong NDC, **fraud** charges against the person who filed the claim may result.

Focus On...

completely or incorrectly. Drug data was often improperly reported to the FDA. Changes to drug products were often made without applying for a new NDC number.

Key Points of the Legislation

This act amended the Food, Drug, and Cosmetic Act of 1938. It requires all drug manufacturers to list all of their commercial products with the FDA. Its jurisdiction reaches from the manufacturer, through every individual or company that handles the drug product, up to the final point of sale. It requires that drug product listings be updated two times per year.

What Would You Do?

David is a pharmacy technician who received a prescription for Valium 50 mg b.i.d. for 30 days, with five refills. After thoroughly reviewing this prescription, if you were David, what would you do?

MEDICAL DEVICE AMENDMENT OF 1976

In 1976, medical devices previously subject to control only under the Food, Drug, and Cosmetic Act's general **adulteration** and misbranding sections were subjected to extensive new requirements. In order to keep up with rapidly expanding scientific and medical technology, devices were classified and subjected to different levels of control, depending upon how their function was evaluated. The safety and effectiveness of life-sustaining and life-supporting devices was required, for the first time, to have the pre-market approval of the FDA.

Focus On...

Medical Devices

Pharmacy technicians must be familiar with many medical devices in the pharmacy. Commonly used devices in the pharmacy include scales, pill-counting devices, wheelchairs, and crutches.

What Led to the Legislation?

Failures and problems surrounding pacemakers and intrauterine devices (IUDs) were among the chief factors influencing this act. Prior to this legislation, the FDA had little ability to regulate medical devices for safety, effectiveness, or proper use.

Key Points of the Legislation

The Medical Device Amendment of 1976 classified medical devices according to their risk levels. It set up three different classes of devices. While Class I and II devices do not require pre-market approval, Class III devices have to pass unique regulatory requirements.

RESOURCE CONSERVATION AND RECOVERY ACT OF 1976

The Resource Conservation and Recovery Act of 1976 is also referred to as the Solid Waste Disposal Act. It regulates the handling of solid wastes and authorizes environmental agencies to handle the cleanup of contaminated sites. It also regulates solid waste landfills. It focuses on the protection of human, animal, and environmental health and welfare by reducing and eliminating pollution.

What Led to the Legislation?

This act was required because of large-scale disposal of hazardous wastes in ways that could lead to environmental pollution and poisoning of humans and animals. Before the Resource Conservation and Recovery Act, there was little forethought or planning prior to the dumping of hazardous waste.

Key Points of the Legislation

This act regulates the disposal of hazardous wastes. It gives environmental agencies the power to order approved methods of cleaning up improperly disposed wastes. It encourages elimination of open dumps and landfills and development of comprehensive solid waste management programs.

DRUG REGULATION REFORM ACT OF 1978 AND PROVISIONS

This act was intended to revise the Food, Drug, and Cosmetic Act on many different levels. It did not pass in 1978. In 1979, the act was approved by the Senate. Ultimately however, the House did not pass it. The Drug Regulation Reform Act of 1978 ....

7. To increase the FDA's public accountability

8. To make additional drugs available

9. To encourage research and training

What Led to the Legislation?

Lack of drug regulation and the need for fairer consumer protection prompted this revision of the Food, Drug, and Cosmetic Act. High drug prices, resulting from a lack of competition in the industry, were also instrumental motivators of its development.

Key Points of the Legislation

The Drug Regulation Reform Act and its provisions were designed to encourage fairer FDA regulation of the pharmaceutical industry. It was focused on shortening the time required to develop new drugs, get approval, and bring them to market. It was also intended to reduce the costs involved in the development of new drugs so that manufacturers would be able to develop more drug products at lower cost.

DRUG RECALLS

Manufacturers may determine that a drug they manufacture has been shown to be harmful to the public. When this occurs, they may issue a drug recall and inform the FDA. Also, the FDA may recommend that a drug be recalled by its manufacturer. However, though the FDA can withdraw approval of a drug, products marketed prior to the withdrawal of approval may remain on the market. The FDA may obtain a warrant to seize defective products, but this is not a drug recall. The FDA can recall defective animal foods, medical devices, and infant formulas. Because the FDA can take legal action against a manufacturer of a harmful drug product, it is best for the manufacturer to voluntarily announce the recall and inform the FDA. Serious injury and even death have resulted from several drugs on the market, and over a dozen drugs have been recalled or withdrawn in recent years. Some of these are the following:

- Avandia—It was withdrawn until a black box warning could be added, because it has been shown to cause or worsen heart failure in some patients.

- Ortho Evra birth control patch—The manufacturer was required to withdraw this product and update its warning label after patients experienced blood clots, deep vein thrombosis, heart attack, pulmonary embolisms, and stroke.

- Vioxx—It was recalled due to the filing of thousands of lawsuits by patients and their families alleging fatal arrhythmias and heart diseases.

- Ceclor suspension—It was recalled because of drying agent (desiccant) packets that were found in some bottles; the manufacturer feared potential adulteration of the product.

Focus On...

Drug Recalls

The manufacturer may issue a drug recall on its own, or it may do so in response to a request by the FDA.

There are three classes of drug recalls:
- Class 1—The most severe type of FDA recall; these occur when there is a serious potential for injury or death.
- Class 2—These occur when there is a less serious potential for injury or death, but there still is a possibility of serious adverse effects whose consequences may be irreversible.
- Class 3—These occur where there is a potential for adverse effects, even though they are not very likely.

Market withdrawal is another option. A manufacturer may remove from the market or correct a distributed product in the following circumstances:
- There is a minor violation that is not subject to legal action by the FDA.
- There is no actual violation, but the manufacturer nevertheless decides to correct something about the product.

When a drug recall is issued, the pharmacy technician must assist the pharmacist in removing all of the drug product from the shelves, packaging the recalled drug product for return to the manufacturer, and contacting everyone who has received the drug product in question from the pharmacy so that they can be alerted about the recall. In these circumstances, technicians must follow all of the guidelines of the pharmacy concerning drug recalls, which should be listed in the pharmacy's policies and procedures manual.

lected only a small number of people were not being a... , manufacturers did not want to invest the money and time needed to secure approval. A drug that falls into this category is called an **orphan drug**. These drugs are used to treat diseases affecting fewer than 200,000 people in the United States. This act offers tax breaks and a seven-year monopoly on drug sales in order to induce companies to undertake the development and manufacturing of such drugs. Since the Act went into effect in 1983, more than 100 orphan drugs have been approved. Orphan drugs include those used for the treatment of acquired immunodeficiency syndrome (AIDS), cystic fibrosis, blepharospasm (uncontrolled rapid blinking), and snakebite.

Focus On...

Orphan Drugs

The law provides exclusive licensing and tax incentives for manufacturers to develop and market orphan drugs.

What Led to the Legislation?

This act was established because of the many different diseases and conditions that exist in the United States but affect 200,000 or fewer individuals. These diseases and conditions include ALS (Lou Gehrig's disease), Huntington's disease, muscular dystrophy, myoclonus (abnormal muscle contraction), and Tourette's syndrome. Prior to this act, there were few medications that could treat these and other rare conditions.

Key Points of the Legislation

This act offers tax breaks and a seven-year monopoly to manufacturers of orphan drugs, and therefore helps to make the manufacture of these drugs profitable for their makers. It covers about 5,000 different rare conditions.

DRUG PRICE COMPETITION AND PATENT TERM RESTORATION ACT OF 1984

The Drug Price Competition and Patent Term Restoration Act of 1984 gave marketers of a generic drug the ability to file an abbreviated new drug application (ANDA) to seek FDA approval of the generic drug. This act was created to give more incentives to drug manufacturers in order to offset the time and money required to bring new, innovative drug products to market. In most cases, it allows previous patents to be extended by five years. Overall, this act has greatly helped in the generic drug approval process.

Currently, drug companies get patent protection starting 20 years from the date that a new drug begins being developed. The 20-year period is designed to allow the manufacturer enough time to bring the drug to market, which can take several years, leaving enough time for profitability and recovery of costs. Drug patents help ensure that competing companies cannot infringe on this process. They protect the drug inventor's business interests and help to offset the extremely high costs involved in bringing a new drug to market. When a drug patent is about to expire, other companies may apply (through the FDA) to sell the drug. These generic drugs must meet the same specifications as the original drug. They may be of less cost to consumers, since the cost to bring them to market was absorbed by the original patent holder.

In the pharmacy, the "Orange Book" is used for the approval of drug products with therapeutic equivalence. This book evaluates these drug products to ensure safe substitutions. Now also in electronic format, the Orange Book allows searching by active ingredients, proprietary name, applicant holder, or applicant name. There are different versions of this book, and updates are available as frequently as every month.

What Led to the Legislation?

Drug manufacturers did not, prior to this act, have good patent protection for new drugs that they brought to market. They also did not have enough market exclusivity to ensure that their new drug products remained unique to them. Without a sufficiently long period of drug product exclusivity, manufacturers could not recoup their drug development costs.

Key Points of the Legislation

This act amended the Food, Drug, and Cosmetic Act. It created a formal generic drug approval process and established the abbreviated new drug application approval process. Under this act, generic versions of innovator drugs that have already been approved could get FDA approval without the manufacturer having to submit a full NDA.

Focus On...

How a Drug Comes to Market

There are three clinical phases that must be completed before a drug is made available in the United States. Phase 1 studies are designed to determine the drug's safety, adverse effects, and metabolism. Phase 2 studies target the

PRESCRIPTION DRUG MARKETING ACT OF 1987

The Prescription Drug Marketing Act of 1987 was enacted to ensure that prescription drug products are safe and effective, and to prevent tainting, counterfeiting, and misbranding of drugs. Its main purpose is to protect the ability of drug manufacturers to offer different pricing to different segments of the market. It also allows for effective control over drug sources. This act regulates the methods of selling specific drugs and controls those companies and individuals who participate.

What Led to the Legislation?

The development of a "diversion market" (a wholesale sub-market) of prescription drugs was the main factor in this act's passage. This sub-market consisted of many unauthorized distributors marketing prescription drugs to buyers who intended to use them recreationally, and operated with little government intervention. Another influencing factor was that certain facilities that dealt with blood products were distributing blood-derived products with no regulation.

Key Points of the Legislation

This act established specific prescription drug distribution standards. It encouraged the distribution of authentic, properly labeled, and effective prescription drugs. It required that wholesalers of prescription drugs be state licensed. It also regulated blood centers that provided certain healthcare services and controlled their ability to distribute blood-derived products.

OMNIBUS BUDGET RECONCILIATION ACT OF 1990

The Omnibus Budget Reconciliation Act of 1990, also known as OBRA-90, contained important amendments affecting Medicare and Medicaid. Its main purpose was to reduce Medicaid costs by reducing inappropriate use of drugs by Medicaid recipients. Though there is currently no cap on Medicare taxes, this act imposed a cap on taxable income. As of 2008, this cap was $102,000. The act is administered by the Centers for Medicare and Medicaid Services. It requires Medicaid pharmacy providers to obtain, record, and maintain basic patient information, including disease history. Pharmacy technicians assist in the maintenance and updating of patient profiles.

OBRA-90 expanded rules about drug products to ensure the utmost safe and effective drug therapy, effectively prohibiting the prescription of legend drugs for unapproved uses. It helps patients to save money while obtaining the quality medications they need through rebates, scientific studies, and drug use review. OBRA-90 expanded on the legislation known as OBRA-87, which included the Nursing Home Reform Act of 1987. This act required monthly review of Medicare and Medicaid patients in nursing homes, and periodic reviews of psychotropic drug use in nursing homes. It was designed to provide the highest quality care for residents of nursing homes.

OBRA-90 also requires that each state require its pharmacists to offer to counsel each of their patients (including Medicaid patients) and review the drugs the patients have been taking. Pharmacy technicians should ascertain that the pharmacist has counseled each and every patient. Medicaid demands that these procedures, as well as pharmacist maintenance of Medicaid patient profiles and the performance of prospective drug use reviews, are completed for every covered patient, and makes these procedures a condition of continued funding. Significantly, OBRA-90 requires that manufacturers provide the lowest prices to Medicaid patients by rebating each state Medicaid agency the difference between the average price and the lowest available price. (This requirement does not directly help patients to save money.) Each state is required to establish a board that reviews drug use in order to detect fraud or inappropriate care by physicians or pharmacists.

Focus On...

Drug Use Review

In order to make sure that drug therapy for patients is as safe and effective as it can be, OBRA-90 requires drug use evaluation (DUE). This process consists of analyzing a patient's medications to ensure that there is no duplication, as well as checking any and all contraindications, interactions, patient allergies, correct dosages, and proper term of usage.

What Led to the Legislation?

Prior to this act, many Medicaid patients received less than quality care, and experienced high medical costs. Lack of prospective drug use review, poor patient counseling, and bad maintenance of patient records also prompted the enactment of this law.

Key Points of the Legislation

The FDA Safe Medical Devices Act of 1990 gave the FDA increased ability to regulate medical devices and products used for medical diagnosis. Also known as the SMDA, it requires medical device reports to be filed on a timely basis. It established an approval procedure that manufacturers of new medical devices must follow prior to putting such devices on the market. The SMDA also increased civil penalties for anyone violating the Food, Drug, and Cosmetic Act's policy on medical devices.

What Led to the Legislation?

Prior to this act, medical devices were subject to little regulation. When these devices caused patient harm or death, the injured parties had inadequate federal support for their cases.

Key Points of the Legislation

This act requires facilities that use medical devices to report the devices if illness, injury, or death occurs because of their use. It controls the method of reporting such devices and protects those that report them. It also requires better manufacturer quality control and tracking of the devices that manufacturers bring to market.

ANABOLIC STEROIDS CONTROL ACT OF 1990

This act extended the Controlled Substances Act to anabolic steroids. These hormonal substances promote muscle growth, and are often used illegally by athletes. Also known as "performance-enhancing drugs," anabolic steroids have been shown to cause serious health consequences when overused. The Anabolic Steroids Control Act is considered significant because it sparked a new era in the control of drug abuse. This act offered harsher penalties for the abuse and misuse of anabolic steroids by athletes than had previously been imposed.

You Be the Judge

A pharmacy technician who is also an avid basketball player has begun using anabolic steroids, which he obtains illegally from the pharmacy in which he works. Slowly, his behavior begins to change as a result of these drugs, and he eventually is fired from his job. What are the most common adverse effects of using anabolic steroids? Is the pharmacist liable for not noticing that these drugs were missing? What would be the consequences of stealing anabolic steroids?

What Led to the Legislation?

Prior to this act, anabolic steroids were obtained and used with more ease, and with less regulation, than they are now. The abuse of anabolic steroids by athletes and others who were interested in increasing muscle growth led to serious consequences and even death.

Key Points of the Legislation

This act put anabolic steroids into Schedule III of the CSA. It raised penalties for illegal distribution of these agents, as well as human growth hormone. It resulted in the prosecution of many foreign companies who were distributing these types of products into the U.S. market.

AMERICANS WITH DISABILITIES ACT OF 1990

This act prohibits discrimination against disabled persons in areas such as employment, public services and transportation, public accommodations and commercial facilities, and telecommunications. The Americans with Disabilities Act, also known as the ADA, regulates issues concerning devices and accommodations that disabled persons need in order to live as normally as possible, and establishes rights surrounding these devices and accommodations. Additionally, under the ADA, disabled persons cannot be subjected to medical examinations prior to employment that would not be given to all prospective employees.

Focus On...

ADA

This law prevents discrimination against potential employees who possess a disability.

What Led to the Legislation?

Companies that denied fair treatment to those with disabilities became the focus of many groups who were advocates for the disabled; this led to Congress's adoption of this act.

DIETARY SUPPLEMENT HEALTH AND EDUCATION ACT OF 1994

The Dietary Supplement Health and Education Act of 1994 (DSHEA) was intended to amend the Food, Drug, and Cosmetic Act. Its purpose was to change the way in which dietary supplements are labeled and regulated. It is important to remember that dietary supplements have always been, and still are, treated as foods, not drugs. The DSHEA holds dietary supplement manufacturers responsible for the safety of the supplements they manufacture. It controls many types of dietary supplements, including amino acids, herbs and botanicals, some hormones, minerals, vitamins, and other dietary supplements.

This act affects pharmacy technicians with respect to the displaying, stocking, and recommendation of supplements. In the pharmacy, technicians are not allowed to recommend dietary supplements, just as they are not allowed to recommend OTC or legend drugs. Additionally, under this act, pharmacy technicians are not allowed to attach extraneous labeling or stickers to packages of dietary supplements.

What Led to the Legislation?

Before the DSHEA, various substances and formulations were sold as supplements with little or no regulation. This led to dangerous interactions with prescription and OTC drugs, and caused patient harm. It was clear that some sort of regulation of dietary supplements was necessary.

Key Points of the Legislation

This act clearly defined the term "dietary supplement." It imposed sanctions against any manufacturer of a dietary supplement that claimed that the supplement actually treated or cured a specific condition.

HEALTH INSURANCE PORTABILITY AND ACCOUNTABILITY ACT (HIPAA) OF 1996

HIPAA was designed to improve continuity and portability of health insurance, to reduce fraudulent activities, to establish medical savings accounts, to improve long-term healthcare access, and to simplify health-care administration. It also sought to improve the effectiveness of Medicare and Medicaid by improving the system used to store and share private health information. HIPAA provides for healthcare coverage for workers who lose or change their jobs. It created a system of national provider identifiers (NPIs) for healthcare providers, employers, and health insurance plans. An NPI is a unique identification number for covered healthcare providers. An NPI consists of 10 digits with no letters or other characters. These numbers are easy to obtain and are free. They are especially essential for providers who bill Medicare for services.

HIPAA regulations are divided into three parts: privacy regulations, security regulations, and transaction standards. The privacy regulations give patients specific rights, which pertain to access to their records, tracking of disclosures, hospital privacy, amendments to their records, communication of health information, and use and disclosure of information. The security regulations are designed to ensure the confidentiality of protected health information. The transaction standards require common code sets, common electronic claims standards, and unique health identifiers. This act is discussed in greater detail in Chapter 6.

What Would You Do?

Mary Jo, an inexperienced pharmacy technician, started working in a retail pharmacy last week. Many customers were in close proximity to the counter. While dispensing a prescription for a certain patient, she called out to her by name, asking, "Mrs. Corby, can you please give me your Medicaid card so that I can make a copy?" What would you do in this situation, and what law was violated by Mary Jo?

What Led to the Legislation?

Prior to HIPAA, many employees who changed or lost jobs could not maintain their health insurance coverage. There was a lack of cohesiveness in how standards concerning healthcare and insurance were administered. The healthcare system needed some sort of consistency and better overall organization.

Key Points of the Legislation

HIPAA protects a patient's health insurance coverage after the loss or change of a job. It established national standards for healthcare transactions, and national identifiers for individuals and companies within the ~~system. It encouraged~~ electronic data interchange of private health infor-

medical products, ~~...~~

pounding, food safety, and regulation of medical devices. It increased patient access to experimental drugs and medical devices. This act also included incentives giving manufacturers six-month extensions on new pediatric drugs that had drug trial testing data on file. Importantly, it also mandated risk assessment reviews of all foods and drugs in the United States that contain mercury. The FDA Modernization Act of 1997, also known as the FDAMA, changed the promotion of off-label uses for drugs significantly. This law required that manufacturers of legend drugs must label their packaging with the "R$_x$" symbol.

Medicare Part D was established to subsidize prescription drug costs for Medicare beneficiaries. This drug benefit may be obtained by joining either a prescription drug plan (PDP) or a Medicare Advantage (MA) plan. Enrollment is voluntary and occurs annually. Plans can be tailored to cover different drugs, or classes of drugs, and various co-payment amounts. Medicare Part D does not cover drugs that are not approved by the FDA, those not intended for their approved indications, those not available for prescribing within the United States, and those already covered by Medicare Parts A or B. Also excluded are drugs and drug classes excluded from Medicaid coverage.

What Led to the Legislation?

Prior to this act, the drug approval process was slow and rather cumbersome. This act was intended to speed up the process so that the public could enjoy the benefits of new medications and therapies on a timely basis.

Key Points of the Legislation

This act was passed to improve FDA regulation of drugs, biological products, food, and medical devices, with the main aim of speeding up the approval process. It was poised to address the changing technologies and marketing of these products to the growing, diversifying public.

MEDICARE PRESCRIPTION DRUG, IMPROVEMENT, AND MODERNIZATION ACT OF 2003

Also known as the Medicare Modernization Act (MMA), this legislation overhauled the Medicare program more than any other act has done. It introduced tax breaks and subsidies for prescription drugs. This act authorized new Medicare Advantage plans, which offered patients better choices about their terms of care, providers, other types of coverage, and federal reimbursements. Significantly, the MMA established a trial, partially privatized Medicare system, offered pre-tax medical savings accounts, and imposed certain fees for wealthier senior citizens.

What Led to the Legislation?

Newer and more expensive drugs have regularly come to market since 1965, when Medicare was created. Many patients, especially senior citizens, found it hard to afford these new drugs. This act was passed to help them.

Key Points of the Legislation

This act provided an entitlement benefit for prescription drugs. It used subsidies and tax breaks to help patients afford the medications they needed. It also offered employers the opportunity to offer drug benefits to their employees through drug subsidies.

ISOTRETINOIN (ACCUTANE®) SAFETY AND RISK MANAGEMENT ACT (PROPOSAL ONLY) OF 2005

This act, which was proposed but not passed, attempted to establish certain restrictions concerning drugs that contained isotretinoin (Accutane®). It was designed to restrict the distribution of Accutane and monitor the drug's side effects. The act was proposed because this drug, used to treat acne, can cause severe birth defects in the fetuses of patients who take Accutane during pregnancy. This drug has also caused spontaneous abortions to occur. Because Congress failed to pass this act, the FDA has initiated a program known as SMART (System to Manage Accutane-Related Teratogenicity). However, the SMART program has not significantly reduced cases of Accutane-related birth defects and fetal deaths.

What Led to the Legislation?

Accutane, a powerful anti-acne drug, was shown to cause birth defects in the babies of mothers who used the drug. It also caused the spontaneous abortion of many fetuses. Other studies showed links to depression,

reporting of all adverse effects.

THE COMBAT METHAMPHETAMINE EPIDEMIC ACT OF 2005

This act focused on the methamphetamine provisions of the Patriot Act extension, which was titled "The USA Patriot Act Improvements and Reauthorization Act." It was intended to stop the illegal use of the drug known as methamphetamine. Drug trafficking, one source of financial support for terrorism, is now regulated by this act, which imposes stiff penalties on anyone found in violation. When methamphetamine is involved in terrorist activities in any way, the government can now confiscate the personal property of people involved. Other drugs, such as crack cocaine, are also named in this act.

Drug products that fall under this legislation must be kept behind a counter or in a locked case. The law limits sales of pure ephedrine or pseudoephedrine (which are precursors of methamphetamine) to nine grams per month per person. Customers purchasing these products must provide identification and sign a sales log. Pharmacy technicians must assist the pharmacist in making sure that the sales log is maintained correctly, and that the products are placed out of reach of customers as required. Everyone involved in the selling of these products is required to register with the U.S. Attorney General's office and be trained about the provisions of the law.

What Led to the Legislation?

The use of methamphetamine and similar drugs has been on the increase, and their use has often crossed over the lines of other criminal activities, including terrorism. This act was intended to curb the manufacture and distribution of these drugs, as well as severely punish those individuals involved with these activities and other crimes.

Key Points of the Legislation

This act introduced safeguards to make ingredients used in the creation of methamphetamine and similar drugs harder to access. It also gave the government heightened powers to combat drug smuggling, manufacture, and distribution. The terrorism connection enables the government to pursue terrorists more effectively by using drug-related legislation to improve its law enforcement efforts.

REGULATORY AGENCIES

The following regulatory agencies each have specific activities that relate to public use and governmental control of specific substances. They are listed alphabetically by their abbreviations where applicable.

Bureau of Alcohol, Tobacco, and Firearms (ATF)

The ATF is dedicated to preventing terrorism, reducing violent crime, and protecting the United States. It regulates alcohol, tobacco, firearms, and even explosives. The ATF also investigates acts of arson.

State Boards of Pharmacy (BOP)

The board of pharmacy in each state is designed to regulate and control the practice of pharmacy. These boards adopt laws that affect pharmacy practice. The focus of each board's activities is protecting the health of the public.

Centers for Medicare and Medicaid Service (CMS)

The CMS works to promote healthcare coverage that is both effective and up-to-date. It also promotes quality healthcare for beneficiaries. The CMS intends to modernize the U.S. healthcare system.

Drug Enforcement Agency (DEA)

The DEA strives to enforce controlled-substances legislation, and to bring offenders to justice, while also promoting the reduction of illicit substances. The DEA cooperates with local, regional, national, and international agencies in order to accomplish its mission. The DEA investigates and prosecutes major violators of controlled substance laws, with serious focus on those individuals or groups (including gangs) who use violence as part of their illegal activities. It also manages a national drug intelligence program that reaches into many other countries via liaisons with major crime-fighting agencies. The assets of violators are regularly seized by the DEA as part of its enforcement actions against illegal drug activities.

Department of Transportation (DOT)

The EPA strives to protect ... human beings. It develops and enforces environmental legislation, and offers grants to state environmental programs. It publishes information designed to educate the public and establishes voluntary environmental partnerships and programs.

Food and Drug Administration (FDA)

The FDA was created from the Food, Drug, and Insecticide Administration in 1930. The FDA's intent is to promote public health. It controls the safety and effectiveness of foods, drugs, biological products, medical devices, cosmetics, and radioactive substances. It also provides information about better, safer, and more cost-effective products. The FDA should be notified when adverse reactions, problems with product quality, or product-use errors occur. The system that they have in place for this reporting is called MedWatch. This system serves both healthcare professionals and the public. Information about MedWatch and directions for making reports to the FDA can be found at http://www.fda .gov; click on "Safety Alerts (MedWatch)" on the "Drugs" menu.

The FDA approves new drugs for sale in the United States. Within the FDA, there is a center for drug evaluation and research, which is the largest division of the organization. The other centers are responsible for medical and radiological devices, foods, cosmetics, biologics, and veterinary drugs. The FDA drug and evaluation research center ensures that drugs are safe and effective.

Five types of drug applications exist, as follows:

- *Investigational new drug application*—This requires a drug to be the subject of an approved marketing application before it is transported or distributed across state lines; the purpose of this application is to obtain an exemption from the FDA to ship the investigational drug to clinical investigators in different states.

- *New drug application*—This is used to help the FDA determine if a drug is safe and effective in its proposed uses, whether the benefits of the drug outweigh the risks, whether its proposed labeling is appropriate, what its proposed labeling should contain, and whether methods used in its manufacture and the controls used to maintain quality are adequate to preserve the drug's identity, quality, purity, and strength.

- *Abbreviated new drug application*—This involves the approval of generic drugs, meaning those that are comparable to an innovator drug product in dosage form, strength, and route of administration, quality, performance characteristics, and intended use. These applications generally do not require preclinical (animal) or clinical (human) data to establish safety and effectiveness; instead, applicants must scientifically demonstrate that their product is bioequivalent (performs in the same manner as the innovator drug) by measuring how long the generic drug takes to enter the bloodstream.

- *Over-the-counter drug application*—This application requires three phases of review and approval.
  - The first phase involves a review of ingredients for each class of findings based on a panel's review:
    - Category 1—generally recognized as safe and effective for the claimed therapeutic indication
    - Category 2—not generally recognized as safe and effective, or having unacceptable indications
    - Category 3—insufficient data available to permit final classification
  - The second phase involves FDA review of ingredients in each class of drugs based on a panel's findings, public comment, and newly available data.
  - The third phase is issuance of final regulations establishing conditions under which the OTC product is generally recognized as safe and effective.

- *Biologic license application*—The FDA requires a firm that manufactures a biologic for sale in interstate commerce to hold a license for the product; it contains specific information on the manufacturing processes, chemistry, pharmacology, clinical pharmacology, and medical effects of the biologic product. If the application is approved, a license is issued allowing the manufacturer to market the biologic product.

The Joint Commission

The Joint Commission accredits and certifies healthcare organizations in the United States. Its ultimate goal is to improve the safety and quality of healthcare. The Joint Commission is not a government agency, but an independent, not-for-profit organization that is recognized nationwide. It strives continually to improve the quality of its programs so that accredited organizations may offer increased patient safety.

National Association of the Boards

Institutional Review Boards (IRB)

Institutional review boards are designed to oversee biomedical and behavioral research to protect the public. They can approve or reject new research, or even ask for modifications to the research. They are regulated by the Office for Human Research Protection (OHRP), which is part of the HSS.

SUMMARY

Many laws and amendments were enacted over the past 100 years to shape the current Food, Drug, and Cosmetic Act. In the practice of pharmacy, laws, regulations, and standards govern the control of drugs. Pharmacy technicians should understand the different terminology used in the law, and which punishments may be imposed for certain violations.

The U.S. Congress passed the first important federal law governing pharmacy, the Pure Food and Drug Act, in 1906. Because of the tragedy involving sulfanilamide in 1937, which caused more than 100 patient deaths from the ingesting of Elixir Sulfanilamide, the Food, Drug, and Cosmetic Act was passed in 1938.

The Durham-Humphrey Amendment of 1951 prohibited dispensing of legend drugs without a prescription. The Federal Food, Drug, and Cosmetic Act was amended again by the Kefauver-Harris Amendment of 1962 to require that drug products, both prescription and nonprescription, be effective as well as safe.

Since 1970, Congress has passed several important laws, including the Poison Prevention Packaging Act (to prevent and protect children from accidental poisoning through the use of child-resistant packaging), the Controlled Substances Act, and the Medical Device Amendment of 1976 (for the safety and effectiveness of life-sustaining and life-supporting devices).

The Orphan Drug Act, passed in 1983, offers tax breaks and a seven-year monopoly on drug sales in order to induce companies to undertake the development and manufacturing of drugs used for rare diseases or conditions (such as the treatment of AIDS, cystic fibrosis, blepharospasm, and snakebite).

OBRA-90 was enacted to reduce Medicaid costs. Most significantly, it requires manufacturers to provide the lowest possible prices by rebating each state Medicaid agency the difference between the average price of a drug and the lowest available price. It also requires DUE and the offer to counsel patients in order to make sure that drug therapy is as safe and as effective as it can be.

The FDA's Safe Medical Devices Act (SMDA) requires all medical devices to be tracked and records maintained for durable medical equipment.

The Anabolic Steroids Control Act allows the CSA to regulate anabolic steroids, which are often used illegally by athletes to promote muscle growth.

The ADA was established to prohibit discrimination against disabled persons.

The DSHEA controls many different supplements, including amino acids, herbs and botanicals, some hormones, minerals, and vitamins.

The HIPAA was designed to regulate patient privacy, security, and transaction standards relating to electronic health records.

Separate statutes were enacted that modernized the FDA and added Medicare Part D.

The Combat Methamphetamine Epidemic Act was intended to stop the use of illegal drugs such as methamphetamine, crack cocaine, and other drugs, especially because their sale is often used to finance terrorism.

SETTING THE SCENE

The following discussion and responses relate to the opening "Setting the Scene" scenario:

- The pharmacy technician must not package the prescription in a non-child-resistant container.

- Both the pharmacy technician and the pharmacist ignored the Poison Prevention Packaging Act of 1970. This act requires that child-resistant containers be provided unless an adult patient spe- ~~~ ~on-child-resistant containers.

~~~ ~ut liability rests

Multiple Choice

1. The Food, Drug, and Cosmetic Act was passed in

   A. 1906.
   B. 1914.
   C. 1938.
   D. 1962.

2. The Harrison Narcotics Tax Act was part of

   A. the Internal Revenue Code.
   B. toxicity tests after the sulfanilamide tragedy.
   C. internal regulations to create classifications of prescriptions.
   D. toxicity tests after the thalidomide tragedy.

3. The labeling of a medication in a way that is false or misleading is referred to as

   A. adulteration.
   B. distribution.
   C. fraud.
   D. misbranding.

4. The first U.S. act prohibiting the interstate distribution or sale of adulterated or misbranded food and drugs was passed in

   A. 1906.
   B. 1912.
   C. 1914.
   D. 1938.

5. The FDA is a branch of a government department that controls all drugs for legal use. Which one?

   A. U.S. Department of Health
   B. U.S. Department of Health and Human Services
   C. U.S. Department of Agriculture
   D. U.S. Department of Labor

6.   Which of the following acts was designed to protect the public health by requiring that only safe and properly labeled drugs may be introduced into interstate commerce?

A.   Durham-Humphrey Amendment
B.   Kefauver-Harris Amendment
C.   Harrison Narcotics Tax Act
D.   Pure Food and Drug Act

7.   In 1937, the Massengill Company introduced Elixir Sulfanilamide into the market. It contained a solution containing which of the following substances?

A.   glycerin
B.   chloroform
C.   diethylene glycol
D.   methyl alcohol

8.   Which act required that pharmaceutical manufacturers file an NDA with the FDA?

A.   Durham-Humphrey Amendment
B.   Kefauver-Harris Amendment
C.   Poison Prevention Packaging Act
D.   Food, Drug, and Cosmetic Act

9.   Which of the following acts offers federal financial incentives to commercial and nonprofit organizations for the development of drugs?

A.   Medical Device Amendment
B.   Drug Listing Act
C.   Orphan Drug Act
D.   Poison Prevention Packaging Act

10.   Which of the following laws was passed to establish clear criteria for classifications of legend and OTC drugs?

A.   Kefauver-Harris Amendment
B.   Durham-Humphrey Amendment
C.   Harrison Narcotics Tax Act
D.   Pure Food and Drug Act

11.   When patients agree to be part of a study that tests a new drug, they must be thoroughly educated about its possible medical risks. This is referred to as

A.   informed consent.
B.   a black box warning.
C.   post-drug approval.
D.   drug review.

12. Orphan drugs are used for all of the following disorders or conditions, except

    A. cystic fibrosis.
    B. hepatitis A.

14. The five controlled substance schedules were established by which statute?

    A. Harrison Narcotics Tax Act
    B. Comprehensive Drug Abuse Prevention and Control Act
    C. Drug Regulation Reform Act
    D. Drug Listing Act

15. Which of the following laws requires that most legend drugs be packaged in child-resistant containers?

    A. Drug Listing Act
    B. Food, Drug, and Cosmetic Act
    C. Harrison Narcotics Tax Act
    D. Poison Prevention Packaging Act

Fill in the Blank

1. The act that restricted the sale of drugs by requiring a prescription was the _____ .

2. The Kefauver-Harris Amendment required that drug products be _____ and _____ as well as _____ .

3. The act that required employers to provide safe and healthy working environments was known as _____ .

4. The FDA uses a special code to maintain a database of drugs; this code is made up of numbers that represent usage, manufacturer, drug product, and type of packaging. This code is known as the _____ .

5. The act that regulates solid waste landfills to protect humans, animals, and the environment is known as the _____ .

6. The Drug Regulation Reform Act and its provisions were designed to encourage _____ FDA regulation of the _____ industry.

7. The drug that was recalled due to thousands of lawsuits related to fatal arrhythmias and heart diseases was called _____.

8. Orphan drugs are used to treat diseases affecting fewer than _____ people in the United States.

9. OBRA-90 requires that manufacturers provide reduced Medicaid costs by rebating the difference between a drug's _____ price and the _____ available price.

10. The organization that accredits healthcare organizations is known as _____.

CASE STUDY

A pharmacy technician asks the pharmacist if it is suitable to substitute Fiorinal No. 3 for Sedapap, which was prescribed, because of the nearly identical chemical properties of the two drugs. He explains to the pharmacist that the pharmacy is out of Sedapap, and that the prescribing physician did indicate that a suitable substitution medication was allowed. After taking the Fiorinal No. 3, which contains codeine (to which the patient is allergic), she is hospitalized after going into anaphylactic shock. It is later found that Fiorinal No. 3 (a Schedule III drug because of its codeine content) is vastly different than the drug simply referred to as Fiorinal, a non-narcotic agonist analgesic.

1. Is this error the fault of the pharmacy technician only?

2. Is it the fault of the physician?

3. What are the potential outcomes of this error?

RELATED INTERNET SITES

At the websites listed, search for the various laws outlined in the chapter.

http://aspe.hhs.gov

http://depts.washington.edu; Search for "hiprc", then click on "HIPRC: Best Practices" and then "HIPRC PUBLICATIONS", "Search (By Topic)", "Alcohol and Drugs."

http://library.findlaw.com

http://www.ada.gov

annals.org

http://www.fda.gov; search

http://www.hhs.gov

http://www.jointcommission.org

http://www.justice.gov

http://www.osha.gov

http://www.usdoj.gov; Search for "drug abuse."

http://www.uspharmd.com

REFERENCES

Abood, R. (2011). *Pharmacy Practice and the Law* (6th ed.). Burlington, MA: Jones and Bartlett.

Allport-Settle, M. J. (2010). *Federal Food, Drug, and Cosmetic Act: The United States Federal FD&C Act Concise Reference.* Raleigh, NC: PharmaLogika.

Friedhoff, L. T. (2009). *New Drugs: An Insider's Guide to the FDA's New Drug Approval Process for Scientists, Investors, and Patients.* Columbia, SC: PSPG Publishing.

Hawthorne, F. (2005). *Inside the FDA: The Business and Politics Behind the Drugs We Take and the Food We Eat.* Hoboken, NJ: John Wiley & Sons Inc.

Pisano, D. J., & Mantus, D. (eds.) (2003). *FDA Regulatory Affairs: A Guide for Prescription Drugs, Medical Devices, and Biologics.* London: Informa Healthcare.

Reiss, B. S., & Hall, G. D. (2010). *Guide to Federal Pharmacy Law* (7th ed.). Boynton Beach, FL: Apothecary Press.

Voet, M. A. (2008). *The Generic Challenge: Understanding Patents, FDA & Pharmaceutical Life-Cycle Management* (2nd ed.). Boca Raton, FL: Brown Walker.

Comprehensive Drug Abuse and Prevention Control Act: A Closer Look

OBJECTIVES

Upon completion of this chapter, the reader should be able to:

1. Distinguish between Schedule I and Schedule II drugs.
2. Identify the significance of each controlled substance schedule.
3. Distinguish among prescription drugs, non-prescription drugs, and controlled substances.
4. Explain the Controlled Substances Act and scheduled drugs.
5. Describe labeling of controlled substances.
6. Explain the importance of recording refills for controlled substances.
7. Describe the importance of record keeping for controlled substances.
8. Explain DEA Forms 41, 106, and 222.
9. Describe the process of returning controlled substances.
10. Identify state and federal law regarding controlled substances.

KEY TERMS

Anabolic steroids—Schedule III controlled substances (either drugs or hormonal substances) that are often misused by athletes seeking to enhance their bulk (by increasing muscle mass) and physical prowess.

"C" symbol—A marking that indicates a controlled substance, and is printed on a drug's label, its box, and/or its packaging insert.

Data processing system—An alternative, computerized method for the storage and retrieval of prescription refill information for controlled substances on Schedules III and IV.

Drug Enforcement Administration (DEA)—The bureau within the United States Department of Justice that is primarily responsible for enforcing federal laws that concern controlled substances. In addition to investigating the sellers, producers, and smugglers of illicit drugs, the DEA also monitors physician prescribing patterns and pharmacy purchases.

Facsimile—A copy of an official document (such as a prescription or medication order) that is transmitted via fax machine.

Schedules—The five classifications of controlled substances; the drugs with the highest potential for abuse and no medical use are listed in Schedule I, and those with progressively less abuse potential are listed in Schedules II, III, IV, and V.

rizing him to sign for Schedule II drugs. He signs and faxes it to his supplier. The supplier calls the pharmacist and asks for an explanation as to why an unauthorized signature appears on the form. The pharmacist questions Anthony about these events.

Critical Thinking

- What did Anthony do wrong?

- Is his job in jeopardy because of this situation?

- Briefly explain the DEA's procedures related to ordering Schedule II drugs.

OVERVIEW

The **Drug Enforcement Administration (DEA)** was established in 1973 as part of the Department of Justice to enforce federal laws regarding the use of illegal drugs. According to the federal Controlled Substances Act (CSA), drugs or other substances that have the potential for illegal use (and abuse) must be included in the controlled substances list. Any new drugs with similar action to drugs already on the controlled substances list are considered to have the same potential for abuse.

Pharmacy technicians must be familiar with the Comprehensive Drug Abuse and Prevention Control Act. They should understand its guidelines concerning controlled substances, their storage, security, and keeping of controlled substance records. Federal and state laws require all personnel, including pharmacy technicians, to help in the management of controlled substances located in the workplace. They must take precautions to monitor patient drug use, maintain correct records (as required by law), and report any known or suspected theft or diversion of drugs.

CLASSIFICATION OF SCHEDULED DRUGS

The drugs that come under the jurisdiction of the Controlled Substances Act (CSA) have been categorized according to their potential for abuse and their addictive abilities. They are divided into five **schedules**, which range from Schedule I (illegal drugs and those that cannot be prescribed) to Schedule V (drugs that have the least potential for addiction and abuse). Scheduling requests may be initiated by the Department of Health and Human Services (DHHS), by the DEA, or by petition of a manufacturer, medical society, pharmaceutical association, public interest group, or individual citizen.

The states with the harshest penalties for controlled substance convictions are New York and Michigan. Because of drug laws initiated by Nelson Rockefeller, drug convictions involving Schedule I or II controlled substances brought punishments nearly as severe as those for murder. These punishments included life imprisonment in certain circumstances. It is important to note that when a state law conflicts with the federal government's position concerning a specific drug, the stricter law takes precedence. Discrepancies should be handled by contacting the closest DEA office to determine your state's regulations, as well as the federal government's regulations concerning any controlled substance in question.

Schedule I

Schedule I agents are not accepted for medical use in the United States. They possess an extremely high potential for abuse. Properly registered people may use Schedule I substances for research purposes. Examples of Schedule I drugs are opiates and opium derivatives (such as heroin); crystal methamphetamine; hallucinogens such as lysergic acid diethylamide (LSD), marijuana, and mescaline; peyote; stimulants such as methcathinone, hashish, and crack cocaine; depressants such as methaqualone and gamma-hydroxy butyrate (GHB); and dihydromorphine.

In recent years, *medical marijuana* has been prescribed to relieve the pain and suffering caused by a variety of conditions, or to treat specific symptoms, without debilitating side effects. Conditions for which medical marijuana has been prescribed include cancer (for chemotherapy-induced nausea), AIDS, neuropathic pain, spasticity associated with multiple sclerosis, and glaucoma. Individual states have approved the use of medical marijuana, though the federal government maintains its listing as a Schedule I agent. Officially, the U.S. government ranks marijuana as an unapproved new drug that has not been approved for medical use. However, safer dosage forms of cannabinoids have been approved (Marinol® and Cesamet®), which contain active ingredients that are present in botanical marijuana. These drugs are in capsule form, and are indicated for nausea and vomiting associated with cancer chemo-therapy, as well as for the anorexia associated with weight loss in AIDS patients.

adone, morphine, meperidine

lants such as amphetamine and methylphenidate; and depre-

as amobarbital, pentobarbital, secobarbital, and various combinations of depressants.

The quantity of the substance in a drug product often determines the schedule that will control it. For example, amphetamines and codeine usually are classified in Schedule II. However, Schedules III and IV control specific products containing smaller quantities of Schedule II substances, most often in combination with a non-controlled substance.

Schedule III

These agents have accepted medical uses, and have less abuse potential than Schedule I and II drugs. **Anabolic steroids** were and are misused by athletes seeking to enhance their bulk and physical prowess. Competitive and peer pressure to use these drugs is constant. In 1988, Congress responded by amending the Food, Drug, and Cosmetic Act, declaring that distribution or possession of anabolic steroids with intent to distribute for human use, *other than for the treatment of disease upon the order of a physician,* was punishable by not more than three years' imprisonment, a fine, or both. If the person possessed such drugs as anabolic steroids with the intent to distribute them to a minor under 18 years of age, the penalty was increased to six years of imprisonment.

In 1990, anabolic steroids were added to Schedule III as controlled substances. Some feel that anabolic steroids were swept into the controlled substance category simply to take advantage of the broad enforcement arm of the DEA as well as the penalties that attach to the violation of the CSA. Other examples of Schedule III drugs include nalorphine, buprenorphine, buprenorphine with naloxone, acetaminophen with codeine, aspirin with codeine, acetaminophen with hydrocodone, ibuprofen with hydrocodone, butabarbital, and other barbiturates combined with non-controlled drugs such as aspirin.

Focus On...

Anabolic Steroids

Anabolic steroids are substances (other than estrogens, progestin, and corticosteroids) that are chemically and pharmacologically related to testosterone and promote muscle growth.

Focus On...

Hydrocodone / APAP

Hydrocodone with acetaminophen (hydrocodone/APAP) is a highly abused drug. It is a readily available and relatively inexpensive prescription narcotic medication approved to treat pain. As a narcotic, hydrocodone/APAP leads to physical dependence. Having a prior history of drug or alcohol abuse, or even having a family history of abuse, increases the likelihood of hydrocodone/APAP abuse. Those who drink alcohol while taking this combination drug are likely to develop liver failure.

Schedule IV

The abuse potential for Schedule IV drugs is less than those in Schedule III. However, abuse of Schedule IV drugs can still lead to physical or psychological dependency. Schedule IV drugs are generally long-acting barbiturates, certain hypnotics, and minor tranquilizers. For all practical purposes, there are no regulatory differences between Schedules III and IV. Examples of Schedule IV drugs are benzodiazepines (alprazolam, temazepam, clonazepam, diazepam); fenfluramine; phenobarbital; chlordiazepoxide; ethinamate; diethylpropion; and meprobamate.

Schedule V

Schedule V agents have the lowest abuse potential of the controlled substances and consist of preparations containing limited quantities of certain narcotic drugs, generally used for antitussive and antidiarrheal purposes. Examples of Schedule V drugs are antidiarrheals, analgesics, cough syrups that contain codeine, diphenoxylate mixtures, certain strengths of opium mixtures, pseudoephedrine, and phenergan with codeine. While a few Schedule V drugs do not require a prescription, there are still requirements for their sale, and some states do not allow such sales at all. As controlled substances, they may be sold OTC, but the sale must be recorded in a logbook. The entry must include information about the person making the purchase, the quantity, and the strength of the drug. The pharmacy's name and date and the pharmacist's initials must be placed on the bottle containing the medication. Of the Schedule V drugs, phenobarbital, various prescription cough syrups containing codeine, and acetaminophen with codeine elixir all require prescriptions. Table 5-1 shows drug schedules and some examples.

TABLE 5-1 Drug Schedules

Schedule	Abuse Potential	Examples
(...)	High—No accepted medical use	Fenethylline (also spelled "...thylline") • Hallucinogens ... • Hydrocodone
III (5 refills permitted within 6 months)	Moderate—Accepted medical use	Anabolic Steroids • Barbiturates (moderate-acting) • Butabarbital (Butisol®) • Codeine mixtures (most of them) • Glutethimide • Hydrocodone/APAP
IV (5 refills permitted within 6 months)	Low—Accepted medical use	Alprazolam (Xanax®) • Chloral hydrate (Noctec®) • Diazepam (Valium®) • Pentazocine HCl (Talwin®)
V (No prescription required for individuals who are 18 or older for most of these drugs; however, they may only be sold at pharmacies and require pharmacist involvement in their sale)	Low—Accepted medical use	Cough syrups with codeine (Cheracol® with codeine) • Guaifenesin mixtures (such as Naldecon Dx®) • Lomotil® • Parepectolin® • Robitussin AC® • Pseudoephedrine

DEA REGISTRATION FOR CONTROLLED SUBSTANCES

Individuals who manufacture, dispense, or distribute any controlled substance are obligated to register with the DEA, unless they are exempted. Pharmacy registrations are issued for three years. A DEA number must be assigned to those who are registered under the law as manufacturers, distributors, wholesalers, or practitioners, such as physicians, dentists, veterinarians, scientists, pharmacies, and hospitals. Each state regulates which medical professionals may prescribe controlled substances. If an individual is authorized by his or her state to order controlled substances, he or she may apply for a DEA number. Some states allow certified nurse practitioners to prescribe, and a few states allow optometrists to prescribe.

All pharmacies must have a valid DEA registration, which grants them the authority to handle controlled substances as specified in their registration documents. This is determined by both state and federal laws. To register, new pharmacy applicants are required to complete DEA Form 224 and submit it to the following address: DEA, Registration Unit, Central Station, PO Box 28083, Washington, D.C. 20038-8083. DEA registrations must be renewed every three years.

If the DEA registrant is not the same person who controls the pharmacy's day-to-day operations, or who orders controlled substances, a power of attorney may be used, which requires two signatures in order to be valid. Records of transactions made using a power of attorney must be kept on file for two years.

A DEA number can be checked for legitimacy in two ways. The first method is a simple calculation that checks its authenticity. A DEA number is made up of a two-letter prefix, followed by seven digits. The first letter is an "A" if the practitioner began practice before 1988, and a "B" if they began practice later. The second letter comes from the practitioner's last name—if the last name were "Smith," it would be an "S." To verify accuracy of the digits, add up the first, third, and fifth numbers. Then add up the second, fourth, and sixth numbers, after which you multiply this result by two. Add this new total to the total of the first, third, and fifth numbers. Look at this new total—the last digit of this total will be the same as the seventh digit in the DEA number.

Focus On...

Verifying a DEA number

Dr. Smith's DEA number is BS3076216. Using the instructions indicated above, to check the digits you would do the following:

Add the first, third, and fifth digits (3 + 7 + 2 = 12).

Add the second, fourth, and sixth digits (0 + 6 + 1 = 7).

Multiply by 2 (7 × 2 = 14).

Add the first total to the second total (12 + 14 = 26).

The last digit of this total, which is a 6, is the same as the seventh digit in the DEA number BS3076216.

The second method is online verification for the actual DEA registrant. This provides the registrant's name, DEA number, and DEA address of record. Data on registrants is updated monthly by the Department of Justice. Healthcare providers and other entities can subscribe to various systems to verify DEA numbers. An example of one of these online services is located at www.dealookup.com.

Focus On...

DEA Registration

When a DEA registration is terminated, revoked, or suspended for any
_____ DEA forms must be returned to the closest DEA office.

previous applications may now a...

Registration Certificate

Falsification of an application will result in the suspension or revocation of the applicant's registration by the DEA. If the applicant has a previous felony conviction related to controlled substances, a suspended registration, or a suspended state license, the applicant will no longer be allowed to dispense controlled substances.

Except in emergency situations, registrants are assured of a hearing and due process of law prior to suspension or revocation of registration. In addition, anyone who discontinues his or her business or professional practice, ends his or her legal existence, or dies automatically has his or her registration terminated.

Security of Personnel

Background checks should be carried out for all potential employees who will work in the proximity of controlled substances. Interviewees must supply truthful information about past convictions or criminal charges against them. They must also answer questions about any illegal drug use. Lying or providing incomplete answers concerning these topics may lead to future legal situations between the prospective employee and employer, and even between the prospective employee and the state.

You Be the Judge

Glenn, a pharmacy technician who has been working for a year, was required because of new pharmacy rules to take drug-screening tests upon starting his second year at work. The new rules also required a full background check to be made. When Glenn's test results were returned, he had a positive result for cocaine in his system, and the background check revealed that he had a previous conviction for drug possession. In your judgment, what will be the result of Glenn's positive drug test and his background check?

Form-224	APPLICATION FOR REGISTRATION Under the Controlled Substances Act	APPROVED OMB NO 1117-0014 FORM DEA-224 (10-06) Previous editions are obsolete

INSTRUCTIONS — Save time - apply on-line at *www.deadiversion.usdoj.gov*

1. To apply by mail complete this application. Keep a copy for your records.
2. Print clearly, using black or blue ink, or use a typewriter.
3. Mail this form to the address provided in Section 7 or use enclosed envelope.
4. Include the correct payment amount. FEE IS NON-REFUNDABLE.
5. If you have any questions call 800-882-9539 prior to submitting your application.

IMPORTANT: DO NOT SEND THIS APPLICATION **AND** APPLY ON-LINE.

DEA OFFICIAL USE :

Do you have other DEA registration numbers?
☐ NO ☐ YES

MAIL-TO ADDRESS Please print mailing address changes to the right of the address in this box.

FEE FOR THREE (3) YEARS IS $551
FEE IS NON-REFUNDABLE

SECTION 1 APPLICANT IDENTIFICATION ☐ Individual Registration ☐ Business Registration

Name 1 (Last Name of individual -OR- Business or Facility Name)

Name 2 (First Name and Middle Name of individual - OR- Continuation of business name)

Street Address Line 1 (if applying for fee exemption, this must be address of the fee exempt institution)

Address Line 2

City   State   Zip Code

Business Phone Number   Point of Contact

Business Fax Number   Email Address

DEBT COLLECTION INFORMATION
Mandatory pursuant to Debt Collection Improvements Act

Social Security Number (*if registration is for individual*)

Provide SSN or TIN.
See additional information note #3 on page 4.

Tax Identification Number (*if registration is for business*)

FOR Practitioner or MLP ONLY:

Professional Degree : *select from list only*   Professional School :   Year of Graduation :

National Provider Identification: Date of Birth (*MM-DD-YYYY*):
M M - D D - Y Y Y Y

SECTION 2
BUSINESS ACTIVITY

Check one business activity box only

☐ Central Fill Pharmacy
☐ Retail Pharmacy
☐ Nursing Home
☐ Automated Dispensing System

☐ Practitioner (DDS, DMD, DO, DPM, DVM, MD or PHD)
☐ Practitioner Military (DDS, DMD, DO, DPM, DVM, MD or PHD)
☐ Mid-level Practitioner (MLP) (DOM, HMD, MP, ND, NP, OD, PA, or RPH)
☐ Euthanasia Technician

☐ Ambulance Service
☐ Animal Shelter
☐ Hospital/Clinic
☐ Teaching Institution

FOR Automated Dispensing System (ADS) ONLY: DEA Registration # of Retail Pharmacy for this ADS

An ADS is automatically fee-exempt. Skip Section 6 and Section 7 on page 2. You must attach a notarized affidavit.

SECTION 3
DRUG SCHEDULES

Check all that apply

☐ Schedule II Narcotic
☐ Schedule II Non-Narcotic

☐ Schedule III Narcotic
☐ Schedule III Non-Narcotic

☐ Schedule IV
☐ Schedule V

☐ Check this box if you require official order forms - for purchase or transfer of schedule 2 narcotic and/or schedule 2 non-narcotic controlled substances.

NEW - Page 1

Figure 5-1 DEA Form 224.

SECTION 4

STATE LICENSE(S)

You MUST be currently authorized to prescribe, distribute, dispense, conduct research, or otherwise handle the controlled substances in the schedules for which you are applying under the laws of the **state** or jurisdiction in which you are operating or propose to operate.

Be sure to include both state license numbers if applicable

State License Number (required)

Expiration Date (required) / /
MM - DD - YYYY

What state was this license issued in? _____

Expiration / /

revoked, suspended, denied,

Date(s) of incident MM-DD-YYYY:

4. If the applicant is a **corporation** (other than a corporation whose stock is owned and traded by the public), association, partnership, or pharmacy, has any officer, partner, stockholder, or proprietor been **convicted of a crime** in connection with controlled substance(s) under state or federal law, or ever surrendered, for cause, or had a **federal** controlled substance registration revoked, suspended, restricted, denied, or ever had a **state** professional license or controlled substance registration revoked, suspended, denied, restricted or placed on probation, or is any such action pending?

Date(s) of incident MM-DD-YYYY: *Note: If question 4 does not apply to you, be sure to mark 'NO'. It will slow down processing of your application if you leave it blank.*

EXPLANATION OF "YES" ANSWERS

Applicants who have answered "YES" to any of the four questions above **must provide a statement to explain each "YES" answer.**

Use this space or attach a separate sheet and return with application

Liability question # _____   Location(s) of incident: _____

Nature of incident:

Disposition of incident:

SECTION 6   EXEMPTION FROM APPLICATION FEE

☐ Check this box if the applicant is a federal, state, or local government official or institution. Does not apply to contractor-operated institutions.

Business or Facility Name of Fee Exempt Institution. **Be sure to enter the address of this exempt institution in Section 1.**

FEE EXEMPT CERTIFIER

Provide the name and phone number of the certifying official

The undersigned hereby certifies that the applicant named hereon is a federal, state or local government official or institution, and is exempt from payment of the application fee.

Signature of certifying official **(other than applicant)**   Date

Print or type name and title of certifying official   Telephone No. (required for verification)

SECTION 7

METHOD OF PAYMENT

Check one form of payment only

☐ Check   Make check payable to: **Drug Enforcement Administration** See page 4 of instructions for important information.

☐ American Express ☐ Discover ☐ Master Card ☐ Visa

Credit Card Number   Expiration Date

Sign if paying by credit card

Signature of Card Holder

Printed Name of Card Holder

Mail this form with payment to:

U.S. Department of Justice
Drug Enforcement Administration
P.O. Box 28083
Washington, DC 20038-8083

FEE IS NON-REFUNDABLE

SECTION 8

APPLICANT'S SIGNATURE

Sign in ink

I certify that the foregoing information furnished on this application is true and correct.

Signature of applicant **(sign in ink)**   Date

Print or type name and title of applicant

WARNING: Section 843(a)(4)(A) of Title 21, United States Code states that any person who knowingly or intentionally furnishes false or fraudulent information in the application is subject to imprisonment for not more than four years, a fine of not more than $30,000, or both.

NEW - Page 2

Figure 5-1 *continued.*

REGULATION OF CONTROLLED SUBSTANCES

There are specific CSA regulations concerning controlled substances that govern record keeping, physician and pharmacy registrations, and inventory. All scheduled drugs used in any ambulatory care setting must have complete and accurate records kept concerning their purchase, storage, management, and distribution.

Focus On...

State Law and Controlled Substances

State governments regulate certain substances not controlled at the federal level. These include substances such as toluene, amyl or butyl nitrite, and nitrous oxide. Many states enforce age limits concerning the sale of products that contain these substances.

Controlled substances may also be regulated by individual states, and pharmacists must comply with the regulations of their state regarding the handling of controlled substances. Because of this, pharmacy technicians must understand their state's legal requirements. Specific guidelines for controlled substance prescriptions include the following:

- Prescription forms must be filled out in ink or typed, except for hospice and nursing home prescriptions, which may be faxed to the pharmacy; the fax may then be used as the hard copy.

- Federal law does not require a physical prescription, but individual states may choose to do so.

- Prescriptions must include the date prescribed, patient's name and address, and physician's DEA number.

- The amount prescribed should be written out in order to avoid errors; for example, "fifteen" should be used instead of "15."

- The physician must physically sign every written controlled substance prescription, but can verbally order Schedule III, IV, and V controlled substances.

Focus On...

Roles of Pharmacy Technicians

If state law allows, pharmacy technicians may count scheduled drugs, do inventory, and conduct record keeping. In many states, they can only have access to the pharmacy safe, room, or cabinet that contains scheduled drugs if supervised by the pharmacist, and the pharmacist must keep the keys to the safe. Federal regulations do not actually restrict access to controlled substance containment areas by pharmacy technicians. However, only a licensed pharmacist is able to dispense scheduled drugs.

ORDERING CONTROLLED SUBSTANCES

DEA Form 222 is used to order controlled substances from Schedules I or II. This form, which is filled out in triplicate, may be ordered from the ~~central agency by mail~~, or online, and is free of charge. However, the DEA ~~...~~

Form 222 requires the person ordering the substances to supply the following information: company name and address, ordering date, number of packages of each item, size of package of each item, name of each item, signature of purchaser or his or her attorney or agent, and DEA registration number. It is important to note that not every pharmacist in a given pharmacy can sign DEA 222 forms. There must be someone dedicated to do this or a power of attorney in place. A maximum of 10 different items may be ordered on one form, with 1 item per numbered line. After all the items are entered, the DEA registrant must notate the number of lines completed using a designated space on the left side of the form. This helps to assure that no other person enters any substances onto the form after it is completed. In order to prevent fraudulent activities, this form should never be signed or dated prior to ordering. Each book of order forms contains seven sets of these forms. A pharmacy may have no more than six books of forms at a given time, unless the pharmacist can prove the need to have more.

When a supplier receives a form and processes an order, he or she must add the following information to the form: his or her DEA registration number, the national drug code of each item, an indication of the packaging being shipped, and the date of each shipment. In most states, the supplier keeps a copy of the purchasing company or individual's DEA certificate on file prior to shipping any order. This is good practice, but not required by federal regulations. The supplier can only ship to the purchaser's address that is listed on both the Form 222 and his or her DEA certificate. Form 222 is shown in Figure 5-2.

Focus On...

Form 222

When Form 222 is used, the first copy stays with the pharmaceutical supplier. The second copy goes to the DEA from the pharmaceutical supplier. The third copy remains with the pharmacy or entity that is ordering the pharmaceutical.

BLANK DEA FORM-222
U.S. OFFICIAL ORDER FORM—SCHEDULES I & II

See Reverse of PURCHASER'S Copy for Instructions	No order form may be issued for Schedules I and II substances unless a completed application form has been received, (21 CFR 1305.04).	OMB APPROVAL NO. 1117-0010

TO: *(Name of Supplier)*	STREET ADDRESS

CITY and STATE	DATE	TO BE FILLED IN BY SUPPLIER
		SUPPLIERS DEA REGISTRATION No.

LINE No.	TO BE FILLED IN BY PURCHASER					
	No. of Packages	Size of Packages	Name of Item	National Drug Code	Packages Shipped	Date Shipped
1						
2						
3						
4						
5						
6						
7						
8						
9						
10						

NO. OF LINES COMPLETED	SIGNATURE OF PURCHASER OR HIS ATTORNEY OR AGENT

Date Issued	DEA Registration No.	Name and Address of Registrant
Schedules	2, 2N, 3, 3N, 4, 5	
Registered as a PHARMACY	No. of this Order Form	

DEA Form-222

U.S. OFFICIAL ORDER FORMS—SCHEDULES I & II
DRUG ENFORCEMENT ADMINISTRATION
SUPPLIER'S COPY 1

Figure 5-2 DEA Form 222.

If a Form 222 is defective, or contains errors or omissions, corrections may be made only under these circumstances: the drug's name is misspelled, the date of the order is missing, the package size is missing, the strength of the drug is missing, the number of line items completed is missing, or if the items are placed in incorrect locations on the order form. Other than the above items, the order cannot be processed without a correct, new order form being submitted. Suppliers are instructed not to fill any order if the Form 222 is illegible, not endorsed (signed), or shows signs of being changed, erased, or altered.

Partial filling of a Form 222 order is allowed, but the balance of the order must be supplied within 60 days of the original order date.

What Would You Do?

Joe, a pharmacist, gave a list of 13 Schedule II drugs to Betty so that she could write them onto a DEA Form 222. Betty wrote all 13 items on the 10-line form so that Joe could then sign it. Joe told her she would have to redo the form. What should Betty have done in this situation?

Electronic ordering is also available on an electronic version of Form 222 called "e222." The use of e222 helps to prevent illegal ordering of controlled substances, because identifiers are used that make it very difficult for any non-authorized person to use this mode of ordering. The website used for electronic ordering is http://www.deadiversion.usdoj.gov. While the use of e222 is not required, it is suggested to use it instead of the traditional paper forms because of the potential reduction in fraudulent activities.

When using e222, the following information is required: a unique number that the purchaser has created for themselves, the supplier's name/address/DEA number, the date the order is signed, the name of the controlled substance(s), the NDC number, the quantity (in a single package or container), and the number of packages or containers ordered. The "digital certificate" that is attached to the order provides the following: the purchaser's name, registered location, DEA number, his or her business activities, and his or her authorized schedules.

Focus On...

Ordering Controlled Substances

After a pharmacy orders and receives Schedule III, IV, or V drugs, the invoice must be confirmed as accurate and dated. Though not required, it is often stamped with a red "C" to signify "controlled substance." The invoice or packing slip must be kept in a separate, secure location in the pharmacy for a minimum of two years.

PRESCRIPTIONS FOR CONTROLLED SUBSTANCES

A practitioner must issue a prescription for a controlled substance for a valid medical purpose. If a practitioner attempts to resupply office stock by writing prescriptions for such a purpose, it is a violation of the law. DEA Form 222 must always be used to order drugs. Also, a practitioner ordering a controlled substance to maintain drug-dependent individuals who do not have legitimate prescriptions is in clear violation of the law. Practitioners cannot order drugs for their office using prescription pads—they must use an order form or a purchase order. Prescriptions for Schedule II drugs must be written, not faxed or called in, unless an absolute emergency exists that requires a telephone prescription order. Exceptions are made for hospices and nursing homes. No prescription for a Schedule II controlled substance may be refilled. Prescriptions for Schedule III or IV controlled substances may be refilled if a practitioner gives authorization. These prescriptions may not be filled or refilled more than six months after the date issued, nor can they be refilled more than five times after the date issued. After six months or after five refills, the practitioner may renew the prescription.

The advent of technology has brought "electronic prescribing" or "e-prescribing" to the forefront in order to reduce medication errors. The accuracy that e-prescribing allows will become instrumental in reducing errors due to illegible handwriting, wrong dosing, and missed drug interactions. In e-prescribing, prescriptions are generated electronically through automated data entry and a pharmacy-linked transmission network. It features warning/alert systems, access to full medical histories, reduction of telephonic and faxed requests, streamlined authorizations, increased patient compliance, and better reporting of the entire prescription process.

Though e-prescribing is evolving into the best, most accurate form of prescribing, it is not fully able to support controlled substance prescriptions. Many physicians find e-prescribing systems to have incomplete data and limited usefulness. Medication histories and formulary information may be difficult to access due to formatting issues. E-prescribing may also introduce unforeseen problems, and give physicians the possibility of ordering the wrong drug. Depending on how large the formulary is and how many drugs it lists, if the wrong key is pushed and the error is not recognized there could be a significantly bad outcome.

Currently, certain pharmacies are not linked to all e-prescribing systems. Also, prescriptions for controlled substances cannot be sent electronically. Mail-order pharmacies may not be able to receive electronic prescriptions. The e-prescribing process does not allow patients to shop for the best price, or to get prescriptions months ahead of time before filling ~~_____ transmitted and then filled immediately.~~

portion dispensed can be ...
a new prescription is needed to obtain any additional quantities. The pharmacist should notify the physician if the remaining amount is not available. Verbal prescriptions are only allowed in an emergency. The pharmacist must identify the physician, who is required to follow up with a written prescription within 72 hours. The amount dispensed for an emergency should only be that which is necessary until the written prescription can be presented. All prescriptions for controlled substances must be maintained in one of the following manners:

- A three-file system

  - One file for all Schedule II prescriptions
  - One file for all Schedule III, IV, and V prescriptions
  - One file for all other types of prescriptions

- A two-file system

  - One file for Schedule II prescriptions
  - One file for Schedules III, IV, and V prescriptions

- An alternate two-file system

  - One file for all controlled drug prescriptions
  - One file for prescription orders for all non-controlled drugs that are dispensed

LABELING OF CONTROLLED SUBSTANCES

Federal law and state statutes regulate the labeling of controlled substance prescriptions. These types of prescription orders must include the dispensing pharmacist's name and address, the pharmacy's name, the drug's serial number, and the date the prescription was filled. The prescribing physician's name, the patient's name, directions for use, and any cautionary statements must also be included. Most states have adopted laws requiring additional information to be included on the label, for example, the telephone number of the pharmacy.

The law requires labeling of controlled substances. The containers of controlled substances must have a special symbol, printed by their manufacturer, on the label of their stock bottle designating which schedule applies. The following symbols are designed for stock bottles containing controlled substances in Schedules I through V:

CI	or	C-I
CII	or	C-II
CIII	or	C-III
CIV	or	C-IV
CV	or	C-V

The word "Schedule" does not need to be used. Each symbol must be at least twice as large as the largest letter printed on the label. If the container is too small to have a printed label, only the box and the package insert must contain the **"C" symbol**. Drugs in Schedules II, III, and IV must bear this label when dispensed by a pharmacy: *Federal law prohibits the transfer of this drug to any person other than the patient for whom it is prescribed.* See Figure 5-3 for an example of a controlled substance label.

Focus On...

Labeling Controlled Substances

These symbols are not required on prescription containers dispensed by a pharmacist to a patient in the course of his professional practice, although laws of some states may require such symbols on prescriptions dispensed to extended-care facilities.

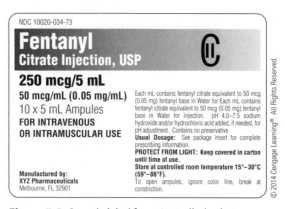

Figure 5-3 Sample label for a controlled substance.

Exemptions from Labeling Requirements— Schedule II Substances

Unit doses dispensed to an inpatient hospital or in a nursing home or other long-term care facility are exempt from prescription container labeling requirements as long as the following conditions exist:

1. A maximum of a seven-day supply is dispensed at one time.

2. The patient does n... ...

A separate DEA registration is needed for manufacturing, distributing, dispensing, or conducting research. However, a pharmacy registered to dispense a controlled substance can distribute (without being registered as a distributor) a given amount of controlled substances to a physician, hospital, nursing home, or another pharmacy for general dispensing. These distributions must meet the following conditions:

1. The pharmacy or practitioner to which the controlled substance is distributed must be listed.

2. If the substance is listed in Schedules I or II, the transfer must be made with an official DEA order on Form 222.

3. The distribution must be recorded as being distributed by the pharmacy, and the pharmacist or practitioner must record the substance as being received. The pharmacy who is distributing a controlled substance must record the following information:

   - The name of the medication
   - The dosage form
   - The amount of the substance
   - The name and address of the pharmacy
   - The DEA registration number of the practitioner or the pharmacy
   - The date of distribution

4. The total number of dosage units of controlled substance distributed by a pharmacy may not exceed 5 percent of all controlled substances dispensed by the pharmacy during the 12-month period in which the pharmacy is registered. If at any time it does exceed 5 percent, the pharmacy is required to register as a distributor as well as a pharmacy.

The DEA maintains strict controls concerning the transfer of controlled substances. If, for example, a pharmacy goes out of business, or is purchased by another company, its controlled substances may be transferred to the new owner, the supplier, the manufacturer, or a distributor that is registered to dispose of controlled substances. A pharmacy that is intending to terminate business must notify the closest DEA field office in writing prior to termination. The DEA registrant who will be receiving Schedule I or II controlled substances must issue a DEA Form 222 to the registrant who will be transferring the drugs. For Schedule III to V controlled substances, the transfer must be documented in writing, showing the drug name, dosage form, strength, quality, date transferred, and the complete names, addresses, and DEA numbers of any parties involved in the transfer.

What Would You Do?

Nicole had a back injury and was suffering from severe back pain. Her neurologist prescribed oxycodone for her. Two days later, her brother came to visit from out of state, planning to stay with Nicole for one week. Upon his arrival, he complained about a severe headache. Nicole gave some of the oxycodone to her brother to relieve his pain, which he then crushed up and snorted, similar to cocaine. Several days later, she found that five more oxycodone tablets were missing from her bottle. If you were Nicole, what would you do in this situation? Did she break the law?

RECORD KEEPING

Any pharmacy that handles controlled substances must keep complete and accurate records of all drugs received and dispensed. The records must be kept for two years. Some states require that the records be kept for at least five years. Schedule II drug records must be kept separately from all other records. Any record that includes controlled substances must be made available for inspection by DEA officials. Records required to be kept include a record of inventory, a record of received drugs, and a dispersal record.

Inventory Records

The CSA requires that, every two years, each registrant create a complete, accurate controlled substances stock record. When the inventory of

Schedule II controlled substances is taken, an exact count or measure must be made. Before a new pharmacy opens, a complete inventory of all controlled substances must be made. This is known as the "initial inventory."

After a pharmacy opens for business, an exact count of all Schedule II substances must be made every two years. An estimated count of all Schedule III, IV, and V substances must also be made every two years, though Schedule III and IV substances in bottles of 1,000 or

---

What Would You Do?

Teresa, a pharmacy technician, was doing an initial inventory of scheduled drugs for a new pharmacy, including Schedule II drugs. She estimated the content of the scheduled drugs and recorded her estimates. When the pharmacist checked her inventory records later, he noticed that the inventory for the Schedule II drugs was not accurate. If you were Teresa, what would you have done differently?

Keeping Receipts

DEA Form 222 is used as the official form of receipt for all Schedule I and II substances. Invoices are acceptable to use as receipts for all Schedule III, IV, and V substances. Each type of receipt must have the date the items were received written upon them. Controlled substances are usually clearly indicated (with red ink) on a specific page of any invoice that contains both controlled and non-controlled substances.

Receipts must contain the name and strength of each substance, dosage forms, number of dosage units, container volumes, number of received containers, and dates of receipt. The supplier's name, address, and DEA number must also be included.

Dispersal Record

Records of all drugs dispensed from the pharmacy, as well as records of all drugs removed from the pharmacy for any reason, are considered "dispersal records." Dispersal records include DEA Form 222, invoices, record books, disposal records, and theft or loss records.

RETURNING CONTROLLED SUBSTANCES

When controlled substances from Schedule II are returned, DEA Form 222 must be used. These substances may only be returned from one DEA registrant to another. Any facility that does not have a DEA number cannot return controlled substances. All returned controlled substances must be properly labeled with product descriptions, quantities, product names, product sizes, strengths, NDC numbers, and manufacturer names.

DEALING WITH OUTDATED CONTROLLED SUBSTANCES

When controlled substances become out of date, DEA Form 41, which can be obtained online, must be used. The pharmacist must write a cover letter explaining the situation and requesting DEA permission to destroy these substances. Though these substances do not have to be destroyed by the pharmacy, they must be listed separately in its biennial inventories. Approval for destruction of these drugs is not required from the DEA if a Board of Pharmacy investigator witnesses the destruction. The cover letter must be attached to the completed Form 41 with signed copies of Form 41 sent to the DEA (see Figure 5-4).

Retail pharmacies may request DEA permission to destroy these substances once per year. The request must be sent to the DEA two weeks prior to the intended date of destruction. Two witnesses (either physicians, pharmacists, mid-level practitioners, nurses, or law enforcement officers) must witness the destruction of the substances. Many pharmacies use a product-return system wherein they may be reimbursed for part of the drug product's original cost.

THEFT OR LOSS OF CONTROLLED SUBSTANCES

The DEA office nearest the pharmacy must be notified if a controlled substance is lost or stolen. Significant losses must be reported by phone immediately. When lesser amounts are reported in writing, DEA Form 106 must be used. The report must include the company's name and address, its DEA number, the date the theft or loss occurred, the type of theft or loss, a complete list of the missing controlled substances, and the local police department's contact information, as well as an explanation of the pharmacy's container-marking system and related costs. An original copy of the report should be kept by the pharmacy, two copies should be sent to the DEA, and in most states, one copy should be sent to the Board of Pharmacy. The pharmacy may also be required to send a copy to the local police department. See Figure 5-5 for an example of DEA Form 106.

OMB Approval No. 1117 - 0007	U. S. Department of Justice / Drug Enforcement Administration **REGISTRANTS INVENTORY OF DRUGS SURRENDERED**	PACKAGE NO.

The following schedule is an inventory of controlled substances which is hereby surrendered to you for proper disposition.

FROM: *(Include Name, Street, City, State and ZIP Code in space provided below.)*

Signature of applicant or authorized agent

NAME OF DRUG OR PREPARATION		Number of Containers	CONTENTS (Number of grams, tablets, ounces or other units per container)	Controlled Substance Content, (Each Unit)	FOR DEA USE ONLY		
					DISPOSITION	QUANTITY	
Registrants will fill in Columns 1,2,3, and 4 ONLY.						GMS.	MGS.
	1	*2*	*3*	*4*	*5*	*6*	*7*
1							
2							
3							
4							
5							
6							
7							
8							
9							
10							
11							
12							
13							
14							
15							
16							

FORM DEA-41 (9-01)   Previous edition dated **6-86** is usable.   *See instructions on reverse (page 2) of form.*

© U.S. Drug Enforcement Agency

Figure 5-4 DEA Form 41

DEA-41 (6/1986) Pg. 2

NAME OF DRUG OR PREPARATION	Number of Con- tainers	CONTENTS (Number of grams, tablets, ounces or other units per con- tainer)	Con- trolled Sub- stance Con- tent, (Each Unit)	FOR DEA USE ONLY		
				DISPOSITION	QUANTITY	
Registrants will fill in Columns 1,2,3, and 4 ONLY.					GMS.	MGS.
1	*2*	*3*	*4*	*5*	*6*	*7*
17						
18						
19						
20						
21						
22						
23						
24						

The controlled substances surrendered in accordance with Title 21 of the Code of Federal Regulations, Section 1307.21, have been received in _____ packages purporting to contain the drugs listed on this inventory and have been: ** (1) Forwarded tape-sealed without opening; (2) Destroyed as indicated and the remainder forwarded tape-sealed after verifying contents; (3) Forwarded tape-sealed after verifying contents.

DATE _____   DESTROYED BY: _____

** *Strike out lines not applicable.*

WITNESSED BY: _____

INSTRUCTIONS

1. List the name of the drug in column 1, the number of containers in column 2, the size of each container in column 3, and in column 4 the controlled substance content of each unit described in column 3; e.g., morphine sulfate tabs., 3 pkgs., 100 tabs., 1/4 gr. (16 mg.) or morphine sulfate tabs., 1 pkg., 83 tabs., 1/2 gr. (32mg.), etc.

2. All packages included on a single line should be identical in name, content and controlled substance strength.

3. Prepare this form in quadruplicate. Mail two (2) copies of this form to the Special Agent in Charge, under separate cover. Enclose one additional copy in the shipment with the drugs. Retain one copy for your records. One copy will be returned to you as a receipt. No further receipt will be furnished to you unless specifically requested. Any further inquiries concerning these drugs should be addressed to the DEA District Office which serves your area.

4. There is no provision for payment for drugs surrendered. This is merely a service rendered to registrants enabling them to clear their stocks and records of unwanted items.

5. Drugs should be shipped tape-sealed via prepaid express or certified mail (**return receipt requested**) to Special Agent in Charge, Drug Enforcement Administration, of the DEA District Office which serves your area.

PRIVACY ACT INFORMATION

AUTHORITY: Section 307 of the Controlled Substances Act of 1970 (PL 91-513).
PURPOSE: To document the surrender of controlled substances which have been forwarded by registrants to DEA for disposal.
ROUTINE USES: This form is required by Federal Regulations for the surrender of unwanted Controlled Substances. Disclosures of information from this system are made to the following categories of users for the purposes stated.
 A. Other Federal law enforcement and regulatory agencies for law enforcement and regulatory purposes.
 B. State and local law enforcement and regulatory agencies for law enforcement and regulatory purposes.
EFFECT: Failure to document the surrender of unwanted Controlled Substances may result in prosecution for violation of the Controlled Substances Act.

Under the Paperwork Reduction Act, a person is not required to respond to a collection of information unless it displays a currently valid OMB control number. Public reporting burden for this collection of information is estimated to average 30 minutes per response, including the time for reviewing instructions, searching existing data sources, gathering and maintaining the data needed, and completing and reviewing the collection of information. Send comments regarding this burden estimate or any other aspect of this collection of information, including suggestions for reducing this burden, to the Drug Enforcement Administration, FOI and Records Management Section, Washington, D.C. 20537; and to the Office of Management and Budget, Paperwork Reduction Project no. 1117-0007, Washington, D.C. 20503.

© U.S. Drug Enforcement Agency

Figure 5-4 *continued*

REPORT OF THEFT OR LOSS OF CONTROLLED SUBSTANCES

Federal Regulations require registrants to submit a detailed report of any theft or loss of Controlled Substances to the Drug Enforcement Administration. Complete the front and back of this form in triplicate. Forward the original and duplicate copies to the nearest DEA Office. ... your records. Some states may also require a copy of this report.	**OMB APPROVAL** No. 1117-0001

2. Phone No. (Include Area Code)

9. Number of Thefts or Losses Registrant has experienced in the past 24 months	10. Type of Theft or Loss (Check one)

10. Type of Theft or Loss (Check one)

1 ☐ Night break-in   3 ☐ Employee pilferage   5 ☐ Other (Explain)

2 ☐ Armed robbery   4 ☐ Customer theft   6 ☐ Lost in transit (Complete Item 14)

11. If Armed Robbery, was anyone:	12. Purchase value to registrant of Controlled Substances taken?	13. Were any pharmaceuticals or merchandise taken?
Killed? ☐ No ☐ Yes (How many) _____ Injured? ☐ No ☐ Yes (How many) _____	$	☐ No ☐ Yes (Est. Value) $

14. IF LOST IN TRANSIT, COMPLETE THE FOLLOWING:

A. Name of Common Carrier	B. Name of Consignee	C. Consignee's DEA Registration Number
D. Was the carton received by the customer? ☐ Yes ☐ No	E. If received, did it appear to be tampered with? ☐ Yes ☐ No	F. Have you experienced losses in transit from this same carrier in the past? ☐ No ☐ Yes (How Many) _____

15. What identifying marks, symbols, or price codes were on the labels of these containers that would assist in identifying the products?

16. If Official Controlled Substance Order Forms (DEA-222) were stolen, give numbers.

17. What security measures have been taken to prevent future thefts or losses?

FORM DEA - 106 (11-00) *Previous editions obsolete*   **CONTINUE ON REVERSE**

© U.S. Drug Enforcement Agency

Figure 5-5 DEA Form 106.

FORM DEA-106 (Nov. 2000) Pg. 2   **LIST OF CONTROLLED SUBSTANCES LOST**

Trade Name of Substance or Preparation		Name of Controlled Substance in Preparation	Dosage Strength and Form	Quantity
Examples:	Desoxyn	Methamphetamine Hydrochloride	5 mg Tablets	3 x 100
	Demerol	Meperidine Hydrochloride	50 mg/ml Vial	5 x 30 ml
	Robitussin A-C	Codeine Phosphate	2 mg/cc Liquid	12 Pints
1.				
2.				
3.				
4.				
5.				
6.				
7.				
8.				
9.				
10.				
11.				
12.				
13.				
14.				
15.				
16.				
17.				
18.				
19.				
20.				
21.				
22.				
23.				
24.				
25.				
26.				
27.				
28.				
29.				
30.				
31.				
32.				
33.				
34.				
35.				
36.				
37.				
38.				
39.				
40.				
41.				
42.				
43.				
44.				
45.				
46.				
47.				
48.				
49.				
50.				

I certify that the foregoing information is correct to the best of my knowledge and belief.

_____   _____   _____
Signature   Title   Date

Figure 5-5 *continued.*

filled, except in certain limited circumstances. Federal law allows the partial filling of Schedule II prescriptions, and prescriptions for Schedules III or IV controlled substances may be refilled if so authorized. The DEA has published information about partial refills of Schedule III and IV substances on its website. These are permissible as long as each partial filling is dispensed and recorded in the same manner as a refilling. The total quantity dispensed in all partial fillings cannot exceed the total quantity prescribed. No dispensing can occur after six months past the date of issue. Some states allow for partial refills of Schedule II drugs to ambulatory patients, often within 72 hours of the original prescription.

Focus On...

Refills

Schedule II drugs are not refillable. However, in certain circumstances (such as nursing homes), when individual patients need multiple, sequential prescriptions up to a 90-day supply, partial refills are allowed. There are rules for issuing multiple prescriptions on the same day for the same drug and patient. Generally, multiple prescriptions are still required. Schedule III and IV prescriptions may not be refilled more than five times after the date issued.

Recording Refills

A pharmacist, after refilling a prescription for any controlled substance in Schedules III, IV, or V, must enter (on the back of the prescription) his or her initials, the date the prescription was refilled, and the amount of drug dispensed. If the pharmacist merely initials and dates the back of the prescription, he or she shall be deemed to have dispensed a refill for the full face amount of the prescription. This initialing, dating, and adding of the amount of drug dispensed is not required if the pharmacy is using electronic data retrieval, and today this process is used only rarely, since computerization makes it unnecessary.

Computerization of Refilling

A pharmacy is allowed to use a **data processing system** for the storage and retrieval of prescription refill information for controlled substances in Schedules III and IV. The computerized system must allow immediate retrieval of original prescription information for prescriptions that currently are authorized for refilling. The information that must be readily retrievable must include, but is not limited to, the original prescription number; date of issuance of the prescription by the practitioner; full name and address of the patient; practitioner's name and DEA registration number; the name, strength, dosage form, and quantity of the controlled substance prescribed; the quantity dispensed, if different from the quantity prescribed; and the total number of refills authorized by the prescriber.

In addition, the system must provide for immediate retrieval of the current refill history for Schedules III and IV controlled substance prescriptions that have been authorized for refills during the past six months. Backup documentation (such as the daily logbook or printout) can be used to show that the refill information is correct. Pharmacy technicians can help assure that this backup documentation is signed by all pharmacists who worked during the period in question. The backup documentation must be stored in a separate file at the pharmacy and maintained for two years from the dispensing date.

FACSIMILE PRESCRIPTIONS

DEA regulations permit prescriptions for Schedule II, III, IV, and V drugs to be sent via **facsimile** (a copy of an official document transmitted electronically via a fax machine) from the practitioner directly to the pharmacy. The pharmacist must review original, signed prescriptions for Schedule II substances. The only cases where this is not required are listed below.

- A Schedule II narcotic requiring compounding for direct parenteral or intraspinal infusion with specific instructions for a home infusion pharmacy.

- A Schedule II prescription for a patient in a long-term care facility.

- A Schedule II prescription for a patient in a Medicare-certified or state-certified hospice facility. The pharmacy must keep this fax for its records. Faxed prescriptions may also be used for hospice patients who are at home but receiving services from a certified hospice; they do not have to reside in the hospice facility.

In addition to written or oral prescribing of Schedule III, IV, and V substances, DEA regulations permit the facsimile of a written, signed prescription transmitted by the prescribing practitioner or the practitioner's agent to serve as the authority for, and record of, the dispensing of a Schedule III, IV, or V substance.

Although federal DEA regulations allow for facsimile prescriptions for controlled substances, they do not authorize a practitioner to prescribe or a pharmacist to dispense controlled substances via faxed prescriptions unless *expressly provided for under the state law* in the jurisdiction in

ing chemical analysis may disperse them throughout their non-controlled substances stock in order to obstruct theft or diversion of the controlled substances. This information can be found at http://www.deadiversion .usdoj.gov (click on "Regulations and Codified CSA"; "Code of Federal Regulations"; "Section 1301"; "Section 1301.75"). Security regulations must be stringent to prevent theft of controlled substances. All of the following help to assure strict control and security concerning controlled substances:

- An electronic alarm system

- Perimeter security

- Self-closing and locking doors

- A system of key control

- Controlled accessibility

Other security controls that affect manufacturers, distributors, shippers, and carriers include the following:

- The manufacturer or distributor must make a diligent effort to determine that persons ordering from them are registered.

- The distributor must develop and maintain a system for detecting suspicious orders and reporting them.

- The distributor must report all losses of controlled substances, including goods lost in transit, to the DEA on Form 106, even if the substances are recovered. It is *the responsibility of the shipper, not the carrier,* to report such losses.

- The registrant is responsible for selecting a reputable and secure warehouse for storage as well as a reputable and security-conscious carrier to transport controlled substances.

3. Which of the following agencies oversees controlled substances and recommends prosecution of individuals who illegally distribute them?

   A. FDA
   B. CDC
   C. HIPAA
   D. DEA

4. Anabolic steroids are classified on which of the following schedules?

   A. II
   B. III
   C. IV
   D. V

5. Diphenoxylate (with atropine) is listed on which of the following schedules?

   A. I
   B. II
   C. IV
   D. V

6. Which of the following drugs is classified on Schedule IV?

   A. diphenoxylate
   B. anabolic steroids
   C. methadone
   D. benzodiazepines

7. Drugs on Schedules II, III, and IV must bear which of the following statements?

   A. Federal law prohibits the transfer of this drug to any person other than the patient for whom it was prescribed.
   B. Federal law allows partial refilling.
   C. May be refilled up to 10 times.
   D. May be refilled up to 5 times.

8. How and when must significant losses of controlled substances be reported?

   A. in writing to the DEA within seven days
   B. in writing to the DEA within 72 hours
   C. immediately, by phone, to the nearest DEA office
   D. none of the above

9.   Which of the following statements is not true regarding the maintenance of files for scheduled drugs?

   A.   One file is used for Schedule II drugs dispensed.
   B.   One file is used for Schedule III, IV, and V drugs dispensed.
   C.   One file is used for Schedule I and II drugs dispensed.
   ... used for prescription orders for all other drugs.

11.   The CSA requires each DEA registrant to controlled substances stock record

   A.   every two years.
   B.   every year.
   C.   every three years.
   D.   every five years.

12.   In most types of pharmacy practice, controlled substances should be kept in a

   A.   locked cabinet.
   B.   refrigerator.
   C.   laminar airflow hood.
   D.   freezer.

13.   The total number of dosage units of controlled substances distributed by a pharmacy to another registrant during a 12-month period should not exceed

   A.   1 percent of their total amount.
   B.   5 percent of their total amount.
   C.   10 percent of their total amount.
   D.   15 percent of their total amount.

14.   In most states, pharmacists are usually given certificates of registration, which are granted for

   A.   10 to 12 years.
   B.   10 to 12 months.
   C.   1 to 3 years.
   D.   3 to 5 years.

15. Schedule III and IV prescriptions may not be refilled more than

    A.   one time.
    B.   two times.
    C.   three times.
    D.   five times.

Fill in the Blank

1. Controlled substances have been categorized according to their potential for _____ and their _____ abilities.

2. Amphetamines and codeine are usually classified in _____.

3. Acetaminophen with codeine, and hydrocodone with APAP, are examples of _____.

4. Diphenoxylate hydrochloride with atropine sulfate (Lomotil) is a Schedule V preparation that requires a _____.

5. Controlled substances from Schedule II are ordered by submitting DEA Form _____.

6. The total number of dosage units of controlled substances distributed to other registrants by a pharmacy may not exceed _____ of all controlled substances dispensed by the pharmacy during a _____ -month period.

7. Inventory records for Schedule II drugs must be kept on file for at least _____ years following the date the inventory was taken.

8. Though this is not required, controlled substances are often marked with red ink on any invoice that contains both controlled and _____ substances.

9. For destroying controlled substances, DEA Form _____ must be used.

10. When controlled substances are stolen or lost, DEA Form _____ must be used.

CASE STUDY

Jackie is a pharmacy technician. She receives a faxed prescription for a Schedule II drug for a patient in a long-term care facility. She questions her supervisor about the prescription. Robert, her supervisor, asks

to fill a faxed prescription for

assumption.

1. Without knowing anything else about this case, who do you think is correct?

2. What else could Robert, Jackie, and John have done to verify the correct information?

3. What agency would regulate Schedule II prescriptions in their state?

RELATED INTERNET SITES

Use the following key words to search for additional information at these sites: "controlled substances act," "controlled substances," "Schedule II drugs," and "DEA."

http://www.deadiversion.usdoj.gov Click "Search," then search for "Section 1301.75."

http://www.deadiversion.usdoj.gov Click "Search," then search for "Pharmacist's Manual."

http://www.deaecom.gov

http://www.dealookup.com

http://www.fda.gov Search for "databases."

http://www.fdalawblog.net

http://www.justice.gov

http://www.napra.org

http://www.nationalsubstanceabuseindex.org

http://www.nccusl.org

http://www.ntis.gov

REFERENCES

Abadinsky, H. (2010). *Drug Use and Abuse: A Comprehensive Introduction* (7th ed.). Bellmont, CA: Wadsworth Cengage Learning.

Abood, R. (2010). *Pharmacy Practice and the Law* (6th ed.). Burlington, MA: Jones and Bartlett.

Carter, G. T., Gieringer, D., & Rosenthal, E. (2008). *Marijuana Medical Handbook: Practical Guide to Therapeutic Uses of Marijuana* (rev. ed.). Piedmont, CA: Quick American Archives.

Cole, M. D. (2003). *The Analysis of Controlled Substances.* Hoboken, NJ: John Wiley & Sons Inc.

Fincham, J. E. (2008). *E-Prescribing: The Electronic Transformation of Medicine.* Burlington, MA: Jones and Bartlett.

Fink, J. L., Vivian, J. C., & Keller Reid, K. (2005). *Pharmacy Law Digest* (40th ed.). Philadelphia: Lippincott, Williams, & Wilkins.

Fred, L. Y. (2005). *Manual for Pharmacy Technicians* (3rd ed.). Bethesda, MD: ASHP.

Mizner, J. J. (2009). *Mosby's Review for the PTCB Certification Examination* (2nd ed.). Philadelphia: Mosby.

Reiss, B. S., & Hall, G. D. (2010). *Guide to Federal Pharmacy Law* (7th ed.). Boynton Beach, FL: Apothecary Press.

The Health Insurance Portability and Accountability Act (HIPAA)

1. Explain how the HIPAA Privacy Rule ben...

2. Identify the difference between Title I and Title II of HIPAA.

3. List the rights that patients have under the Privacy Rule.

4. Explain what is expected of pharmacy technicians in relation to the Privacy Rule.

5. Describe how to protect patient confidentiality.

6. Explain why a technician cannot discuss protected health information with a patient's friends and family.

7. Discuss the general purpose of the HIPAA-mandated administrative code sets.

8. State the purpose of the HIPAA Electronic HealthCare Transactions and Code Sets standards.

9. Describe the purpose of the Office of Inspector General.

10. Compare fraud and abuse.

KEY TERMS

Compliance program guidelines—HIPAA-related privacy, training, and security regulations designed to focus on, correct, and maintain good healthcare practices.

Disclosure—Transferring information, releasing information, providing access to information, or divulging information in any manner.

Electronic data interchange (EDI)—A set of standards for structuring electronic information intended to be exchanged between different entities.

Electronic medical records (EMR)—Method of record storage preferred over paper records because the electronic format can be accessed more quickly and takes less room to store.

Encryption—Transforming information via an algorithm to make it unreadable to anyone who does not possess the decryption information required to read it.

Extranet—A private network that uses Internet protocols, network connections, and sometimes

OUTLINE
(continued)

Medical Code Sets

Administrative
Code Sets

HIPAA Enforcement

HIPAA Enforcement
Agencies

Fraud and Abuse
Regulation

The Compliance Plan

Violations and
Penalties

telecommunication devices to share information with outside entities.

Medical code sets—Sets of alphanumeric codes used for encoding medical conditions, diseases, procedures, and other information.

Notice of Privacy Practices (NOPP)—A document that explains to patients how his or her PHI may be used and disclosed.

Office of Inspector General (OIG)—Governmental office that investigates various organizations, including healthcare organizations, to assure integrity and efficiency in their operations.

Protected health information (PHI)—All stored health information that relates to a past, present, or future physical or mental health condition.

Security Rule—A HIPAA-related regulation that specifies how PHI is protected on computer networks, the Internet, the extranet, and disks and other storage media.

Treatment, payment, and healthcare operations (TPHCO)—This concerns PHI that may be shared in order to provide treatment, process payment, and operate the medical business.

SETTING THE SCENE

Katie, a pharmacy technician with 15 years of experience, works for an institutional pharmacy. Her sister is a nurse, and her brother is a cardiovascular technician. Katie's mother-in-law has been a nurse for 40 years, and she has worked for a local internist for more than 25 years. At a family picnic, Katie's mother-in-law asked Katie if she was aware that their neighbor Joe had been diagnosed with HIV and syphilis. Katie asked her how she knew this, and her mother-in-law told her that Joe had been in the medical office where she worked, and she had looked at his lab results in his medical record. Katie told her husband about Joe's condition, and at their next golf game, he told Joe he was so sorry to hear about his diagnosis. Joe was angry, and asked how he knew about this.

Critical Thinking

- What should Katie and her relatives have done?
- How could their discussion of Joe's private health information jeopardize their careers?

OVERVIEW

The creation of privacy and security laws was aimed at more efficient pharmacy practice and faster reimbursement. The advent of technology has increased the practice of and efficiencies of pharmacy. However, electronic records and electronic data processing led to concerns related to maintaining the privacy of patients. HIPAA laws were put into place to standardize controls over the dissemination of private health records. Many healthcare professionals feel that they can't discuss anything about any patient at all—no matter where they are or when the topic arises. If pharmacy technicians understand HIPAA compliance, they can feel ~~l other individuals~~ in the pharmacy.

groups and individuals, and is ~~intended~~ in healthcare delivery and insurance. HIPAA strives to promote the use of medical savings accounts, improve access to long-term healthcare coverage and services, and simplify health insurance administration.

Under HIPAA, healthcare providers ensure that patient confidentiality is always maintained. The use and disclosure of **protected health information (PHI)** by covered entities is controlled by HIPAA. PHI must be identified to be protected, and it is important to understand that all health information, whether verbal, written, or electronic, should be protected. Patients have the right to be told how their PHI can be used. HIPAA allows employees to take their health coverage with them when they change jobs. It allows patients to have better access to their own health information while controlling how others can access it. HIPAA consists of two parts. Title I focuses on continuation of health insurance coverage. Title II controls the private health information of individuals.

Title I: Health Insurance Reform

Before HIPAA, people who had private health insurance did not have as many rights as did people who were covered by Medicare or Medicaid. Most private insurance comes from employers, individual healthcare plans, or from the Federal Employees' Health Benefits Program. State law regulates many types of health insurance. In addition, employer-offered health plans are regulated by the federal Employee Retirement Income and Security Act of 1974 (ERISA).

The Consolidated Omnibus Budget Reconciliation Act of 1985 (COBRA) allows employees who are leaving a job to elect to continue their previous employer's health coverage for a limited time. Under COBRA, employees must pay the premium for their coverage themselves, and it is usually higher than what they were paying when still employed at their previous job. COBRA was modified by Title I of HIPAA, which limited exclusions for pre existing health conditions. Title I also gave certain people the ability to enroll in new healthcare plans of different types.

Title II: Administrative Simplification

Title II of HIPAA restricted electronic transfer of healthcare data, gave patients more rights regarding their own personal health information, and put in place better security of this information. Due to rising costs, Title II sought to reduce paperwork, simplify Internet form processing, and standardize the administration of healthcare information.

The use of **electronic data interchange (EDI)** was encouraged so routine business information exchange could be exchanged between computers. Title II of HIPAA promoted the establishment of national electronic healthcare transaction standards. It established national identifiers for healthcare providers, employers, and even health insurance plans. The five basic provisions of HIPAA Title II are as follows:

- Electronic health information transaction standards—includes healthcare benefits coordination, claims, eligibility, enrollment, payment, and security.

- Penalties—assigned fines and imprisonment to specific violations.

- Privacy—gave the federal Department of Health and Human Services the task of establishing health information standards, and the ability to set privacy regulations if Congress did not put privacy legislation into place.

- Provider and health plan mandate and timetable—gave providers and health plans two years to start using the new HIPAA standards.

- State law preemption—allowed HIPAA to supersede state laws unless Health and Human Services decided otherwise; however, when a state law is stronger, it must be followed.

COMPLYING WITH HIPAA

Those who must comply with HIPAA are referred to as "covered entities" (CEs). These entities provide healthcare services regularly and send HIPAA-protected information electronically. HIPAA governs three types of covered entities: clearinghouses (claims handlers and companies that manage electronic medical records), health insurance plans, and healthcare providers. State laws that relate to HIPAA should be followed because they may be more stringent than the actual related HIPAA requirements. A state law is more stringent when it

- grants better access rights to a patient's own PHI

- prohibits a use or disclosure of PHI that a HIPAA regulation would allow

Medicare policies, long term, CHAMPVA, the Indian Health Service, the Federal Employees Health Benefits Program, approved child health plans, high-risk plans, and others. Healthcare providers include hospitals, nursing facilities, rehabilitation facilities, hospices, home health care, pharmacies, private practices, dental practices, labs, chiropractors, osteopaths, podiatrists, and therapists.

Direct providers are those that provide direct treatment to patients. Indirect providers include labs that handle patient test results. HIPAA also works with business associates (BA) that relate to healthcare, including accreditation agencies, accountants, information technology (IT) contractors, lawyers, medical transcription services, coding services, collection agents, third-party claimants, and independent contractors.

PRIVACY STANDARDS

Pharmacies have increased controls over the way they manage and store patient information. This is a result of the Privacy Rule of 2003. Patients have a right to confidentiality and the protection of their PHI. Under the HIPAA Privacy Rule, this information belongs to patients, and they have the right to control who is able to view it. However, healthcare providers who create medical records about patients also have some legal claim as to how these records are used. Access to medical records must be protected by healthcare personnel, including pharmacy technicians, who must know which types of information they can release.

Discarded patient information (DPI) must be handled with great care. When patient records (either electronic or paper) are to be discarded, they should be destroyed by a licensed, bonded company. Computer storage media containing patient records must be completely wiped (erased) of all data so that no trace of patient information may remain. It is not sufficient to simply delete patient files, because computer hard drives and other storage media devices retain files in various forms, even though they may no longer appear in the file directories. DPI must never be thrown into the trash, because documented cases exist of individuals who have stolen both paper records and computer disks containing hundreds or thousands of patient records. From these, thieves may obtain Social Security numbers, account information, and more. Identity theft is rampant in today's society, and the proper methods of discarding patient information must be undertaken.

Focus On...

Protected Health Information

PHI is health information that relates to a past, present, or future physical or mental health condition.

The Medical Record

Medical records contain information about a patient's health over time. They are shared among the healthcare professionals who need them to provide accurate patient care. The medical record documents all the medical history of a patient in chronological order. The medical standards of care in each state ensure that every patient receives the best quality care. Since medical records are legal documents, their accuracy is vital in documenting that appropriate medical care has been given to each patient. Visits to healthcare providers are documented thoroughly, and the same form of documentation is undertaken for every visit (also known as an "encounter"). Aside from the patient's name, the other information that is documented for each encounter is the date and reason for the visit, related medical history, physical exam, review of medications, review of tests, diagnosis, review of procedures and treatments, care plan, advice that was given to the patient, and the healthcare professional's signature.

More healthcare providers are using electronic medical records today, and paper records are becoming rarer. **Electronic medical records (EMR)** are preferred over paper records because they can be accessed more quickly, and take less room to store. They also may be shared between authorized healthcare professionals more easily than paper records can. *Electronic health records (EHR)*, which are often confused with EMR, are actually not the same at all. An EHR relies on an EMR being in place. An EMR is the legal record of a care delivery organization upon which an EHR is based. An EMR is owned by the care delivery organization, while an EHR is owned by the patient or person who has a stake in the outcome.

Although an EMR is not really interactive with the patient, an EHR provides interactive patient access.

Protected Health Information

HIPAA privacy standards were established in 2003 to protect personal health information. These standards require that privacy poli-

providers.

Often, a pharmacy has a designated privacy and security officer who handles disclosure of PHI. This officer usually receives referred requests from patients to access or amend their records, and strives to handle them in a timely manner.

Only the minimum amount of PHI should be disclosed in any situation. This *minimum necessary standard* protects against too much information being given to any specific person or entity. A group of medical records is known as a *designated record set (DRS)*, and includes a provider's medical and billing records. Insurance companies include other information, such as payments and claims, in their designated record sets. Providers must create a **Notice of Privacy Practices (NOPP)**, which details their policies and procedures, and make it available to anyone who requests it. Patients must sign an additional document stating that they have read and reviewed the provider's NOPP.

Focus On...

Protected Health Information

When a patient requests that his or her health information not be disclosed to anyone, the healthcare provider must follow through on this request. Example: A woman requested that her PHI not be disclosed to anyone. Soon after, her husband, who was in the process of divorcing her, asked for her PHI from their pharmacy because he said he needed it for tax purposes. A young attendant gave him the information, which he proceeded to use in court against his wife to prove that she was taking prescribed drugs that impaired her judgment and ability to function normally. Her PHI should not have been given to him under any circumstances, since she had requested no disclosure.

Providers must be very careful when deciding if a person is allowed to have the PHI of any patient. Parents' or guardians' approval should be obtained before disclosing a child's PHI. However, in some cases, a child must give permission for his or her records to be disclosed. Children's access to their own records is governed by state law. In recent years, many new laws have been enacted that protect the disclosure of the PHI of emancipated, married, pregnant, and other minors—even to their parents. It is a good idea for pharmacy technicians to refer issues related to the disclosure of a child's PHI to the pharmacist or privacy officer.

Certain disclosure always requires the patient's approval. This usually means the patient will have to sign an authorization form. For example, insurance companies sometimes require medical history of drug use, mental disorders, and sexually transmitted diseases. Providers must have written authorization from the patient in order to share this type of information with insurance companies.

Judicial orders can override a patient's preferences regarding the release of PHI. Subpoenas for court appearances and testimony can authorize disclosure of PHI. In addition, PHI may be released to researchers who are studying patient data for clinical reasons. State and federal prisoners have less protection concerning the disclosure of their PHI, though state statutes may overrule HIPAA in certain circumstances. In-depth PHI about a patient's psychotherapy cannot be disclosed in most cases. However, national security entities may have access to PHI generally any time they request it.

Focus On...

Disclosure

Information is disclosed when it is transmitted between or among organizations.

Patients' Rights

Patients have the right to view and copy their PHI within 30 days of requesting it, either free or for a reasonable fee as per HIPAA regulations. They can request amendments (changes) to any incorrect parts of their PHI, and these must usually be completed within 30 days. Patients may request an "accounting of disclosures," though many disclosures (such as those made for TPHCO) do not have to be included in what the patient is shown. Patients can also ask for confidential communications that use different addresses, phone numbers, e-mail addresses, etc., than are listed in their medical record. Complaints against providers' handling of PHI may be made to the federal Office for Civil Rights (OCR). Additionally, certain restrictions against uses or disclosures of PHI may be requested.

Many states have more stringent rules, as well as shorter time limits for responses to requests.

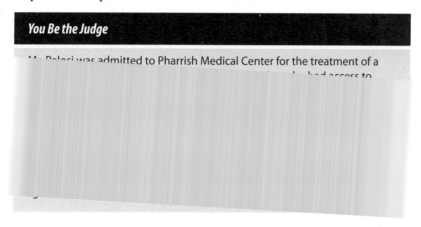

Patient Notification

The HIPAA Privacy Rule changed the way patients are informed about the HIPAA compliance of covered entities. Using the Notice of Privacy Practices (NOPP), providers explain to patients how their PHI may be used and disclosed. These NOPPs discuss the patient's access to his or her own information, patient rights in full, and how to register complaints. These notices explain how the covered entity operates, and give points of contact for patients who need help concerning their PHI, as well as stating when the NOPP became effective for each patient. An NOPP also covers how the covered entity gets authorization regarding the use and disclosure of PHI. It explains that patients must sign and date authorization forms giving specific entities access to their PHI. Patients must sign an acknowledgement of the receipt of an NOPP or receive an explanation if it cannot be obtained.

Security Standards

The HIPAA security standards describe how electronic PHI must be safeguarded. It is important to understand these security standards. All healthcare professionals participate in the protection of patient records.

Focus On...

Physical Safeguards

Physical safeguards are security measures designed to protect a covered entity's electronic information system. They relate to the protection of buildings and equipment from natural and environmental hazards and unauthorized intrusion.

HIPAA Security

HIPAA security standards focus on electronic PHI, not those records that are kept on paper. Electronic protected health information is also referred to as *ePHI*. These records may be stored in computers and related peripheral devices, and transmitted over computer networks, over the Internet, and on removable media that interfaces with computers.

The goals of ePHI include availability, confidentiality, and integrity of the information included within. Covered entities must use *risk analysis* to determine potential security threats to ePHI. They must then manage these risks with policies and procedures designed to protect against them. Security risks that may threaten ePHI include computer system changes, identity theft, malware (harmful computer programs), natural disasters, power outages, and subversive threats. Computer systems and networks should have security measures implemented to protect them from threats that occur from outside or within the organization.

In February 2003, final regulations were issued regarding the administrative, physical, and technical safeguards that protect HIPAA-regulated health information and its confidentiality, integrity, and availability. The **Security Rule** specifies how patient information is protected on computer networks, the Internet, the **extranet**, and disks and other storage media.

Focus On...

HIPAA Training

Federal law requires that all employees of covered entities be trained on policies and procedures for the protection of the confidentiality, integrity, and security of individually identifiable health information.

Mobile Devices and Media

Devices that are termed "mobile" or "portable" include backup media, home computers, laptop computers, memory cards, personal digital assistants (PDAs), public workstations, remote access devices, smartphones, USB flash drives, and wireless access points. HIPAA has established further guidelines known as the *HIPAA Security Guidance for Remote Use of and Access to Electronic Protected Health Information*. These guidelines focus on the off-site use of ePHI. They advise covered entities to limit all forms of remote access, use **encryption** and virus protection, and back up all ePHI that is used by remote systems.

Faxes and E-mail

HIPAA also requires protection of PHI when using faxes and e-mail. People on the receiving end of these communications may be unauthorized to view the contents, but may have the opportunity to see them ~~dless~~ HIPAA suggests that all fax numbers and e-mail addresses be ~~~~ ~~ddition.~~ HIPAA recommends the in- ~~receives~~

Faxes and ~~E-mail~~

A drug manufacturer accidentally reveals its entire ~~patie~~ when sending out promotional e-mails to its customers. Because the drug in question is an antidepressant, this inadvertent publication of private health information could have disastrous consequences affecting these patients' employment, families, and more. Faxes and e-mails containing PHI are dangerous because of the possibility of someone else on the receiving end seeing this information.

HIPAA TRANSACTIONS

HIPAA sets forth requirements concerning electronic data interchange (EDI) to simplify administration information exchange. Healthcare professionals should understand the related code sets and national identifiers (such as Social Security numbers and numbers derived from them) used in these transactions.

HIPAA Electronic Healthcare Transactions

All providers are required by HIPAA to use the same code sets, identifiers, and transaction when healthcare information is transmitted. These include claims, claim status, encounter information, inquiries, and payment or remittance advice. These standards are codified as *The HIPAA Electronic Health Care Transactions and Code Sets (TCS)*.

Transaction Standards

HIPAA requires that transfers of ePHI for specific business purposes must comply with specific transaction standards. These standards apply to all methods of electronic transmission, including special "extranet" links to authorized connected parties, the Internet, leased or dial-up lines, networks, or mobile storage media. HIPAA transactions are divided into areas of medical business, including but not limited to the following: benefits, claims and equivalent encounters; claim status; eligibility inquiries; enrollment/disenrollment; payments and remittance; and referrals.

The National Council for Prescription Drug Programs (NCPDP) creates and promotes data transfer standards relating to the practice of pharmacy. Members of the NCPDP may receive education tailored to their pharmacy practice, and also receive database services. The NCPDP standards focus on diverse areas of pharmacy practice, such as telecommunications, product identification, standard identifiers, manufacturer rebates, government programs, professional pharmacy services, electronic prescribing, long-term care, safety concerns, and insurance. As it relates to HIPAA, the NCPDP has subsections that focus on the National Provider ID (NPI), the Strategic National Implementation Process, HIPAA transactions and code sets, privacy, enforcement, security, employer IDs, and Designated Standard Maintenance Organizations (DSMOs).

Medical Code Sets

Medical code sets are used to encode data elements concerning specific diagnoses and clinical procedures. Alphanumeric codes are used. Diseases, procedures, supplies, treatments, and other data have unique codes. There are six code sets used for clinical information:

- ICD-9-CM (for identifying diseases and conditions)
- HCPCS (for items, supplies, and non-physician services)
- CPT-4 (for medical procedures and services)
- ICD Volume 3 codes (for inpatient hospital services)
- NDC (for drug products)
- CDT-4 (for dental services)

The ICD-9 codes were developed as part of the *International Classification of Diseases, Ninth Revision, Clinical Modification (ICD-9-CM)*.

Administrative Code Sets

Non-medical code sets are also known as "administrative code sets." These are used for administrative information, and include simple and complex codes. For example, simple codes include abbreviations for states and locations. Complex codes may refer to payments, claims, providers, and places of service.

HIPAA ENFORCEMENT

The HIPAA Security Rule requires that covered entities implement policies and procedures that will prevent, detect, contain, and correct security violations. HIPAA standards and regulations are enforced by the Department of Health and Human Services, which also enforces situations of related abuse and fraud. Healthcare professionals should under-

Justice (DOJ) prosecutes criminal violations. The Centers for Medicare and Medicaid Services (CMS) enforce non-privacy standards, the Electronic Health Care Transaction and Code Set Rule (TCS), the National Employer Identifier Number Rule (EIN), the Security Rule, and rules that relate to national identifiers. The Office for Civil Rights (OCR) enforces civil violations of HIPAA privacy standards. The **Office of Inspector General (OIG)** prosecutes fraud and abuse in the healthcare industry while overseeing Medicare and Medicaid.

Fraud and Abuse Regulation

Healthcare fraud and abuse may harm patients financially and even medically if unsafe procedures are performed as a result. The *Health Care Fraud and Abuse Control Program* enforces HIPAA regulations and government standards, and is conducted by the Office of Inspector General and the Department of Justice. The *False Claims Act* prohibits false claims or misrepresentations, and rewards "whistle-blowers" who alert the government to cases of fraud. Other regulations focus on "kickbacks" (incentives given to those who defraud others), "self-referrals" (referring patients to an entity in which the referrer receives some monetary compensation), and fraud compliance education.

The Compliance Plan

Compliance plans are designed to prevent illegal practices. Many healthcare providers create compliance plans to stay in line with government regulations, develop consistent policies and procedures, train their staff, and eliminate errors. Compliance plans also serve as legal defense in the case of prosecution for fraud. The OIG has created **compliance**

program guidelines for many areas of healthcare, including pharmacies, laboratories, home health agencies, medical billing companies, nursing facilities, private practices, hospitals, and manufacturers.

Compliance plans should contain written policies and procedures, appointments of officers and a committee, auditing/monitoring measures, communication measures, systems of discipline, error correction methods, and employee training methods. Codes of conduct should be established in order to comply with government regulations, maintain accurate records, and provide high-quality and ethical patient care. Internal audits should be conducted regularly to assure that the compliance plan is being followed.

Violations and Penalties

All healthcare employees who deal with PHI must comply with HIPAA. Ethical or legal breaches of confidentiality may result in many different penalties, including fines, termination, and imprisonment. Criminal penalties, which are usually assessed for intentional misuse of PHI, can be as high as $250,000 in fines and up to 10 years in prison. These types of penalties are given for knowing misuse of PHI, misuse involving false pretenses, and profiting from misuse of PHI that causes malicious harm. Civil penalties can be as high as $25,000 in fines per year if repeated violations occur. These types of penalties are given for violating privacy on an unintentional basis.

Examples of recently reported violations of HIPAA disclosure regulations include the following:

- A hospital published a woman's PHI regarding an abortion online. This action resulted in her being harassed by an anti-abortion group. She successfully sued the hospital that published the information.

- A man was automatically enrolled in a depression counseling program by his employer after his medical records were released to it by his drug management company; he had taken antidepressants previously but was no longer in need of them.

- A famous entertainer's PHI was released to her manager; later, after the two ceased their working relationship, he released her records to a national tabloid.

- A pharmacist discussed a patient's PHI over a speaker phone in the pharmacy, mentioning her Social Security number, medications she was taking, and the disease she was being treated for. Several customers overheard all of this, one of whom knew the patient and alerted her.

- A pharmacy technician went on a break without logging off of his computer terminal, while patient information was displayed on its screen. A delivery man who was bringing vaccines to the pharmacy recognized a name on the screen as his sister-in-law's, and read that she was currently being prescribed medications for a sexually transmitted infection; when he told his brother, the situ-

  ~~lawsuit~~ against the pharmacy for disclosing the

continuity of healthcare coverage.

prove access to long-term healthcare coverage and services, promote the use of medical savings accounts, and simplify health insurance administration.

HIPAA is made up of two parts. Title I focuses on continuation of health insurance coverage, while Title II controls private health information for individuals. Title II also restricts electronic transfer of healthcare data, allows patients more rights concerning their protected health information (PHI), and improves security measures for this information.

HIPAA regulates clearinghouses, healthcare providers, and health insurance plans. In 2003, the Privacy Rule was established, which changed the ways that pharmacies stored and managed PHI. This basically means that it changed the way pharmacies transmitted information to insurance companies.

Patients have a right to confidentiality as well as protection of their PHI. Disclosure (the release of PHI to any outside entity) can be done by e-mail, by fax, orally, or in writing. If the use of PHI does not focus on treatment, payment, and operations (TPHCO), then written authorization must be obtained before it can be shared.

Patients also have the right to examine and copy their PHI within 30 days of requesting to do so. HIPAA's 30-day rule is longer than the similar rules of many states. Patients can do this for free or for a small fee, as described in HIPAA. The security standards set forth in HIPAA are mostly concerned with electronic PHI, not records kept on paper. The goals of using electronic PHI include better availability, stricter confidentiality, and preserving the integrity of the information. To assure that timelines are met, prompt referral to the privacy officer is critical.

SETTING THE SCENE

The following discussion and responses relate to the opening "Setting the Scene" scenario:

- Katie and her mother-in-law must not discuss private health information of any patient, as this does not respect the privacy and confidentiality of the patient.

- According to the Privacy Rule of 2003, patients have a right to confidentiality and the protection of their private health information.

REVIEW QUESTIONS

Multiple Choice

1. Title II of HIPAA is referred to as which of the following?

    A. COBRA
    B. NPPM
    C. Administrative Simplification
    D. Health Insurance reform

2. Hospitals, pharmacists, physicians, and therapists are examples of

    A. business associates.
    B. health plans.
    C. providers.
    D. none of the above.

3. Which of the following is protected under the HIPAA privacy standards?

    A. patient information communicated over the phone.
    B. patient data that is printed and mailed.
    C. patient information sent by e-mail.
    D. all of the above.

4. A Notice of Privacy Practices is given to

    A. pharmacists.
    B. patients.
    C. business associates.
    D. other covered entities.

5. Patients' PHI may be released without authorization to

    A.   family and friends.

    B.   social workers providing services to the patient.

    C.   local newspapers.

    D.   online tabloids.

                     is an example of fraud?

7. Which of the following medical codes is used to identify drug products?

    A.   CPT-4

    B.   NDC

    C.   HCPCS

    D.   CDT-4

8. Which of the following specifies how patient information is protected on computer networks?

    A.   HIPAA Privacy Rule

    B.   quality control and assurance

    C.   Notice of Privacy Practices

    D.   Security Rule

9. The Health Insurance Portability and Accountability Act of 1996 deals with the patient's right to

    A.   get information prior to treatment.

    B.   refuse treatment.

    C.   preserve privacy.

    D.   choose a physician.

10. Violations of HIPAA can result in which of the following penalties?

    A.   criminal penalties

    B.   civil penalties

    C.   both

    D.   neither

11.   Disclosure of a patient's health information usually requires
      which of the following, except in the case of TPHCO?

      A.   the patient's approval
      B.   the physician's approval
      C.   the family's approval
      D.   all of the above

12.   *Protected health information* is defined as the stored informa-
      tion that is identified about

      A.   a federal agency.
      B.   an insurance provider.
      C.   a patient.
      D.   none of the above.

13.   Title I of HIPAA is referred to as which of the following?

      A.   electronic health information transaction standards
      B.   privacy and state law preemption
      C.   health insurance reform
      D.   all of the above

14.   Which of the following is referred to as a "covered entity"?

      A.   health insurance plans
      B.   healthcare providers
      C.   clearinghouses
      D.   all of the above

15.   Healthcare covered entities include which of the following?

      A.   providers
      B.   accreditation agencies
      C.   lawyers and collection agents
      D.   B and C

Fill in the Blank

1.   The release of PHI to any outside entity is referred to as
     _____.

2.   A "Notice of Privacy Practices" explains to patients how their
     PHI may be _____ and _____ by
     providers.

3.   The Office for Civil Rights enforces civil violations of HIPAA
     _____ standards.

4. The Employee Retirement Income and Security Act of 1974 (ERISA) regulates _____ -offered health plans.

5. Patients have a right to _____ and the protection of their private health information.

_____ confused with

9. ICD-9-CM codes are used to identify _____ _____ and conditions.

10. Civil penalties for misuse of PHI can be as high as _____ _____ in fines per year if repeated violations occur.

CASE STUDY

A pharmacy technician is asked to fax a patient's PHI to a pharmacy out of state because the patient will be traveling and will need medications there. He confirms the fax number to which he is to send the information. However, when he dials the number on the fax machine, he transposes two of the numbers and the fax goes to a different location than intended.

1. What should the pharmacy technician have included with this fax to ensure that the correct person would receive it?

2. What should the person who received this information do?

RELATED INTERNET SITES

Search for "HIPAA" at these sites for additional information related to this act.

http://aspe.hhs.gov

http://www.aafp.org

http://www.ama-assn.org

http://www.cms.hhs.gov

http://www.hhs.gov

http://www.himssanalytics.org

http://www.hipaacompliancejournal.com

http://www.privacyrights.org

REFERENCES

Abood, R. (2010). *Pharmacy Practice and the Law* (6th ed.). Burlington, MA: Jones and Bartlett.

Fink, J. L., Vivian, J. C., & Keller Reid, Kim (2005). *Pharmacy Law Digest* (40th ed.). Philadelphia Lippincott, Williams, and Wilkins.

Fred, L. Y. (2005). *Manual for Pharmacy Technicians* (3rd ed.). Bethesda, MD: ASHP.

Hopper, T. (2011). Philadelphia *Mosby's Pharmacy Technician: Principles & Practice* (3rd ed.). Saunders.

Krager, C., & Krager, D. (2008). *HIPAA for Health Care Professionals.* Clifton Park, NY: Cengage Learning.

LearnSomething (author group). (2003). *HIPAA Privacy RX: The Privacy Rule and Pharmacy Practice.* Upper Saddle River, NJ: Prentice Hall.

Peden, A. (2011). *Comparative Health Information Management* (3rd ed.). Clifton Park, NY: Cengage Learning.

Reiss, B. S., & Hall, G. D. (2010). *Guide to Federal Pharmacy Law* (7th ed.). Boynton Beach, FL: Apothecary Press.

Wager, K. A., Lee, F. W., & Glaser, J. P. (2009). *Health Care Information Systems: A Practical Approach for Health Care Management.* (2nd ed.). Hoboken, NJ: Jossey-Bass.

Workplace Safety Laws

1. Explain the bloodborne pathogen
2. Summarize the management of post-exposure evaluation and follow-up.
3. Differentiate among disinfection, sanitization, and sterilization procedures.
4. Identify sexual harassment as a form of sexual discrimination.
5. Identify four areas for which standards are mandated by the Occupational Safety and Health Administration (OSHA) for work done in a pharmacy setting.
6. Discuss the role of pharmacists and technicians in following OSHA standards in the pharmacy.
7. Summarize standard precautions.
8. State the purpose of workers' compensation laws.
9. Discuss exposure control plans.
10. Briefly describe the guidelines of an exposure control plan.

KEY TERMS

Airflow hoods—Workstations that emit a stream of highly filtered air that reduces possible contamination of the substances being used.

Biohazard symbol—An international symbol that is used to designate any substance harmful to human health, including bloodborne pathogens and medical wastes.

Bloodborne pathogen—Any infectious microorganism present in blood or other body fluids and tissues.

Chemical hygiene plan—A laboratory standard established by OSHA to reduce employees' exposure to chemicals they handle.

Compensation claim—A claim filed with the state that addresses an on-site workplace injury or illness.

Federal Register—A U.S. government publication that contains all administrative regulations, and is the primary source of information for OSHA standards.

Fire safety plan—A workplace plan detailing locations of fire alarm pull boxes, fire extinguishers, and fire sprinklers, as well as a plan for continued fire prevention training and drills.

Germicides—Agents that kill germs; also known as disinfectants.

Hazard communication plan—A system of notifying personnel of hazards by applying warning labels that signify the types and ratings of hazardous chemicals and substances.

Hazardous waste—A solid, chemical, radioactive, or infectious material that may transmit pathogens or other hazardous substances.

Material Safety Data Sheet (MSDS)—A form that is required for all hazardous chemicals or other substances that are used in laboratories or pharmacies. This form contains information about a product's name, chemical characteristics, ingredients, guidelines for safe handling, physical and health hazards, and procedures to be followed in the event of exposure.

Medical Waste Tracking Act—An act that gives OSHA the authority to inspect hazardous medical waste and cite offices for unhealthy or unsafe practices regarding such waste.

Occupational Safety and Health Administration (OSHA)—A division of the U.S. Department of Labor.

Radioactive waste—Any waste that contains or is contaminated with liquid or solid radioactive materials.

Workers' compensation—Laws that establish procedures for compensating workers who are injured on the job, with the employer paying the cost of the insurance premium for the employee.

SETTING THE SCENE

Sheila, a 26-year-old, has been working as a pharmacy technician in a chain pharmacy for 16 months. The pharmacist's name is Brad, and he is Sheila's supervisor. He is 45 years old and was divorced three years ago. For some time, Brad has been sexually harassing Sheila. Fearing for her job, she doesn't tell anyone after Brad fondles her in the storage room. Upset at what happened, Sheila takes an indefinite sick leave, which leads to Brad firing her.

Critical Thinking

- If you were in Sheila's situation, what would you do?

- After she was fired, what steps do you think Sheila could take?

- Do you think sexual harassment is, in general, considered a felony or a misdemeanor?

OVERVIEW

Many federal and state laws govern the workplace. Some federal laws ~~~ only to those businesses with a certain number of employees (such ~~~ ~~~ number of weeks per year.

Major areas include workplace safety, medical ~~ related injuries and illnesses, and unemployment or reemployment. The Occupational Safety and Health Act (OSHA) was developed to maintain a reporting system for job-related injuries and illnesses, and to reduce hazards in the workplace. In the pharmacy, this law affects the following:

- Air contaminants
- Eye and skin protection
- Flammable and combustible liquids
- The hazard communication standard

Safe working conditions must be ensured by pharmacies because biologic, electrical, chemical, and radiation hazards are encountered in pharmacy settings on a daily basis. It is important for pharmacy technicians to be aware of hazards, and to have knowledge about safety precautions. They need to know the rules necessary for eliminating or minimizing hazards.

OCCUPATIONAL SAFETY AND HEALTH ADMINISTRATION (OSHA)

In 1970, President Nixon signed the Occupational Safety and Health Act, which created the **Occupational Safety and Health Administration (OSHA)**. OSHA is a division of the U.S. Department of Labor. Workplace injuries, illnesses, and fatalities have been significantly reduced since OSHA was enacted. OSHA's mission is to ensure workplace safety and a healthy work environment for all employees.

This act created compulsory standards for health and safety in the workplace, which are enforced by OSHA. Its regulations include the following:

- Administrative requirements
- First aid
- Machinery and equipment
- Materials
- Physical workplace
- Power sources
- Processing
- Protective clothing

All employees must know the OSHA standards that apply to their business. The **Federal Register** is a U.S. government publication that contains all administrative laws and is the primary source of information for OSHA standards.

OSHA is authorized to do the following:

- Establish "separate but dependent responsibilities and rights" for employers and employees for the achievement of better safety and health conditions.
- Encourage employers and employees to reduce workplace hazards and to implement new and improved health programs.
- Develop mandatory job safety and health standards, and enforce them effectively.
- Maintain a record-keeping system to monitor job-related injuries and illnesses.

OSHA established the Occupational Exposure to Hazardous Chemicals Standard and the Bloodborne Pathogens Standard. The primary goal of the Bloodborne Pathogens Standard was to reduce occupation-related cases of HIV and hepatitis B infection among health-care workers.

Occupational Exposure to Hazardous Chemicals Standard

OSHA requires that risk assessments be performed in workplaces that use hazardous chemicals. Standard operating procedures should include the use of protective equipment, clearly defined steps to be taken in case of exposure, storage of antitoxins for emergencies, proper storage of hazardous materials, and approved methods of waste disposal.

The Occupational Exposure to Hazardous Chemicals Standard requires the following tasks to be performed by employers:

1. Inventory any and all hazardous chemicals regarding quantity, manufacturer's name, address, and chemical hazard

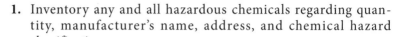

4. Develop and evaluate a chemical hygiene plan to address how to handle any spills or exposures.

Bloodborne Pathogens Standard

The term **bloodborne pathogen** refers to any infectious microorganism present in blood or other body fluids and tissues. Bloodborne pathogens are one of the most significant biohazards faced by healthcare workers. The most publicized bloodborne pathogens are human immunodeficiency virus (HIV), hepatitis B virus (HBV), and hepatitis C virus (HCV). Though pharmacy technicians usually have less chance of exposure to bloodborne pathogens in the pharmacy setting, they should still have knowledge about the dangers of these pathogens.

OSHA requires medical facilities to comply with the Bloodborne Pathogens Standard, and to prove their compliance to OSHA inspectors if necessary. This standard protects OSHA personnel who may face potential bloodborne pathogen exposure at work, and addresses the following:

1. Control and determination of exposure
2. Universal precautions
3. Administration of HBV vaccine to those potentially exposed to bloodborne pathogens while on the job
4. Post-exposure follow-up
5. Labeling and disposal of biologic wastes
6. Housekeeping and laundry functions
7. Employee training

Aseptic Technique

The goal of aseptic technique is to minimize contamination by pathogens. It involves a carefully controlled, specific set of practices and procedures. Good aseptic technique also protects healthcare workers, as well as patients, from contamination. Aseptic technique includes the practices of cleaning, sanitizing, and disinfecting to remove impurities on equipment or personnel, and to reduce the amount of microorganisms to the greatest possible extent. It is important to use aseptic technique to prevent contamination of an otherwise sterile medication. Aseptic technique is of the utmost importance during surgery, as well as in many other practical applications. Healthcare personnel and equipment, as well as the environment, are capable of transferring microorganisms. In the pharmacy, the use of aseptic technique is generally referred to as "medical asepsis" or "clean technique" for sterile compounding (mainly of parenteral products to decrease risk to patients).

The United States Pharmacopeia (USP) details the procedures and requirements for compounding sterile medications and sets standards applicable to all practice settings in which sterile preparations are compounded. USP Chapter 797 is considered a requirement for good aseptic technique, and therefore, pharmacies may be subject to inspection against these standards by the Joint Commission, FDA, and other accreditation organizations. High-risk compounding is the area of most concern. This includes non-sterile ingredients such as bulk powders (morphine, other narcotics, etc.) and final containers that are nonsterile and must be terminally sterilized (nuclear pharmaceuticals). High-risk compounding requires preparation in Class 100 clean rooms or areas and separate anterooms between these clean areas and the rest of the facility.

According to the USP, the responsibilities of the person who supervises compounding activities include the following:

- Personnel must be adequately educated, instructed, and skilled.
- Ingredients must have correct identity, quality, and amount.
- Open or partial containers must be properly stored.
- Bacterial endotoxins must be minimized.
- Proper and adequate sterilization must be used.
- Equipment must be clean, accurate, and appropriate.

- Potential harm from added substances must be evaluated before dispensing.

- Packaging must be appropriate (for sterility and stability).

- Workers in the compounding environment must maintain sterility of pre-sterilized items.

- Labels must be appropriate and complete.

Personal Protective Equipment (PPE)

Under OSHA's guidelines, personal protective equipment (PPE) is used to protect employees from bodily fluids, including blood. It can prevent contamination through the skin, wounds, and mucous membranes. Personal protective equipment includes the following, put on in this sequential order:

- Gowns or lab coats—worn over regular clothing; they may be laundered and reused.

- Face shields, goggles, and masks—used when there is a risk of splashing or splattering with bodily fluids. Face shields and goggles may be reused; masks may either be single-use or made for multiple uses.

- Gloves—used when there is a possibility of hand contamination. Gloves are to be used one time only.

Eyewash stations should be provided so that workers can wash out their eyes, or flush mucous membranes with water, in cases of accidental exposure to bodily fluids or chemicals. Figure 7-1 shows PPE, while Figure 7-2 shows an eyewash station.

What Would You Do?

While John was compounding in the laboratory, he was splashed in the eyes with a chemical. He went to the men's room and washed his face in the sink. He did not use the eyewash station. After returning to work, he found that his eyes remained irritated, and he could not see very well. If you were John, what would you do in this situation?

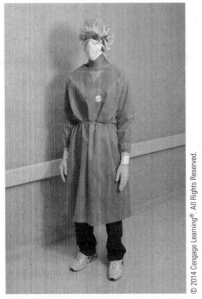

Figure 7-1 Proper personal protective equipment.

Figure 7-2 Eyewash station.

Exposure Control Plan

Exposure control plans should be printed so that they can be readily referred to. Per OSHA guidelines, they should be updated annually. These plans are intended to lower the risks for exposure to dangerous or infectious materials, and to prevent bloodborne diseases from being transmitted. OSHA has regulations about a variety of hazardous substances, including those that are radioactive. A "universal precautions statement" should be included that explains the type of precautions that are to be taken by every employee who may be exposed to hazards. Exposure control plans usually include the following hazards:

- Sharps

- Bins and pails

- Broken glassware

- Laundry

- Substances used for vaccinations

  Exposure control plans focus on several areas:

- The types of exposure that may occur in the workplace

- Personal protective equipment

- Housekeeping requirements for the workplace

- Provision of hepatitis B vaccines at no cost for employees who have had a potential bloodborne pathogen exposure at work

- Warning labeling and training about exposure and post-exposure procedures

- Good documentation concerning medical records, training ses-

cur in a variety of ways, including the following:

- Needle sticks (or sticks with other potentially contaminated sharp objects)

- Splashing of substances into mucous membranes or other body areas

- Contact with intact or non-intact skin

In the pharmacy, exposure can commonly occur during compounding by contact with sharps, splashing, and even inhalation of hazardous substances. Eyewash facilities should be available so that the technician can thoroughly rinse out the body area of possible contamination. Immediately after exposure, the technician should clean the area of exposure with water or soap and water (if possible), and inform his or her supervisor of the need to be evaluated and/or treated because of the exposure.

What Would You Do?

Mary, a pharmacy technician working in a hospital pharmacy, was splashed when she accidentally dropped a glass medication bottle into an airflow hood. The moving air carried the medication onto her face. She was not wearing a mask but was wearing protective glasses. The medication partially entered her nose. If you were Mary, what would you do in this situation?

Pharmacy Hazard Regulation

Potential hazards in the pharmacy should be addressed by a pharmacy hazard regulation standard. OSHA provides clear instruction about possible hazards as they relate to the practice of pharmacy, and will conduct a free assessment of the workplace upon request. Personnel in the pharmacy should be familiar with OSHA's guidelines concerning hazardous substances, and methods that can help them avoid contamination regardless of the transmission pathway (by inhalation, via the mouth, or through the skin).

Good worker training upon hiring, and thereafter on an annual (or even more regular) schedule, can minimize pharmacy hazards. Specific worker training, focusing on the actual individual job requirements, is critical so that each employee is thoroughly prepared for his or her own job's potential hazards, and knows which particular hazardous substances he or she may encounter. Retraining may be required if an employee has not received OSHA training for more than one year, and is no longer familiar with all of the basic OSHA training requirements related to his or her workplace. Retraining may be required when employees change job duties, because the hazards they must be familiar with may change along with their duties. When new hazardous substances are introduced into a workplace, it is also recommended that further training be given. After an accident or near-accident occurs, further training should take place.

OSHA generally requires that individuals who teach employees about OSHA safety requirements have the following credentials, related to the individual subjects that they teach:

- Thorough experience with the subject

- Strong knowledge about the subject

- Previous training about the subject prior to their own ability to teach it.

In most workplaces, safety managers or supervisors conduct OSHA training. OSHA provides training for instructors through videos and software. The OSHA reference materials library is located at http://www.osha.gov (click on "Compliance Assistance"; "Training and Reference Materials Library").

Along with proper training, the use of warning labels and MSDS complement a safe pharmacy setting. Chemicals or drugs that are considered hazardous include those that are carcinogenic, corrosive, irritating, sensitizing, or toxic. Every year, an updated list of potentially hazardous drugs is released by the National Institute for Occupational Safety and Health (NIOSH).

You Be the Judge

A compounding pharmacy provided its workers with gowns, goggles, gloves, and similar equipment on a regular basis, but did not provide an airflow hood because the types of substances compounded there did not require such a device. Because of a fire that had occurred in a nearby compounding pharmacy, this pharmacy was asked to quickly handle the compounding of cytotoxic agents required for several different patients. A pharmacy technician who knew that an airflow hood was required for work with these agents refused to complete the compounding, and was reprimanded. He notified OSHA that the pharmacist was completing the compounding of cytotoxic agents without the proper equipment. What do

dled in the workplace. A chemical hygiene p details the ways that each employee should handle the chemicals that are used. Included in the plan should be sections that focus on administrative and engineering controls, as well as PPE. The plan should outline emergency preparedness procedures concerning acceptable and unacceptable procedures; the use of compressed gases, particularly hazardous ones; potential explosions; proper labeling; laminar **airflow hoods**; and safety equipment.

Fire Safety Plan

Pharmacy technicians and other pharmacy employees should be aware of procedures to follow in case of fire. They should know where fire extinguishers are located, and be familiar with their use. Technicians should understand how to use fire blankets or heavy toweling to smother fires on clothing. In addition, they should be familiar with the location of emergency exits. Every **fire safety plan** must be compliant with OSHA regulations. These plans should include written (and posted) procedures with clearly marked escape routes. OSHA requires employers to provide the following as part of their fire safety plan:

- Fire alarm pull boxes, tested on a regular basis
- Fire extinguishers
- Fire sprinklers, tested on a regular basis
- Fire prevention training
- Fire drills, conducted on a regular basis

Figure 7-3 shows a clearly marked escape route for use in the case of a fire.

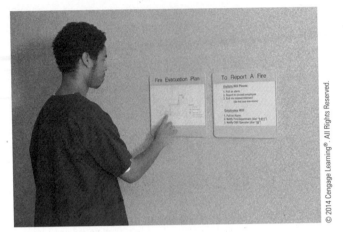

Figure 7-3 Fire evacuation plan.

What Would You Do?

Shannon was working with electronic equipment in her pharmacy when a power cord caught fire. She was extremely nervous, and could not remember what she should do in case of fire. If you were Shannon, what procedures would you follow?

Electrical Safety

Pharmacy technicians must be familiar with electricity and how it relates to the pharmacy setting. All electrical equipment holds the potential for becoming a fire hazard if used improperly or if in poor working condition. Electrical shocks can and do occur, but can be minimized by good training and maintenance of equipment. Extension cords and multi-outlet electrical plugs should be used minimally. Overloaded electrical circuits can result in fires, so outlets should never be overused. Every employee should know the location of the circuit breaker box for the pharmacy. Spills of various drugs or chemicals should be avoided at all locations, but especially near electrical outlets, equipment, or power strips.

Radiation Safety

Radioactive waste is any waste that contains or is contaminated with liquid or solid radioactive materials. This waste must be clearly labeled as radioactive and never placed in an incinerator, down a drain, or in public areas. It should be removed only by a licensed removal service.

Radiation hazard symbols are used to inform personnel of areas where radiation is in use. Storage areas of radioactive materials and radioactive material containers are likewise labeled. To be safe from radiation, it is important to maintain good standards of radiation exposure protection. Exposure times must be no longer than the minimum required for the procedure to be performed. Proper shielding must be worn, and correct distances from the radiation source maintained. Pharmacy technicians must be trained in the use of radioactive materials if they are required to work with them in any manner.

A hazard communication plan details the hazardous substances that are present in the workplace. It explains to employees the potential health risks. Material safety data sheets (MSDS) are part of a hazard communication plan, and pharmacy technicians must be familiar with the MSDS for each chemical or substance used. (MSDS will be discussed in more detail later in this chapter.) Chemicals must be properly contained, sealed, and labeled. Figure 7-4 shows clear and accurate labeling of a chemical in the workplace.

The National Fire Protection Association (NFPA) is the world's primary advocate of fire prevention and safety. Its mission is to set codes and standards, conduct research, and provide training and education about safety from fire and other hazards. The NFPA provides a colored, numbered hazard identification symbol for every chemical that may be potentially hazardous. The top diamond indicates the flammability potential of the chemical. The left diamond indicates the potential health hazard of the chemical. The right diamond shows the stability or reactivity potential of the chemical. The bottom diamond features specialized information, such as biohazard or radioactivity information. The numbers used in this system range from 0 (meaning "no hazard") to 4 (meaning "extremely hazardous"). The NFPA hazard identification system is demonstrated in Figure 7-5.

Medical Waste Tracking Act

Hospitals, laboratories, pharmacies, nursing homes, and other healthcare facilities generate 3.2 million tons of hazardous medical waste each year. Much of this waste is dangerous, especially when it is potentially infectious or radioactive. OSHA may, under the authority of the **Medical Waste Tracking Act**, inspect hazardous medical wastes and cite offices for unhealthy or unsafe practices regarding them.

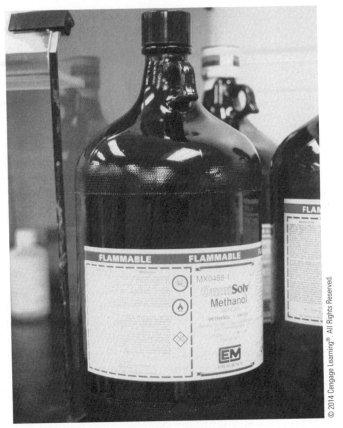

Figure 7-4 Proper labeling of chemical substances.

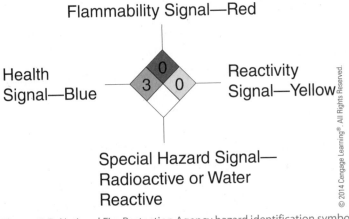

Flammability Signal—Red

Health
Signal—Blue

Reactivity
Signal—Yellow

Special Hazard Signal—
Radioactive or Water
Reactive

Figure 7-5 National Fire Protection Agency hazard identification symbol.

Hazardous medical wastes include four major types of medical waste: solid, chemical, radioactive, and infectious. An approved sharps container that is puncture-proof must be provided for disposal of sharp objects. These containers are very important for infectious medical wastes such as bloodborne pathogens. Chemical wastes include **germicides**, cleaning solvents, and pharmaceuticals. These wastes can create a hazardous situation (a fire or explosion) in either an institutional or a com-

which also must provide specific information of chemicals safely.

Other hazardous wastes must be contained in leak-proof plastic biohazard bags. These materials should only be handled by reputable and licensed medical waste handlers. Medical wastes are often disposed of by incineration.

Focus On...

Solid Wastes

Solid waste is not considered hazardous, but can pollute the environment. Mandatory recycling programs have helped reduce some of the solid wastes produced in the United States.

Focus On...

The Medical Waste Tracking Act

The federal law that authorizes OSHA to inspect hazardous medical wastes and to cite pharmacies for unsafe or unhealthy practices regarding these wastes is the Medical Waste Tracking Act.

Disposal of Hazardous Materials and Spill Cleanup

Containers that hold hazardous wastes must be labeled with the **biohazard symbol** to alert employees to the dangerousness of the materials within. Figure 7-6 shows the biohazard symbol.

Figure 7-6 Biohazard symbol.

The term **hazardous waste** includes many different substances and materials, including those that have been exposed to blood or body fluids. Other potential hazardous wastes include the following:

- Gloves and other protective clothing or equipment
- Dressings and equipment from medical procedures
- Paper towels and other cleaning equipment
- Sharps, including needles, syringes, and blades
- Microscope slides

Hazardous waste containers are available in a variety of different sizes and thicknesses, and are made from hard and soft plastics and other substances. Pharmacy technicians who work with hazardous waste containers must wear full protective equipment, and general cleaning staff should not have access to these containers. Often, an outside company is hired to remove and dispose of all hazardous waste. Laws and regulations concerning the transportation, storage, and handling of hazardous materials can be found at http://phmsa.dot.gov (click on "Hazmat Safety Community"; "Hazardous Materials Information Center"). Figure 7-7 shows hazardous waste containers.

When a spill occurs, the specific policies and procedures of the workplace must be followed carefully. Spill kits are used to properly clean up a variety of spills. These kits contain protective equipment and clothing that keep workers safe from various types of contamination from materials that may be spilled at work. They usually contain most of the following items:

- Disposable scoops
- Eye protection
- Gauze or toweling (disposable after use)
- Gloves (usually both latex gloves and utility gloves)

Figure 7-7 (a) Biohazard and (b) sharps containers.

- Disposable gowns or coveralls
- Plastic containers that are leak- and puncture-resistant
- Powder designed for absorption
- Protective equipment
- Respirators
- Sealable bags made of thick plastic
- Shoe covers
- Spill pads
- Warning signs that indicate a spill has occurred

When a spill occurs, all broken fragments of containers and equipment should be put into thick plastic bags or containers. Liquid substances should be absorbed using pads or towels. Dry substances such as powders should be cleaned up with wet gauze or towels. The spill area should be rinsed off with water. Then, a detergent should be used to wash the area, followed by a second rinse with water. Work from the outer edges of the spill, moving inward. If the area is carpeted, special absorbent powder is often used to lift the spilled substances from the carpeting. It is important to have special vacuum cleaners on hand that are to be used only for hazardous materials that have been spilled. Every spill should be documented in an incident report and filed at the workplace. OSHA forms for reporting and summarizing work-related injuries and illnesses can be found at http://www.osha.gov (click on "Recordkeeping").

Training and Accident Report Documentation

Each pharmacy must have a written training program detailing how pharmacy technicians will be provided with information and training related to workplace hazards. OSHA dictates that training should include information about hazards in the work area, locations of hazard lists and MSDS manuals, and explanations of MSDS manuals and hazardous chemical labeling systems, as well as any measures that pharmacy technicians may use to protect themselves. Training logs should be kept, signed, and dated upon completion of each type of training. Accident reports are required if accidents occur and must contain the following:

- The pharmacy's name and address
- The pharmacy technician's name, address, and phone number
- Where, when, and how the accident occurred, and what was involved
- The nature of the injury
- Medical treatment, hospitalization, or other follow-up information

A log of all occupational injuries and illnesses must be kept by employers for five years following the end of the calendar year to which they relate, and these must be available for inspection by the U.S. Department of Health and Human Services, the U.S. Department of Labor, and state officials. OSHA standards for healthcare settings may be obtained from state or regional OSHA offices, or from OSHA at the following address:

U.S. Department of Labor, Occupational Safety and Health Administration

Directorate of Health Standards Programs

200 Constitution Avenue NW

Washington, D.C. 20210

What Would You Do?

Mark is a pharmacy technician. Three weeks after he was hired, his pharmacist set up an OSHA training class. Mark was sick during this time, and unable to attend. On his first day back at work, he was attempting to clean up a corrosive chemical spill on the floor. Since he had missed the training, Mark was unsure of the proper procedures to follow, and wore latex gloves while cleaning up the spill. If you were Mark, what would you do in this situation?

OSHA Record-Keeping Regulations

OSHA may make unannounced visits to the workplace, and may issue citations or penalties of up to $1,000 per violation to an employer who does not provide a safe environment. The OSHA regulations contain a clinical hygiene plan that addresses training, information requirements, and provisions that must be implemented for chemical exposure in the pharmacy setting. Chemical inventories must be taken, and **material**

sheets pertinent to the workplace.

Employers are required to provide a hazard communication program to employees within 30 days of hire. A hazard communication program is designed to inform employees about hazardous substances in the workplace, their potential harmful effects, and appropriate control measures.

Violations of OSHA

Some of the most common violations of OSHA regulations are the following:

- No eyewash facilities available at facilities that are required to have them
- No labeling (or improper labeling) of hazardous chemicals
- No MSDS for each hazardous chemical

Employee Responsibilities

Some states follow OSHA regulations regarding the responsibilities of employees, while others adopt their own regulations. OSHA does not directly cite employees when they breach the organization's regulations. However, in most states, regulations are similar to those established by OSHA concerning employee responsibilities. Employees should do the following so that they understand their responsibilities:

- They should read all OSHA posters.
- They should follow all OSHA standards for proper compliance.

- They should follow the regulations of their employer concerning the use of protective equipment while at work.

- They should report any hazardous conditions to their supervisor.

- They should report any on-the-job injuries or illnesses to their supervisor and ask for prompt treatment.

- They should cooperate with OSHA inspectors if they are questioned about workplace safety and health conditions.

- They should understand and exercise their rights as set forth by OSHA.

You Be the Judge

Joshua took a special OSHA course and understood his responsibilities on the job. One day, when he was doing his routine work and dealing with chemical substances, he did not use protective equipment for safety. What could be the result of Joshua's actions?

WORKERS' COMPENSATION

Workers' compensation laws establish procedures for compensating workers who are injured on the job, with the employer paying the cost of the insurance premium for the employee. These state and federal laws allow claims for compensation to be filed with state or federal governments in lieu of lawsuits against employers. The laws require workers to accept workers' compensation as the exclusive remedy for on-the-job injuries. Federal laws cover workers in Washington, D.C., coal miners, federal employees, and maritime workers. State laws cover those workers not protected under federal statutes. There are five types of state compensation benefits for which workers may apply:

1. Medical treatment, including hospitalization, medical and surgical services, medications, and prosthetic devices

2. Temporary disability indemnity in the form of weekly cash payments to the injured or ill employee

3. Permanent disability indemnity, comprising either a lump-sum award or a weekly or monthly cash payment

4. Death benefits for survivors, consisting of cash payments to dependents of employees killed while on the job

5. Rehabilitation benefits paid for vocational or medical rehabilitation

One area of concern in the pharmacy workplace is in the physical design of the facility, and how it relates to the employees' ability to conduct normal day-to-day tasks without straining their backs, legs, arms, etc. This should be an ergonomic design so that items may be easily reached and are not too high to be easily accessed by the employees (Figure 7-8). Packages should not be of excessive size or weight; this will help prevent strains caused by lifting or moving them. Easy-access shelv-

workplace to his or her supervisor. An injury report and **compensation claim** are then filed with the correct state workers' compensation agency, along with forms from the attending or designated physician who examines and treats the employee. When a claim is filed, all questions must be fully and thoroughly answered. A pharmacy employee may be required to file the physician's report with the state workers' compensation agency. Each state has different requirements concerning waiting periods and other filing specifics.

Workers' compensation originated shortly after the turn of the 20th century, and was among the first social insurance programs. Most states had adopted workers' compensation laws by 1920. Before these

© Tyler Olson/www.Shutterstock.com

Figure 7-8 Physical layout of the pharmacy requires that items be easily reached by employees.

laws, workers who were injured on the job could ask their employers for compensation for their injuries, but there was no guaranteed outcome for their requests. Many employers avoided paying for their workers' injuries by claiming that the workers understood job-related dangers and hazards, and accepted these working conditions when they were employed. Some workers accepted more dangerous jobs in exchange for higher pay, and thus received no compensation from their employers when an accident occurred.

After workers' compensation laws were enacted, most claims no longer required the worker to prove that the employer was at fault and therefore responsible for the injuries they sustained. After an injury, most employees could receive up to two-thirds of their weekly pay while they were recovering. Families of workers who died on the job would usually receive reimbursement for burial costs, plus up to two-thirds of the deceased worker's weekly pay, every week, up to a predetermined total amount.

Focus On...

Workers' Compensation

Workers' compensation is a form of insurance established by federal and state statutes that provides reimbursement for workers who are injured on the job.

SEXUAL HARASSMENT

Sexual harassment occurs in a variety of circumstances. Anyone may be sexually harassed. A man or a woman may be either the victim or the harasser. A victim and their harasser do not need to be of the opposite sex. A victim may be either the person actually being harassed or a coworker who overhears the harassment.

The Civil Rights Act of 1964 protects employees from sexual harassment that occurs on the job. The employer is strictly liable for the acts of supervisors who sexually harass employees that they are in charge of, as well as for some acts of harassment by coworkers and clients. Employers must provide a written policy on sexual harassment.

Written pharmacy policies about sexual harassment should include the following:

1. A statement that sexual harassment of employees will not be tolerated

2. A statement that any employee who feels harassed must bring the matter to the immediate attention of specially designated person within the company

3. A statement about the confidentiality of all related incidents and specific disciplinary action against harassers

4. Procedures that will be followed if harassment occurs

Traditionally, sexual harassment has involved the trading of sexual favors for advancement or rewards within a company. Sexual harassment is a form of discrimination. It is the responsibility of all employees not to discriminate against their fellow employees in any manner, including

These steps for stopping sexual harassment are suggested, and should be followed in this order:

1. Tell the harasser to stop the behavior.

2. Tell another colleague, or tell the harasser that you will tell another person—your Human Resources representatives are usually the best initial choice, followed by senior management. Your employee handbook should list the steps that you can take.

3. Document the harassment.

4. If no help is given by your company, seek legal advice.

Individuals who are prosecuted for sexual harassment can experience a variety of consequences if their actions are proven. These include loss of employment (which may seriously affect future employment opportunities), fines, imprisonment, remedial classes, court costs, and publication throughout the community of the individual's actions. Websites exist today that publish the names, photos, and addresses of convicted sexual offenders of many different types. An example of this type of website is http://www.familywatchdog.us.

What Would You Do?

Richard was talking to one of his coworkers, Nicole, in the pharmacy. He told her a rather rude joke of a sexual nature. Nicole was offended by the joke. If you were Nicole, what would you do?

SUMMARY

Federal and state laws specifically provide for employee safety and welfare. These laws include workplace safety regulations. Congress passed the Occupational Safety and Health Act in 1970 to prevent workplace disease and injuries. This act includes regulations for the physical workplace, machinery and equipment, materials, power sources, processing, protective clothing, and first aid, as well as administrative requirements.

In the pharmacy, pharmacy technicians should use PPE. They should be familiar with their pharmacy's exposure control plan, and follow post-exposure procedures. Safety in the pharmacy should be maintained by establishing and following fire, electrical, and radiation safety plans. OSHA has established record-keeping methods that must be followed concerning exposure to hazardous materials, as well as fire and safety training documentation.

OSHA may make unannounced visits to the workplace and may issue citations or penalties of up to $1,000 per violation to employers who do not provide safe environments. OSHA may also, under the authority of the Medical Waste Tracking Act, inspect hazardous medical wastes and cite pharmacies or medical offices for unhealthy or unsafe practices regarding them.

Each employer must have a written training program detailing how employees will be provided with information about hazards in the work area, locations of hazard lists and MSDS manuals, and hazardous chemical labeling systems. Hazardous materials must be disposed of properly by using protective equipment, approved containers, and correct labeling. Special removal agencies are usually employed to transfer hazardous materials out of the workplace. Common hazardous chemicals found in the pharmacy include pharmaceuticals such as epinephrine, nitroglycerin, physostigmine salicylate, chemotherapy agents, reserpine, chromium, and more.

Pharmacy technicians should have information about workers' compensation in case any on-the-job injuries occur. They should understand the correct methods of filing workers' compensation claims and understand the benefits of their pharmacy's plan. The Civil Rights Act protects employees from sexual harassment that occurs on the job. Employers must provide a written policy on this matter.

SETTING THE SCENE

The following discussion and responses relate to the opening "Setting the Scene" scenario:

- Sheila should have told Brad to stop all of the harassment or she would report him to the proper authorities.

Multiple Choice

1. How long must pharmacies keep logs of occupational injuries available for inspection?

   A. 1 year
   B. 3 years
   C. 5 years
   D. 10 years

2. Workers' compensation includes which of the following types of laws?

   A. state law
   B. federal law
   C. both state and federal law
   D. civil (private) law

3. Which legislation protects against sexual harassment?

   A. OSHA
   B. Equal Employment Opportunity Act
   C. Civil Rights Act
   D. both B and C

4. The blue quadrant of the National Fire Protection Association diamond-shaped symbol for hazardous materials indicates a

   A. health hazard.
   B. fire hazard.
   C. reactivity hazard.
   D. specific hazard.

5. The OSHA regulations contain a clinical hygiene plan that addresses which of the following?

    A. training and provisions that must be implemented for chemical exposure in the pharmacy setting

    B. training and information requirements that must be implemented for equipment and computer parts

    C. training and information requirements that must be provided for pharmacy technicians to be licensed

    D. all of the above

6. Which of the following is required for accident reports when accidents occur?

    A. pharmacy's name and address

    B. when, where, and how the accident occurred

    C. the nature of the injury

    D. all of the above

7. OSHA may issue citations or penalties of up to what amount per violation to employers who do not provide safe environments?

    A. $1,000

    B. $5,000

    C. $10,000

    D. $50,000

8. The general purpose of OSHA 1970 was to require all employers to ensure employee

    A. security and a clean environment.

    B. safety and health.

    C. enjoyment and productivity.

    D. none of the above.

9. Radioactive wastes should be removed by which of the following methods?

    A. placing them into an incinerator

    B. pouring them down the drain

    C. storing them in public areas

    D. engaging a licensed removal service

10. All of the following are state compensation benefits that may be applied for, except

    A. medical treatment.

    B. rehabilitation benefits.

    C. death benefits for survivors.

    D. exemptions from state and federal taxes.

11. Standard precautions should be followed if the pharmacy technician is exposed to which of the following?

    A. chemical materials
    B. human body fluids
    C. dangerous gases
    D. radioactive substances

12. When pharmacy technicians change hazardous waste bags,

    B. maintain records of all work-related injuries and illnesses.
    C. keep records only if they feel it necessary.
    D. maintain vacation records.

14. Pharmacies must provide safety training to pharmacy technicians

    A. upon firing them.
    B. upon hiring them.
    C. at least once a month.
    D. if they are expectant mothers.

15. Which of the following forms is required for all hazardous chemicals or substances used in the pharmacy?

    A. CMS-1500
    B. IRS Form 941
    C. TRICARE
    D. MSDS

Fill in the Blank

1. OSHA was developed to maintain a reporting system for job-related _____ and reduce hazards in the _____.

2. Hazardous medical wastes include four major types of medical waste: solid, chemical, infectious, and _____.

3. Radioactive waste must be clearly _____ as radioactive and never placed into an incinerator, down a drain, or in _____ areas.

4. Record management of workers' compensation cases varies by _____ .

5. Eyewash stations should be available for _____ decontamination if a technician is exposed to _____ _____ or blood substances.

6. Biohazard symbols alert the pharmacy technician to _____ materials.

7. Proper personal protective _____ must be worn at all times.

8. The single most important means of preventing the spread of infection is _____ and _____ hand hygiene by all pharmacy technicians.

9. Each MSDS contains basic information about the specific _____ or product.

10. The exposure control plan is designed to minimize risk of exposure to _____ material and bloodborne disease.

CASE STUDY

Brian is a pharmacy technician who was asked by his supervisor to take compounded medicinal fluids to a local nursing home.

On the way, he was involved in a car accident that was not his fault and was injured. He was hospitalized for one week with mild head injuries and a fractured left leg. After being released from the hospital, he had to do physical therapy for four months. Though he lost a total of four and a half months of work, Brian did not have any health insurance.

1. Who must Brian report to in order to obtain workers' compensation?

2. Who must pay for Brian's medical expenses?

3. What must Brian's supervisor do on his behalf?

RELATED INTERNET SITES

http://phmsa.dot.gov; **Search for** *"Hazardous Materials."*

http://www.cdc.gov

http://www.eeoc.gov

http://www.osha.....

http://www.workerscompensation.com

REFERENCES

American Academy of Orthopedic Surgeons (author group). (2007). *Bloodborne Pathogens (American College of Emergency Physicians)* (5th ed.). Burlington, MA: Jones and Bartlett.

Boland, M. L. (2005). *Sexual Harassment in the Workplace. Naperville, IL:* Sphinx.

Fink, J. L., Vivian, J. C., & Keller Reid, K. (2005). *Pharmacy Law Digest* (40th ed.). Philadelphia: Lippincott Williams & Wilkins.

Johnston, M., & Gricar, J. (2010). *Sterile Products and Aseptic Techniques for the Pharmacy Technician* (2nd ed.). Englewood Cliffs, NJ: Prentice Hall.

Kennamer, M. (2006). *Basic Infection Control for Healthcare Providers* (2nd ed.). Clifton Park, NY: Cengage Learning.

Moini, J. (2010). *The Pharmacy Technician—A Comprehensive Approach* (2nd ed.). Clifton Park, NY: Cengage Learning.

Moran, M. (2011). *The OSHA Answer Book* (10th ed.). Orange Park, FL: Moran Associates.

Priz, E. (2010). *Worker's Compensation: A Field Guide for Employers.* Charleston, SC: BookSurge.

Uselton, J. P., Kienle, P., & Murdaugh, L. B. (2010). *Assuring Continuous Compliance with Joint Commission Standards: A Pharmacy Guide* (8th ed.). Bethesda, MD: American Society of Health-Systems Pharmacists.

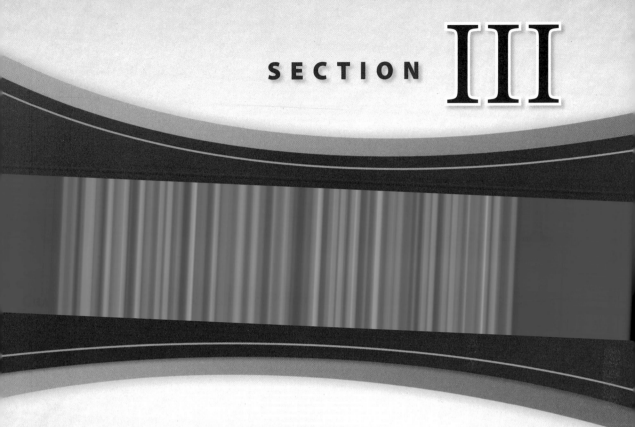

SECTION III

State Laws and Pharmacy Practice

2. Explain the role of pharmacy technicians in the processing of prescriptions.

3. List drug labeling requirements.

4. Explain state law as it relates to pharmacy ownership.

5. Discuss patient records and drug review.

6. List computer regulations.

7. Give the minimum requirements for a pharmacy.

8. Define electronic files.

9. Describe patient counseling under OBRA-90.

10. Explain prescription drug orders.

KEY TERMS

Auxiliary labels—Labels applied to drug containers that supply additional information, such as whether to take the medication with or without food, potential adverse effects, whether to avoid taking with alcohol, etc.

DEA number—A multi-digit number assigned to a healthcare practitioner that allows him or her to write prescriptions for controlled substances.

Downtime—A period of time when a computer or computer system is not operational, for any of a variety of reasons.

Drug history—A history of a patient's medication use over a reasonable period of time, usually for at least the last five years; it includes all documented information on prescription medications, non-prescription (OTC) medications, and supplements.

Fax paper—A special paper that burns a thermal image of a transmitted document without using regular paper and printer ink or toner; this type of paper usually causes the burned text and/or images to fade over time.

NDC number—A product identifier used for drugs intended for human use; "NDC" stands for "National Drug Code."

Pharmacy compounding—Creating a new mixture or compound by blending or mixing two or more medications and other substances in a licensed pharmacy.

SETTING THE SCENE

Mrs. Johnstone brings a prescription to your pharmacy. As a pharmacy technician, you realize that she is covered by Medicaid. You dispense her prescription, the pharmacist checks it, and initials the prescription. Mrs. Johnstone takes her medication and leaves the pharmacy.

Critical Thinking

- What should the pharmacist have done differently to best benefit the patient?

- Did the pharmacist ignore any state or federal laws? Explain fully.

- If the patient had a severe adverse effect and ended up in the emergency department, who would be responsible: the pharmacist, physician, pharmacy technician, or patient?

OVERVIEW

State laws vary widely. They regulate pharmacy practice, minimum requirements, and how pharmacists and pharmacy technicians are qualified so that they can legally practice. Pharmacists and pharmacy technicians must learn and understand how their state's laws differ from federal law, which is regularly addressed in most publications of the industry. Under state law, pharmacists must be licensed, and must follow the rules and regulations of their state board of pharmacy. In each state, this agency determines how prescriptions are processed, how practitioners may place drug orders, and how the Drug Enforcement Administration (DEA) will handle the use of controlled substances. The use of computerized dispensing systems is now the standard in many practices because of improved dispensing time, accuracy, and cross-checking of information.

Most states have their own regulations for electronic transmission of prescriptions, which usually require the prescriber's full information to appear. Drug product selection laws, drug product substitution laws, and generic substitution laws are designed to regulate how pharmacists may dispense a different drug product than the one that was prescribed.

Both state and federal legislatures have enacted mandatory Medicaid patient counseling requirements for pharmacists. OBRA-90 dictates how pharmacists must counsel Medicaid patients, whether in person or by telephone. The practice of pharmacy compounding is also regulated by OBRA-90, which limits payments for unlabeled indications. This may affect compounded prescriptions under Medicaid but, otherwise, there is no actual restriction on the practice of compounding.

STATE LAWS AFFECTING PHARMACY PRACTICE

Pharmacists and pharmacy technicians need to be informed about the state and federal regulations that regulate pharmacy practice. The FDA regulates medications, including controlled substances, and medical devices. State agencies, including the state boards of pharmacy, regulate pharmacy practice on a daily basis. A *board of pharmacy* is a government organization that creates uniform regulations to protect public health in a state or other jurisdiction. Boards of pharmacy in the United States are found in all 50 states, the District of Columbia, Guam, Puerto Rico, and the Virgin Islands. Boards of pharmacy are discussed in greater detail in Chapter 9.

State laws regulating pharmacy vary widely. Because of this, the National Association of Boards of Pharmacy (NABP) has created informative, well-organized tables of information that enable pharmacists and pharmacy technicians to quickly find their state's position on a variety of pharmacy-related activities. These tables include information about state boards of pharmacy, examination requirements, internships, registration, training, licensure, transfers, renewals, continuing education, disciplinary actions, status of pharmacy technicians, places of practice, wholesaling, distributing, drug control, drug product selection, prescription requirements, transmissions, patient counseling, prescribers, non-controlled and controlled substances, and more.

The NABP developed and published the *Model Pharmacy Practice Act* to promote, preserve, and protect the public safety, health, and welfare by effectively controlling and regulating the practice of pharmacy. This act addresses the licensure of pharmacists, registration of pharmacy technicians, and control of the activities of all people or businesses that manufacture, sell, or distribute drugs or devices used in the dispensing of drugs, along with many other equipment and materials related to the pharmacy field.

What Would You Do?

Tara is a pharmacy technician who recently moved from Maine to Florida. According to the NABP, if you were Tara, what would you have to do in order to be able to practice in Florida? (For reference, see Chapter 9.)

MINIMUM REQUIREMENTS FOR A PHARMACY

Pharmacies are required to have enough space to conduct all of their needed activities, and must have designated patient counseling areas. These are not required to be separate rooms, but simply areas where patient counseling may occur without too much distraction or interference from normal pharmacy activities (Figure 8-1). They must supply reference materials for patients to educate them about medications and other products. Drug storage must be controlled and orderly, and compliant with proper temperature and storage requirements.

All facilities, equipment, and personnel must adhere to Occupational Safety and Health Administration (OSHA) requirements. Proper sinks must be installed, with hot and cold running water. A comprehensive security system must be in place. A complete fire-safety plan, including training of all pharmacy staff, must be in place. A hazard communication plan must be established. The pharmacy must be completely stocked with needed equipment and supplies.

Figure 8-1 Patient counseling areas are required in all pharmacies.

Patients must be able to privately disclose their PHI. There must always be a pharmacist on duty when the pharmacy is open, though a sign may be placed at the counter for short periods if the pharmacist is temporarily unavailable. Quality control and training programs must be in place. Policies and procedural manuals must be created and followed in an orderly fashion. Licensure must be maintained continually. Prescription drug orders must be received, verified, and processed in a manner consistent with

authorities, as directed by the state board of pharmacy.

You Be the Judge

A new drugstore was about to open in Minnesota. The pharmacist tried to follow the minimum requirements of his state. The store opened and, soon after, was inspected by the state board of pharmacy. The inspector discovered that fire safety and hazard communication plans were not in place. What are the likely consequences of this situation?

PROCESSING OF PRESCRIPTIONS

The role of pharmacy technicians in the processing of prescriptions requires concentration in order to ensure that all steps are completed properly. According to state law, when a prescription is submitted to a pharmacy for processing, the pharmacy technician must do the following:

- Receive the prescription and verify that all of the information it contains is completed and clear so that it will be correctly filled. Prescriptions may be handwritten on prescription pads, sent electronically to the pharmacy, or even called in by telephone. In some states, only licensed pharmacists or pharmacist interns can take prescriptions over the phone.

- Translate the prescription so that the information it indicates can be correctly entered into the computer system, and so that the prescription can be labeled with clear instructions for the patient. If there is any question about what was intended by the prescriber, he or she should be called and asked for clarification.

- Enter the prescription information into the computer system correctly and completely and make sure that the information in the computer exactly matches the printed labels (one for the medication container and one for the packaging that holds the container). The pharmacist should initial both of these labels, either via computer or by hand, after verifying that they are correct.

- Verify the patient's insurance information and eligibility. If the patient has Medicaid, the prescription must be written on a tamper-proof prescription blank. Some states requiring special prescription blanks for controlled substances.

- Fill the prescription and verify that it is correct and packaged according to the standards of the pharmacy and state law. The label should be sent to the counter for filling only after it has been checked against the original order.

- Pharmacy technicians should check the stock bottle's labeling and the National Drug Code (**NDC number**) in the computer system, and compare them to the original prescription. It is good practice to mark stock bottles with an "X" across the front label, which lets other employees know that the bottle has already been opened and no longer contains the entire labeled amount.

  - Never touch the medication when dispensing it.
  - Verify that the correct type of lid is affixed onto the correct container properly and firmly.
  - Check the labels against the original order and, if correct, apply one to the medication container and one to the packaging that holds the container (usually a paper bag). Make sure labels are completely intact, not smeared, and placed evenly.
  - Apply any **auxiliary labels** that may be required by specific medications. These labels, chosen by the pharmacist, may include instructions about certain adverse effects, whether the medication should be taken with or without food, and interactions. Figure 8-2 shows examples of auxiliary labels.
  - Verify that the packaging is correct and initial it.
  - Put the packaged medication on the original prescription so that the pharmacist can verify them both. In total, the prescription should be checked and verified at least three times during the filling process.

The pharmacist can then counsel the patient about the prescription and make sure that the patient understands everything about the proper administration of the drug contained within. The pharmacist is the only person allowed to conduct patient counseling, and pharmacy technicians must always refer patients to the pharmacist when they have a question about a prescription.

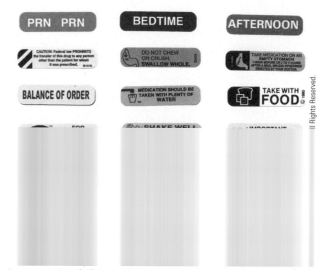

Computerized dispensing systems can greatly improve dispensing time and accuracy, because they contain many built-in functions that cross-check and verify information. They also interact with computer inventories to give an up-to-the-minute accounting of all medications in stock. These systems can interact with robotic dispensing equipment to instruct the machinery on which medications, amounts, strengths, and forms need to be dispensed.

Focus On...

Schedule II Prescriptions

Faxed prescriptions for Schedule II drugs must be followed up by a written prescription; these written follow-ups must be received by the pharmacy within seven days after the faxed Schedule II prescription was submitted. Faxed prescriptions without a written follow-up are allowed for nursing homes or hospices in some states.

What Would You Do?

Tina, a pharmacy technician, was dispensing a sulfa drug prescription. She forgot to put a required auxiliary label onto the container. The pharmacist noticed that there was no auxiliary label and told Tina that she must put the appropriate label onto the container. If you were Tina, what should you know about sulfa drugs and related auxiliary labels?

Prescription Drug Orders

State law regulates prescribers of medications. Each practitioner, whether he or she is a physician, osteopath, dentist, or podiatrist, must be state-licensed. If required, the practitioner must also register with the DEA. For example, all individuals who prescribe controlled substances must be registered with the DEA. In some states, certified nurse practitioners, physician's assistants, and even pharmacists may prescribe medications. Certain states allow these individuals to prescribe all forms of legal drugs, while others allow them to prescribe all non-controlled substances.

Prescribers should write prescription drug orders only for diseases and conditions with which they directly deal. For example, a dentist should not prescribe medication for back pain. Pharmacists should be aware of any prescription that appears to be outside the scope of practice of the prescriber. The amount of a controlled substance should be within the standards of accepted prescribed amounts for a given condition. Doses and combinations of drugs should be looked at closely. Patients who ask for refills more frequently than is normally accepted should be questioned, and their refills investigated if they seem out of the ordinary (Figure 8-3).

Prescription drug orders for controlled substances should contain the same standard information as other prescriptions, with the addition of the prescriber's **DEA number**. They should only bear the date of issue, and not any previous dates or post-dates. The practitioner who wrote the prescription must sign the prescription by hand on the actual date of issue, rather than using a stamp that bears the likeness of his or her signature.

Focus On...

Prescriptions

Prescriptions are written orders for a drug or treatment that are usually dispensed by a pharmacist or a technician. The prescription process depends on the statutes of the state in which the pharmacist practices.

Figure 8-3 Patients asking for refills more frequently than normal should be questioned.

Electronic Files

Most states have adopted their own regulations for the electronic transmission of prescriptions. Most states now allow controlled substance prescriptions to be faxed, though individual states have their own restrictions, such as requirements that the prescription be written in the prescriber's own handwriting, that the name of the pharmacy that will be ~~... ... be written~~

~~...~~

~~prescription...~~ ting prescriptions becomes more popular.

Drug Product Selection

Drug product selection laws, drug product substitution laws, and generic substitution laws are designed to regulate the ability of pharmacists to dispense a different drug product than the drug that was prescribed. A good amount of cost savings can be attained by the substitution of generic drugs for brand-name drugs. The law requires that the generic drug be identical to the brand-name drug in order for the substitution to be allowed. If a generic drug is prescribed, the pharmacist can dispense any product that has identical ingredients.

> ### You Be the Judge
>
> Your pharmacist received a prescription for Zocor® 20 mg for 30 days. He selected the generic drug simvastatin instead of Zocor. Based on your knowledge, why did the pharmacist make this substitution? Is he allowed to do this?

Labeling

Though differences exist in drug labeling requirements among hospital settings, institutional settings, and others, these requirements are, in general, as follows:

- Single-unit packages of individual-dose or unit-dose drug products must include:
  - The drug's generic or trade name
  - The route of administration if other than oral
  - The strength and volume of the drug (preferably in metric measurements)

- The drug's control number and expiration date
- The re-packager's name or license number (which must be clearly distinguishable from the rest of the label information)
- Any special storage conditions

- Multiple-use drug packages must include:

  - Identifying information about the dispensing pharmacy
  - The patient's name
  - The dispensing date
  - The generic and/or trade name of the drug
  - The strength of the drug (preferably in metric measurements)

- Ambulatory or outpatient drug packages must include:

  - The name and address of the dispensing pharmacy
  - The name of the patient
  - The name of the prescriber
  - Directions for use
  - The dispensing date
  - Any federal or state cautions
  - The prescription number
  - The name or initials of the dispensing pharmacist
  - The generic or trade name of the drug
  - The strength of the drug (if more than one strength of the drug is available)
  - The manufacturer or distributor of the drug
  - The beyond-use date of the drug

Focus On...

Labels for Stock Medications

The manufacturer's label found on stock medication bottles contains information about the size of the bottle, the strength of the medication, the expiration date, the NDC number, and other important facts necessary for providing the correct and safe medication needed by the patient.

Patient Records and Drug Review

The maintenance of patient medication records is intended to facilitate monitoring of patients' drug therapy. Good record keeping is important. These records must indicate that the pharmacist properly counseled the patient, and indicate whether the pharmacist contacted the prescriber about possible problems concerning the patient's prescription or prescriptions.

Patient records should contain the patient's full name, address, and telephone number. The patient's age or date of birth should be included, as well as gender. Each pharmacy should make sure that every patient's record shows his or her entire available **drug history**, covering at least the past five years, with the most recent prescriptions listed first. Any comments by pharmacists should be included, ... allergies, reactions, diseases, or

The pharmacist has the responsibility to ... tient's medication use and verify that there is no abuse or misuse of medications. The patient's allergies must always be verified to avoid medication errors and potential interactions with other medications, foods, or supplements. Certain medications are not indicated for individuals with certain diseases or conditions, and these issues must be carefully evaluated. Drug dosages must be checked for effectiveness, and the duration for which the medication should be taken must be appropriate. Overuse or underuse of medications should be prevented, and there should be no unneeded duplication of medications. All of these verifications lead to quality therapeutic care and prevent harm to the patient.

Patient Counseling

Patient counseling is to be performed only by licensed pharmacists—not pharmacy technicians or any other pharmacy staff members. Under OBRA-90, most states have enacted mandatory patient counseling requirements for pharmacists. These requirements are expanding the pharmacist's standards of practice. OBRA-90 requires pharmacists to offer counseling to all Medicaid patients. It is wise for pharmacists to provide patient counseling in order to ensure that each patient understands the possible adverse effects, drug and food interactions, contraindications, and warnings concerning each prescription. During patient counseling, the pharmacist must explain the name of the drug, its dosage form, its route of administration, the duration of the drug therapy, directions for use, and side effects. The pharmacist should also emphasize how to properly store the medication, and discuss refill information should a refill be required.

Focus On...

Patient Counseling

Pharmacists are required to offer counseling to every Medicaid patient regarding his or her prescription medications; such counseling may occur in person, by telephone, or in writing, depending on the individual laws of each state.

COMPUTER REGULATIONS

Secure computer systems are required more than ever for pharmacy record keeping. The NABP publishes rules for use of computer systems for the protection and confidentiality of PHI. PHI must be able to be retrieved online for all prescriptions that may be refilled. All prescription and refill information must be able to be printed out, and include the complete medication history of a given patient. Computer systems used for pharmacy record keeping must have secure backup systems in place should the primary system become compromised or inaccessible. Pharmacists have final authority and responsibility to make sure that the correct decisions are made about patient refills if an automated computer system is not in proper operation, and any prescriptions filled or refilled during computer **downtime** must be entered into the computer system within four business days of when it becomes operable.

PHARMACY OWNERSHIP

Though state laws may restrict who is allowed to own a pharmacy, these restrictions are rare. In general, anyone who has proven their qualifications and is of good moral character may own a pharmacy in most states. The ownership of a pharmacy is usually only of concern if any of the following conditions exists:

- Unlicensed or untrained individuals manage the pharmacy.
- A physician owns a pharmacy and such ownership causes a conflict of interest with his or her medical practice.
- Unethical or undignified pharmacy practices are conducted.
- Incorrect or uninformed drug stocking practices are conducted.

SALE OF HYPODERMIC NEEDLES AND SYRINGES

The pharmacist must carefully control the sale of hypodermic needles and syringes to avoid their illegal use. Individual states regulate the sale of OTC needles and syringes, with some states only allowing them to be sold if prescribed by a physician. Other states allow needles and syringes to be legally purchased without a prescription as long as the patient is at least 18 years of age. These states require that pharmacies not advertise or promote the fact that they sell hypodermic needles and syringes. Many pharmacy chains and independent pharmacies in these states follow these guidelines and legally sell hypodermic needles and syringes. In some states, only 10 needle/syringe combinations may be sold to an indi-

COMPOUNDING

Both state and federal laws regulate the practice of **pharmacy compounding**. The U.S. Supreme Court has ruled that advertising of compounding services cannot be prohibited because this would violate rights to commercial free speech. The FDA has stepped in regarding cases of community pharmacies compounding certain drugs that are available in commercial preparations. Previously, pharmacists often compounded drug products without being required to obtain a new drug approval (NDA) from the FDA. The administration stated that this practice created "unapproved compounds" that could be dangerous. Thus, pharmacists cannot advertise compounding services if they are compounding drug products that are otherwise commercially available in approved compounded products that have an NDA on file.

Much litigation between consumer groups and governmental bodies has occurred since the FDA became more focused on the compounding activities of pharmacists. As a result, pharmacists must follow their state's laws as well as the FDA's guidelines concerning compounding very closely. Compounding outside of these guidelines may bring legal complications at either state or federal levels. Regardless, the issue of compounding is one that will see continued focus and revision as new medications are brought onto the market. The roles of pharmacy technicians will be affected as new laws are developed and amended concerning compounding and those individuals who are allowed to participate. Pharmacy technicians will most likely see an increase in their approved duties in assisting pharmacists in compounding a variety of medications.

The United States Pharmacopoeia (USP) has consistently updated sterile compounding regulations. The USP <795> is an the FDA constantly monitoring the compounding activities of pharmacies. Because of increased regulation, pharmacy technicians will see an increase in their approved duties in assisting pharmacists.

SETTING THE SCENE

The following discussion and responses relate to the opening "Setting the Scene" scenario:

- The pharmacist should have consulted with the patient to explain the medication and all details.

- The pharmacist is in violation of the law because consultation with all Medicaid (and Medicare) patients is required.

- The pharmacist has the ultimate responsibility for patient care.

REVIEW QUESTIONS

Multiple Choice

1. The rules of pharmacy practice are set forth by which of the following agencies?

   A. National Association of Boards of Pharmacy
   B. Food and Drug Administration
   C. state boards of pharmacy
   D. Drug Enforcement Administration

2. All of the following components are required on a prescription label, except

   A. dispensing date.
   B. address of the dispensing pharmacy.
   C. any special third-party payer.
   D. any federal or state cautions.

3. Who must make decisions about patient refills if a hospital's automated computer system is not properly operational, or is experiencing downtime?

   A. nurses
   B. pharmacists
   C. pharmacy technicians
   D. none of the above

4. Pharmacy technicians must make sure that the prescription information in the computer matches which of the following?

    A.   the printed labels
    B.   the fax numbers
    C.   the prescription
    D.   the USP

without a prescription if the patient is

    A.   over 18 years of age.
    B.   under 18 years of age.
    C.   a U.S. citizen.
    D.   none of the above.

7. All drug products must be properly labeled and conform to the requirements of which of the following?

    A.   Drug Enforcement Administration
    B.   State Health Department
    C.   state board of pharmacy
    D.   all of the above

8. According to state law, when a prescription is submitted to a pharmacy for processing, the pharmacy technician must do all of the following, except

    A.   verify that all of the information on the prescription is complete and clear.
    B.   translate the prescription information for the practitioner.
    C.   enter the prescription information into the computer system.
    D.   fill the prescription and have the pharmacist verify that it is correct and is packaged according to the standards of the pharmacy and state law.

9. Pharmacy technicians should check the stock bottle's labeling and the NDC number in the computer system and compare these to the original prescription. A good step to follow upon

first use of the contents of the stock bottle is to mark its front label with which of the following letters?

A. Z
B. W
C. X
D. C

10. Faxed prescriptions for Schedule II drugs must be followed up by a written prescription, which must be received by the pharmacy within

A. one day.
B. two days.
C. three days.
D. seven days.

11. Prescriptions that are received on machines using fax paper must be immediately

A. dispensed to the patient.
B. photocopied and filed.
C. recorded in the pharmacy's computer system.
D. translated into English.

12. Each pharmacy should make sure that every patient's record shows his or her entire available drug history for at least

A. one year.
B. two years.
C. three years.
D. five years.

13. While most states allow pharmacies to sell hypodermic needles and syringes in any quantity, there are some states that allow pharmacies to sell no more than

A. three at a time.
B. five at a time.
C. ten at a time.
D. two dozen at a time.

14. A product identifier used for drugs intended for human use is called a

A. National Drug Code number.
B. Drug Enforcement Administration number.
C. United States Pharmacopoeia number.
D. Food and Drug Administration number.

15. The state monitors the operation of long-term care facilities and the amount of medication that the pharmacist or technician dispenses because of

    A. the potential for misuse.
    B. the potential for addiction.
    C. the price and cost of the medication.
    D. all of the above.

2. Pharmacy technicians must understand both the state and _____ laws that regulate the practice of pharmacy.

3. Tables of information that enable pharmacists and pharmacy technicians to quickly find their state's position on a variety of pharmacy-related activities have been created by the _____.

4. Unprofessional conduct must be _____ to the proper _____, as directed by the state board of pharmacy.

5. Computer dispensing systems can interact with robotic dispensing equipment to tell the machinery which _____ are needed to be dispensed.

6. Most states now allow that controlled substance prescriptions can be _____.

7. A good amount of cost savings can be attained by the substitution of _____ drugs for _____ drugs.

8. The patient record should contain his or her full name, address, and _____ number.

9. Patient allergies must always be verified to avoid _____.

10. Computer systems used for pharmacy record keeping must have secure _____ systems in place in case the primary system becomes compromised or inaccessible.

CASE STUDY

Hillary, a certified pharmacy technician, dispensed a prescription for a patient. Jeremy, the pharmacist, knew that the prescriber's license had been revoked during the previous month.

1. What should Hillary have done before dispensing this medication?

2. What steps should Hillary take to examine the prescription to prevent forgeries?

3. What should the pharmacist ask the patient about the prescription?

RELATED INTERNET SITES

http://www.drugpolicy.org

http://www.drugsafetyinstitute.com

http://www.fda.gov

http://www.medscape.com

http://www.nabp.net

http://www.ncpanet.org

http://www.ncsl.org

http://www.pharmacytimes.com

http://www.uspharmacist.com

REFERENCES

Abood, R. (2010). *Pharmacy Practice and the Law* (6th ed.). Burlington, MA: Jones & Bartlett.

Allen, L. V. (2008). *The Art, Science, and Technology of Pharmaceutical Compounding* (3rd ed.). Washington, DC: American Pharmacists Association.

Darvey, D. L. (2008). *Legal Handbook for Pharmacy Technicians*. Bethesda, MD: American Society of Health-System Pharmacists.

CHAPTER 9

State Boards of Pharmacy and the Joint Commission

OBJECTIVES

Upon completion of this chapter, the reader should be able to:

1. Describe the state board of pharmacy.

2. List the roles and responsibilities of the state board of pharmacy.

3. Describe the purpose of the state board of pharmacy.

4. Explain the enforcement powers of the state board of pharmacy.

5. Define the major responsibilities of the state board of pharmacy.

6. Describe the Joint Commission and its responsibility regarding the pharmacy and the pharmacist.

7. Discuss pharmacist licensure renewal.

8. Describe disciplinary action against a pharmacist.

9. Explain pharmacy technician liability.

10. Identify the requirements for pharmacy licensure.

KEY TERMS

Continuing education—Instructional programs that keep an individual up to date on advancements in his or her field.

Infringements—Violations of laws, regulations, or agreements.

Licensure—The practice of granting licenses to practice a profession.

Magistrates—Civil officers with the power to enforce laws.

National Formulary (NF) standards—Standards concerning medicines, dosage forms, drug substances, excipients (inactive substances used as carriers for active medicinal ingredients), medical devices, and dietary supplements.

Pharmacy internship—A period of service in a pharmacy during which a pharmacy student works under supervision to gain practical experience.

Prosecution—A legal proceeding by the state against an individual.

Revocation—Recall of authority or power to act.

Revoked—Voided, annulled, recalled, withdrawn, or reversed.

United States Pharmacopoeia (USP)—The officially recognized authority and standard on the prescription of drugs, chemicals, and medicinal preparations in the United States.

OUTLINE

SETTING THE SCENE

Jeff, a licensed hospital pharmacist, is on the phone, talking with a physician. After the phone call, the pharmacy technician, Jackie, tells Jeff that there are two men waiting to see him. They are inspectors from the

- If the inspectors found that the locking mechanism on the door to the storage area for controlled substances was broken and could not be locked, what could be the penalty?

OVERVIEW

The regulation of the practice of pharmacy is primarily a state function and not a function of the federal government. The legal responsibilities of pharmacies vary from state to state. To provide better uniformity of state regulations, the National Association of Boards of Pharmacy (NABP) published a book entitled **Model Rules for Pharmaceutical Care.** However, states may enact laws and board of pharmacy rules independent of the federal government, as long as they do not conflict with federal law. While pharmacy laws of the different states do vary, they agree as to the fundamental principles, purposes, aims, and objectives of pharmacy practice. State boards of pharmacy also issue licenses for retail, hospital, and other types of pharmacies.

No one may practice pharmacy unless he or she is licensed according to state law. Individuals achieve such licensure by successfully completing the qualifications that their state has established. In most states, the board of pharmacy can take disciplinary action against any pharmacist or pharmacy, but each state has different approaches to regulation of pharmacy technicians. Today, more states than ever before require that pharmacy technicians become certified before they are allowed to work in the pharmacy setting.

The State Board of Pharmacy

The board of pharmacy in each state is established by statutes (pharmacy practice acts). These boards strive to protect the health, safety, and welfare of the public. They are mostly made up of a combination of pharmacists, consumers, and healthcare professionals. Members of a state's board of pharmacy are usually appointed by the governor of the state.

State Board of Pharmacy's Functions

The board of pharmacy is usually a sub-agency that exists as part of a larger state agency, such as the department of health or department of licensing. The board of pharmacy is charged with the enforcement and administration of pharmacy practice laws. This agency has powers delegated to it by the legislature under pharmacy practice statutes to put into effect rules or regulations to implement the statutes. A certain amount of enforcement discretion is vested in the board of pharmacy. While the board is authorized to make rules and regulations for the enforcement and administration of pharmacy law, it must do so according to the purposes of the law.

The board is an administrative agency, and not a legislative entity. It may not exercise any power or authority that has not been clearly delegated to it. The board of pharmacy will grant licenses to qualified pharmacists, pharmacies, technicians, and interns. It also has the power to impose sanctions against those who do not follow all applicable laws. Licensure or registration may be canceled, **revoked** (withdrawn), or suspended according to conditions specified in certain statutes or regulations. Likewise, offenders may be placed on probation by the board.

Many boards of pharmacy have other disciplinary sanctions available. These include civil fines and the imposition of a community service requirement. Some state laws specify that violations of the pharmacy act are punishable as criminal misdemeanors.

Drug distribution within a state is regulated by that state's board of pharmacy, which controls the practice of pharmacy for the protection of public health, safety, and welfare. It accomplishes this with rules and regulations. When these rules and regulations are violated, such action constitutes grounds for refusal, suspension, or **revocation** of any license or permit issued.

The board may also conduct hearings or proceedings to revoke, suspend, or refuse renewal of any license or permit issued under the authority of the pharmacy act. The board of pharmacy assists state law enforcement agencies in enforcing all laws that pertain to drugs, narcotics, and pharmacy practice.

Most states issue licensure permits for pharmacy practice that last one to two years. Pharmacists must be periodically re-licensed. Certificates of licensure must always be prominently displayed at the pharmacy. Pharmacists who are licensed in one state may obtain licensure in another state

Pharmacy Practice Act (MSPPA). A copy of this act may be viewed online at http://www.nabp.net.

ENFORCEMENT POWERS

Most situations wherein the board of pharmacy can institute actions involve violations that are civil in nature. Their powers may also include authority to arrest (when a felony is committed in the presence of an enforcement officer), though warrants for such arrests must be issued by **magistrates** or judges. In criminal cases, the board conducts investigations and turns over evidence to state or county prosecutors. Similarly, the Food and Drug Administration (FDA) and Drug Enforcement Administration (DEA) enforce federal drug laws by investigating matters and turning them over to the U.S. Attorney's office for **prosecution**.

Boards of pharmacy can enforce statutes, state drug control acts, and their own regulations by suspension, revocation, or withholding of licenses or permits; by imposing monetary penalties; or by seeking injunctions, restraining orders, or other court orders. They may also refuse to renew a pharmacist's license or a pharmacy's permit due to **infringements.** State boards of pharmacy are responsible for all of the following:

1. Licensing by examination or license transfer—State boards of pharmacy are responsible for granting pharmacist licenses and pharmacy technician certificates. They accomplish this by holding examinations, such as the NAPLEX, which an individual must pass in order to practice. They also transfer licenses from other states so that an individual can practice in a new location. During this

process, the background of each applicant is thoroughly checked. In some states, pharmacy technicians must be registered to practice.

2. Renewal of licenses—In most states, licenses are granted for two years. Renewal of licenses can occur after an individual has applied for renewal on a timely basis, and completed continuing education since the previous licensure. After review, the state board of pharmacy determines if the individual has met all necessary requirements in order to have his or her license renewed. Other states simply require the individual to update all of his or her information on file and pay the renewal fee. Pharmacists in certain states can even renew their licenses via the Internet.

3. Establishment and enforcement of compliance in pharmacy practice—State boards of pharmacy assess penalties against those who violate their regulations of practice. They establish standards of behavior that must be followed by pharmacy technicians and pharmacists alike. Penalties include fines, revocation, or suspension of pharmacist licenses, legal actions, and even imprisonment in severe cases.

4. Approval of degree programs to teach the practice of pharmacy— State boards of pharmacy offer accreditation for pharmacy degree programs offered by colleges and universities. These programs are rigidly controlled so that each school conforms to the requirements of the board of pharmacy in its state. State laws also uniformly allow state boards of pharmacy to recognize national accreditation from the American Council on Pharmaceutical Education (ACPE) throughout the United States. No state accredits specific pharmacy schools.

5. The suspension, revocation, or restriction of pharmacy licenses—State boards of pharmacy review individual cases and can determine that an applicant's license may need to be suspended, revoked, or even restricted. Suspension of a pharmacy license means that it is placed "on hold" for a specific period while the individual or company fulfills the requirements of the state board, after which the license is reactivated. Revocation of a license means that the license has been nullified by the state board and cannot be reactivated. Restriction of a license means that the individual or company may continue to practice, but only within certain parameters allowed by the state board; certain activities are allowed, while others are not.

6. Control of the training, qualifications, and employment of pharmacy personnel—The state boards of pharmacy monitor the quality of pharmacies and their personnel, requiring specialized training that is of a certain approved level. Unqualified

or untrained personnel cannot legally practice until they fulfill these requirements. Pharmacies can only employ properly qualified and trained personnel, including pharmacy technicians.

7. Collection of demographic data—State boards of pharmacy collect ~~graphic~~ data about the staff members of each pharmacy in ~~may be provided by the state~~

~~medi~~
lates to drugs and therapies.

9. Establishing specifications for pharmacy facilities and equipment—State boards of pharmacy control the types of facilities required by each pharmacy, as well as the equipment that can be used within pharmacies. All items used in the pharmacy setting must conform to the state board of pharmacy's listing of approved equipment. Each state has its own specifications for pharmacy facilities and equipment.

10. Establishing standards for purity and quality—The board of pharmacy in each state establishes purity and quality standards for compounding, which may be further regulated by federal standards. Usually, the more restrictive standard (either state or federal) prevails when there is a discrepancy.

11. The issuance and renewal of licenses related to manufacturing and distribution of pharmaceutical drugs and devices—State boards of pharmacy issue and renew the licenses of pharmaceutical manufacturers and distributors, as regulated by the FDA. Severe penalties exist if these companies do not fully adhere to the guidelines of the state. Individualized regulations apply to both prescription and OTC drugs and devices.

12. Inspection of pharmacy personnel, facilities, and equipment—State boards of pharmacy may conduct unannounced inspections of pharmacies, paying attention to the facilities themselves, the equipment they use on a regular basis, and even the personnel within. They may check for proper display of licenses; conditions of the workplace; potential hazards; and proper storage of medications, medical devices, and other equipment; they may even question pharmacy staff members about their daily job duties.

13. Establishing standards for the integrity and confidentiality of patient information—The private health information of patients requires protection. This is accomplished by the state boards of pharmacy through the regulations and standards they establish concerning the integrity and confidentiality of patient information. Those who violate protected health information (PHI) confidentiality standards may face severe penalties, with the most serious penalties given for intentional misuse of PHI. Those who unintentionally misuse PHI may receive minor penalties intended to correct their future behavior while still allowing them to practice and increase their knowledge of pharmacy.

What Would You Do?

Sean has been working as a pharmacy technician in a retail pharmacy for 10 years. His certification expires and he must renew it quickly in order to continue to practice. If you were Sean, what would you need to do to renew your certification?

EXAMINATION REQUIREMENTS

Applicants for a pharmacist license must pass some or all of the following, within differing periods of time per state law, after graduating from a state-approved school of pharmacy:

- Part I—North American Pharmacist Licensing Exam (NAPLEX)
- Part II—Multistate Pharmacy Jurisprudence Exam (MPJE)
- Part III—Written and Practical (Compounding) Exam (only 10 states currently require this part)

For the NAPLEX, applicants must submit a completed **licensure** application and have their completed education documentation approved before they are allowed to take the exam. Once their application is approved, they can apply to take the exam online at http://www.nabp .net. In addition, some states require applicants to have their college or school submit a tentative graduation date to the NABP, plus a "Form 2— Certification of Professional Education" with an official education transcript.

Focus On...

NAPLEX

As of 2008, all states were using the North American Pharmacist Licensing Exam (NAPLEX).

For the MPJE, the same requirements exist; in addition, applicants must have their completed internship experience submitted and approved. For the Written and Practical (Compounding) Exam, applicants must meet all requirements for the MPJE.

rience working under a licensed pharmacist's direction." The purpose of a pharmacy internship program is to acquire the knowledge and practical experience that is necessary if one is to function competently and effectively upon licensure. The supervising pharmacist must submit proof of an intern's completion of required clock hours on a *practical experience affidavit.*

During a pharmacy internship, interns receive comprehensive instruction and experience in these (and possibly other) important areas of pharmacy practice:

1. Receiving and interpreting prescriptions and medication orders
2. Compounding prescriptions and medication orders
3. Dispensing prescriptions and medication orders
4. Reviewing patient medication profiles
5. Communicating with patients
6. Consulting with other healthcare professionals
7. Managing the pharmacy

LICENSURE OF THE PHARMACIST

State boards of pharmacy issue licenses to pharmacists and pharmacies. The NABP represents state pharmaceutical licensing authorities. All states have standards dealing with pharmacy practices. In order to become a licensed pharmacist, most states require each applicant to have done the following:

- Graduated from an ***accredited*** school of pharmacy
- Completed a required internship

- Passed the state's pharmacy licensure exam
- Achieved a documentable history of good moral character

Ten states require pharmacists to be 21 or older, with most of the rest requiring pharmacists to be at least 18 years of age.

Each pharmacy location is issued a separate license by its state's board of pharmacy. Some states grant licensure by transfer from another jurisdiction (reciprocity), though many states do not allow reciprocity based on a Florida license. These states include Arkansas, Connecticut, Georgia, Hawaii, Idaho, Louisiana, Minnesota, Ohio, Oklahoma, Tennessee, West Virginia, and Wyoming. Florida itself only allows reciprocity if the NAPLEX exam was taken within the prior 12 years. California only allows reciprocity if the applicant took the NAPLEX after 2004.

While some states do not regulate who can actually own a pharmacy, other states do not allow physicians to own pharmacies because of possible conflicts of interest. An example would be a physician's office referring its patients exclusively to the pharmacy that it owns.

Focus On...

Licensing of Pharmacists

Pharmacists may become licensed in most states by simply transferring their license from another state, depending on the states involved. In general, this removes the requirement of taking the board of pharmacy examination in a new state.

PHARMACIST LICENSURE RENEWAL

Periodically, pharmacists must renew their licenses by paying a fee and, in some states, by completing a certain number of continuing education credits. Renewal of a license usually requires the revealing of in-depth personal information, continuing education record forms, the pharmacy's permit information, verification of any disciplinary actions taken during the previous licensure period and explanation of outcomes, and the renewal fee.

Some states currently offer online renewal, which can expedite the process. All states require completely correct filing of paperwork or online renewal information and usually will refuse to renew an applicant if anything is still incomplete at the end of the allowed renewal period.

Focus On...

Licensure Renewal

It is not the responsibility of the state boards of pharmacy to deliver a license renewal to a licensee. Instead, it is the responsibility of each pharmacist to ~~~~~~~ licensure renewal.

practi
both in formal courses given
courses. Appropriate subjects for pharmacy practi
clude, but are not limited to, the following:

- Techniques for the reduction of medication and prescription errors

- Knowledge of drug interactions

- Pharmacology of new or developing drugs

- Infection control

- Reporting of suspected child abuse

- Public health issues

- Legal and regulatory issues (one hour of continuing education credits must now focus on pharmacy law)

- Proper patient counseling

- Sterile procedures

    Approved providers of continuing education generally include the following:

- American Council on Pharmaceutical Education (ACPE)–approved sponsors or providers (this list is available at http://www .acpe-accredit.org)

- State board of pharmacy–approved sponsors or providers

- Colleges, universities, and other degree-granting institutions (these are usually listed under individual state websites, but the degrees they offer must include A.A.S., B.S., M.S., Pharm.D., or Ph.D. in pharmacy)

STATE BOARD INSPECTIONS

Periodically, pharmacy board inspectors conduct routine inspections of pharmacies for compliance with various laws and regulations. These laws and regulations for pharmacy operation vary per state. All licensed personnel as well as appropriate records may be inspected, and employees are expected to cooperate with inspectors. Though most inspections are more educational than investigative, the pharmacist should be aware of any inspections that involve searches for incriminating evidence.

CERTIFICATION OF PHARMACY TECHNICIANS

States regulate pharmacy technician certification, and differ from each other in their requirements. To ensure that pharmacy technicians in every state have at least a minimum level of skill, the Pharmacy Technician Certification Board (PTCB) has been established. The overall goal of the PTCB is to improve the proficiency of pharmacy technicians in every state so that they may serve patients, co-workers, and pharmacists more competently.

The PTCB offers an examination called the Pharmacy Technician Certification Examination (PTCE) three times per year. This examination is divided into the following three areas of competence:

- Assisting the pharmacist
- Maintenance of medication/inventory control systems
- Helping with administration and management of the pharmacy

The examination includes questions that focus on drug names and classifications, federal pharmacy law, mathematics (as used in the pharmacy), and pharmacy operations. Certified pharmacy technicians may use the initials "CPhT" following their names. Pharmacies in some states pay certified pharmacy technicians higher wages than those who are not certified, though this is not yet true everywhere.

Renewal of pharmacy technician certification requires continuing education. In order to have his or her certification renewed, a pharmacy technician must complete 20 hours of continuing education credits every two years. Continuing education may be obtained at a variety of pharmacy seminars, through pharmacy organizations and journal publications, and even over the Internet. The individual requirements of each state are not the same, so it is important that pharmacy technicians verify what the state board of pharmacy requires them to do. Every year, more states are increasing their requirements for pharmacy technicians, and more are requiring that they become certified.

The other nationally accredited pharmacy technician certification exam is the ExCPT, which is given by the Institute for the Certification of Pharmacy Technicians (ICPT). The mission of the ICPT is to recognize ... the knowledge and skills needed to assist

Focus On...

State Certification, Registration, and Licensure Requirements

Most states now require pharmacy technicians to be registered in order to practice. There are now eight states that require pharmacy technicians to obtain a license: Alaska, Arizona, California, Massachusetts, Oregon, Rhode Island, Utah, and Wyoming.

For the latest updates, go to http://www.nationaltechexam.org (under "ExCPT exam," click on "State by State Tech Requirements").

DRUG CONTROL REGULATIONS

Pharmacists who violate the federal Controlled Substances Act are sanctioned according to whether they knowingly and intentionally violated the act. Unintentional violations, such as those related to bookkeeping, are punished with a civil (not criminal) penalty. Harsher penalties await those who knowingly and intentionally violate the act, with criminal adjudication occurring commonly. Federal or state violations involving controlled substances can have severe implications for a pharmacist's licensure and can even keep him or her from practicing pharmacy at all in the future.

HOSPITAL PHARMACY

The state regulation of hospital pharmacy is quite different from the regulation of community pharmacy. Areas of difference that have prompted new hospital pharmacy regulations include in-hospital dispensing of drugs, the licensure of hospital pharmacy personnel, and the appropriate functions of the hospital pharmacy technician. The PTCB has unique state-by-state regulations for pharmacy technicians working in hospital or institutional pharmacies. In general, pharmacy technicians in these pharmacies are not allowed to accept called-in prescriptions from physicians, check the work of other pharmacy technicians, or transfer prescription orders. However, they are allowed to enter prescriptions into the pharmacy computer system and compound medications for dispensing. Also, many states require that directors of hospital pharmacies possess special training or expertise.

REGULATION OF LONG-TERM CARE PHARMACIES

Under current legislation, pharmacies in long-term care facilities may be separately licensed under state law. Pharmacists in these facilities are usually required by state law to have special training or expertise, and must complete individualized continuing education in order to recertify their licenses. Pharmacists must be very careful to correctly dispense medications in these facilities under the full approval of their state laws. The pharmacist must comply with rules about the use of strong (often Schedule II) medications, even though a patient resides in a long-term care facility and may need these medications until the end of his or her life. The long-term care pharmacist supervises all aspects of the drugs required by residents of these facilities, as regulated by the laws of their state and Omnibus Budget Reconciliation Act (OBRA) drug review requirements. He or she must maintain strict drug control, regular drug regimen reviews, cost controls, review committees, and detailed pharmacy policies and procedures. Techniques such as personal patient supervision and infusion therapy teams help to control medication use. Comprehensive medication reviews help to identify and prevent adverse outcomes.

THE JOINT COMMISSION AND ACCREDITATION

The Joint Commission is an independent, not-for-profit organization that surveys and accredits healthcare services to ensure high standards of patient care. This accreditation process is conducted in all healthcare organizations every three years, and the organization also helps companies become accredited. The Joint Commission identifies very specific guidelines for all departments within hospitals, including the hospital pharmacy. It also publishes standards concerning the control of pharmaceuticals, their manufacturers, and the ways they are stored and delivered. Based on very focused inspections, Joint Commission standards are reviewed and revised on a regular basis.

There are more than 250 different standards set by the Joint Commission. They address a wide variety of subject areas, including patient rights and education, medication management, infection control, prevention of medical errors, verification of staff competency, emergency preparedness, data collection, and improvement standards. When the Joint Commission conducts a survey of a healthcare organization, the ~~included doctors, nurses, hospital administrators, laboratory~~

ment" (RFI) for anything that does not meet its standards, and this is the topic for which most RFIs are issued. There are three elements in medication storage: security, safety, and integrity. The security element is also addressed by federal standards. Security involves safe storage, including the locking of controlled substances, disposition of drugs, and proper handling of drugs. Written policies must define security measures and list all personnel who are authorized to access medications. Controlled substances must be kept in locked areas and other medications must be stored safely. Disposition must occur by the end of each shift. Special attention must be paid to the storage of concentrated electrolytes, look-alike and sound-alike medications, ready-to-use formulations, and standard concentrations. Medication integrity must be safeguarded through inspections, written logs, and/or electronic logging systems.

- Prescriptions and medication orders—These must be written clearly and transcribed accurately. They must be complete, have clear intent, be legible, and include any special precautions. Items required to be included are the patient's name, medication name, its strength, the route, its rate, and the dosing frequency. Special precautions are required for pediatric weight-based orders, telephone orders, and orders for look-alike/sound-alike drugs.

- High-alert medications—High-alert medications must be identified. These include chemotherapy medications, narcotics, and anticoagulants.

- Safe medication preparation—All staff members who prepare medications must use techniques to ensure accuracy and avoid contamination. These include double-checking calculations; using clean or aseptic technique as appropriate; maintaining cleanliness;

using laminar airflow hoods or other class 100 environments to prepare all IV admixtures, sterile products made from nonsterile ingredients, and sterile products that will not be used within 24 hours; keeping the hoods uncluttered and functionally separate in order to minimize contamination; and visually inspecting integrity of medications. Staff must use safety materials and equipment while preparing hazardous medications such as cytotoxic drugs.

- Appropriate medication labeling—To minimize errors, medications must be labeled in a standardized manner based on organizational policy, applicable laws and regulations, and standards of practice. Labels must, at a minimum, include the drug name, strength, and amount; expiration date if the drug is not to be used within 24 hours; expiration time, when expiration occurs less than 24 hours after preparation; date prepared; diluent used for all compounded IV admixtures and parenteral nutrient solutions; patient's name and location (when preparing individualized medications for multiple patients, or when the preparer is not the person who will administer the medication); directions for use; and any applicable cautionary statements (such as "requires refrigeration" or "for IM use only").

- Pharmacist review of orders—All prescriptions and medication orders must be reviewed for appropriateness. The elements that must be reviewed include appropriateness, interactions, complicating allergies, and contraindications. Access to certain areas is restricted when a pharmacist is not present. Usually in this situation, only a trained, designated staff member is allowed to access a limited set of medications that have been approved by the hospital.

- Safe medication dispensation—Medications must be dispensed in quantities that meet patient needs but minimize diversion. Dispensing must occur in a timely manner and in compliance with laws, regulations, licensure requirements, and professional standards of practice. Medications must be dispensed in the most ready-to-administer forms available, or in unit doses that have been repackaged by the pharmacy or by a licensed repackager. Dose-packaging systems should be consistent, and if they are not, education about different systems must be provided.

- Providing medications when the pharmacy is closed—This concerns the ability to provide medications to meet urgent needs such as emergency situations. Access must be limited to authorized individuals, and to a limited set of medications approved by the organization. Open access to the entire pharmacy by a non-pharmacist is not allowed. Related medications may be stored in night cabinets, automated medication storage and distribution devices, or in a limited section of the pharmacy. Quality control procedures must be in place to prevent medication retrieval errors. Qualified pharmacists who can answer questions or provide medications from locations other than those accessible to non-pharmacist staff members must be on call at all times.

- Recalled medications—Medications dispensed by an organiza-
  t̶i̶o̶n̶ ̶m̶u̶s̶t̶ ̶b̶e̶ ̶r̶e̶t̶r̶i̶e̶v̶e̶d̶ when recalled or discontinued for safety

as well as those

managed. The pharmacy must have procedures in place for preventing diversion of medications. Any outside sources used for destruction of returned medications must be properly managed by the pharmacy. Accountability for these medications is at a gross level, not an individual tablet level.

STANDARDS OF THE JOINT COMMISSION

The Joint Commission sets certain voluntary standards for hospitals and provides accreditation based on hospitals' compliance with Joint Commission standards. These important standards serve as a guide to the proper method of operating a hospital and ensuring competence, licensure, controls, records, accuracy, and evaluation. Though the Joint Commission standards are voluntary, not being accredited by them is detrimental to a hospital's survival, as many insurance companies will not pay a non-accredited hospital. There are six basic Joint Commission standards:

1. The hospital pharmacy must be staffed with competent, legally qualified personnel, and have a pharmacist available at all times on duty, on call, or as a consultant. Non-pharmacist personnel must be assigned only duties that are consistent with their training. Clerical services must be provided. The pharmacy must be licensed as required. If there is no pharmacy at the hospital, pharmaceutical services must be obtained from another hospital pharmacy.

2. Drugs for external use only must be separated from drugs for internal use only and stored and controlled in accordance with the **United States Pharmacopoeia (USP)** and **National Formulary**

(NF) standards (see Appendix G). Provisions must be made for emergency drugs on carts or in kits. The metric system must be used for all medications. Conversion charts must be made available.

3. Adequate record-keeping systems and procedural guidelines for pharmaceutical preparation must be developed. Pharmacy personnel must participate in applicable patient care programs. Patient medication profiles should be maintained and reviewed for potential drug interactions. Patients must be instructed in correct drug use.

4. The pharmacist must review inpatient drug orders before initial dosage dispensation except in an emergency. There must be proper drug recall procedures. Drug defects must be reported to the USP/FDA drug defect program. Proper labeling of inpatient and outpatient medications must be initiated. Outpatient labels must contain the pharmacy's name, address, and phone number; the date; the drug's serial number; the patient's full name; the drug's name, strength, and amount dispensed; patient directions; the name or initials of the dispensing individual; and any required cautionary labeling.

5. There must be automatic cancellation of standing orders when a patient goes to surgery. A system of drug stop orders must be in existence. Identification of each patient must be made before drug administration. The use of abbreviations when ordering drugs must be discouraged. Drugs must be ordered by a practitioner and properly labeled when given to a patient upon discharge.

6. The pharmacy's activities must be monitored and evaluated in accordance with the hospital's quality assurance program.

You Be the Judge

Betty, a pharmacy technician, is working in a hospital pharmacy. While she is repacking drugs, she discovers that some of them have defective packaging. However, she ignores this and repacks the drugs anyway. What do you think that Betty should have done in this case?

DISCIPLINARY ACTION

In most states, the board of pharmacy can take disciplinary action against any pharmacist upon proof of the following:

1. The pharmacist's license was obtained through fraud, misrepresentation, or deceit.

2. The pharmacist has been determined to be mentally incompetent.

3. The pharmacist has knowingly violated or allowed the violation of any state or federal provision or law, rule, or regulation concerning drug possession, use, distribution, or dispensation.

4. The pharmacist has knowingly allowed an unlicensed or unauthorized person to run the pharmacy or engage in the practice of pharmacy.

~~~caused the com~~

Florida. Recently, the state board of pharmacy ... planning to move to the state of New York within a short period of time. What do you think Karen will be required to do in order to practice pharmacy in New York?

You Be the Judge

Vincent is a pharmacy technician who refused to submit to a random drug screen for his employer. He had been working at the same pharmacy for 18 months, and had never been drug tested, except during his pre-employment screening. Vincent argued that the pharmacy had no right to "spring this on him" since he had been a faithful employee ever since he was hired. The employer argued that, as stated in the documents Vincent signed when he was hired, it was their policy to conduct random drug screening. *Eventually, the pharmacy fired Vincent, who intends to seek legal action against it.* Who do you think will prevail in this case, and why?

You Be the Judge

Jaime worked for a local pharmacy for three years. On two occasions, she diverted a prescription cream without a valid prescription and dispensed it to herself, compromising the purity of other drugs in the pharmacy. When confronted by an investigator for the pharmacy, she admitted her actions and voluntarily surrendered her registration as a pharmacy technician. Jaime's employer did not fire her, but instead made her a cashier with the condition that if she worked for one year without any other problems, he would consider allowing her to resume work as a pharmacy technician. A year later, with her employer's approval, she requested that her state board of pharmacy reinstate her registration. Do you think that her state board of pharmacy will allow reinstatement of her pharmacy technician registration?

STATUS OF PHARMACY TECHNICIANS

Every pharmacy technician should know and understand the regulations of his or her state board of pharmacy. In order to practice as a pharmacy technician, some states require pharmacy technicians to be registered. Their status must be maintained continually by completing continuing education requirements as set forth by the state board of pharmacy. All statutes, both state and federal, must be continually obeyed. Regulations concerning the status of pharmacy technicians differ from state to state. As the duties of pharmacy technicians have expanded in response to the growth of the pharmacy industry, regulatory changes in what they can and cannot legally do have followed. Each state has different approaches to how pharmacy technicians are regulated. More states than ever before require that pharmacy technicians become certified before being allowed to work in the pharmacy setting.

Traditional pharmacy technician activities include, but are not limited to, the following:

- Accepting written prescriptions
- Checking prescriptions for accuracy and completeness
- Creating patient profiles
- Determining patient benefit plan information
- Retrieving patient profiles
- Entering prescription information on patient profiles
- Obtaining drug products to use in filling prescriptions
- Counting numbers of tablets and other drug forms
- Manually filling prescriptions
- Using appropriately sized containers

Many states now allow pharmacy technicians to call physicians for refill authorization (Figure 9-1). However, few states allow pharmacy technicians to accept new called-in prescriptions from a physician's office, and those that do have instituted many regulations concerning this practice. One area of extreme change is the allowing of pharmacy technicians to reconstitute oral liquids. Other newer areas of pharmacy technician duties include managing new automated technology, implementing or revising policies and procedure manuals, and training other technicians by providing in-service and other types of training programs.

Figure 9-1 Pharmacy technicians can call physicians for refill authorization in many states

Focus On...

Pharmacy Technicians

The pharmacist on duty is responsible for the supervision of non-pharmacist support personnel. This particularly applies to the supervision of pharmacy technicians.

PHARMACY TECHNICIANS IN RETAIL SETTINGS

About 7 out of 10 pharmacy technician jobs are in retail settings, including both independently owned and chain stores. These settings may be in dedicated pharmacies or in drug stores, grocery stores, department stores, or mass retailers. An increasing number of job openings are resulting from the expansion of retail pharmacies and similar settings, and from the need to replace workers who change occupations or leave the labor force.

As the population grows and ages, demand for pharmaceuticals, and therefore for the trained individuals required for their preparation and dispensation, will increase dramatically. Because of this growth, pharmacist-to-technician ratios have changed in many states. It is common for a pharmacist to supervise three or more pharmacy technicians in today's pharmacy practice. Many retail pharmacies are now open 24 hours, requiring pharmacists and pharmacy technicians to work varying shifts, and also leading to more employment opportunities.

PHARMACY TECHNICIANS IN HOSPITAL SETTINGS

About 2 out of 10 pharmacy technician jobs are in hospital settings. In the hospital, pharmacy technicians (in most states) are responsible for the following:

- Unit dose and other medication preparation
- Checking patient charts in conjunction with prescriptions
- Preparing, packaging, and labeling medications
- Delivering medications to nurses
- Managing robotic stocking systems
- Organizing 24-hour supplies of medications for all patients
- Cataloguing information in the hospital computer system

Focus On...

State Boards of Pharmacy

Each state board of pharmacy regulates the roles, duties, and expectations of pharmacy technicians who practice in the state.

PHARMACY TECHNICIANS' LIABILITIES

Most states require pharmacy technicians to work under the close, direct observation of a licensed pharmacist (Figure 9-2). Usually, the supervising pharmacist is responsible for any negligence committed by the pharmacy technician. As technicians take over an increasing proportion of drug dispensing functions, their opportunities to be involved in medication errors increase.

Figure 9-2 Pharmacy technicians work under the direct supervision of a pharmacist

Other common areas where pharmacy technicians may be liable are the following:

- Not advising the pharmacist of known drug interactions

- Providing incorrect information to patients

- Providing advice to patients when the state does not allow them to do so

Pharmacy technicians may be suspended from work, be fined, be fired, and even receive jail sentences depending on their negligent or criminal actions. Though pharmacists have the utmost authority over and responsibility for the actions of their pharmacy technicians, the technicians themselves can be in serious legal trouble if their duties are not conducted properly at all times. Liability insurance is available for pharmacy technicians, and it is recommended that they purchase it in order to protect themselves. It is important to always remember that patients' lives hang in the balance.

Focus On...

Disciplinary Action

State boards of pharmacy have the authority to discipline pharmacy technicians for improper behavior.

SUMMARY

Pharmacists must attend a pharmacy school and pass rigorous examinations in order to be able to obtain licensure. Pharmacy internships are also required, to ensure that pharmacists have plenty of experience in the pharmacy setting before being allowed to practice on their own. Once they are ready, pharmacists obtain their licenses to practice from the state in which they will work. Continuing education credits are required in all states so that pharmacists will continue to learn about their field, ensuring better patient care. Disciplinary action can be taken by the state board of pharmacy against pharmacists who violate regulations of practice. Likewise, now that pharmacy technicians are allowed to perform many of the duties traditionally handled by pharmacists, regulatory control of their activities is on the rise. Pharmacy technicians must receive specialized training in the areas of pharmacy in which they will work, be it in the community setting, the hospital, or other settings.

In all states, the board of pharmacy can discipline pharmacists and pharmacy technicians if they violate state or federal laws. Each state has its own regulations concerning pharmacy technician certifications, and regulates pharmacy technicians in different ways. All states also require pharmacy technicians to work under close, direct observation of licensed pharmacists. These pharmacists are usually held responsible for any negligent acts of pharmacy technicians. Criminal and/or negligent actions by pharmacy technicians may result in suspension, termination, fines, and even imprisonment.

The Joint Commission surveys and accredits healthcare services to ensure high standards of patient care. It also publishes standards concerning pharmaceuticals, drug manufacturers, and how drug products are stored and delivered. Joint Commission standards are reviewed and revised on a regular basis. There are more than 250 different standards set by the Joint Commission. Top issues focused on by this organization include medication storage, prescriptions and medication orders, high-alert medications, safe medication preparation, labeling, pharmacist review of orders, safe dispensation, provision of medications when a pharmacy is closed, recalled medications, and returned medications.

SETTING THE SCENE

The following discussion and responses relate to the opening "Setting the Scene" scenario:

- Pharmacy board inspectors commonly check all licensure documents of the pharmacy and its staff, as well as the pharmacy records.

- The inspectors will charge the pharmacist with practicing with-

REVIEW QUESTIONS

Multiple Choice

1. All of the following are powers of the board of pharmacy, except

   A. to regulate the practice of pharmacy.
   B. to administer and enforce all laws placed under its jurisdiction.
   C. to distribute drugs within the state.
   D. to investigate violations of law under the pharmacy act itself.

2. The pharmacy board may discipline a pharmacy that is in violation of the law by

   A. firing the pharmacist.
   B. not issuing a renewal of the pharmacy permit.
   C. refusing funding for the pharmacy.
   D. prosecuting the pharmacist through the U.S. Attorney General's office.

3. State boards of pharmacy are responsible for

   A. renewal of licenses.
   B. approval of degree programs to teach the practice of pharmacy.
   C. establishment of standards for purity and quality.
   D. all of the above.

4. Which of the following organizations sets certain voluntary standards for hospitals?

   A. NABP
   B. FDA

       C.   DEA

       D.   the Joint Commission

5. The pharmacy department's activities must be monitored and evaluated in accordance with which of the following?

       A.   the hospital's quality assurance program

       B.   the hospital's pharmacy directors

       C.   the hospital's vice president

       D.   the FDA

6. Which of the following are the duties and responsibilities of the NABP?

       A.   coordination of uniformity of the state boards of pharmacy

       B.   control of scheduled drugs

       C.   coordination of the DEA and FDA

       D.   coordination of the CDC to prevent communicable diseases

7. State boards of pharmacy are responsible for all of the following, except

       A.   establishment and enforcement of compliance in pharmacy practice.

       B.   approval of degree programs to teach the practice of pharmacy.

       C.   establishing academic standards for pharmacy technicians.

       D.   inspection of pharmacy personnel, facilities, and equipment.

8. According to the standards of the Joint Commission, non-pharmacist personnel must be assigned duties that are consistent with

       A.   their training.

       B.   staff shortages.

       C.   their skills.

       D.   the demands of nurses.

9. Which of the following statements is *not* true regarding applying for pharmacist licensure?

       A.   The applicant must have knowledge in medicine at the level of a practitioner.

       B.   The applicant must have graduated from an accredited pharmacy school or college.

       C.   The applicant must be over 18 years of age.

       D.   The applicant must have demonstrated a good moral character.

10. A pharmacist may complete his or her continuing education in which of the following ways?

    A. formal courses
    B. self-training courses
    C. self-study courses
    D. A and C

D. all of the above

12. Which of the following currently allow(s) pharmacy technicians to call physicians for refill authorization?

    A. only the state of Florida
    B. the states of Florida and New York
    C. many states
    D. none of the above

13. Pharmacy technicians may be liable for which of the following areas?

    A. providing advice to patients
    B. providing patients' insurance information
    C. advising the pharmacist of known drug interactions
    D. advising co-workers about medication errors

14. Which of the following unintentional violations of the federal Controlled Substances Act is punished with a civil penalty?

    A. selling narcotic drugs
    B. purchasing non-narcotic drugs
    C. bookkeeping of controlled substances
    D. all of the above

15. Which of the following is *not* a responsibility of pharmacy technicians in the hospital setting?

    A. delivering medications to nurses
    B. preparing, packaging, and labeling drugs
    C. providing advice to nurses and patients
    D. checking patient charts in conjunction with prescriptions

Fill in the Blank

1. The board of pharmacy is a legislative body that has the authority to pass _____ regulations.

2. Many states have adopted provisions that were set forth by the National Association of _____.

3. In most states, the board of pharmacy can take disciplinary action against any pharmacist whose license was obtained through _____ , misrepresentation, or deceit.

4. State boards of pharmacy are responsible for approval of degree programs to teach the practice of _____.

5. State boards of pharmacy are mostly made up of pharmacists, healthcare professionals, and _____.

6. The pharmacist must review inpatient drug orders before initial dosage dispensation except in an _____.

CASE STUDY

A pharmacy technician practicing in the state of Oregon, which requires both active certification and licensure, remembers to recertify herself, but ignores the requirement to renew her license on time. After two months, the state board of pharmacy contacts her about her expired license.

1. What will this pharmacy technician have to do in order to become re-licensed?

2. Which examination or examinations must she take in order to become re-licensed?

3. How long will the new license last before it expires?

RELATED INTERNET SITES

http://careers.pharmacytimes.com

http://drugtopics.modernmedicine.com

http://www.bls.gov

http://www.iohpharm.com

http://www.pharmacychoice.com

http://www.ptcb.org

REFERENCES

American Pharmaceutical Association (author group). (2007). *Pharmacy Compounding Accreditation: A How-To Manual.* Washington, DC: American Pharmacists Association.

Fink, J. L., Vivian, J. C., & Keller Reid, K. (2005). *Pharmacy Law Digest* (40th ed.). Philadelphia: Lippincott Williams & Wilkins.

Moini, J. (2010). *The Pharmacy Technician—A Comprehensive Approach* (2nd ed.). Clifton Park, NY: Cengage Learning.

Moini, J. (2011). *Comprehensive Exam Review for the Pharmacy Technician* (2nd ed.). Clifton Park, NY: Cengage Learning.

Reiss, B. S., & Hall, G. D. (2010). *Guide to Federal Pharmacy Law* (7th ed.). Boynton Beach, FL: Apothecary Press.

Tietze, K. J. (2011). *Clinical Skills for Pharmacists: A Patient-Focused Approach* (3rd ed.). Philadelphia: Mosby.

University of the Sciences in Philadelphia. (Ed.). (2005). *Remington: The Science and Practice of Pharmacy* (21st ed.). Philadelphia Lippincott Williams & Wilkins.

Uselton, J. P., Kienle, P., & Murdaugh, L. B. (2010). *Assuring Continuous Compliance with Joint Commission Standards: A Pharmacy Guide* (8th ed.). Bethesda, MD: American Society of Health-System Pharmacists.

CHAPTER 1

What Would You Do?

Brian has had three traffic violations in the past three months. He has also been charged with domestic violence against his girlfriend. You are the pharmacist for whom Brian works, and you are aware of some of these events. One day, you hear him verbally provoking another worker until an argument breaks out. Brian becomes very agitated. Knowing his background, what would you do in this situation?

In this situation, it would be wise for the pharmacist to ask Brian to leave the pharmacy and take the rest of the day off. The next day, the situation should be discussed with Brian, and a letter written explaining that his behavior cannot be tolerated at work. This letter can serve as a legal notice to Brian that the pharmacy can terminate his employment should his adverse behavior continue.

You Be the Judge

Mark has been working in a retail pharmacy for 17 years. He is a senior technician, and a reliable person at work. About a year ago, his wife died, causing him to become very depressed. Last week, he made a mistake while he was compounding two medications. The pharmacist found out about his failure to exercise reasonable care while working. He told Mark that this was a case of negligence and that legal action could be brought based on his error. Mark responded rudely and even pushed the pharmacist.

In your judgment, what would be the possible consequences for Mark, taking his entire situation into account? What could he be charged with for being physically violent with the pharmacist?

In this situation, since Mark has been a good employee and only recently had problems because of the death of his wife, it may be a good idea to suggest grief counseling to Mark. However, the pharmacist was correct about Mark's potential liability for negligence. If the pharmacist chose to press charges against Mark, he could be charged with battery, though it is unlikely Mark would be convicted since there was no actual injury to the pharmacist. In most jurisdictions, Mark's actions against the pharmacist would be considered a misdemeanor, especially since there was no threat of a weapon being used.

CHAPTER 2

You Be the Judge

Pamela is a pharmacy technician who recently dispensed eyedrops for a patient with glaucoma. The patient used the eyedrops per the enclosed instructions, but experienced no positive effects, and after one week, was still experiencing minor but continuing visual impairment. The patient went back to her physician and complained about the eyedrops she had used. He checked the eyedrops, and found out that they were long past their expiration date. In your judgment, what would the possible consequences be for Pamela since she did not check the expiration date before the medication was dispensed by the pharmacist?

In addition, what would happen to the pharmacist because of this error?

Both Pamela and the pharmacist are responsible for the failure to check the expiration date; this product should have been removed from stock. The pharmacist is legally responsible for the actions of the pharmacy technician, and could be fined or even have his license revoked.

You Be the Judge

Greg, a pharmacy technician, was asked to fill a prescription by a man who entered the pharmacy. However, the prescription was, according to the man, for his girlfriend who was too ill to bring it herself. The man asked Greg what the medication was intended to treat. Greg told him it was used to treat sexually transmitted diseases. Which laws were violated by Greg's response? Could Greg be legally liable for a breach of confidentiality?

Greg violated the confidentiality of the patient's health information by telling the man that the medication was used to treat sexually transmitted diseases. He violated the HITECH Act and HIPAA. Greg could definitely be held liable if the female patient brought a breach of confidentiality lawsuit.

CHAPTER 3

You Be the Judge

Phil is a pharmacy technician who is asked by a customer about Plan B®, a medication intended for use as a morning-after pill. Because Phil believes that the use of a morning-after medication to prevent conception is wrong, he describes all sorts of serious adverse effects and states that they happen to most of the people who take the drug. As a result, the patient calls her doctor, who later calls the pharmacy and speaks with the pharmacist, telling him what Phil said and asking for an explanation. In your judgment, was Phil ethically correct in his actions? What sorts of legal repercussions do you think could await Phil as a result of his misstatements about Plan B?

Phil was not ethically correct in misrepresenting the facts about Plan B to the patient or in his failure to respect the patient's autonomy. He was not legally correct in advising this patient; he should have immediately referred her to the pharmacist. Because counseling a patient is outside the scope of a pharmacy technician's practice, he could lose his job as a result.

What Would You Do?

It is a busy afternoon, and the pharmacy has only one pharmacy technician on duty. The pharmacist does not consult with two patients because of all his other responsibilities, and they leave the pharmacy. If you were the pharmacist in this situation, what should you have done?

The pharmacist is ethically, morally, and legally responsible for consulting with patients. Consulting and supporting patients is more important than other activities, and he should have given it higher priority. A pharmacist's role as a patient advocate is of the utmost importance in preventing medication errors. It is important to prioritize in the pharmacy—with patient consultation being most important.

You Be the Judge

Molly, a young pharmacy technician, goes into work early Monday morning after spending Sunday night out late at a nightclub with her friends. She has a bad hangover. How could Molly's condition affect her ability to provide good patient care? What could Molly have done instead of coming to work in this condition? What may be the consequences of this type of behavior?

Molly's condition could impair her ability to make accurate judgments and concentrate on providing high-quality service to patients, and potentially could lead to her making errors that could harm them. She could have called in and asked for sick

leave or traded shifts with a co-worker—this way, the patients would not be compromised by her impaired conditi~~on. B~~...

a real concern because of his statem~~ents~~ ...
~~ph~~...

...this happen. Quickly, she picked the capsules off the floor and put them back onto the tray, after which she included them in the container of dispensed medication. If you were Sheila, what would you do in this situation? If you were another pharmacy worker who saw this happen, what would you do?

In this situation, the pharmacist should be notified about the capsules that were dropped on the floor. They should not be used for patients after they were spilled because of possible contaminants on the floor. If Sheila had been seen dropping the pills, the person who saw this should explain to her that the pills must be discarded and not used for patients—it would be morally wrong to use them. She should be reminded that the honesty and integrity of the pharmacy staff is of utmost importance.

What Would You Do?

Mr. Johnson, who has been coming to your pharmacy for many years, approaches you. You know that his wife died the previous year, and that he is taking medications for depression as well as cancer. When he arrives with a new prescription, he asks about the prescribed medication and comments, "I sure wouldn't want to take too much of this stuff. How much of this do you think would kill me if I wasn't careful?" Do you think Mr. Johnson may be contemplating suicide? What should you do first in this situation?

Given his state of health, the death of his wife, and his depression medication, suicide may be

A pharmacy technician is working on a Saturday morning. His pharmacist decides to take a break since there are no customers in the pharmacy. During the pharmacist's break, a friend of the pharmacy technician enters the pharmacy and asks if he can have a few Percocet tablets because of back pain. The pharmacy technician gives his friend six Percocet tablets out of a container in the pharmacy. His friend takes these tablets and leaves. What do you think the pharmacy technician did wrong in this situation? If the pharmacist finds out about this, what do you think the consequences will be? What possible legal action could ensue against this pharmacy technician?

The pharmacy technician has no authority to give medications to any person without a prescription. If the pharmacist finds out, the pharmacy technician will probably be fired. The pharmacist could even report the pharmacy technician to the authorities. The pharmacy technician could be charged with felony diversion of a controlled substance, and could be prosecuted for illegally dispensing a prescription drug. A conviction such as this would bar the pharmacy technician from participating in Medicare or Medicaid—which, in reality, means that no pharmacy would hire him in the future.

What Would You Do?

David is a pharmacy technician who received a prescription for Valium 50 mg b.i.d. for 30 days, with five refills. After thoroughly reviewing this prescription, if you were David, what would you do?

In this situation, the pharmacy technician should recognize that this prescription is out of the ordinary because Valium tablets are available in 2 mg, 5 mg, and 10 mg sizes, but not in 50 mg. David might assume that the physician meant to write "5.0 mg" but left out the decimal point. Also, the maximum amount of Valium usually suggested for a one-day period is 40 mg. The pharmacy technician should report this prescription to the pharmacist immediately.

You Be the Judge

A pharmacy technician who is also an avid basketball player has begun using anabolic steroids, which he obtains illegally from the pharmacy in which he works. Slowly, his behavior begins to change as a result of these drugs, and he eventually is fired from his job. What are the most common adverse effects of using anabolic steroids? Is the pharmacist liable for not noticing that these drugs were missing? What would be the consequences of stealing anabolic steroids?

Anabolic steroids commonly cause hypertension, cardiac problems, mental depression, suicidal behavior, and psychosis. The pharmacist should have been aware of the missing steroids, and could be held accountable for not keeping adequate records of the drug supply in the pharmacy. The theft of anabolic steroids is a felony, punishable by five years or longer in prison.

What Would You Do?

Mary Jo, an inexperienced pharmacy technician, started working in a retail pharmacy last week. Many customers were in close proximity to the counter. While dispensing a prescription for a certain patient, she called out to her by name, asking, "Mrs. Corby, can you please give me your Medicaid card so that I can make a copy?" What would you do in this situation, and what law was violated by Mary Jo?

In this situation, the pharmacy technician should ask the patient for the Medicaid card without anyone else being able to hear. Though it is not a violation of HIPAA or any other federal statute to publicly ask a patient for insurance documentation, it is polite to keep the patient's name and their insurance as confidential as possible.

CHAPTER 5

You Be the Judge

Glenn, a pharmacy technician who has been working for a year, was required because of new pharmacy rules to take drug-screening tests upon starting his second year at work. The new rules also required a full background check to be made. When Glenn's test results were returned, he had a positive result for cocaine in his system, and the background check revealed that he had a previous conviction for drug possession. In your judgment, what will be the result of Glenn's positive drug test and his background check?

If Glenn's positive drug test means he has broken the pharmacy's rules of employment, which is likely, he will probably be fired. If he had filled out information about his background before being hired initially, and never mentioned his drug conviction, this would also most likely result in him being fired. It is important to tell the truth about previous convictions whenever questioned about them in regard to employment.

What Would You Do?

Joe, a pharmacist, gave a list of 13 Schedule II drugs to Betty so that she could write them onto a DEA Form 222. Betty wrote all 13 items on the 10-line form so that Joe could then sign it. Joe told her she would have to redo the form. What should Betty have done in this situation?

Betty should have known that only 10 items in total could be ordered on one DEA Form 222. The other three items will have to be written on a second form.

What Would You Do?

Nicole had a back injury and was suffering from severe back pain. Her neurologist prescribed bottle. If you were Nicole, what would you do in this situation? Did she break the law?

Nicole should not have given the oxycodone, which is a scheduled drug, to anybody else. Distribution of this type of drug is against the law, punishable by fines and imprisonment. Though the circumstances in this situation are difficult, Nicole did break the law by giving her brother this medication.

What Would You Do?

Teresa, a pharmacy technician, was doing an initial inventory of scheduled drugs for a new pharmacy, including Schedule II drugs. She estimated the content of the scheduled drugs and recorded her estimates. When the pharmacist checked her inventory records later, he noticed that the inventory for the Schedule II drugs was not accurate. If you were Teresa, what would you have done differently?

Schedule II drugs must be counted exactly, one by one, rather than estimated. In general, Schedule III, IV, and V substances may be estimated; however, Schedule III and IV bottles of 1,000 pills (or more) must be counted exactly. Teresa should have known that the Schedule II drugs required an exact count.

You Be the Judge

Monica, a pharmacy technician, has assisted the pharmacist in completing an inventory of her pharmacy's medications. She found out that one bottle containing 20 Percocet tablets was missing. She notified the pharmacist, who told her to fill out the correct DEA form, which he would then sign. Which DEA form should Monica use? What would be the next step that Monica should take?

You Be the Judge

Mr. Pelosi was admitted to Pharrish Medical Center for the treatment of a sexually transmitted disease. A pharmacy technician who had access to his chart did not comply with the HIPAA Privacy Rule, and joked with a hospital janitor about Mr. Pelosi's condition. Later, the janitor, working in Mr. Pelosi's hospital room, told Mr. Pelosi not to worry, because he had had the same condition at one time, and that the hospital would take good care of him. Mr. Pelosi asked him how he knew about his condition, and the janitor mentioned the pharmacy technician who told him. Infuriated at this breach of his privacy, Mr. Pelosi called his lawyer and told him to file a lawsuit against the technician. In your judgment, can Mr. Pelosi sue the technician?

The HIPAA Privacy Rule does not give patients the express right to sue. A patient can file a written complaint with the Secretary of Health and Human Services through the Office of Civil Rights. The HHS Secretary will then decide whether to investigate the complaint.

CHAPTER 7

What Would You Do?

While John was compounding in the laboratory, he was splashed in the eyes with a chemical. He went to the men's room and washed his face in the sink. He did not use the eyewash facilities. After he went back to work, he found that his eyes remained irritated, and he could not see very well. If you were John, what would you do in this situation?

OSHA requires that eyewash facilities be available in laboratories. John should have used the eyewash facilities and notified his employer of the accident. He should have gone to the emergency room because he was still unable to see very well. His eyes could have permanent damage as a result.

What Would You Do?

Mary, a pharmacy technician working in a hospital pharmacy, was splashed when she accidentally dropped a glass medication bottle into an airflow hood. The moving air carried the medication onto her face. She was not wearing a mask but was wearing protective glasses. The medication partially entered her nose. If you were Mary, what would you do in this situation?

After exposure, Mary should immediately follow the post-exposure procedures of her hospital pharmacy, and should also notify her supervisor.

You Be the Judge

A compounding pharmacy provided its workers with gowns, goggles, gloves, and similar equipment on a regular basis, but did not provide an airflow hood because the types of substances compounded there did not require such a device. Because of a fire that had occurred in a nearby compounding pharmacy, this pharmacy was asked to quickly handle the compounding of cytotoxic agents required for several different patients. A pharmacy technician who knew that an airflow hood was required for work with these agents refused to complete the compounding, and was reprimanded. He notified OSHA that the pharmacist was completing the compounding of cytotoxic agents without the proper equipment. What do you think the OSHA inspectors would do in this case?

In this case, OSHA would hold the pharmacist accountable for the illegal compounding of cytotoxic agents without the proper equipment. The pharmacy technician was correct in his assumption about OSHA rules. Most likely, the pharmacist would be fined for his actions.

What Would You Do?

Shannon was working with electronic equipment in her pharmacy when a power cord caught fire. She was extremely nervous, and could not remember what she should do in case of fire. If you were Shannon, what procedures would you follow?

Shannon should pull the fire alarm box to alert her fellow employees of the fire. She should then locate the closest fire extinguisher by using the fire safety plan (which should show fire extinguisher locations).

What Would You Do?

Mark is a pharmacy technician. Three weeks after he was hired, his pharmacist set up an OSHA training class. Mark was sick during this time, and unable to attend. On his first day back at work, he was attempting to clean up a corrosive chemical spill on the floor. Since he had missed the training, Mark was unsure of the proper procedures to follow, and wore latex gloves while cleaning up the spill. If you were Mark, what would you do in this situation?

If Mark had attended his OSHA training, he would have known that special thick gloves are required to be used when cleaning up corrosive chemical spills, rather than ordinary latex gloves, which these types of chemicals can burn through. Therefore, only special utility gloves that resist corrosive chemicals should be used. If Mark were injured as a result, the pharmacy would be responsible. They should not have allowed Mark, who did not receive the training, to clean up the spill.

You Be the Judge

Joshua took a special OSHA course and understood his responsibilities on the job. One day when he was doing his routine work and dealing with chemical substances, he did not use protective equipment for safety. What could be the result of Joshua's actions?

Richard was talking to one of his co-workers, Nicole, in the pharmacy. He told her a rather rude joke of a sexual nature. Nicole was offended by the joke. If you were Nicole, what would you do?

Nicole has several options in this situation. She could ask Richard not to tell her any more jokes of this nature. If Richard persisted with these kinds of jokes, Nicole could report his actions to her supervisor, and even the authorities.

CHAPTER 8

What Would You Do?

Tara is a pharmacy technician who recently moved from Maine to Florida. According to the National Association of Boards of Pharmacy, if you were Tara, what would you have to do in order to be able to practice in Florida?

In this situation, a pharmacy technician can simply apply for any open position. The State of Florida previously did not require certification or registration in order to be able to practice as a pharmacy technician. (However, as of July 2008, Florida requires PTCB certification for pharmacy technicians.) If Tara already had previous certification or registration in another state, her qualifications may help her to gain employment more quickly than other applicants who may be uncertified or unregistered. Tara must get information about her board of pharmacy, registration, continuing education, disciplinary actions, and status of pharmacy technicians.

The state board of pharmacy may not allow the pharmacy to open until a correct fire safety plan and hazard communication plan are established, and the proper displays are posted. This includes evacuation routes, fire alarm pull stations, locations of extinguishers, etc.

What Would You Do?

Tina, a pharmacy technician, was dispensing a sulfa drug prescription. She forgot to put a required auxiliary label onto the container. The pharmacist noticed that there was no auxiliary label and told Tina that she must put the appropriate label onto the container. If you were Tina, what should you know about sulfa drugs and related auxiliary labels?

Sulfa drugs can cause severe adverse effects on the kidneys. The auxiliary label should indicate that this drug must be taken with plenty of water. Also, direct sunlight should be avoided as much as possible when taking sulfa drugs, and appropriate labeling regarding this point should be included.

You Be the Judge

Your pharmacist received a prescription for Zocor® 20 mg for 30 days. He selected the generic drug simvastatin instead of Zocor. Based on your knowledge, why did the pharmacist make this substitution? Is he allowed to do this?

The pharmacist followed a generic substitution law allowing simvastatin to be substituted for Zocor (if authorized by the physician) in order to

save the patient money. Simvastatin is identical to Zocor, so the pharmacist is allowed to make this substitution.

What Would You Do?

While you are dispensing a drug product, you hear that a client has asked the pharmacist if he can purchase a dozen hypodermic needles and syringes. The client claims he is a diabetic. You know this client personally, and are sure he has used illegal drugs in the past. What would you do in this scenario?

Morally, you are obligated to alert the pharmacist about the client's request, because sometimes the pharmacist requires a prescription for needles and syringes. However, since some states do not require a prescription for hypodermic or insulin needles and syringes, this patient may be able to obtain them regardless. Certain states' laws hold that these devices need to be available for sale without prescription because patients such as individuals with diabetes may need them quickly. Such an individual would probably know that he should ask for "insulin" syringes and not "hypodermic" syringes.

CHAPTER 9

What Would You Do?

Sean has been working in a retail pharmacy for 10 years. His certification has expired and he must renew it quickly in order to continue to practice. If you were Sean, what would you need to do to renew your certification?

Renewal of certification requires that the applicant complete 20 hours of continuing education credits, 1 hour of which must focus on pharmacy law, every two years; update the applicant's information with the certifying agency; pay a renewal fee; and fill out a renewal application form, which must be submitted within individual state time requirements. If submitted late, the renewal may require an additional fee. Also, it is important to remember that Sean cannot legally practice while his certification is expired.

You Be the Judge

Betty, a pharmacy technician, is working in a hospital pharmacy. While she is repacking drugs, she discovers that some of them have defective packaging. However, she ignores this, and repacks the drugs anyway. What do you think that Betty should have done in this case?

Betty should have notified her pharmacist about the defective packaging. Then, the decision could have been made to return them to the manufacturer or distributor in exchange for properly packaged replacements. If the defective packaging has damaged the drugs in any way, their effectiveness could be compromised, resulting in a medication error. Knowledge of the defective packaging and Betty's actions could result in penalties being assessed against Betty, the pharmacist, and the pharmacy itself.

You Be the Judge

Karen is a pharmacist who has been practicing at a retail pharmacy in Miami, Florida. Recently, the state board of pharmacy revoked her license. She is planning to move to the state of New York within a short period of time. What do you think that Karen will be required to do in order to practice pharmacy in New York?

For Karen to apply for a pharmacist license in New York, she must fill out the correct New York application and pay a fee. Part of the application asks if the applicant has ever had a license revoked. She would need to indicate that she has, and then submit a letter fully explaining the reasons that Florida revoked her license. She would have to list any resultant legal actions, outcomes, penalties, etc. The State of New York would take all of this into account in determining whether to grant Karen a pharmacist license.

during his pre-employ......
argued that the pharmacy had no right to "spring ....
on him" since he had been a faithful employee ever
since he was hired. The employer argued that, as
stated in the documents Vincent signed when he was
hired, it was their policy to conduct random drug
screening. Eventually, the pharmacy fired Vincent,
who intends to seek legal action against it. Who do
you think will prevail in this case, and why?

**In this case, the employer will probably prevail
since Vincent signed the hiring documents, which
indicated his understanding that the employer
had the right to conduct random drug screening
at any time. Vincent's history as a "good" employee
has nothing to do with the employer's right to
conduct these screenings.**

You Be the Judge

Jaime worked for a local pharmacy for three years.
On two occasions, she diverted a prescription
cream without a valid prescription and dispensed

any other ...
to resume work as a pharmac, ...
later, with her employer's approval, she requested
that her state board of pharmacy reinstate her
registration. Do you think that her state board of
pharmacy will allow reinstatement of her pharmacy
technician registration?

**In this case, the state board of pharmacy will
probably reinstate Jaime's registration. Since she
had worked for the same pharmacy for three years,
and only had these two instances of badly chosen
actions, and since she admitted her actions and
voluntarily surrendered her pharmacy technician
registration, the state board of pharmacy would
look closely at the employer's statements about
Jaime. Working as a cashier without any problems
for the employer-imposed one-year period,
and gaining the employer's approval of her
reinstatement, will most likely persuade the state
board of pharmacy to decide in Jaime's favor.**

adverse events involving human medical products. These include potential and actual product use errors and product quality problems. These errors and problems may be associated with the use of FDA-regulated drugs; biologics (human cells, tissues, and cellular and tissue-based products); medical devices (including in vitro diagnostics); and special nutritional products and cosmetics. The MedWatch Online Voluntary Reporting Form (3500) is located at https://www.accessdata.fda.gov/scripts/medwatch/medwatch-online.htm.

Also, manufacturers and distributors of FDA-approved biologics, drugs, special nutritional products, dietary supplements, radiation-emitting devices, infant formulas, and other medical products must report related problems and errors to the FDA. The form that is used to report problems and errors is shown here. (Source: http://www.fda.gov/Safety/MedWatch/default.htm)

U.S. Department of Health and Human Services

MEDWATCH
The FDA Safety Information and Adverse Event Reporting Program

For VOLUNTARY reporting of adverse events, product problems and product use errors

Form Approved: OMB No. 0910-0291, Expires: 10/31/08
See OMB statement on reverse.

Page ____ of ____

FDA USE ONLY

Triage unit sequence #

PLEASE TYPE OR USE BLACK INK

A. PATIENT INFORMATION

1. Patient Identifier
2. Age at Time of Event, or Date of Birth:
   In confidence
3. Sex
   ☐ Female
   ☐ Male
4. Weight
   or ____ lb
   or ____ kg

B. ADVERSE EVENT, PRODUCT PROBLEM OR ERROR

Check all that apply:

1. ☐ Adverse Event ☐ Product Problem (e.g., defects/malfunctions)
   ☐ Product Use Error ☐ Problem with Different Manufacturer of Same Medicine

2. Outcomes Attributed to Adverse Event (Check all that apply)
   ☐ Death: ____ (mm/dd/yyyy)
   ☐ Life-threatening
   ☐ Hospitalization - initial or prolonged
   ☐ Required Intervention to Prevent Permanent Impairment/Damage (Devices)
   ☐ Disability or Permanent Damage
   ☐ Congenital Anomaly/Birth Defect
   ☐ Other Serious (Important Medical Events)

3. Date of Event (mm/dd/yyyy)
4. Date of this Report (mm/dd/yyyy)

5. Describe Event, Problem or Product Use Error

6. Relevant Tests/Laboratory Data, Including Dates

7. Other Relevant History, Including Preexisting Medical Conditions (e.g., allergies, race, pregnancy, smoking and alcohol use, liver/kidney problems, etc.)

C. PRODUCT AVAILABILITY

Product Available for Evaluation? (Do not send product to FDA)
☐ Yes ☐ No ☐ Returned to Manufacturer on: ____ (mm/dd/yyyy)

D. SUSPECT PRODUCT(S)

1. Name, Strength, Manufacturer (from product label)
   #1
   #2

2. Dose or Amount | Frequency | Route
   #1
   #2

3. Dates of Use (If unknown, give duration) from/to (or best estimate)
   #1
   #2
5. Event Abated After Use Stopped or Dose Reduced?
   #1 ☐ Yes ☐ No ☐ Doesn't Apply
   #2 ☐ Yes ☐ No ☐ Doesn't Apply

4. Diagnosis or Reason for Use (Indication)
   #1
   #2
6. Event Reappeared After Reintroduction?
   #1 ☐ Yes ☐ No ☐ Doesn't Apply

6. Lot # | 7. Expiration Date
   #1 | #1
   #2 | #2
   #2 ☐ Yes ☐ No ☐ Doesn't Apply
9. NDC # or Unique ID

E. SUSPECT MEDICAL DEVICE

1. Brand Name
2. Common Device Name
3. Manufacturer Name, City and State

4. Model # | Lot # | 5. Operator of Device
   Catalog # | Expiration Date (mm/dd/yyyy) | ☐ Health Professional
   Serial # | Other # | ☐ Lay User/Patient
                          ☐ Other:

6. If Implanted, Give Date (mm/dd/yyyy) | 7. If Explanted, Give Date (mm/dd/yyyy)

8. Is this a Single-use Device that was Reprocessed and Reused on a Patient?
   ☐ Yes ☐ No
9. If Yes to Item No. 8, Enter Name and Address of Reprocessor

F. OTHER (CONCOMITANT) MEDICAL PRODUCTS

Product names and therapy dates (exclude treatment of event)

G. REPORTER (See confidentiality section on back)

1. Name and Address

Phone # | E-mail

2. Health Professional? 3. Occupation 4. Also Reported to:
   ☐ Yes ☐ No   ☐ Manufacturer
5. If you do NOT want your identity disclosed to the manufacturer, place an "X" in this box: ☐
                              ☐ User Facility
                              ☐ Distributor/Importer

FORM FDA 3500 (10/05) Submission of a report does not constitute an admission that medical personnel or the product caused or contributed to the event.

© U.S. Department of Health and Human Services

ADVICE ABOUT VOLUNTARY REPORTING

Detailed instructions available at: http://www.fda.gov/medwatch/report/consumer/instruct.htm

Report adverse events, product problems or product use errors with:

- Medications *(drugs or biologics)*
- Medical devices *(including in-vitro diagnostics)*
- Combination products *(medication & medical devices)*
- Human cells, tissues, and cellular and tissue-based products
- Special nutritional products *(dietary supplements, medical foods, infant formulas)*
- Cosmetics

Report product problems - quality, performance or safety concerns such as:

- Suspected counterfeit product
- Suspected contamination
- Questionable stability
- Defective components
- Poor packaging or labeling
- Therapeutic failures (product didn't work)

Report SERIOUS adverse events. An event is serious when the patient outcome is:

- Death
- Life-threatening
- Hospitalization - initial or prolonged
- Disability or permanent damage
- Congenital anomaly/birth defect
- Required intervention to prevent permanent impairment or damage
- Other serious (important medical events)

Report even if:

- You're not certain the product caused the event
- You don't have all the details

How to report:

- Just fill in the sections that apply to your report
- Use section D for all products except medical devices
- Attach additional pages if needed
- Use a separate form for each patient
- Report either to FDA or the manufacturer *(or both)*

Other methods of reporting:

- 1-800-FDA-0178 -- To FAX report
- 1-800-FDA-1088 -- To report by phone
- www.fda.gov/medwatch/report.htm -- To report online

If your report involves a serious adverse event with a device and it occurred in a facility outside a doctor's office, that facility may be legally required to report to FDA and/or the manufacturer. Please notify the person in that facility who would handle such reporting.

If your report involves a serious adverse event with a vaccine call 1-800-822-7967 to report.

Confidentiality: The patient's identity is held in strict confidence by FDA and protected to the fullest extent of the law. FDA will not disclose the reporter's identity in response to a request from the public, pursuant to the Freedom of Information Act. The reporter's identity, including the identity of a self-reporter, may be shared with the manufacturer unless requested otherwise.

-Fold Here-

The public reporting burden for this collection of information has been estimated to average 36 minutes per response, including the time for reviewing instructions, searching existing data sources, gathering and maintaining the data needed, and completing and reviewing the collection of information. Send comments regarding this burden estimate or any other aspect of this collection of information, including suggestions for reducing this burden to:

Department of Health and Human Services
Food and Drug Administration - MedWatch
10903 New Hampshire Avenue
Building 22, Mail Stop 4447
Silver Spring, MD 20993-0002

Please DO NOT
RETURN this form
to this address.

OMB statement:
"An agency may not conduct or sponsor, and a person is not required to respond to, a collection of information unless it displays a currently valid OMB control number."

U.S. DEPARTMENT OF HEALTH AND HUMAN SERVICES
Food and Drug Administration

FORM FDA 3500 (10/05) (Back)   Please Use Address Provided Below -- Fold in Thirds, Tape and Mail

DEPARTMENT OF
HEALTH & HUMAN SERVICES

Public Health Service
Food and Drug Administration
Rockville, MD 20857

Official Business
Penalty for Private Use $300

NO POSTAGE
NECESSARY
IF MAILED
IN THE
UNITED STATES
OR APO/FPO

BUSINESS REPLY MAIL

FIRST CLASS MAIL   PERMIT NO. 946   ROCKVILLE MD

MEDWATCH
The FDA Safety Information and Adverse Event Reporting Program
Food and Drug Administration
5600 Fishers Lane
Rockville, MD 20852-9787

NOTE: MedWatch Online Form 3500 does not allow the reporting of vaccines or investigational (study) drugs, nor is it used for mandatory reporting of drugs, biologics, and devices. To report vaccine events, you must use the Vaccine Adverse Event Reporting System (VAERS) at https://vaers.hhs.gov/esub/step1. Investigational (study) drug adverse events should be reported as required in study protocols by sending the report to the address and contact person listed in the study protocol.

Special Tasks for Pharmacy

State	May Prepare Medications in Cards for Nursing Homes	May Reconstitute Oral Liquids	May Place Prescription Labels on Containers	May Call Physicians for Refill Authorization
Alabama	Yes	Yes	Yes	Yes
Alaska	Yes	Yes	Yes	Yes
Arizona	Yes	Yes	Yes	Yes
Arkansas	Yes	Yes	Yes	Yes
California	Yes	Yes	Yes	Yes
Colorado	Yes	Yes	Yes	Yes
Connecticut	Yes	Yes	Yes	Yes
Delaware	Yes	Yes	Yes	Yes, if certified
District of Columbia	Yes	Yes	Yes	Yes
Florida	Yes	Yes	Yes	Yes
Georgia	Yes	Yes	Yes	No
Hawaii	Yes	Yes	Yes	No
Idaho	Yes	Yes	Yes	Yes
Illinois	Yes	Yes	Yes	Yes
Indiana	Yes	Yes	Yes	Yes
Iowa	Yes	Yes	Yes	Yes
Kansas	Yes	Yes	Yes	Yes
Kentucky	Yes	Yes	Yes	Yes
Louisiana	Yes	Yes	Yes	Yes
Maine	Yes	Yes	Yes	Yes
Maryland	Yes	Yes	Yes	No
Massachusetts	Yes	Yes	Yes	Yes
Michigan	Yes	Yes	Yes	No
Minnesota	Yes	Yes	Yes	Yes
Mississippi	Yes	Yes	Yes	Yes
Missouri	Yes	Yes	Yes	Yes

(continued)

State	May Prepare Medications in Cards for Nursing Homes	May Reconstitute Oral Liquids	May Place Prescription Labels on Containers	May Call Physicians for Refill Authorization
Montana	Yes	Yes	Yes	No
Nebraska	Yes	Yes	Yes	No
Nevada	Yes	Yes	Yes	Yes
New Hampshire	Yes	Yes	Yes	No
New Jersey	Yes	Yes	Yes	No
New Mexico	Yes	Yes	Yes	Yes
New York	Yes	No	Yes	No
North Carolina	Yes	Yes	Yes	Yes
North Dakota	Yes	Yes	Yes	Yes
Ohio	Yes	Yes	Yes	No
Oklahoma	Yes	Yes	Yes	Yes
Oregon	Yes	Yes	Yes	Yes
Pennsylvania	Yes	Yes	Yes	No
Rhode Island	Yes	Yes	Yes	Yes
South Carolina	Yes	Yes	Yes	No
South Dakota	Yes	Yes	Yes	No
Tennessee	Yes	Yes	Yes	Yes
Texas	Yes	Yes	Yes	Yes
Utah	Yes	Yes	Yes	Yes
Vermont	Yes	Yes	Yes	Yes
Virginia	Yes	Yes	Yes	No
Washington	Yes	Yes	Yes	Yes
West Virginia	Yes	Yes	Yes	Yes
Wisconsin	Yes	No	Yes	Yes
Wyoming	Yes	Yes	Yes	Yes

Source: Adapted from Strandberg, K. M. (2011). *Essentials of Law and Ethics for Pharmacy Technicians* (3rd ed.). New York: CRC.

State	Accept Prescriptions over the Phone	Enter Prescriptions into Computers
Alabama	No	Yes
Alaska	No	Yes
Arizona	No	Yes
Arkansas	No	Yes
California	No	Yes
Colorado	No	Yes
Connecticut	No	Yes
Delaware	No	Yes
District of Columbia	Yes	Yes
Florida	No	Yes
Georgia	No	Yes
Hawaii	No	Yes
Idaho	No	Yes
Illinois	No	Yes
Indiana	No	Yes
Iowa	Yes	Yes
Kansas	No	Yes
Kentucky	No	Yes
Louisiana	No	Yes
Maine	No	Yes
Maryland	No	Yes
Massachusetts	No	Yes
Michigan	Yes	Yes
Minnesota	No	Yes
Mississippi	No	Yes
Missouri	Yes	Yes
Montana	No	Yes

(continued)

State	Accept Prescriptions over the Phone	Enter Prescriptions into Computers
Nebraska	No	Yes
Nevada	No	Yes
New Hampshire	No	Yes
New Jersey	No	Yes
New Mexico	No	Yes
New York	No	Yes
North Carolina	Yes	Yes
North Dakota	Yes	Yes
Ohio	No	Yes
Oklahoma	No	Yes
Oregon	No	Yes
Pennsylvania	No	Yes
Rhode Island	Yes	Yes
South Carolina	No	Yes
South Dakota	No	Yes
Tennessee	Yes	Yes
Texas	No	Yes
Utah	No	Yes
Vermont	No	Yes
Virginia	No	Yes
Washington	No	Yes
West Virginia	No	Yes
Wisconsin	No	Yes
Wyoming	No	Yes

NOTE: All jurisdictions currently allow pharmacy technicians to enter information into patient files, retrieve stocked medications, prepare prescription labels, and place medications into containers.

Source: Adapted from Strandberg, K. M. (2011). *Essentials of Law and Ethics for Pharmacy Technicians* (3rd ed.). New York: CRC.

State	Certification Required	Registration Required	Licensure Required
Alaba...			
		Yes	No
California	No	No	Yes
Colorado	No	No	No
Connecticut	No	Yes	No
Delaware	No	No	No
District of Columbia	Yes, but this is in some contention with various authorities and is still being researched.	No	No
Florida	No	Yes	No
Georgia	No	Yes	No
Hawaii	No	No	No
Idaho	Yes, for PTs registered after July 1, 2009, and for those registered before that date who change employers.	Yes	No
Illinois	Yes	Yes	No
Indiana	No	Yes	No
Iowa	Yes	Yes	No
Kansas	No	Yes	No

(continued)

State	Certification Required	Registration Required	Licensure Required
Kentucky	No	Yes	No
Louisiana	No	Yes	No
Maine	No	Yes	No
Maryland	Yes	Yes	No
Massachusetts	No	Yes	No
Michigan	No	No	No
Minnesota	No	Yes	No
Mississippi	Yes, upon renewal for any PT who registered with the Board after April 1, 2011.	Yes	No
Missouri	No	Yes	No
Montana	No	Yes	No
Nebraska	No	Yes	No
Nevada	No	Yes	No
New Hampshire	No	Yes	No
New Jersey	No	Yes	No
New Mexico	Yes	Yes	No
New York	No	No	No
North Carolina	No	Yes	No
North Dakota	No	Yes	No
Ohio	No	No	No
Oklahoma	No	Yes	No
Oregon	No, but all PTs will need to be certified in the future.	No	Yes
Pennsylvania	No	No	No
Rhode Island	No	No	Yes
South Carolina	No	Yes	No
South Dakota	No	Yes	No
Tennessee	No	Yes	No

(continued)

State	Certification Required	Registration Required	Licensure Required
Virginia	Yes	Yes	No
Washington	No	Yes	No
West Virginia	No	Yes	No
Wisconsin	No	No	No
Wyoming	No	Yes	Yes

Source: http://www.nhanow.com

State Boards of Pharmacy

Mount Prospect, IL 60056
Phone: (847) 391-4406
Website: http://www.nabp.net
E-mail: exec-office@nabp.net

Alabama
Herbert "Herb" Bobo, Executive Director
P.O. Box 381988
Birmingham, AL 35238
Phone: (205) 981-2280
Website: http://www.albop.com
E-mail: hbobo@albop.com

Alaska
Mary Kay Vellucci, Licensing Examiner
P.O. Box 110806
Juneau, AK 99811-0806
Phone: (907) 465-2589
Website: http://www.commerce.state.ak.us/occ/ppha
.htm
E-mail: mary.kay.velluci@alaska.gov

Arizona
Hal Wand, Executive Director
P.O. Box 18520
Phoenix, AZ 85005-8520
Phone: (602) 771-2740
Website: http://www.azpharmacy.gov/default.asp
E-mail: hwand@azpharmacy.gov

Little Rock, AR 72201
Phone: (501) 682-0190
Website: http://www.arkansas.gov/asbp
E-mail: John.Kirtley@arkansas.gov

California
Virginia "Giny" Herold, Executive Officer
1625 N. Market Blvd., N219
Sacramento, CA 95834
Phone: (916) 574-7900
Website: http://www.pharmacy.ca.gov
E-mail: Virginia_herold@dca.ca.gov

Colorado
Wendy Anderson, Program Director
1560 Broadway, Suite 1350
Denver, CO 80202-5143
Phone: (303) 894-7800
Website: http://www.dora.state.co.us/pharmacy/
E-mail: pharmacy@dora.state.co.us

Connecticut
deLinda Brown-Jagne, Board Administrator
State Office Building, 165 Capital Ave., Room 147
Hartford, CT 06106
Phone: (860) 713-6070
Website: http://www.ct.gov/dcp/site/default.asp
E-mail: delinda.brown-jagne@ct.gov

Delaware
David W. Dryden, Executive Secretary
Division of Professional Regulation
Cannon Building, 861 Silver Lake Blvd., Suite 203
Dover, DE 19904
Phone: (302) 744-4500
Website: http://www.dpr.delaware.gov
E-mail: customerservice.dpr@state.de.us

District of Columbia
Patricia D'Antonio, Executive Director
899 North Capitol Street, N.E., Second Floor
Washington, DC 20002
Phone: (202) 727-9856
Website: http://doh.dc.gov/service
/health-professionals
E-mail: patricia.dantonio@dc.gov

Florida
Mark Whitten, Executive Director
4052 Bald Cypress Way, Bin #C04
Tallahassee, FL 32399-3254
Phone: (850) 245-4292
Website: http://www.doh.state.fl.us/mqa/pharmacy/
E-mail: MQA_Pharmacy@doh.state.fl.us

Georgia
Tanja Battle, Executive Director
Professional Licensing Boards
237 Coliseum Dr.
Macon, GA 31217-3858
Phone: (478) 207-2440
Website: http://www.sos.ga.gov/plb/pharmacy/
E-mail (online form): http://www.sos.ga.gov/cgi-bin
/emailplb.asp

Guam
Eugene Santos, Acting Administrator
651 Legacy Square Commercial Complex, South
Route 10, Suite 9
Mangilao, GU 96913
Phone: (671) 735-7406 ext. 11
Website: http://www.dphss.guam.gov/
E-mail: eugene.santos@dphss.guam.gov

Hawaii
Lee Ann Teshima, Executive Officer
P.O. Box 3469
Honolulu, HI 96801
Phone: (808) 586-2695
Website: http://www.hawaii.gov/dcca/areas/pvl
/boards/pharmacy
E-mail: pharmacy@dcca.hawaii.gov

Idaho
Mark D. Johnston, Executive Director
1199 Shoreline Ln., Suite 303
Boise, ID 83702
Phone: (208) 334-2356
Website: http://bop.idaho.gov/
E-mail: Mark.Johnston@bop.idaho.gov

Illinois
Carol Freligh, Pharmacy Board Liaison
320 W. Washington, 3rd Floor
Springfield, IL 62786
Phone: (217) 782-8556
Website: http://www.idfpr.com
E-mail: fpr.prfgroup10@illinois.gov

Indiana
Phil Wickizer, Director
402 W. Washington St, Room W072
Indianapolis, IN 46204-2739
Phone: (317) 234-2067
Website: http://www.in.gov/pla/pharmacy.htm
E-mail: pla4@pla.IN.gov

Debra L. Billingsley, Executive Secretary
800 S.W. Jackson, Suite 1414
Topeka, KS 66612
Phone: (785) 296-4056
Website: http://www.kansas.gov/pharmacy
E-mail: dbillingsley@pharmacy.ks.gov

Kentucky

Michael A. Burleson, Executive Director
State Office Building Annex, Suite 300
125 Holmes St.
Frankfort, KY 40601
Phone: (502) 564-7910
Website: http://pharmacy.ky.gov/
E-mail: pharmacy.board@ky.gov

Louisiana

Malcolm J. Broussard, Executive Director
3388 Brentwood Dr.
Baton Rouge, LA 70809-1700
Phone: (225) 925-6496
Website: http://www.pharmacy.la.gov
E-mail: info@pharmacy.la.gov

Maine

Geraldine L."Jeri" Betts, Board Administrator
Department of Professional and Financial Regulation
35 State House Station
Augusta, ME 04333
Phone: (207) 624-8603
Website: http://www.maine.gov/professionallicensing
E-mail: geraldine.l.betts@maine.gov

Massachusetts

James D. Coffey, Director
239 Causeway St., 5th Floor, Suite 500
Boston, MA 02114
Phone: (617) 973-0950
Website: http://www.mass.gov/dph/boards
/pharmacy
E-mail: James.d.coffey@state.ma.us

Michigan

Rae Ramsdell, Acting Bureau Director
611 W. Ottawa, First Floor
P.O. Box 30670
Lansing, MI 48909-8170
Phone: (517) 335-7212
Website: http://www.michigan.gov/healthlicense
E-mail: ramsdellr@michigan.gov

Minnesota

Cody C. Wiberg, Executive Director
2829 University Ave. S.E., Suite 530
Minneapolis, MN 55414-3251
Phone: (651) 201-2825
Website: http://www.pharmacy.state.mn.us/
E-mail: pharmacy.board@state.mn.us

Mississippi

Frank Gammill, Executive Director
204 Key Dr., Suite D
Madison, MS 39110
Phone: (601) 605-5388
Website: http://www.mbp.state.ms.us
E-mail: fgammill@mbp.state.ms.us

Missouri
Kimberly Grinston, Executive Director
P.O. Box 625
Jefferson City, MO 65102
Phone: (573) 751-0091
Website: http://www.pr.mo.gov/pharmacists.asp
E-mail: pharmacy@pr.mo.gov

Montana
Ronald J. Klein, Executive Director
P.O. Box 200513
301 S. Park Ave, 4th Floor
Helena, MT 59620-0513
Phone: (406) 841-2371
Website: http://bsd.dli.mt.gov/license/bsd_boards
/pha_board/board_page.asp
E-mail: roklein@mt.gov

Nebraska
Becky Wisell, Administrator
P.O. Box 94986
Lincoln, NE 68509-4986
Phone: (402) 471-2118
Website: http://dhhs.ne.gov/publichealth/Pages
/crl_medical_pharm_pharmlic_pharmindex.aspx
E-mail: becky.wisell@nebraska.gov

Nevada
Larry L. Pinson, Executive Secretary
431 W. Plumb Lane
Reno, NV 89509
Phone: (775) 850-1440
Website: http://bop.nv.gov
E-mail: pharmacy@pharmacy.nv.gov

New Hampshire
Jay Queenan, Executive Secretary/Director
57 Regional Drive
Concord, NH 03301-8518
Phone: (603) 271-2350
Website: http://www.nh.gov/pharmacy
E-mail: pharmacy.board@nh.gov

New Jersey
Anthony Rubinaccio, Executive Director
P.O. Box 45013
Newark, NJ 07101
Phone: (973) 504-6450
Website: http://www.state.nj.us/lps/ca/boards.htm
E-mail: RubinaccioA@dca.lps.state.nj.us

New Mexico
William Harvey, Executive Director/Chief Drug
Inspector
5200 Oakland N.E., Suite A
Albuquerque, NM 87113
Phone: (505) 222-9830
Website: http://www.rld.state.nm.us/boards
/Pharmacy.aspx
E-mail: william.harvey@state.nm.us

New York
Lawrence H. Mokhiber, Executive Secretary
89 Washington Ave., 2nd Floor W.
Albany, NY 12234-1000
Phone: (518) 474-3817 ext. 130
Website: www.op.nysed.gov
E-mail: pharmbd@mail.nysed.gov

North Carolina
Jack W. "Jay" Campbell IV, Executive Director
6015 Farrington Rd., Suite 201
Chapel Hill, NC 27517
Phone: (919) 246-1050
Website: http://www.ncbop.org
E-mail: jcampbell@ncbop.org

North Dakota
Howard C. Anderson, Jr., Executive Director
1906 E. Broadway Ave.
Bismarck, ND 58501-1354
Phone: (701) 328-9535
Website: http://www.nodakpharmacy.com
E-mail: ndboph@btinet.net

Ohio

John A. Foust, Executive Director
4545 Lincoln Blvd., Suite 112
Oklahoma City, OK 73105-3488
Phone: (405) 521-3815
Website: http://www.pharmacy.ok.gov
E-mail: pharmacy@pharmacy.ok.gov

Oregon
Gary A. Schnabel, Executive Director
800 N.E. Oregon St., Suite 150
Portland, OR 97232
Phone: (971) 673-0001
Website: http://www.pharmacy.state.or.us
E-mail: pharmacy.board@state.or.us

Pennsylvania
Melanie Zimmerman, Executive Secretary
P.O. Box 2649
Harrisburg, PA 17105-2649
Phone: (717) 783-7156
Website: http://www.dos.state.pa.us/pharm
E-mail: st-pharmacy@state.pa.us

Puerto Rico
Ernesto Caballero, Executive Director
Department of Health, Call Box 10200
Santurce, PR 00908
Phone: (787) 781-8989 ext 6581
Website: http://www.salud.gov.pr/Pages/default.aspx
E-mail: ecaballero@salud.gov.pr

South Carolina
Lee Ann Bundrick, Administrator
Kingstree Bldg.
110 Centerview Dr.
Columbia, SC 29210
Phone: (803) 896-4700
Website: http://www.llr.state.sc.us/pol/pharmacy
E-mail: bundricl@llr.sc.gov

South Dakota
Randy Jones, Executive Director
3701 West 49th St., Suite 204
Sioux Falls, SD 57106
Phone: (605) 362-2737
Website: http://www.pharmacy.sd.gov
E-mail: randy.jones@state.sd.us

Tennessee
Andrew Holt, Executive Director
227 French Landing, Suite 300
Nashville, TN 37243
Phone: (615) 741-2718
Website: http://health.state.tn.us/Boards/Pharmacy
/index.shtml
E-mail: andrew.holt@state.tn.us

Texas
Gay Dodson, Executive Director/Secretary
333 Guadalupe, Tower 3, Suite 600
Austin, TX 78701
Phone: (512) 305-8000
Website: http://www.tsbp.state.tx.us
E-mail: gay.dodson@tsbp.state.tx.us

Utah
Debra Hobbins, Bureau Manager
Division of Occupational and Professional Licensing
P.O. Box 146741
Salt Lake City, UT 84114-6741
Phone: (801) 530-6789
Website: http://www.dopl.utah.gov/
E-mail: dhobbins@utah.gov

Vermont
Ronald J. Klein, Executive Officer
Office of Professional Regulation
National Life Bldg, North FL2
Montpelier, VT 05620-3402
Phone: (802) 828-2373
Website: http://www.vtprofessionals.org
E-mail: ronald.klein@sec.state.vt.us

Virgin Islands
Deborah Richardson-Peter, Interim Director
1303 Hospital Ground, Suite 10
St. Thomas, VI 00802
Phone: (340) 774-0117
Website: http://www.healthvi.org
E-mail: deborah.richardson@usvi-doh.org

Virginia
Caroline Juran, Executive Director
9960 Mayland Dr., Suite 300
Henrico, VA 23233-1463
Phone: (804) 367-4456
Website: http://www.dhp.virginia.gov/pharmacy
E-mail: pharmbd@dhp.virginia.gov

Washington
Steven M. Saxe, Interim Executive Director
P.O. Box 47852
Olympia, WA 98504-7852
Phone: (360) 236-4946
Website: http://www.doh.wa.gov/hsqa/Professions
/Pharmacy/default.htm
E-mail: wsbop@doh.wa.gov

West Virginia
David E. Potters, Executive Director and General
Counsel
232 Capitol St.
Charleston, WV 25301
Phone: (304) 558-0558
Website: http://www.wvbop.com/
E-mail: david.e.potters@wv.gov

Wisconsin
Dan Williams, Bureau Director
P.O. Box 8935
Madison, WI 53708-8935
Phone: (608) 266-2112
Website: http://www.drl.state.wi.us/
E-mail: drlboards@wisconsin.gov

Wyoming
Mary K. Walker, Executive Director
1712 Carey Ave., Suite 200
Cheyenne, WY 82002
Phone: (307) 634-9636
Website: http://pharmacyboard.state.wy.us/
E-mail: BOP@wyo.gov

Source: http://www.nabp.net

or Pharmacy (AACP)
1727 King Street
Alexandria, VA 22314
(703) 739-2330
http://www.aacp.org
Founded in 1900, the AACP is the national
organization representing pharmacy education
in the United States. The mission of AACP is to
lead and partner with its members in advancing
pharmacy education, research, scholarship, practice,
and service to improve societal health. The AACP
publishes *Academic Pharmacy Now*, a biweekly
E-lert newsletter, news releases, and a variety of
other resources.

American Association of Pharmaceutical Scientists (AAPS)
2107 Wilson Blvd., Suite 700
Arlington, VA 22201-3042
(703) 243-2800
http://www.aaps.org
Established in 1986, the AAPS is a professional
scientific association of approximately 12,000
members employed in industry, academia,
government, and other research institutes
worldwide. The AAPS provides a dynamic
international forum for the exchange of knowledge
among scientists to enhance their contributions
to public health. The AAPS publishes *AAPS
Newsmagazine, Careers, The AAPS Journal, AAPS
PharmSciTech*, and *Pharmaceutical Research*. The
AAPS Press offers a variety of books through its
publishing program, which was created for the
pharmaceutical scientist.

Association of Pharmacy Technicians (AAPT)
P.O. Box 1447
Greensboro, NC 27402
(877) 368-4771
http://www.pharmacytechnician.com
Established in 1979, the AAPT provides leadership
and represents the interests of its members to
the public as well as healthcare organizations.
The AAPT was the first pharmacy technician
association in the United States and remains a
not-for-profit association. It publishes the *AAPT
Newsletter* for its members.

American College of Clinical Pharmacy (ACCP)
13000 W. 87th St. Parkway
Lenexa, KS 66215-4530
(913) 492-3311
http://www.accp.com
Established in 1979, the ACCP is a professional
scientific society that provides leadership,
education, advocacy, and resources that enable
clinical pharmacists to achieve excellence in practice
and research. Its membership is composed of
practitioners, scientists, educators, administrators,
students, residents, fellows, and others committed
to excellence in clinical pharmacy and patient
pharmacotherapy. The AACP publishes a variety
of papers, including petitions, commentaries,
white papers, position statements, guidelines,
opinion papers, and other documents of interest.
Publications include *Pharmacotherapy* and the
ACCP Report.

Accreditation Council for Pharmacy Education (ACPE)
135 S. LaSalle Street, Suite 4100
Chicago, IL 60603-4810
(312) 664-3575
http://www.acpe-accredit.org
The ACPE was established in 1932 and is the national agency for the accreditation of professional degree programs in pharmacy and providers of continuing pharmacy education. It is an autonomous and independent agency whose board of directors is drawn from members of the American Association of Colleges of Pharmacy (AACP), the American Pharmacists Association (APhA), the National Association of Boards of Pharmacy (NABP), and the American Council on Education (ACE). Its publications include the *CPE Provider eUpdate, ACPE Update Newsletter,* and the *International Services Program Newsletter.*

American Pharmacists Association (APhA)
2215 Constitution Avenue, N.W.
Washington, DC 20037
(800) 237-2742
http://www.pharmacist.com
Established in 1852 as the American Pharmaceutical Association, the APhA is a leader in providing professional education and information for pharmacists and is an advocate for improved health of the American public through the provision of comprehensive pharmaceutical care. The APhA consists of three academies:
+ The Academy of Pharmacy Practice and Management (APhA-APPM)
+ The Academy of Pharmaceutical Research and Science (APhA-APRS)
+ The Academy of Students of Pharmacy (APhA-ASP)

American Society of Health-System Pharmacists (ASHP)
7272 Wisconsin Avenue
Bethesda, MD 20814
(866) 279-0681
http://www.ashp.org

Established in 1942, the ASHP is a 35,000-member national professional association that represents pharmacists who practice in hospitals, health maintenance organizations, long-term care facilities, home care, and other components of healthcare systems. The ASHP represents pharmacists who practice in the following environments:
+ Health maintenance organizations
+ Hospitals
+ Home care agencies
+ Long-term care facilities
+ Other institutions

The ASHP publishes continuing education publications and "briefs" that earn CPE hours in an online, electronic format.

National Pharmacy Technician Association (NPTA)
P.O. Box 683148
Houston, TX 72268
(888) 247-8700
http://www.pharmacytechnician.org
Established in 1991, the NPTA is the world's largest professional organization specifically for pharmacy technicians. The organization is composed of pharmacy technicians practicing in a variety of practice settings, including retail chains, independent, hospital, mail-order, home care, long-term care, nuclear, military, correctional facility, formal education, training, management, sales, and many more. It publishes *Today's Technician*, which was the first full-color magazine specifically for pharmacy technicians.

Pharmacy Technician Certification Board (PTCB)
2215 Constitution Avenue N.W.
Washington, DC 20005
(800) 363-8012
http://www.ptcb.org
The PTCB was established in 1995 by five organizations: the American Pharmacists Association, the American Society of

Health-System Pharmacists, the Illinois Council of Health-System Pharmacists, the Michigan Pharmacists Association, and the National

Pharmacy Technician Educators Council (PTEC)
6144 Knyghton Road
Indianapolis, IN 46220
(317) 962-0919
http://www.pharmacytecheducators.com
Established in 1991, the PTEC's mission is to assist the profession of pharmacy in preparing high-quality, well-trained technical personnel through education and practical training. The PTEC publishes a newsletter containing information dedicated to pharmacy technician education, and the *Journal of Pharmacy Technology*, a peer-reviewed publication containing information dedicated to pharmacy practice, training, and technology.

United States Pharmacopeial Convention (USP)
12601 Twinbrook Parkway

, the Food and Drug Administration, and these standards are developed and relied upon in more than 130 countries. The USP publishes *The Standard*, a quarterly newsletter delivering news about the USP's science, people, products, and public health programs. It publishes international quarterly updates in Brazil, China, and India, and also offers electronic newsletter for foods, dietary supplements, biologics, and biotechnology, as well as monthly e-mail notices and compendial updates.

food and drug substances. Monographs consist of the following sections:

- A substance's molecular structure
- A substance's chemical formula and molecular weight
- The required potency for a substance to be considered "USP grade"
- Packaging and storage requirements
- Labeling requirements
- USP reference standards required for testing a substance
- Description of test methods, references to test methods, and references to related monographs

The USP-NF also contains descriptions of analytical procedures, apparatuses that may be used, and reagent monographs. It is published every five years, though continual revisions take place on a regular basis. The USP also sells "reference standards" to use in determining whether substances meet USP requirements.

A sample drug monograph for acetaminophen is shown below.

Acetaminophen Monograph, Illustrated

1. Acetaminophen

HO — $\langle$ ring $\rangle$ — N(H) — C(=O) — CH₃

$C_8H_9NO_2$ 151.17

Acetamide, *N*-(4 hydroxyphenyl)-.4'-Hydroxyacetanilide [103-90-2].

2. Acetaminophen contains not less than 98.0 percent and not more than 101.0 percent of $C_8H_9NO_2$, calculated on the anhydrous basis.

1. The monograph begins with an official title, using the *United States Adopted Name (USAN)*, *as outlined under Nomenclature* <1121> followed by descriptive information, including a graphic formula, chemical formula, molecular weight, chemical names, and Chemical Abstracts (CAS) registry number.

2. The first item, introduced by a boldface double-chevron symbol ($>>$), is the *Definition*. In the Definition, the content of the article is specified. It is usually given as a percentage of the chemical formula, based on the *Assay*, calculated on the anhydrous

269

or dried basis. The assayed content of a synthetic drug substance normally should not be less than 98.0 percent and not more than 102.0 percent. The tightness of the tolerance depends on the precision of the assay used as well as the ability to produce a drug substance of high purity without incurring unreasonable costs. For articles of lesser purity, which are derived from natural sources or fermentations, as well as for biologics (see *Biologics* <1041>), the content might be expressed in micrograms per milligram or in units per milligram.

3. Packaging and storage—Preserve in tight, light-resistant containers.

3. A discussion on packaging and storage is found in the *General Notices* under *Preservation, Packaging, Storage, and Labeling*. The proper packaging and storage conditions should be derived and documented from stability studies on the bulk drug. These standards are also important and applicable to storage and repackaging within the community pharmacy.

4. USP Reference standards <11>—*USP Acetaminophen RS*.

4. The Reference Standards section notifies the analyst of the official USP Reference Standard(s) used in the monograph and refers to the general test chapter *USP Reference Standards* <11> for additional information and instructions. Reference Standards are supplied by USP. (See also the section on *Reference Standards* in the *General Notices*.)

5. *Change to read:*

5. Although technically not part of the monograph, this is a key revision phrase, which denotes that an official revision has occurred (see No. 6). The superscript black box is the beginning of the change and the subscript black box with a numeral signals the end of the change. The number at the end denotes the *Supplement* in which the revision becomes official. (The official date of each *Supplement* is listed on the front cover of each *Supplement*.) Other revision phrases include "*Add the following:*" and "*Delete the following:*"

6. Identification

A: *Infrared Absorption* <197K>.

B: *Ultraviolet Absorption* <197U>—

Solution: 5 μg per mL. *Medium:* 0.1 N hydrochloric acid in methanol (1 in 100).

C: It responds to the *Thin-layer Chromatographic Identification Test* <201>, a test solution in methanol containing about 1 mg per mL and a solvent system consisting of a mixture of methylene chloride and methanol (4:1) being used.

6. Identification tests are discussed in *Procedures* under *Tests and Assays* in the *General Notices and Requirements*. They are "… provided as an aid in verifying the identity of articles. Such tests, however specific, are not necessarily sufficient to establish proof of identity.… Other tests and specifications in the monograph often contribute to establishing or confirming the identity of the article under examination." The most conclusive test for identity is the infrared absorption spectrum (see *Spectrophotometry and Light-scattering* <851>). When taken together, absorption bands characteristic of individual functional groups are unique for a given chemical compound with few exceptions.

Conformance with both infrared absorption and ultraviolet absorption test specifications "leaves little doubt ... regarding the identity of the specimen under examination" (see *Spectrophotometric Identification Tests* ⟨197⟩). If no suitable infrared spectrum can be obtained.

7. Melting range <741>: between 168° and 172°.

7. For many organic compounds, the melting range or temperature is a convenient criterion of identity and purity. Generally, for a melting range to be useful it should not exceed 3° or 4°. This test should not be specified when the substance melts with decomposition; rather, such characteristics are given in *USP* in the *Reference Tables* under *Description and Solubility*.

8. Water, *Method I* <921>: not more than 0.5%.

8. If water is the only residual solvent, or if it is bound as a hydrate, it must be determined for the reasons given for *Procedures* under *Tests and Assays* in the *General Notices*. *Water Determination* <921> describes the various methods that might be applicable for a given article.

9. Residue on ignition <281>: not more than 0.1%.

9. Residue on ignition can be regarded as a purity test because it limits contamination with inorganic matter (salts) in an organic compound. Such contamination would not be readily detectable by the assay, particularly a chromatographic one. It also serves as

10. Chloride <221>—Shake 1.0 g with 25 mL of water, filter, and add 1 mL of 2 N nitric acid and 1 mL of silver nitrate TS: the filtrate shows no more chloride than corresponds to 0.20 mL of 0.020 N hydrochloric acid (0.014%).

10. These tests are provided as general procedures where limits of chloride or sulfate salts are specified.

Sulfate <221>—Shake 1.0 g with 25 mL of water, filter, add 2 mL of 1 N acetic acid, then add 2 mL of barium chloride TS: the mixture shows no more sulfate than corresponds to 0.20 mL of 0.020 N sulfuric acid (0.02%).

Sulfide—Place about 2.5 g in a 50-mL beaker. Add 5 mL of alcohol and 1 mL of 3 N hydrochloric acid. Moisten a piece of lead acetate test paper with water, and fix to the underside of a watch glass. Cover the beaker with the watch glass so that part of the lead acetate paper hangs down near the pouring spout of the beaker. Heat the contents of the beaker on a hot plate just to boiling: no coloration or spotting of the test paper occurs.

11. Heavy metals, *Method II* <231>: 0.001%.

11. This limit test, which actually determines heavy metals relative to a lead standard, should be used whenever contamination with toxic metals introduced during the manufacturing process is suspected. With modern methods of synthesis and modern supplies of acids, the need for such a test requirement seems to have lessened somewhat, at least in developed countries, and it has been possible to lower the limits for heavy metals in a number of articles.

12. Free *p*-aminophenol—Transfer 5.0 g to a 100-mL volumetric flask, and dissolve in about 75 mL of a mixture of equal volumes of methanol and water. Add 5.0 mL of alkaline nitroferricyanide solution (prepared by dissolving 1 g of sodium nitroferricyanide and 1 g of anhydrous sodium carbonate in 100 mL of water), dilute with a mixture of equal volumes of methanol and water to volume, mix, and allow to stand for 30 minutes. Concomitantly determine the absorbances of this solution and of a freshly prepared solution of *p*-aminophenol, similarly prepared at a concentration of 2.5 µg per mL, using the same quantities of the same reagents, in 1-cm cells, at the maximum at about 710 nm, with a suitable spectrophotometer, using 5.0 mL of alkaline nitroferricyanide solution diluted with a mixture of equal volumes of methanol and water to 100 mL as the blank: the absorbance of the test solution does not exceed that of the standard solution, corresponding to not more than 0.005% of *p*-aminophenol.

12. Toxic impurities, arising out of the synthesis or degradation of an article, are those possessing undesirable biological properties. They must be controlled by suitable tests to a level not considered harmful. The manufacturer must notify USP concerning the presence of such impurities and should provide methods and validation data for a limit test. Suitable limit tests employ either chromatographic methods or specific and sensitive spectrophotometric and chemical methods.

Limit of *p*-chloroacetanilide—Transfer 1.0 g to a glass-stoppered, 15-mL centrifuge tube, add 5.0 mL of ether, shake by mechanical means for 30 minutes, and centrifuge at 1,000 rpm for 15 minutes or until a clean separation is obtained. Apply 200 µL of the supernatant liquid, in 40-µL portions, to obtain a single spot not more than 10 mm in diameter to a suitable thin-layer chromatographic plate (see *Chromatography* <621>) coated with a 0.25-mm layer of chromatographic silica gel mixture. Similarly, apply 40 µL of a Standard solution in ether containing 10 µg of *p*-chloroacetanilide per mL, and allow the spots to dry. Develop the chromatogram in an unsaturated chamber, with a solvent system consisting of a mixture of solvent hexane and acetone (75:25), until the solvent front has moved three-fourths of the length of the plate. Remove the plate from the developing chamber, mark the solvent front, and allow the solvent to evaporate. Locate the spots in the chromatogram by examination under short-wavelength ultraviolet light: any spot obtained from the solution under test, at an *Rf* value corresponding to the principal spot from the Standard solution is

14. Organic volatile impurities, *Method V* <467>: meets the requirements.

Solvent—Use dimethyl sulfoxide as the solvent.

15. Assay—Dissolve about 120 mg of Acetaminophen, accurately weighed, in 10 mL of methanol in a 500-mL volumetric flask, dilute with water to volume, and mix. Transfer 5.0 mL of this solution to a 100-mL volumetric flask, dilute with water to volume, and mix. Concomitantly determine the absorbances of this solution and of a Standard solution of USP Acetaminophen RS, in the same medium, at a concentration of about 12 μg per mL in 1-cm cells, at the wavelength of maximum absorbance at about 244 nm, with a suitable spectrophotometer, using water as the blank. Calculate the quantity, in mg, of $C_8H_9NO_2$ in the Acetaminophen taken by the formula: $10C(A_U/A_S)$, in which C is the concentration in mg per mL, of USP Acetaminophen RS in the Standard solution, and A_U and A_S are the absorbances of the solution of Acetaminophen and the Standard solution, respectively.

14. This limit test determines organic volatile impurities relative to a standard preparation containing chloroform, benzene, 1,2-dioxane, methylene chloride, and trichloroethylene. The limits are 50, 100, 100, 500, and 1,000 ppm, respectively. The test is required for bulk substances and excipients that are used in chronic-systemic administered dosage forms. The three main analytical methods used are based on the use of gas chromatography.

15. Tolerances in the Definition are based on the fact that this assay does not have to be stability indicating, but the monograph, taken as a whole, should assure that any degradation would be detected and could be limited by a chromatographic or other specific test. An ideal combination is a chromatographic test for ordinary impurities plus a precise titrimetric assay. Microbial assays for antibiotics (see *Antibiotics—Microbial Assays* <81>)) are currently replaced by HPLC (see *Chromatography* <621>) assays wherever possible. However, for antibiotics that are mixtures of several active components, the microbial assay is still the preferred one and is sometimes coupled with a chromatographic test to quantitate the individual components. Biologics, proteins, and peptides may require very specialized biological assays.

---

* *The explanations of each of the monograph sections are based on an article by Klaus G. Florey, Ph.D. entitled "A Guide to USP Standards" that appeared in Pharmacopoeial Forum 15 (5). Dr. Florey was a member of the USP Committee of Revision from 1970 to 1995.*

Administrative law — The body of law governing the administrative agencies (e.g., Occupational Safety and Health Administration or Department of Public Health) that have been created by Congress or by state legislatures.

Adulteration — Tampering with or contaminating a product or substance.

Airflow hoods — Workstations that emit a stream of highly filtered air that reduces possible contamination of the substances being used.

Anabolic steroids — Schedule III controlled substances (either drugs or hormonal substances) that are often misused by athletes seeking to enhance their bulk (by increasing muscle mass) and physical prowess.

Appeals — Legal proceedings in which cases are brought to higher courts to review decisions of lower courts.

Autonomy — The ability or tendency to function independently.

Auxiliary labels — Labels applied to drug containers that supply additional information, such as whether to take the medication with or without food, potential adverse effects, whether to avoid taking with alcohol, etc.

B

Beneficence — Acting to benefit others.

Bioethics — It is concerned with how ethics apply to biological research and applications.

Biohazard symbol — An international symbol that is used to designate any substance harmful to human health, including bloodborne pathogens and medical wastes.

tissues.

C

"C" symbol — A marking that indicates a controlled substance, and is printed on a drug's label, its box, and/or its packaging insert.

Chemical hygiene plan — A laboratory standard established by OSHA to reduce employees' exposure to chemicals they handle.

Code of ethics — Standards developed to affect quality and ensure the highest ethical and professional behavior.

Compensation claim — A claim filed with the state that addresses an on-site workplace injury or illness.

Compliance program guidelines — HIPAA-related privacy, training, and security regulations designed to focus on, correct, and maintain good healthcare practices.

Confidentiality — The obligation of the healthcare provider to maintain patient information in a way that will not allow dissemination beyond the healthcare provider.

Continuing education — Instructional programs that keep an individual up to date on advancements in his or her field.

Contract law — A system of law that pertains to agreements between two or more parties.

Contributory negligence — Conduct by a plaintiff that is below the standard to which he or she is legally required to conform for his or her own protection.

Criminal law — The body of law that defines offenses against the public.

D

Damages — The sum of money that may be recovered in court as financial reparation for any injury or wrong suffered because of a breach of contract, tort, negligence, or medical malpractice. Damages are divided into three types: nominal, actual, and punitive.

Data processing system — An alternative, computerized method for the storage and retrieval of prescription refill information for controlled substances on Schedules III and IV.

DEA number — A multi-digit number assigned to a healthcare practitioner that allows him or her to write prescriptions for controlled substances.

Deontology — Also known as formalism or duty orientation; a concept that asserts that ethical decision making is based on moral rules and unchanging principles, which are derived from reason and can be applied universally.

Disclosure — Transferring information, releasing information, providing access to information, or divulging information in any manner.

Downtime — A period of time when a computer or computer system is not operational, for any of a variety of reasons.

Drug Enforcement Administration (DEA) — The bureau within the United States Department of Justice that is primarily responsible for enforcing federal laws that concern controlled substances. In addition to investigating the sellers, producers, and smugglers of illicit drugs, the DEA also monitors physician prescribing patterns and pharmacy purchases.

Drug history — A history of a patient's medication use over a reasonable period of time, usually for at least the last five years; it includes all documented information on prescription medications, nonprescription (OTC) medications, and supplements.

Duty of care — An obligation to conform to a particular standard of conduct toward another.

E

Electronic data interchange (EDI) — A set of standards for structuring electronic information intended to be exchanged between different entities.

Electronic medical records (EMR) — Method of record storage preferred over paper records because the electronic format can be accessed more quickly and takes less room to store.

Encryption — Transforming information via an algorithm to make it unreadable to anyone who does not possess the decryption information required to read it.

Ethics — The study of values, or morals and morality; it includes concepts such as right, wrong, good, evil, and responsibility.

Extranet — A private network that uses Internet protocols, network connections, and sometimes telecommunication devices to share information with outside entities.

F

Facsimile — A copy of an official document (such as a prescription or medication order) that is transmitted via fax machine.

Fax paper — A special paper that burns a thermal image of a transmitted document without using regular paper and printer ink or toner; this type of paper usually causes the burned text and/or images to fade over time.

Federal Register — A U.S. government publication that contains all administrative regulations, and is the primary source of information for OSHA standards.

Felony — An offense punishable by death or by imprisonment in a state or federal prison for more than one year.

Fire safety plan — A workplace plan detailing locations of fire alarm pull boxes, fire extinguishers, and fire sprinklers, as well as a plan for continued fire prevention training and drills.

Fraud — The intentional use of deceit to deprive another person of his or her money, property, or rights.

Fraudulent — Deceitful; intending to deceive.

G

Germicides — Agents that kill germs; also known as disinfectants.

H

Hazard communication plan — A system of notify-ing personnel of hazard...

agreements.

Investigational — Drugs used to provide detailed inquiry or systematic examination of their effects.

J

Jurisdiction — The power and authority given to a court to hear a case and to make a judgment.

L

Law — A rule of conduct or procedure established by custom, agreement, or authority.

Legend drug — Prescription drug.

Licensure — The practice of granting licenses to prac-tice a profession.

Loyalty — A faithfulness or allegiance to a cause, ide-al, custom, institution, or product.

M

Magistrates — Civil officers with the power to en-force laws.

Malfeasance — The execution of an unlawful or improper act.

Malpractice — Professional misconduct or demon-stration of an unreasonable lack of skill, with the result of injury, loss, or damage to a patient.

Material Safety Data Sheet (MSDS) — A form that is required for all hazardous chemicals or other substances that are used in laboratories or phar-macies. This form contains information about a product's name, chemical characteristics, ingre-dients, guidelines for safe handling, physical and health hazards, and procedures to be followed in the event of exposure.

Medical code sets — Sets of alphanumeric codes used for encoding medical conditions, diseases, procedures, and other information...

marking.

Misdemeanors — Crimes punishable by fine or by imprisonment in a facility other than a prison for less than one year.

Misfeasance — The improper performance of an act.

Morals — Motivations based on ideas of right and wrong.

N

National Drug Code (NDC) — The federal code that identifies a drug's manufacturer or distributor, its formulation, and the size and type of its packaging.

National Formulary (NF) standards — Standards concerning medicines, dosage forms, drug sub-stances, excipients (inactive substances used as carriers for active medicinal ingredients), medical devices, and dietary supplements.

NDC number — A product identifier used for drugs intended for human use; "NDC" stands for "Nation-al Drug Code."

Negligence — A type of unintentional tort alleged when one may have performed or failed to perform an act that a reasonable person would or would not have done, respectively, in similar circumstances.

Nonfeasance — The failure to act as a reasonably prudent person would in similar circumstances when there is a duty to act.

Nonmaleficence — An ethical principle that asserts an obligation not to inflict harm intentionally; it is sometimes combined with beneficence to form a single principle.

Notice of Privacy Practices (NOPP) — A document that explains to patients how his or her PHI may be used and disclosed.

O

Occupational Safety and Health Administration (OSHA) — A division of the U.S. Department of Labor.

Office of Inspector General (OIG) — Governmental office that investigates various organizations, including healthcare organizations, to assure integrity and efficiency in their operations.

Orphan drug — Drugs used to treat diseases that affect fewer than 200,000 people in the United States.

Over-the-counter (OTC) drug — Nonprescription drug.

P

Patient rights — The recognition that patients are entitled to determine for themselves the extent to which they will receive (or not receive) care and treatment.

Pharmacy compounding — Creating a new mixture or compound by blending or mixing two or more medications and other substances in a licensed pharmacy.

Pharmacy internship — A period of service in a pharmacy during which a pharmacy student works under supervision to gain practical experience.

Phocomelia — A severe birth defect, also known as "seal limbs," involving the malformation or nonformation of arms and legs; it was caused by the drug thalidomide.

Privacy — The right to be left alone, or the right to control personal information.

Private law — The type of law that governs conflicts between private parties.

Product liability — A tort that makes a manufacturer liable for compensation to anyone using its product if damages or injuries occur from defects in that product.

Professional ethics — Moral standards and principles of conduct that guide professionals in the performance of their functions.

Prosecution — A legal proceeding by the state against an individual.

Protected health information (PHI) — All stored health information that relates to a past, present, or future physical or mental health condition.

Proximate cause — An action or event that produces injury in a natural, continuous sequence that is unbroken by any intervening cause.

Public law — The type of law that governs conflicts between private parties and the government.

R

Radioactive waste — Any waste that contains or is contaminated with liquid or solid radioactive materials.

Revocation — Recall of authority or power to act.

Revoked — Voided, annulled, recalled, withdrawn, or reversed.

S

Schedules — The five classifications of controlled substances; the drugs with the highest potential for abuse and no medical use are listed in Schedule I, and those with progressively less abuse potential are listed in Schedules II, III, IV, and V.

Security Rule — A HIPAA-related regulation that specifies how PHI is protected on computer networks, the Internet, the extranet, and disks and other storage media.

Statute of limitations — That period of time established by state law during which a lawsuit or criminal proceeding may be filed.

T

Teratogenic — Causing genetic defects.

Tort — A private wrong or injury, other than a breach of contract, for which the court will provide a remedy.

Treatment, payment, and healthcare operations (TPHCO) — This concerns PHI that may be shared in order to provide treatment, process payment, and operate the medical business.

and society ... g
promote the greatest balance of good over ...
for all.

Index